The Warrior Culture
The Indian Wars and Depredations

By

Edward Osborne

Chronology Books
History Publishing Company Global LLC
Palisades, NY 10964

ISBN 9781940773551

For purposes of bulk purchase contact
History Publishing Media Group LLC
Historypublish@aol.com

SAN:850-5942

First Edition

Published by History Publishing Company Global an imprint of
History Publishing Media Group LLC, Palisades, NY 10964.

Dedicated to my
Frontier Wife and Editor
Dorothy

And

The brave, determined and courageous U.S.
Army soldiers and American settler families,
especially the heroic women and children, who
had to confront the brutalities of the Indian Wars.

And
Mrs. Riordan

Table of Contents

"The young Indian, from childhood is taught to regard "killing" as the highest of virtues."
-Isaac Heard, 1863.

"...the best way to negotiate with hostile Indians is with the rifle...which they will not forget." -
-Osborne Russell, 1834-1843.

Estimates of white Americans murdered began at about 500 and climbed as high as 1,000; highest number of whites killed.

"Remember our wives and children murdered on the Platte and Arkansas."   ----Col. John Chivington, 1864.

"They will not sell their hunting grounds to the white man for a road. They will not give you the road unless you whip them."   ----Chief Standing Elk, Brule' Sioux, 1866.

Historical Quotes

1. "Facts are Stubborn Things!" John Adams.
2. "When the past no longer illuminates the future, the Spirit walks in darkness."

   Alexis de Tocqueville.

3. "Nothing great in the World has been accomplished without passion."
   Wilhelm Friedrich Hegel.

4. "History is the record of an encounter between character and circumstances."

   Donald Creighton.

5. "Education is a private matter between the person and the world of knowledge and experience, and has little to do with school or college."
   Lillian Smith.

6. "History is too serious to be left to historians." Iain Macleod.
7. "If fifty million people say a foolish thing, it is still a foolish thing."

   Anatole France.

8. "It is impossible to defeat an ignorant man in argument."
   William G. McAdoo.

9. "The conventional view serves to protect us from the painful job of thinking."

   John Kenneth Galbraith.

10. "One cannot and must not try to erase the past merely because it does not fit the present."

   Golda Meir.

11. "We want the facts to fit the preconceptions. When they don't it is easier to ignore the facts than to change the preconceptions."
   Jessamyn West.

12. "It is as fatal as it is cowardly to blink (at) the facts because they are not to our taste."
   John Tyndall.

Introduction

"Facts are Stubborn Things."
John Adams.

"Mercy to the Guilty is Cruelty to the Innocent."

Adam Smith.

"Interpretation…is the life-blood of history."

E. H. Carr.

This book is a polemical historical narrative based on past American Indian depredations, especially the Sioux, Cheyenne and Arapahoe. It primarily concentrates on the period from 1850 until 1866. The term "polemic" is defined as a "controversial argument, esp. one refuting or attacking an opinion or a doctrine."[i] The opinion I will be attempting to refute is today's contemporary interpretation which states in general that the American Plains Indians were helpless, innocent, oppressed victims of white brutality. I will argue that the historical American Plains Indians were primarily nothing more than vile butchers. As an example of the gruesome torture that the Indians used, I offer the following description provided by J. P. Dunn in his book, *Massacres of the Mountains,* originally published in 1886. Dunn wrote:

> The Sioux have an unpleasant method of torture. They fasten a man, naked, to the ground, lying on his back, with arms and legs stretched out and fastened to pegs; then they build a fire on his stomach, and keep it up until he dies, occasionally touching a burning brand to other portions of his

body, gouging out an eye, or otherwise adding to the agony of the victim.[ii]

Dunn's description is a classic example of the hideous cruelty of the Plains Indians. In addition to being a polemic, I also consider this book to be an example of historical revisionism. For those of you who are not familiar with the term, it is the "reinterpretation of orthodox views on evidence, motivations, and decision-making processes surrounding a historical event."[iii] As stated above, the orthodox/contemporary interpretation is that the Indians were always innocent victims and only the white man was evil.

Before we begin our examination, for the benefit of the general reader, we need to have a good definition of what history is. An excellent definition of history is presented by a renowned present day historian, James M. McPherson. McPherson is not only a great writer, but he was also past president of the American Historical Association in 2003. He states:

"History is a continuing dialogue between the present and past."[iv]

While I agree with McPherson, I prefer the old masters such as E.H. Carr, who states the following in his classic book, *What is History?* (1961): "My first answer to the question 'What is history?' is that it is a continuous process of interaction between the historian and his facts, in an unending dialogue between the present and the past."[v] Carr goes on to make what I consider to be a profound statement that "interpretation…is the life-blood of history."[vi] I prefer to tweak Carr's statement and make it "interpretation is the essence of history." In many cases, today's books offer their biased interpretations without honestly identifying them. I have found that most of the contemporary western authors basically share the same interpretations. The American Indian is innocent of all wrongdoing because his atrocious mutilating is just a reflection of his cultural value system. He has become and still is the "Noble Red Man" of the academic elites and James Fenimore Cooper types; free from sin and one with nature.

A fundamental aspect of the study of history is "presentism" or "the climate of opinion."
Robert Utley, a renowned author of western books describes presentism as follows: "To impose the ways of today on people to whom they would have been alien, Indian or white, we believe a perversion of history." A "presentist" historian uses today's values to evaluate a past historical event and that becomes the major fallacy in their one-sided argument. They re-write or revise history to serve some contemporary ideology, promote an agenda, goal or group such as the Indians or other minorities. An additional example of presentism is the attempt by many modern-day historians to use today's values about slavery to condemn the founding fathers for owning slaves. Using their own contemporary self-righteousness, everyone from the past is guilty of sin; and every individual in today's world who shares their values is exempt from criticism.

A further factor that greatly influences historical writing is "revisionism." "Revisionist" history is generally thought to be "the reinterpretation of orthodox views on evidence, motivations, and the decision-making process surrounding a historical event."[vii] An additional definition of historical revisionism is considered the "legitimate scholastic re-examination of existing knowledge about an historical event, or the distortion of the historical record such that certain events appear in a more or less favorable light or alternatively in a particularly bad light."[viii] The historical author James McPherson states the following in reference to revisionism:

> Interpretations of the past are subject to change in response to new evidence, new questions asked of the evidence, new perspectives gained by the passage of time. There is no single, eternal, and immutable "truth" about past events and their

meaning. The unending quest of historians for understanding the past—that is "revisionism"—is what makes history vital and meaningful.[ix]

To illustrate revisionist history, I will cite three famous examples: one, by Charles A. Beard, *An Economic Interpretation of the Constitution of the United States,* published in 1913; another by Charles Callan Tansill, the book *Back Door to War: The Roosevelt Foreign Policy, 1933-1941,* published in 1952; and the third, David Bergamini's, *Japan's Imperial Conspiracy*, published in 1971. Beard's book shocked the academic world in 1913 because his interpretation stated that the Constitution was written by men of property who were more concerned with protecting their economic rights and power rather than sharing these rights with the people. Beard stated:

> Suppose, on the other hand, that substantially all of the merchants, money lenders, security holders, manufacturers, shippers, capitalists, and financiers and their professional associates are to be found on one side in support of the Constitution and that substantially all or the major portion of the opposition came from the non-slaveholding farmers and the debtors—would it not be pretty conclusively demonstrated that our fundamental law was not the product of an abstraction known as "the whole people," but of a group of economic interests which must have expected beneficial results from its adoption? [x]

The idea that the Constitution was made by the people, for the people, and to protect the people is nothing more than nonsensical, romantic idealism. It is this idea that, however, has become the accepted interpretation. Even the Preamble to the Constitution begins with a major falsehood: "We the people of the United States, in Order to form a more Perfect Union…" The people had absolutely nothing to do with the writing of the Constitution. Beard, in my opinion, builds a realistic and strong argument that the document is an economic defense of the propertied power elites of the times. One need only read an original copy of the document before it was amended. Article I, Section 3, Clause 1, states: "The Senate of the United States shall be composed of two Senators from each State, chosen by the Legislature thereof, for six Years..."[xi] Clearly, the members chosen to be Senators were not selected directly by the people. They were selected by the moneyed and propertied members of the state legislatures.

This provision of the Constitution was not changed until April 8, 1913. That means that for one hundred twenty-four years the members of the Senate were not elected directly by the people but by each state's legislature who also selected the electors of the Electoral College. This also means that the Senate remained a reflection of the economic and moneyed elites. In 1913, the 17th Amendment was passed which provided for the direct popular election of Senators.[xii] And let us not forget that the President is not directly elected by the people but by electors chosen in each State. The Constitutional Convention was held in the strictest of secrecy and took five months to complete, May until September of 1789. There were no reporters or visitors allowed; and James Madison's notes and correspondence about the convention were not released until 1840, after his death; 51 years after the passing of the Constitution. It is totally ridiculous that the Republican Party obsessively worships the Constitution; obviously, they haven't read Beard!

Charles A. Tansill also writes an example of classic historical revisionism in his book, *Back Door to War: The Roosevelt Foreign Policy, 1933-1944.* His interpretation is based upon the premise that Roosevelt maneuvered the Japanese to firing the first shot so he could get into the fight in Europe and save his beloved England. After World War II, a host of revisionist historians attacked Roosevelt for starting the war. These revisionists included George

Morgenstern, Harry Elmer Barnes and Charles Tansill. Tansill's book provides a revision of the standard interpretation which was that the Japanese were solely responsible for the outbreak of World War II with their sneak attack on Pearl Harbor. A review of his book states the following:

> The Soviet Union, in order to promote its own program, was the instigator of war in both the Far East and Europe. "Russia instigates war in the Far East; Roosevelt blames Japan" is a characteristic chapter heading; "Stalin lights the fuse of World War II" is another. Japan was the natural barrier to the spread of communism in Asia; Germany to its spread in Europe. The United States was guilty of a fatal error in opposing Japan; the democracies similarly erred in backing Poland against Hitler. Roosevelt bears the main guilt, for he not only "maneuvered" Japan into the war in the Pacific, thus entering the European war through the "back door"; he had already "needled" Chamberlin into taking a firm stand against Hitler in Poland, thereby playing a key role in precipitating war in Europe.[xiii]

To reinforce Tansill's analysis, one need only read Robert Dallek's book, *Franklin D. Roosevelt and American Foreign Policy, 1932-1945*. It was published in 1979. Dallek writes that on the 25th of November:

> ...in a discussion with Hull, Knox, Marshall, Stark, and Stimson about the Far East, the President focused on the likelihood of a Japanese surprise attack. "The question was how we should maneuver them [the Japanese] into the position of firing the first shot without allowing too much danger to ourselves." The chief concern was how to justify an American declaration of war to Congress and the public if Tokyo struck only at British and/or Dutch

possessions. Roosevelt later told Churchill and Stalin that if "it had not been for the Japanese attack; he would have had great difficulty in getting the American people into the war."[xiv]

Another example of an important revisionist interpretation is the book written by David Bergamini, *Japan's Imperial Conspiracy: How Emperor Hirohito Led Japan into War Against the West,* which was published in 1971.[xv] This book argues that the Emperor, as the title states, was directly involved in the planning of the war against the West; and it was not just a plan of the Imperial Japanese military. It is an extremely interesting book. I consider all three of these books to meet the definition of revisionist history: "the reinterpretation of orthodox views on evidence, motivations, and the decision-making process surrounding a historical event." As always, "interpretation is the essence of history."

The "presentism" or "climate of opinion" that still prevails today had its origins in the late 1960's and 1970's. It is the repressed minorities' version of history. In this case, the glorification of the Indian minority and the moral obligation to pay for previous white crimes, usually with money; the Yankee dollar. Utley describes his confrontation with this pro-minority "climate of opinion" in the following insightful paragraphs:

The year was 1976, not an auspicious time for balance. In 1969 Vine Deloria had published *Custer Died for Your Sins*. A year later Dee Brown followed with *Bury My Heart at Wounded Knee*. Next came Dustin Hoffman's vivid portrayal of a white man raised by the Indians [Why, Mrs. Pendrake?] in the motion picture *Little Big Man*. Although a transparent metaphor for Vietnam, it was set in the Old West. Blood-lusting cavalry rampaged through Indian villages gleefully slaughtering women and children. Throughout the early 1970s, the red power movement took root and, driven by

the   American Indian Movement (AIM), gained
momentum. At Wounded Knee, South   Dakota, in
1973, it turned deadly.

> These were years of social and intellectual ferment,
> of Black power as well as Red power, of marches
> by poor people as well as Indians, of feminine and
> ethnic activism, and above all of mass
> demonstrations against the Vietnam War. For their
> part, the Indians sought to reestablish their pride
> and identity and to gain justice from government
> and society. They fervently believed in the version
> of Indian-white history set forth by Deloria, Brown
> and Hoffman. White society embraced this
> interpretation too and shouldered a heavy burden of
> guilt for what their forebears had done to the
> Indians. In academia as well as the larger
> population, balance fell casualty to the new Indian
> history. Extensive emphasis fell on whites as
> exploitative conquerors, and the Indians as
> romantic, innocent victims.[xvi]

Utley wrote his poignant introduction in 1976 and,
therefore, could not include the most obvious Indian
propaganda movie ever made, *Dances with Wolves*, which
was released in 1990. It starred Kevin Costner as Lt. John J.
Dunbar who is assigned to a remote post and makes friends
with a suspicious wolf who he names "Two Socks." The
asininity of him staying at this abandoned one shack post is
in and of itself completely ridiculous. Let's hear it for
Hollywood. He then meets a Sioux tribe and goes native
and even marries a white captive woman who has also gone
native. After adopting the language, customs and lifestyle
of the Sioux, he becomes one of the tribe. The movie was a
tremendously popular success and directly affected
American popular opinion, winning 7 Academy Awards. It
made a Box Office gross of over $424,200,000 and only
cost about $22,000,000 to make.

The agenda of the movie, in my opinion, is so obvious that it is totally lacking in integrity. The white freight-hauler that takes Dunbar to his isolated post is an obnoxious, drunken brute, as are most of the white soldiers. The vicious white soldiers even shoot his treasured wolf companion, "Two Socks." This is done to further emphasize the cruel brutality of the evil white men. The Sioux Indians are portrayed as the ever "Noble Red Men" who live in total ecological harmony with their utopian natural world. They worship "Wakan Tanka-The Great Mystery" and live their carefree nomadic life wishing no harm to anyone. Of course, this description of the Sioux is totally unrealistic and untrue. There is no mention of their constant heinous butchery of their innocent white victims or their defeated Indian enemies. The movie says nothing about their taking of defeated victims as slaves, the kidnapped women, both Indian women and white, who they rape and abuse. He makes no reference to their continuous plundering of horses and cattle.

I mention the movie because, in my opinion, it provides the extensively false information about the "so-called" innocent American Indian. It presents the standard interpretation of the "peaceful" environmentally correct Indians living in blissful harmony with nature. It has had an extensive impact of misinforming the American public. In the movie, there is no reference to the fact that one tribe of Indians would wantonly slaughter the buffalo herds of their enemies so that their enemies would have no food supply. These buffalo would be left to rot on the prairie. "…Indian auxiliaries the day before… had come across a herd of buffalo and had made a great slaughter of these helpless animals, killing one hundred and fifty of them, for which they had no use at all."[xvii] So much for loving their sacred buffalo.

There is also no mention of the fact that they would start immense prairie fires to defeat their enemies and burn nature's beautiful green grasses to a black cinder.[xviii] There is also no mention of the extensive practice of polygamy that is a fundamental part of their culture where you buy and sell women for a certain number of horses. In my research, there was a report of an elderly chief with 4 wives and 36 children.[xix] Where are the feminists when you need them? There is no mention of white opinions; no diverse point of view; just the Sioux Indians wallowing in their own self-aggrandizement and self-pity. However, James Fenimore Cooper's romantic and idealistic characterization of Indians as the "Noble Red Man" still infects our present-day sympathizers.

It must be noted that the title, "The Noble Red Man," comes from an article written by Mark Twain, not Cooper. It was written for The Galaxy magazine in 1870. This article was purposely written to challenge the widespread false analysis of the "Noble" Indian. Twain writes that the Indian "is little, and scrawny, and black, and dirty; He is ignoble---base and treacherous, and hateful in every way. Not even imminent death can startle him into a spasm of virtue. The ruling trait of all savages is greedy and consuming selfishness, and in our Noble Red Man it is found in its amplest development."[xx]

An important factor in my historical methodology will be the extensive reliance on primary historical sources, also known as original source material, rather than secondary sources. A primary historical source, for those who are unfamiliar, is one based on the eye-witness observations of an individual in reference to the actual historical incident. Primary source materials include diaries, letters, newspapers, oral interviews, books written by eye-witnesses, autobiographies, memoirs, government documents and archives. In reference to our examination, there has been a recent explosion in the use of Indian sources and interpretations; they are very popular, very biased and very, very profitable.

A secondary source is one that refers to or builds upon primary sources. They are written after the fact or historical incident has happened. Most modern books extensively use secondary sources; a textbook is a great example of a secondary source. As examples of a primary and secondary source, I offer two books, one written by Morse H. Coffin and the other written by Stan Hoig. Coffin's book, *The Battle of Sand Creek,* originally published in 1878, is an outstanding example of a primary source in that he was an eyewitness to the battle of Sand Creek. "During the Indian war of 1864, he enlisted in Company D, Third Colorado Cavalry ."[xxi] The Third Cavalry was supposedly responsible for the mutilation of the Indians at that battle. He fought at the battle of Sand Creek and that is what made him a primary source. Stan Hoig's book, *The Sand Creek Massacre*, published in 1961, on the other hand, is a secondary source. It was written after the fact or historical incident.

I have also used a number of internet-sources to increase the comprehensiveness of the research tools available to me. I was amazed at the scope, accuracy and ease of acquisition of these internet-sources. In many cases, they provided primary source information that I could not locate anywhere else.

For the sake of balance, very few writers of the West could refute the charges of corrupt practices by the federal, state and territorial government officials who managed the Indian affairs. These were the individuals who justly deserved the vengeance and hostility of the Indians. An Indian agent named Andrew Myrick of the Great Uprising of 1862 supposedly told the Indians to "Go eat grass." For his "polite" statement the Sioux killed him and stuffed his mouth full of grass. Now that's what I call justice!

The settlers, on the other hand, were innocent immigrants searching for a small plot of land to grow their crops, tend their animals, and provide a safe place to raise their families. One point I will argue is that the Indians had every right to fight the government officials and even the Army. But their gruesome butchery of the defeated Army troopers and settlers was not, and will never be, acceptable! This is also especially true in reference to the mutilations of the innocent settlers and their women and children. The first main argument I will address is that the Plains Indians were vicious butchers; and the evidence, much to my surprise, was utterly overwhelming. However, the pro-Indian sympathizers disclaim these atrocities and identify them just as aspects of an indigenous Indian culture that must be accepted. I wonder if they would be so understanding to the culture of butchery that the Muslim members of ISIS practice today? What is the difference? There is none!

There are five chapters in the book. The first chapter deals with the problem of the fundamental values of the "Warrior Culture." It also deals with the brutality of women's captivity. Chapter two describes the major contributions of the mountain men and Jesuit priest Father Pierre-Jean De Smet. Their important discoveries of the mountain trails and passes, such as South Pass, the Oregon Trail and the California Trail, made possible the settling of the American West. The third chapter deals with the little known Great Sioux Uprising of 1862 which took place in Minnesota. This Indian uprising is known as the largest killing of American settlers in the history of the West. It is estimated that between 800-1,000 Americans were killed during the Sioux Uprising. Chapter four examines the so-called Sand Creek Massacre of 1864. A Colonel Chivington of Colorado is charged with massacring approximately 108 friendly and unarmed Cheyenne and Arapahoe to include two-thirds which were innocent women and children. The last chapter investigates the Fetterman Massacre of 1866 wherein 81 American soldiers and civilians were ambushed by at least 1,500 Indians. The massacre resulted in the total annihilation and the atrocious mutilation of all of the command.

The causes and results of these battles must be challenged because they have produced an agenda-driven, homogenized pro-Indian propaganda interpretation. They have been extensively written about and analyzed by the P.C. Indian sympathizers and defenders. Especially by the academic elites and, much to my surprise, many of the well-known authors of the American West. They seem to glorify in the bravery of the Indians and continually denigrate the behavior of the white soldiers and the innocent white settlers. They seem to suffer from an extensive white-guilt complex when it comes to thinking and writing about the Indians.

One of the primary focuses of this book is the horrendous and vicious nature of Indian raids. The largest scale mutilation of American and European settlers occurred during the Great Sioux Uprising in Minnesota in August of 1862. The number of settlers killed in this Uprising is generally believed to be between 800 and 1,000 innocent American men, women and children.

Many of the writers of the West continually make excuses for the butchery and brutality of the Indian raids. George Bent, a famous half-breed Cheyenne warrior, who fought on the side of the Indians, had his thoughts presented in the book *HALFBREED* written by David Halaas and Andrew Masich; it was published in 2004. His explanation given for the atrocious raids by the Indians was that it was just the nature of the wild bucks. An additional author, Richard G. Hardorff, in his book, *Hokahey! A Good Day to Die!,* is another example which justifies the brutal acts of the Indians. He and many other Indian writers fabricate the lie that since it is a part of their culture we must accept it. Again, I can't help but wonder what people's opinions would be if they compared the atrocities of the Indians with those of modern day ISIS and made the same claims about culture! An interesting comparison of similar cultures. As for the excuse that the Indian culture justifies these brutal acts, Hardorff makes the following statement:

> To the Caucasian mind, such acts are incomprehensible; however, the Indian frame of mind was not inhibited by such restraint. Indian ideology taught not to expect any quarter, and not to give any in return. The mutilation of an enemy

body, therefore, was not considered an act of cruelty. Instead, this behavior was the accepted expression of a nomadic warrior culture, to which the Lakotas and Cheyennes belonged… By understanding the behavior of the Lakota and Cheyenne warriors, one will get a better appreciation of some of the acts of aggression and deeds of valor described in this volume.[xxii]

Before we begin the book, we must first correct several linguistic mistakes that are usually made in reference to Indian terms. The first major mistake, at least from the Indian point of view, is the use of the word Sioux. They claim that the word "Sioux" is not even a word, at least in their language. It is believed that the word came from a bastardization of the French term "Oux" and the Chippewa, "Nadowessi."[xxiii] When these two words were put together it came out to be "Nadowessioux," which was later reduced to Sioux. It means "two little serpents." In many cases, the Lakota consider it to be a negative slang term that refers to the devil, vipers, adders and snakes.

The next Indian word incorrectly defined is the word "Hokahey" which many non-Indians believe means "It is A Good Day to Die!" This term was supposedly used by Chief Crazy Horse at the battle of the Little Big Horn. The author Richard Hardorff titled one of his books *Hokahey! A Good Day To Die,* published in 1993. Hardorff and many others have not done their homework. Hokahey really means "let's go," "let's roll," or "charge."[xxiv] We will also see the same inept research used in reference to the word, "Wasi'chu." In the native Lakota and Dakota Sioux language, wasi'chu, means white man or a "greedy person who steals the fat." It also means "non-Indian." This is a directly pejorative and insulting way to address or call a white person or non-Indian. Some authors avoid this definition of "wasi'chu" saying it does not pertain to today's white people but only pertains to "corporations and individuals, with the governmental accomplices, which continue to covet Indian lives, land, and resources for private profit."[xxv] Nice try for the "Noble Red Man." That is the deliberate excuse they use to cover up their fabricated Ideology. The Urban dictionary defines it as a Lakota term for a white person, more specifically a greedy white person; "the one who takes the best meat for himself. It is also similar to the derogative, white persons, white boy and honky."[xxvi] A native language internet site states the following: "Today, wasi'chu does sometimes have the connotation of a greedy or dishonorable person, because many Sioux perceive white people as being rather greedy and dishonorable..."[xxvii]

One of the most profoundly misused P.C. terms is "Native-American." The academic Left always needs to manipulate everybody's vocabulary to adhere to their psychological value system of being morally superior to everyone else. This need to be "morally superior" is the paramount value of the Left's agenda of political correctness. Yesterday's gym is today's health and fitness center; the more complicated the better. The dictionary definition of the term native means "Existing in or belonging to one by nature; innate... Being such by birth or origin... Being one's own because of the place or circumstances of one's own birth."[xxviii] Based upon this definition, everyone legally born in the United States is a Native-American.

The correct scientific name for the so-called "Native-American" is Indigenous Aborigine. It must be noted that today's and yesterday's American Indians are not really Native-Americans; they are all North American Indigenous Aborigines who came here from Asia about 15,000 years ago. If you check some of their modern-day websites, you will see that they have readily involved themselves with the Indigenous Aboriginal world power movement, especially http://www/defend blackhills.org/indx.php Their litany of complaints, as listed on the websites,is directly similar to the grievances of all the other "oppressed" minorities, none of which can accept responsibility for their own failures!

Native-American, as stated above, is just another politically correct (P.C.) term fabricated by the academic elites. It is used now-a-days to placate, identify and appease the Indians. If the word "Indians" was good enough for the great explorer Columbus, it's good enough for me. This is just another attempt to rewrite history. The West Indies are still known as the West Indies.

The following English terms are also of importance to understanding the identification of the major battles and so-called massacres that are discussed in the book. To everyone's surprise the two words are "battle" and "massacre." Once one has a clear definition of these terms, it is much easier to identify the various conflicts. A battle is defined as a "hostile meeting between opposing forces or a protracted controversy or struggle."[xxix] Therefore, we can define a battle as a drawn out or prolonged struggle between opposing military forces. The definition of the term massacre is "the act or an instance of cruel, indiscriminate killing of a large number of people; to kill indiscriminately and wantonly."[xxx] Keep these definitions in mind as we read the chapters ahead.

Endnotes for Introduction.

[1] *The American Heritage College Dictionary,* 4th ed., s. v. "polemic." Hereafter cited as *AHCD.*
[1] J. P. Dunn, Jr., *Massacres of the Mountains: A History of the Indian Wars of the Far West,*
    (Mechanicsburg: Stackpole Books, 2002), 489-490. Originally published in 1886. Hereafter
    cited as J. P. Dunn.
[1] Revisionist History, https//en.wikipedia.org/wiki/Revisionist history, pg. 1
[1] James McPherson, "From the President: Revisionist Historians," *Perspectives on History,*
    American Historical Association, (September 2003) pg. 1 of 5.
[1] E.H. Carr, *What is History?* (London: Cox and Wyman Ltd, 1961), 30. Hereafter cited as Carr-
    History.
[1] Ibid., 28.

[7] Utley, *Indian Wars,* vi-vii.

8. http://en.wikipedia.org. wiki/Revisionist_history_1 Hereafter cited as Wikipedia Revisionist.

9. James M. McPherson, "Revisionist Historians," *Perspectives on History,* September, (2003):
    Pg. 1 of 5. http://www.historians.org/publications-and-directories/perspective-on-history/
    september-2003/revisionist-historians. Retrieved 2 August 2016.

[1] Charles A. Beard, *An Economic Interpretation of the Constitution of the United States,*
    (New York: The Free Press, 1913) 17. Hereafter cited Beard.

[1] Brinkley, Appendix, A-12.

[1] Ibid. William A. McClenaghan, *Magruder's American Government,*
    (Newton: Allyn and Bacon, Inc. 1987), 729. Hereafter cited as *Magruder's.*

[1] Julius W. Pratt, *Back Doors to War: The Roosevelt Foreign Policy, 1933-1941, The*
    American Historical Review Vol. 58 No. 1 (Oct., 1952) 150-152. Hereafter cited as Pratt.

[1] Robert Dallek, *Franklin D. Roosevelt and* American Foreign Policy, 1932-1945, (Oxford:
    Oxford University Press, 1979), 307. Hereafter cited as Dallek. R.J.C. Butow, *How*
    Roosevelt Attacked Japan at Pearl Harbor: *Myth Masquerading as History, Prologue: The*
    U.S. National Archives and Records Administratioon. Fall 1996, Vol. 28, No. 3, pg. 3 of 19. Hereafter cited as Butow. https://www.archives.gov/publications/prologue/1996/fall/butow.html

[1] David Bergamini, *Japan's Imperial Conspiracy: How Emperor Hirohito led Japan into War*
    against the West, (New York: William Morrow and Company, 1971), 1079-1081. Hereafter
    cited as Bergimini.

[1] Utley, *Indian Wars,* v-vi.

[1] Cyrus T. Brady. *Indian Fights and Fighters,* (Lincoln: University of Nebraska Press, 1971),
    193. Hereafter cited as Brady-*Indian Fights.*

[1] Utley, *Indian Wars,* 246.

[1] Foley-*Missionary,* 17

[1] Mark Twain, "The Noble Red Man", *The Galaxy,* Vol. 10, Issue 3, Sept. 1870, 426-429.
    http://www.jrbooksonline.com/comparison_burton_twain. htm.
    http://nationalvanguard.org/2015/02//the-noble-red-man/ Hereafter cited as *Twain.*

[1] Morse H. Coffin, *The Battle of Sand Creek,* ed. Alan W. Farley, (Waco: W.M. Morrison-
    Publisher, 1965, originally published in 1878), 4. Hereafter cited as Coffin.

[1] Richard G. Hardorff, *Hokahey! A Good Day to Die: The Indian Casualties of the Custer Fight,*
    (Lincoln: University of Nebraska Press, 1993), 12. Hereafter cited as Hardorff-*Hokahey.*

[1] Stacey Makes Good, "Sioux is Not Even a Word," *Lakota Country Times,* Pine Ridge Indian
    Reservation, no dated provided. Hereafter cited as Stacey Makes Good. Hardorff-*Hokahey,*
        14.
[1] John G. Neihardt, *Black Elk Speaks,* (New York: MJF BOOKS, 1932), 56. Hereafter cited as
    Neihardt, Black Elk. *Setting the Record Straight About Native Languages: A Good Day To*
        Die, Hokahey.
http://www.answers.com/Q/How_do_you_say_today_is_a_ good_day_to_
    die_in_the_Indian language. Hereafter cited as www.answers.
http://www.native-
    languages.org/iaq20.htm.
[1] http://dickshovel.com/wasichu.html, pg. 1.
[1] Aaron Huey, "The Black Hills Are Not for Sale," *Harpers,* 26 November 2011,
    http://nativeamericannetroots.net/diary/tag/He%20Sapa, pg. 4 of 35.
[1] www.native-languages, pg. 1.
[1] *AHCD., s. v. "native."*
[1] *AHCD., s. v. "battle."*
[1] Ibid., s. v. "massacre."

Chapter 1

Warrior Culture and Women's Captivity

"The young Indian from childhood is taught to regard 'killing' as the highest of virtues."

Isaac V.D. Heard. September, 1863.

"Then they took me by force, to an unoccupied tipi, near the house, and perpetrated the most horrible and nameless outrages upon my person. These outrages were committed at different times during my captivity."

Mary Schwandt, 14-year old captive, 1862.

"One day the Indians entered into a house where they found a woman baking bread. Her infant child lay in the cradle unconscious of its fate. Snatching it from its little bed they thrust it into the heated oven, its screams torturing the mother..."

Fanny Kelly, captive, July, 1864.

This chapter will examine some of the basic tenets of the Indian culture of killing and the treatment of captive women. The Indian culture of warfare has been used as an excuse to explain away the mutilation and brutal-ity of the American Indians. The correct scientific term for the American Indians is Indigenous Aborigines, but Indians is much simpler. The "Left-ist" politically correct academics in today's universities prefer the words Native-Americans. They use this term to protect their favorite "innocent," oppressed minority from any type of objective criticism. Every time some-one comes along and raises a question about the Indians violent behavior, the "Left" always attributes it to, "they were just practicing their Indian culture." Just think if we applied the same logic to Al-Qaida or ISIS. We would not excuse these Arab terrorists for cutting off heads, murdering innocent victims by the hundreds, possibly thousands, and burning victims alive. I would suggest that many of the violent and heinous acts that the American Indians committed between the early 1500's through the 1890's are not different than the acts of today's terrorists. Just stop and reflect on the comparisons of these two violent terrorist cultures. There are a great many similarities between them.

To begin our examination of the Indian culture, we must start at one of the earliest instances of historic brutality and that would be by the Aztec Indians. I have selected the Aztec because they were the first major Indian culture to confront the arrival of the Spanish Europeans in the early 1500's. Another reason for selecting the Aztec of the 1500's is to show how far back in history the culture of violence and unconscionable behavior existed.

One of the first extensive encounters between the New World Indi-ans and the Europeans was the conquest of the Aztec by Hernan Cor-tes between 1519 and 1521. The examples of the Aztec brutality involved decapitation, mutilation and human heart sacrifice. Cortes was a Spanish leader of a group of brutal conquistadors who went looking for gold on the mainland of Mexico and encountered the Aztec empire. An eye-witness to this fascinating adventure was Bernal Dias del Castillo. Diaz was one of Cortes' soldiers and chronicled his experiences in a manuscript titled, *The True History of the Conquest of New Spain*. An expanded version of his book was published in 1632[1]. This book is a must read for anyone seriously interested in Mexican history. In essence, you actually ride with Cortes and Diaz as they do battle and conquer the cannibalistic Aztec. It is like traveling backwards in H.G. Well's "Time Machine"; it is an enthralling real world adventure.

There are numerous encounters between the Spanish and Aztec in this experience, but I will only present a brief sample to illustrate my point. Cortes initially landed in Mayan territory and then worked his way up the coast to Vera Cruz. The Indians were awestruck by the first arrival of Cortes and his troops by the ships they saw and the mounted horses which they initially believed were gods. The Indians believed that the mounted horse-men were one united creature, half man and half horse. The Aztec had never seen horses before. They also believed that Cortes was the feathered serpent god, Quetzalcoatl. These mistakes were quickly corrected when several of the Spanish troops were killed on the coast.

Cortes' march from the coast to the hinterland brought him directly in contact with the Tlaxcalan, Indians whom he conquered. They then joined him as allies in the conquest of the Aztec empire. The Tlaxcalan Indians were a continuing enemy of the Aztec because the Aztec fought them not to win, but to capture a source of victims for their religious sacrifices.[2] While heading inland, he came upon the City of Cholula and reported: "I cannot omit to mention the cages of stout wooden bars that we found in the city full of men and boys who were being fattened for the sacrifices at which their flesh would be eaten."[3] "The valor of a warrior was estimated by the number of prisoners; and no ransom was large enough to save the devoted captive."[4] No one can understand the deep hatred that the Tlaxca-lans and other nearby Indians had for the Aztec; the Aztec practiced capture and cannibalism.

Cortes had two very important people who helped him in the conflict and conquest of the Aztec. One was a Franciscan priest, Aguilar, who had been shipwrecked and captured by the Mayans. He learned the Mayan lan-guage and became a translator for Cortes. The other individual was a female named La Malinche, generally referred to as Dona Marina. She knew the Aztec language (Nahuatl) and also Mayan. Cortes described Dona Marina as follows: "But let me say that Dona Marina, although a native woman, possessed such manly valor that though she heard every day that the Aztec were going to kill us and eat our flesh with *chillis*, and though she had seen us surrounded in recent battles and knew that we were all wounded and sick, yet she betrayed no weakness but a courage greater than that of a woman."[5] These two individuals were of paramount importance in that it allowed Cortes to communicate with the Aztec king, Montezuma. Now, for the heinous mutilation that Cortes and his Conquistadors confronted during their military campaign: They came upon some Aztec priests who were coming out of a religious temple. There were "ten Indians wearing long white cotton cloaks which fell to their feet. Their hair was very long, and so clotted with blood that it would have needed cutting before it could be combed or parted."[6] As they continued up the coast, they came upon an island and decided to explore it.

> We found two stone temples of good workmanship, each with a flight of steps leading to a kind of altar, and on those altars, were evil-looking idols, which were their gods. Here we found five Indians who had been sacrificed to them that very night. Their chests had been struck open and their arms and thighs cut off, and the walls of these buildings were covered with blood. All of this amazed us greatly, and we called this island the Isla de Sacrificios, as it is now named on the charts.[7]

Cortes was once invited to meet with Montezuma on the top of the main temple in the middle of the capital city, Tenochtitlan; today it is Mex-ico City. This city was a booming metropolitan city with many temples, shops and commercial stalls. It supposedly had a daily population of over 20,000 Indians and was the largest city in Pre-Columbian America. Cortes and some of his men climbed the 114 steps to the top of the temple and went into one of the buildings. "Below them were human hearts, freshly plucked from the living victims. The walls of the oratory were so splashed and encrusted with blood that they were black and the floor was the same. The place stank so abominably that we could hardly wait the moment to get out of it."[8] Cortes and his men:

> ...climbed down the pyramid and on their way out through the courtyard below saw more horrors. They were shown the room where the dead bod-ies of victims rolled down the pyramid after the hearts had been cut out, were collected and cut up, and where the limbs reserved for the priests were cooked. The skull-racks were also shown, a repository where the skulls of all victims were spitted and preserved. "They were arranged in perfect order," says Bernal, "but one could not count them because there were too many."[9]

Cortes also describes the human heart sacrificial process in greater detail below:

> They strike open the wretched Indian's chest with flint knives and hastily tear out the palpitating heart, which, with the blood, they presented to the idols in whose name they have performed the sacrifice. They then cut off the arms, thighs and head, eating the arms and thighs at their ceremonial banquets. The head they hang up on a beam, and the body of the sacrificed man is not eaten but given to the beasts of prey. They also had many vipers in this accursed house, and poisonous snakes which have something that sounds like a bell in their tails.[10]

This is probably the first European observation of the New World rattle-snakes. Cortes, with reinforcements from Cuba and thousands of Tlaxcalan auxiliary allies, between 80,000 and 100,000, defeated the Aztec in August of 1521.[11]

One of the most horrible historical occurrences in Aztec history took place in Tenochtitlan when Montezuma's predecessor, Auitzotzin, sacrificed 20,000 victims on the dedication at the temples of the Humming Bird. The approximate year of this massive sacrifice was 1486. They were not all sacri-ficed at one temple, that would have been impossible. They must have been divided amongst several of the Humming Bird temples. For twenty days, long queues of captives waited below these pyramids to have their hearts ripped out of their chests. The priests operated until they were exhausted. There were great public banquets of human arms and legs. The carnivores in the zoo were gorged with the trunks.[12]

Based upon the information above, one can readily conclude that the Aztec culture was one of the most brutal and inhumane cultures in the New World. Its practice of decapitation, human heart sacrifice, mutilation and cannibalism in the early 1500's clearly shows that even one of the most advanced Indian cultures in the New World could be clearly identified as overwhelmingly cruel. However, there is not any evidence to support the idea that they ever practiced scalping.[13] It also reveals the reality of inter-tribal warfare which was a fundamental aspect of all Indian cultures whether it be Mexican or the American Plains Indians.

Having examined the grotesque and murderous society of the Aztec, we will now explore some of the fundamental factors in the life and culture of the American Plains Indians. Their fundamental power and status came from war, violence, bloodshed and thievery. His crown of feathers, his ultimate dis-play of power, comes from the bloody hand of war. As one Indian agent stated:

> The young Indian from childhood is taught to regard "killing" as the highest of virtues. In the dance and at the feasts, the warriors recite their deeds of theft, pillage, and slaughter as precious things, and, indeed, the only ambition of the young Indian is to secure the "feather," which is but the record of his having murdered, or participated in the murder of some human being— whether man, woman or child is immaterial; and after he has secured his first feather, his appetite is whetted to increase the number in his hair, as an Indian brave is estimated by the number of his feathers. Without the feather the young Indian is regarded as a squaw, and, as a general rule, cannot get a wife, and is despised, derided, and treated with contumely by all. The head-dress filled with feathers and other insignia of blood is regarded as "wakan" (sacred), and no unhallowed hand of man nor any woman dare touch it.[14]

It becomes obvious that the only way a young warrior could attain power and a respectful position in the social hierarchy of the tribe is by the murder and the scalping of victims, sometimes living victims. The male warriors were also known as thieves especially for the practice of stealing horses, cat-tle and plundering settlers' homes.

An important part of this cruel culture is the practice of scalping the victims. There is definitely a controversy as to who started it, the Indi-ans or the English colonists. The Indian academic, politically-correct (P.C.) apologists, of course, blame the white man, the colonial English, for initi-ating the process and offering a bounty on Indian scalps. These apologists offer up their usual agenda-driven analysis. An Indian supporter, Diane E. Foulds, offered the following defense of her protected wards: "Buddy Gwin, a Mashantucket Pequot spokesman stated that 'scalping was not a prac-tice traditional to first nations peoples...'"[15] "Jim Brown, who is a tribal historical-preservation officer for Rhode Island's Narragansett Indians, said that bodily mutilation was considered 'dishonorable' until it was learned from Europeans in the mid-17th century."[16] Does anyone really believe that a "tribal historical-preservation officer" is going to present objective facts about the Indians? This is another obvious P. C. agenda-driven comment to embellish Indian society.

Another spokesman for the Indians, Colin Calloway, a history teacher at Dartmouth College, defends the Indians by stating, in reference to scalp-ing, that the misconceptions are part of "complex process of dehumanizing Indians to take away their land and culture, and attributing the brutality of frontier race wars to the 'other side.'"[17] Here is another one of the favorite words of the P. C. academicians, "dehumanizing"; they glorify in blaming the brutality of the frontier wars only on the white settlers and soldiers. Never is the "Noble Red Man" scrutinized for any blame in evaluating his role in the Indian wars.

All these pseudo-intellectuals need to do is basic research on the Great Minnesota Sioux Uprising of 1862. That would allow them to evaluate the evidence to prove that their "sacred" Indians were the real perpetrators of the "dehumanizing" atrocities. They do not have to go to any special government archives or to any super-duper academic university library. They just need to do good old-fashioned research using primary source materials. There is a wealth of excellent classic books, government documents, and personal letters which have been reprinted on the internet and readily available on Amazon and state historical societies.

An Indian defender, Sam Ball, a National Park Service archeologist, says that, "Most people have bought into the concept that Indians are savages."[18] However, the American Indians of the western plains did murder innocent white settlers. In many cases entire families, husbands, wives, children and even infants were butchered. Their gruesome heinous crimes knew no limits. They kidnapped and raped white women and, in many cases, sold them into slav-ery. The reason many Americans believed they were savages was because they "WERE SAVAGES." The obvious question is, what else would you expect from Indian apologists and academic sympathizers? They are, of course, going to proclaim their special protected minority, the Indian, as innocent and free from sin. They are the ones who lived in total harmony with nature and were the first environmentalists. The research proves this all to be wishful thinking. In many cases, Indians killed buffalo just for their tongues, the most tender and delicious part, and then left the rest of the carcass to decompose in the sun. The also killed many buffalo of their enemies and left them to rot on the prairies.

On the other side of the issue, we have James Axtell, a historian at the College of William and Mary, located in Williamsburg, Virginia. Axtell published a book in 1981 titled *The Europeans and the Indians* and argues that the practice of scalping in North and South America predated the arrival of Columbus.[19] Axtell goes on to state:

> Scalps were not mere trophies or booty of war, however. The whorl hair on the crown and especially male scalp locks, braided and decorated with jewelry, paint and feathers, represented the person's "soul" or living spirit. To lose that hair to an enemy was to lose control over one's life, to become socially and spiritually "dead," whether biological death resulted or not. The crucial distinction was the transference of power and identity into the vic-tor's hands.[20]

Axtell explains that the English colonists did pay for scalps in New England as early as 1675 during King Phillip's War. Originally, bounties were offered as an incentive to kill the Indian allies of your enemy and frighten them. This is a reflection of the idea of fighting the Indians the way they fought you. During the Revolutionary War, the English Americans and their Indian allies participated in the practice.

Axtell stated: "On his second voyage up the St. Lawrence in 1535, Jacques Cartier was shown by the Stadaconans at Quebec 'the skins of five men's heads, stretched on hoops, like parchment...' His host Donnacona told him 'they were Toudamans [Micmacs] from the south, who had waged war con-tinually against his people.'"[21] The complete and original quote can be found in Cartier's own manuscript titled the *Voyages of Jacques Cartier.* Additional evidence provided by Axtell included the fact that the following Spanish explorers also witnessed Apalachee Indian scalping: In 1540, two of Her-nando De Soto's men were captured by the Apalachee Indians; and one of them was scalped as the other watched. In 1549, near Tampa Bay on the west coast of Florida, a missionary reported that "I even saw skin of the crown (el pellejo de la corona) of the man, exhibited to me by an Indian who had brought it to show...the skin of the head...of the monk."[22] "In 1560 a party from the Luna expedition...accompanied local warriors on a raid of the Indian town of 'Napochies.' They found it abandoned, but in the plaza, was a pole...known to be associated with scalps—which was full of hair locks..."[23]

Paul Schneider, who wrote the book, *Brutal Journey*, published in 2006, stated that when the Spanish explorers investigated the west coast of Florida in the late 1520's, they encountered the Apalachee and Timucua Indians. Schneider wrote:

> Their facility with their weapons came from a lifetime spent hunting game, but they knew how to hunt men, too. Border warfare was endemic, and despite persistent rumors that the Europeans introduced the practice to

America, the collection of enemy scalps was already an important status marker before the Spanish arrived. The tool of choice was a sharp reed, and among the Apalachee, a single scalp entitled a young man to enter the *tascaia* or entry-level warrior class.[24]

The more scalps he possessed the higher the status he acquired; ten scalps identified him as a great warrior. This is, of course, exactly similar to the behavior of the American Plains Indians. Another author who disputes the charge that the English introduced the practice of scalping is Charles C. Mann. His book, *1491: New Revelations of the Americas Before Columbus,* was published in 2005. He stated: "Some of the activists have claimed that scalping was actually invented by the white colonists. But European visitors witnessed the practice in the 1530s and 1540s, before any colonies existed north of Florida. "'Hanging, disemboweling, beheading, and draw-ing and quartering were commonplace' in Europe, James Axtell observed, but not scalping. Each continent had its own form of mutilation, and 'it hardly seems worth arguing' which is worse."[25] As one remembers, the first English colony in the New World was established at Jamestown, Virginia, in 1607.

An outstanding defense of the premise that scalping began with the early eastern Indians is a quote made by Scott Weidensaul in his book, *The First Frontier,* published in 2012. He cogently presents the facts that prove that scalping was not originated by the English colonists, although they did make use of it as the colonies developed, in scalping of the Indians. Weiden-saul offers the following in-depth statement to argue his point.

> Starting in the nineteenth century, but especially since the 1960s, a myth has taken root that scalping was a European invention, to which the Natives were introduced after contact. Although there is certain appeal to this view of history—after all, the list of wrongs committed against the American Indi-ans by European invaders is long and bitter—it is demonstrably false. Scalp-ing had an ancient and incontrovertible history throughout North America.
>
> Scalping leaves diagnostic cut marks in the skull, and such wounds have been found by archaeologists at sites dating back thousands of years in places such as Kentucky,Tennessee, Ohio and North Dakota. More recently, but still well before European contact, almost five hundred people were massacred at Crow Creek, South Dakota, during an attack around 1325, most of them mutilated and virtually scalped after death. (In fact, a few of the victims had been scalped in some earlier attacks and survived.)
>
> Scalps were hardly the only parts taken as trophies. Entire heads were often removed, and early observers noted that scalps were sometimes

preferred only when distance precluded taking the whole thing. The lodge of a Huron war captain, in fact, was known as otinontsiskiaj ondaon, "the house of cutoff heads." Scalping, especially among Algonquians and other tribes in the Northeast, needs to be seen within the widespread cultural framework of ritual torture (and sometimes ritual cannibalism), enslavement, and the customary adoption of women, children, and occasionally men as replacements for lost relatives. Through torture, an enemy's spiritual strength could be assumed by his captors—a force also tapped through the possession of a scalp, which was far more than a mere trophy.[26]

The above quote clearly explains that Indian scalping had begun as early as 1325. We also have the statement of the French explorer Cartier in 1535 and the Spanish explorers from 1540 to 1560.

The fact that the Indians derived power from scalping their enemies was reflected in the Plains Indian culture. They thought the scalped victims became their slaves in the afterlife.The Plains Indians also believed that muti-lating their victims would prevent them from using the parts they mutilated. "With the muscles of the arms cut out, the victim could not pull a bow string or a trigger..."[27] Eyes were gouged out to make the enemy blind, and the ultimate insult was cutting of the penis and stuffing it in the victim's mouth. Victims of this sort of grotesque mutilation will be found when we examine the battle of Fort Phil Kearney, also known as the Fetterman Massa-cre. The battle took place on December 21, 1866. This same sort of butchery was also found on the Little Big Horn battlefield, Custer's fatal battle on the 25th of June 1876. In this battle, Custer's black scout, Isaiah Dorman, had his penis stuffed into his mouth and also had his testicles pinned to the ground with a picket pin.[28] So these are the innocent Indians who never mutilated American soldiers and settlers; I think the evidence proves otherwise.

Robert B. Caverly in his book, *Heroism of Hannah Duston,* describes the scalping practices in the 1690's. Hannah Dustin is famous for escaping from an Indian camp where she had been taken prisoner. Her young 6-day-old infant had its head smashed against a tree. When she got an opportunity to escape, she killed and scalped ten of the Indians in their sleep. She became one of the most famous women in New England.

This feat is performed by the savages as follows: Placing his foot upon the neck of his prostrate victim, he twists the fingers of his left hand into the scalp lock; and then, cutting with a knife in his right hand a circular gash around the lock, he tears the scalp from the head, and fastens it to his girdle with a yell of triumph. The scalp upon their belts on public occasions were worn to designate warriors.[29]

A second major factor in the Indian culture was the practice of polygamy. It was widespread and universally practiced by the Sioux, Cheyenne, Arapahoe and most other Indian tribes. In reality, it was a form of female slavery. Since it was a male dominated warrior society, women were not held in very high esteem. Where are our politically correct feminist academics? One never hears a word about Indian polygamy when there is a discussion about Indian society; there is very little condemnation. A warrior could take as many wives as he could afford or tolerate.

It must be noted that many female captives became the wife and slave of the warrior who captured her. Indian marriage, based on which tribe they belonged to, could be a simple or complicated process. Most Indian marriages were arranged by the parents, unless it was an elopement. The marriage process began with the obvious attraction of a male for a female. Upon the male asking the girl if he could marry her and if she agreed, she informed her parents and requested the young man's family to prepare a feast for her family. The boy had to "buy" the girl by presenting a certain number of horses and gifts at her family's tipi; the more important the girl's social status, the higher the price he had to pay. However, once the girl became his wife, she virtually became a slave.

The women were given the menial tasks of providing for the maintenance of the family unit. "Women performed the vital if unheroic labor of cooking, preparing skins and robes, making clothing and preparing lodgings, and moving the camp."[30] They also had to do the additional tasks of chopping firewood and getting water. Divorce depended on the tribe that the husband and wife belonged to. In some Sioux tribes, "all a man needed to do was publicly 'beat the drum' and announce that he had thrown his wife away, for no vows were involved. Marriage was not sanctified, but rather an agreement of the moment, a bargain to which both parties paid a set price for the commodity 'as is.' If the marriage worked, it worked because it was mutually satisfactory to the partners and their families. If it failed, it was the partners' affair and the family must needs adjust."[31]

Royal B. Hassrick, in his book, *The Sioux: Life and Customs of a Warrior Society*, presents a comprehensive explanation of the practice of polygamy. The primary reasons being physical attraction and economic status.

Polygamy was recognized as an acceptable adjustment for those men whose desire was not satisfied by a single spouse… "A man could marry num-ber of women—it mattered only if he could support them. Some women could be bought cheaply; for others one had to pay a great deal." A man might marry as many as six wives, although it was unusal since the matter of supporting this many wives, in two or more tipis, created, if nothing else, a discouragingly heavy economic responsibility. Men desiring plural marriage generally contented themselves with two wives, frequently marrying a younger sister of their first mate.

Polygamy for the Sioux in no way implied a lower status for women or inferred any jeopardy of their rights. In many instances it was the woman who suggested that her husband take a younger wife, realizing that this would relieve her of some of the housekeeping burdens while giving her added status as the senior spouse of a well-to-do man. For it was common knowledge that only the wealthy could afford more than one wife. [32]

In the Blackfeet tribe, in addition to polygamy, we have specific references to adultery. This procedure is much more brutal and may even result in death.

Among the Blackfeet the law in regard to adultery is death for the adulteress, and forfeiture of all the property of the adulterer. His lodge is cut to pieces, his horses are either killed or taken from him, and the woman must suffer death...

When an Indian sees his wife makes too free with young men, the penalty for such offense is a piece of the nose. I have seen several who have undergone that punishment, and awful did they look. After cutting off her nose the husband says, "Go now and see how fond the young men will be talking to you."

Among the Assiniboine's there is no particular law in regard to adultery. This is left at the disposition of the injured individual, who sometimes revenges himself...Some give the woman a flogging, and then either drive her away or keep her. Nothing will be said about it, but the woman then bears a bad name—in their language Wittico Weeon, which means a prostitute... [33]

Now for an explanation of how Indian warriors treated women captives, red or white.

The treatment of women, by any Indians, is usually bad, but by the plains Indians especially so. When a woman is captured by a war party she is the common property of all of them, each night, till they reach their village, when she becomes the special property of her individual captor, who may sell her or gamble her away when he likes. If she resists she is "staked out," that is too say, four pegs are driven into the ground and a hand or a foot tied to each, to prevent struggling. She is also beaten, mutilated, or even killed, for resistance. If a woman gives out under this treatment, she is either tied so as to prevent escape, or maimed so as to insure death in case of rescue, and left to die slowly. [34]

Here is another specific example of the brutal behavior that one Indian carried out against a while woman captive. In this case, a woman named Lucinda Ewbanks who lived on the Little Blue River in Colorado. These atrocious actions were carried out by an old Cheyenne chief:

> He forced me, by the most horrible threats and menaces, to yield my person to him. He treated me as his wife. He then traded me to Two Face, a Sioux, who did not treat me as a wife, but forced me to all menial labor done by squaws and he beat me terribly. Two Face traded me to Black Foot (a Sioux) who treated me as his wife, and because I resisted him his squaws abused and ill-used me. Black Foot also beat me unmercifully, and the Indians gener-ally treated me as though I was a dog, on account of my showing so much detestation towards Black Foot.[35]

Now, we will examine one of the better known white captivity sto-ries related to this time period. The first famous captivity story we will examine is that of Sarah Wakefield, a victim of the Great Sioux Uprising of 1862. Sarah wrote the first edition of her book, *Six Weeks in the Sioux Tepees*, in November of 1863. She published a second edition in 1864. The length of her book varies depending upon the edition. I highly recom-mend the first edition rather than the second; it has the ungarnished and accurate words of Sarah's captivity. The second edition added 3 additional pages interestingly stating sympathy for the Indians who had lost their land. In reference to a republished second edition, 1997, one, June Namais, who is an Associate Professor of History, has edited and annotated the 1997 book with a 39-page introduction. After this extensive introduction, she reprints Sarah Wakefield's original second edition which was published in 1864.

In reference to Namais' edition, I suggest you do not read any of the introduction to Sarah's book. Read them afterwards so Sarah's actual words will not be distorted. Generally, left-wing introductions are usually crammed with fabricated nonsense from our politically correct feminist "friends." They always stress the Indians' positive virtues of cooperation, a shared-community life style, and their environmentally correct culture. In reference to a comparison between the Indians and whites, they always see the Indians as far superior to the greedy and acquisitive values of white society. They also surreptitiously promote the idea that all of the women who are sympathetic to the "Noble Red Man" are heroines and "empow-ered women"; empowered being one of their most worn out clichés.

Sarah's experience is not typical of most of the captivity narratives. She is one of the few that was not sexually abused. Sarah Wakefield, her husband

John and their children had lived amongst the Indians for approximately 6 years, 1858 to 1862. They were married in 1856. They had two children, one son James, who was about 5 years old at the time of the Uprising, and one young daughter, Lucy, who was often called Nellie. She was about 18 months old at that time and still nursing. One of the main reasons she stayed alive was that her husband, John, was one of the agency physicians. Both of them had helped feed and minister to the Indians.

The Christianized and friendly Indians immediately recognized her as his wife. Many of the old squaws happily greeted her and her children and tried to make them as comfortable as they could. Another reason for her survival was the crucial assistance she received from a friendly Sioux Indian named Chaska. His direct intervention prevented her death by a hostile Indian named Hapa. Chaska rightly deserved Sarah's praise and undying gratitude. She tried to save his life but was unsuccessful. She did, however, strongly defend him during the trial after the Uprising. She earned the condemnation of many of her fellow Minnesotans for this defense. Some wrongly called her an "Indian lover" and charged that she was his "wife." She states that, "All the time I was with the Indians the women seemed envious of me, saying that the Indians thought more of me than any other female."[36] Her reputation suffered for her courageous actions. Chaska was mistakenly hung after the trial due to the confusion of the spelling and pro-nunciation of his name. Sarah questioned whether it was done on purpose or was it truly a mistake.

This trial is one of the most famous, or infamous if you prefer, in that 38 Indians were hanged at one time on December 26, 1862. Originally, some 300 Indians had been selected for hanging; but President Lincoln dramatically reduced that number to 38. It was the largest simultaneous one-day execution in American history. This execution was for their heinous participation in the Great Sioux Uprising of 1862. The Sioux murdered between 750 and 1000 white men, women and children; and they also had been tortured and mutilated by them. It is considered by many to be the greatest massacre of white people by Indians in American history.

I would challenge the idea of using U. S. constitutional law to try Indian savages as simply ridiculous. They are clearly not citizens of the United States. It would be like using constitutional law to try modern-day terror-ists. In my humble opinion, neither group is deserving of constitutional law. The Indians had also captured 269 white and half-breed captives who they tried to use as a bargaining chip at the end of the war. The most concen-trated fighting took place between the 17th and the 24th of August, 1862. It is estimated that 200 to 300 settlers were killed in that first week. The fighting continued until September 23, 1862, when Colonel Henry Sibley and his troops defeated the Indians at the Battle of Wood Lake.

The murdering of the settlers began of the 17th of August in the small town of Acton, Minnesota, and involved a hunting party of between 3 to 5 Sioux warriors. They had been unsuccessful on their trip and, upon return-ing, spied upon a farmer's fence with some eggs in it. They argued amongst themselves whether to eat the eggs or not, one warrior accusing another of cowardice because the eggs belonged to a white man. He said that the other was afraid of white men. This insult caused the warriors to attack the settle-ment of Acton, and they killed five white settlers. The unwarranted attack is often referred to as the "Chicken Egg" war. This incident, in addition to the incompetent and corrupt annuities program run by the government, led to a full-scale attack led by Chief Little Crow against the Lower Indian agency, known as the Redwood agency. This war is also known for the famous quote, "if they are hungry, let them eat grass or their own dung," suppos-edly made by Andrew Myrick. Myrick was one of the agency's supply store owners. But recent research by Gregory Michno and Gary C. Anderson has generated serious doubt that Myrick really made that infamous state-ment. Although when his brother, Nathan, discovered him dead after the brutal first week of the Uprising, he was found shot full of arrows with an old scythe pushed through his body. He was supposedly found later with grass stuffed in his mouth. This fact would seem to back up the charge that Myrick had made the statement. More specific and detailed information will be presented in Chapter 3 on the Great Sioux Uprising of 1862.

For Sarah, the insanity known as the Great Uprising erupted a day later on the 18th of August. "Monday, the 18th, they began their work of destruc-tion at an early hour, killing traders in their stores; after this was done they began their outrageous murder and mutilation. The wine and spirits found in the general stores added drunken madness to the madness of despairing vengeance..."[37] She was protected by an Indian named Chaska from the very beginning of her captivity. She had originally been captured by two Indians, Hapa and Chaska. "Chaska was a farmer Indian, and had worn white man's dress for several years; had been to school and could speak some English..."[38] Hapa was the hostile Indian who Chaska said was drunk and an evil man. Once Hapa aimed his gun at Sarah and Chaska knocked the gun down and saved her life. Hapa kept threatening Sarah and said that, "She must die; all whites are bad, better bedead."[39]

Chaska and his mother dressed Sarah as an Indian to help hide and protect her. When dangerous Indians came to camp, the mother wiped dirt Sarah's skin to make her look more like an Indian. Throughout Sarah's six week stay Chaska, his mother, many of the Christianized squaws and even Chaska's grandfather helped Sarah and her children hide. If you thought that her stay amongst the Indians was a quiet and peaceful experience you would be wrong. There were many instances of her Indian friends having to hide her and her nursing baby, Nellie, and also her son, James. There were many drunken and hostile Indians who wanted to kill all the white captives. In one instance, Chaska's grandfather had to hide her in a haystack; she remained there all day without any food or water thinking she was going to die.[40] In many of these captivity stories, only the hardships of the adult men and women are discussed; few address the dangers and fright felt by the children. In this case, Sarah had been separated from her oldest child, James. When they were finally reunited, Sarah described the joy she experienced and said:

> Presently he came in; what a joyful moment for a mother's heart. He rushed into my arms and cried if his little heart would break, "Oh, mamma, I thought you was dead, and I was left alone with the Indians. I have cried until I am sick. Oh, dear mamma have you got back? Do kiss me, and keep your arms around me. I thought that you and Nellie had gone to heaven and left your boy all alone..." I could not get him out of my arms that night. He clung to me in his sleep, and trembled with fear if I would make an attempt to lay him down. I sat all night and held him, and watched the stars through the opening of our tepee, and wondered if his father could see him and me in my captivity.[41]

Later on, James made a very pertinent observation about his Indian captors: "Oh, dear me! mamma, what do you suppose God made Indians for? I wish they were all dead, don't you mamma?"[42] This is an excruciating example of the wrenching pain and suffering that the Indians inflicted on their white captives, especially the innocent and sensitive children! It is this heartless enduring torment that will haunt them forever. It is these unbearable nightmares that today's leftist social scientists purposely want to ignore.

In reference to Sarah Wakefield's experience, the author, June Namias, has written an edited and annotated copy of *Six Weeks in the Sioux Tepees* which was published in 1997. Namias, in my opinion, dwells on the usual politically correct feminist-driven agenda in her introduction. Sarah must be eulogized as the perfection of the "empowered" frontier woman. Namias writes that Sarah had "retained a taste for eastern fashion. She followed contemporary trends in both clothing and culture...Her wardrobe included silk, cashmere, linen, and chenille dresses and even a green velvet hat with feathers. For cold weather she had kid and beaver gloves, an otter muff and cuffs."[43] This seems to be an attempt to associate Sarah's social class to sup-port the credibility of her observations. Observations that must be above doubt. Namais wrote that Sarah had "tasted freedom" and was an inde-pendent, daring woman who was ready to explore her physical and cultural surroundings. She is also a woman of high morality with pro-Indian sympa-thies. Namais describes her as everything our feminist friends hold near and dear to their hearts, an independent "empowered woman."

Another attempt to glorify Sarah states:

> She wrote with a flair. She expanded her second edition written in 1864 because she recognized her talent and gained confidence in her ability to create powerful scenes of human drama…This second edition more fully articulates a pro-Indian emphasis; in the tradition of the alternative captivity narrative; it argues for compassion and understanding. Sarah Wakefield wrote with a moral message.[44]

It is more likely that Sarah experienced tremendous guilt because she did not or could not save her friend Chaska's life, her Dakota protector and friend.

One of the most tragic incidents to happen to Sarah takes place after the Sioux had surrendered. It has to do with Sarah's attempts to save Chaska's life during and after the trial. When Sarah was a captive, she found it neces-sary to claim that she was Chaska's wife to save her and her children's lives. In reference to a battle that the Indians were going to fight against the white men, they said if they lost they would come back and kill all of the white prisoners and half-breeds. Sarah stated:

> When I heard this I dropped as one struck with apoplexy; I could not speak for a while, my teeth chattered and I shivered with fear. I then thought of what Chaska had many times told me, that if I were in danger, to tell the Indians I was his wife, and I would be saved. So, I said to an Indian, "I am Chaska's wife, will they kill me?" He said, "No," but he believed I was tell-ing an untruth. I went back to the old woman's and told Chaska. He said I had done very wrong in saying so, for there was no truth in the story. He was very angry with me for saying so. But I did not consider how it would sound. I would have called myself the evil spirit's wife if I thought by doing so I could save my life. I suppose many Indians really thought I was his wife, for there was such an excitement all the time I forgot all about contradicting it. One day before this a half-breed woman came in and a white woman was with her. They said that Little Crow was going to destroy all the whites, but would spare all that had Indian blood in them. I made up this story, which I relate here. I said I was safe, as I was part Indian. I knew the lady who had

known me in Shakopee many years and she said she did not believe me. I said I was an eight-breed; that my grandfather married a squaw many years ago, in the West, and took her East, and I was one of her descendants...I was sure this half-breed woman would tell it all around, and I would be spared. I knew it was wrong to tell such falsehoods, but I felt as my God knew my thoughts, and he would pardon me for doing as I did. Now to this day that woman believes me part Indian, because I never had an opportunity to con-tradict it.[45]

There were several stories that got Sarah into trouble with her fellow Minnesotans during and after the trial. Many of the women captives had also noticed that Sarah was treated and lived in more comfortable conditions than they did, and they held that against her. Mary Schwandt stated:

I remembered Mrs. Dr. Wakefield (Sarah) and Mrs. Adams. They were painted and decorated and dressed in full Indian costume, and seemed proud of it. They were usually in good spirits, laughing and joking, and appeared to enjoy their new life. The rest of us disliked their conduct, and would have little to do with them. Mrs. Adams was a handsome young woman, talented and educated, but she told me she saw her husband murdered, and that the Indian she was then living with had dashed out her baby's brains before her eyes. And yet she seemed perfectly happy and contented with him![46]

Mrs. Adams reaction to her new circumstances makes for a curious and unfathomable response to the death of her husband and baby. I cannot help but wonder what mystical power, psychological or physical, this new Indian husband had over her.

Chaska, on the other hand, was afraid to be captured; but Sarah and another captive, Ellen Brown, were able to convince Chaska to stay and told him they would protect him from Colonel Sibley and the soldiers.[47] Chaska was afraid of being held wrongly accused by the Army and stated to Sarah: "'You are a good woman, you must talk good to your white people, or they will kill me; you know I am a good man, and did not shoot Mr. Gleason, and I saved your life'... I assured him he need not fear, they would not injure him; but how vain were all my promises; poor man, he found the white deceitful, even until his death."[48] Sarah made several concerted efforts to defend Chaska before and during the trial. She identified him as the Indian who had protected her and her family and even called him by name. When her time came to offer testimony during the trial, she again repeated the same favorable story, convincing herself that all would turn out alright; but she was tragically mistaken.

The Commission modified the rules of law; and although Mr. Steven R. Riggs, the interpreter, translated the charges against each Indian, many have considered the trial unfair. The terrible misfortune for Chaska was that he was misidentified for another Sioux with the name Chaskadon. The sad reality was that Chaska's name was supposedly on the list that was recom-mended for mercy.[49] The relationship between Chaska and Sarah deterio-rated because Chaska believed that Sarah had told lies to the soldiers and that these lies had gotten him imprisoned. Sarah tried to convince him otherwise and was somewhat successful. Their last contact was a final silent farewell handshake. Just the night before she left, a Captain Grant had informed Sarah that Chaska would not be hung. He told her that Chaska would instead be put in prison for five years. Sarah was very saddened to hear that her Chaska was accidently hung. In a letter written from Mr. Riggs to Sarah, he said:

Mrs. Wakefield:

Dear Madam: In regard to the mistake, by which Chaska was hung, instead of another, I doubt whether I can satisfactorily explain it. We all felt a solemn responsibility, and a fear that some mistake should occur. We had forgotten that any other (except Robert Hopkins, who lived by Dr. Williamson's) was so called. On that fatal morning we never thought of the third one. When Chaska was called, your protector answered by the name and came out, & c.[50]

Respectfully yours,
S.R. Riggs

Although Sarah did defend Chaska, in my opinion, she should have followed through and been there for the hanging so there would be no chance of a mistake. After finding her husband alive, she left the area trave-ling down the Minnesota River from Camp Release to Fort Ridgely and then to Mankato and on to Shakopee. It took her several days to complete this journey. The mass executions took place at Mankato on December 26, 1862. I fear that Sarah, once finding her husband alive, was overjoyed with the renewal of her family. As stated, she was informed that Chaska was only going to be imprisoned and put it out of her mind. In my opinion, the main culprit of Chaska's mistaken hanging was Mr. Riggs. He had been involved with the Sioux Indians since 1837 when he and his wife Mary moved into the area as missionaries. He and his wife lived there for twenty-five years before the Uprising took place. Riggs was very familiar with these Indians. As stated before, he had acted as the interpreter during the controversial trial. His duties as interpreter would have made him capable of understanding the confusion of the two names, and he could have prevented a tragic mistake.

Sarah Wakefield's captivity was an atypical example of a white woman's captivity story. She was a special case due to the simple fact that she and her husband, a doctor, had befriended and ministered to many of the Christian-ized and farmer Indians, especially Chaska and his family. She was immedi-ately identified as a special white woman and one to be protected by some of the friendly male and female Indians. So, to attempt to use this example of Indian kindness is totally deceptive.

In reference to the number of unfortunate women raped and murdered, many of them were unable to testify or write their memoirs. This is due to the obviously horrible circumstances beyond their control; they were either dead or their rapists had escaped with Little Crow. Little Crow was the Indian chief who led the Indians in the Great Sioux Uprising of 1862. So, their tragic fate kept the reported rape numbers down. It was not the theo-ries of "white hysteria" or "rape rhetoric!" These two bizarre concepts have been developed by the politically correct social scientists, especially femi-nists, to discredit the numbers of rapes perpetrated by the Indians against the white female settlers. "Rape Rhetoric" refers to the fabricated idea that the rapes reported by the captured white women were nothing more than white hysteria; they never happened. According to the politically correct feminists, the number of white women who were supposedly raped by Indians was purposely inflated to incite the local white population. Rape Rhetoric also refers to the ridiculous idea that the more these women talked about rape, the more they reported rape.

The feminists like to utilize the Military Commission trial results of two proven rape cases to prove their contention that rape was almost non-existent. One must remember that Little Crow and about 300 of his brutal followers had escaped. They were probably the ones who participated in much of the rape, murder, plundering and mutilation. So, the feminists' per-verse delight does not ring true based upon a more thorough investigation.

> Most of the Indians who had committed the murders and atrocities during the uprising had, indeed, gotten away, some heading north with Little Crow and still on the move. Others had not gone so far but had merely crossed the river where they could keep in touch with the situation and return to the Indian camp if all seemed well. Others set up their tepees out on the prairie and waited.[51]

The rapists and murders had escaped with Little Crow and therefore were not present during the surrender or the trial. How can you identify someone who is not there? The escape of Little Crow's warriors would reduce the number of actual rapes reported. One would also have to take into consideration the murdered victims who were raped; their murders would obviously reduce the number of surviving witnesses.

The next primary source book we will investigate is the story of Mary and John Renville written by Stephen R. Riggs in 1880. Mary Renville's story was originally published in 1862 as a thirteen-part series in a local news-paper, the *Berlin City Courant*, the title being, "The Indian Captives: Leaves from a Journal." The book was later published in July of 1863 under the title, *A Thrilling Narrative of Indian Captivity: Dispatches from the Dakota War*.

This book was also republished in 2012 and contains two politically correct, propagandistic introductions that will cause you a terrible migraine headache.[52] The first one is titled "Historical Perspectives," by Carrie Reber Zeman, an independent historian specializing in the context and historiography of the U.S.-Dakota War of 1862. To specialize in such minutia further reinforces the concept that today's academics concentrate on ridiculously narrow subject matters. The second introduction is titled "Literary Perspectives" by Kathryn Zabelle Derounian-Stodola. She is a professor of English. There is also a brief Forward written by Gwen N. Westerman who also is a professor of English and the director of the annual Native American Literature Symposium. She ends her Forward in the Dakota language. I am sure many of us know the meaning of the phrase, "Henana epe kte. Winjuna de miye."

Just to give you a sample of the politically correct, gobbledygook language they use, I will present some of the words used. (Remember, the goal of good writing is to write clearly!) The words are: amanuensis, missiology, contextualize, holographs, the Dakota language by Gwen N. Westerman, quantum, monogenist, acculturationist, exogamous, ABCFM, polygenism, blood quantum, extant, oyate, poly-vocal, ennui, hyperbole, platen, thematic entrée, intertextuality, textual mediation, the three uses of "we," morph into a moral exemplum, trope, and a culture of belonging-bell hooks. These are the nonsensical words used in the two introductions that would, of course, enlighten the average reader. What we must remember is that they are only writing amongst themselves, and what they are attempting to do is impress each other with their pseudo-sophisticated vocabulary.

Westerman is also a member of the Sisseton-Wahpeton Dakota Oyate and a speaker of the Dakota language. The Sisseton-Wahpeton tribes were two of the four involved in the Uprising. I am sure that Westerman, with her background, is completely UNBIASED in reference to the role of the Sioux Indians. The original book consisted of 13 chapters and 58 pages. The

Renvilles were a mixed-blood couple. John was part French and Dakota Indian. His father's heritage is difficult to trace, but he was definitely a French fur trader. The father, Joseph, named his sons John Baptiste, Michael and Antoine; they do not sound like Dakota names to me. Mary was 100% white.

So, this is what our politically correct friends in the academic world like to conclude, as they write, that John was three-quarters Dakota. How they came up with the convoluted number is utterly beyond me. It seems to me that he is more likely one-half French. He was definitely of mixed-blood, and they were a mixed-blood couple. It is interesting to note that even with their mixed-blood relations, both of them were taken and held captive. Her book does an excellent job of describing the two main different groups of Sioux, the Lower band hostiles or "Blanket" Indians, and the friendly Peace Coalition and Christian Indians, known as the "Farmer" Indians, who helped the victims of this massacre.

In my opinion, the Indians suffer as much from ethnocentrism as the whites or any other culture. Our Indian defenders only concentrate on the white ethnocentrism and never identify or explain any of the negative stereotyping that the Indians exhibited. Well, Mary Renville does mention two examples of this negative view that the Indians had of the whites. In the first one she states that, "The Indians dressed them (white captives) up in the poorest kind of Dakota clothes, and then laughed at them, saying, 'these are the people who used to dress in silks so rich and fine'... "[53] Obviously, if one race of people like to embarrass, denigrate, make fun, and belittle another race of people, I would call that Indian ethnocentrism. She goes on to report:

> Chande, an old wicked heathen woman, said to Catherine, "Where is your God? Why don't he come and help you? You see now that our gods are strong and mighty, and have driven away all your teachers. You had better renounce your worship, and serve our idols."[54]

I consider the above statement to be one of the bigoted ethnocentric views of the Indians. When one group humiliates the religious system of another and challenges their very sacred religious deities, they are bigots. Be assured if white men had done the same things, our pro-Indian advocates would have been viciously condemning the whites as "ethnocentric," which they often do.

It is sometimes stated by our Indian advocates that the Indians supposedly treated the captive children as if they were their own. However, Mrs.

Renville cites an example that proves this to be a false assertion. Sometime between September the 15th and September 21st, the following murder of a white boy took place. "It was reported about camp that a white boy has been shot. The woman who had taken him was always at variance with him, and the boy, being very resolute, would not obey her. She became enraged, and tried to kill him, but she did not succeed. When her husband came in she told him about the boy. He led him very coolly out of the tent and shot him."[55]

Another example of the detestable actions of the Indians reveals how the white victims of the Indian brutality felt about the Uprising:

> Mrs. Adams took up her child and hid while the Indians were pursuing her husband, but they soon found her, and caught hold of the child's feet and dashed it to the ground. They then shot him through the body. Mrs. Adams said she believed the child was dead before it reached the ground, for they jerked it so she thought the breath left its body, but was not sorry they shot it for then she knew positively it was dead. She said a little way from her they shot a mother, leaving her helpless infant alive by her side in the road... We learned afterwards that Mr. Adams found the child's body and buried it. Mrs. Adams said she knew her husband would seek revenge on the Indians as long as his life was spared, and that she joined heartily with him. This is the feeling that pervades the minds of the majority of the people of Minnesota. We cannot blame them for feeling injured, for their homes have been made desolate.[56]

These observations indicate the inhumane and gruesome acts that the Indi-ans committed. One must recall that modern Indian advocates consider many of the captivity narratives as examples of white women's "hysteria and imagination." I would suggest that their own books and writings are manifestations of their own intellectual hysteria and defensive imaginations to protect their selected Indian wards.

One of the interesting things about Mary's narrative is that even when describing these brutalities, she still manages to maintain her thanks and belief in the friendly Indians who put their lives in danger to assist her. Mary Renville's story of Indian protection is very similar to that of Sarah Wake-field, who defended her Indian friend Chaska. Sarah offered a remarkably brave defense, in the wake of hostile white criticism, of the friendly Indians and openly attacked the government policies as unfair and ill-conceived.[57]

These two sources confirm that there was much done by the friendly Indi-ans and also stated positive things about Agent Galbraith, the same Galbraith who was much criticized by many of the secondary sources. That's why it is so important to extensively use primary source materials.

The end of her book describes the dates from September 21st through the 25th of 1862. Here she relates the hopeful activities of the captives while waiting for their rescue by Gen. Sibley and his troops:

> ...the friendly Indians, especially the Christians manifested much happiness that the time had come to deliver the captives and themselves from the cruel war waged by Satan's emissaries, who are, or least the most wicked ones, flee-ing from the pursuit of justice, while those who delivered themselves up as prisoner of war, the most of whom are not guilty in crime, are condemned. The friends even that protected the suffering ones, are doomed to an exile almost as cruel as that which the captives suffered, for they had long had the opportunity of hearing the gospel before they were taken prisoner; and if they were Christians the rebels could only destroy the body but could not harm the soul.[58]

She further writes that, "May God guide the people of Minnesota, who have suffered deeply, to act wisely in the present instance, and not drive even the friendly Indians to homeless desperation by driving or sending them among the warlike tribes..."[59] Clearly, Mary Renville's conclusion pre-sents a message of sincere concern for the future well-being of the friendly Indians and a request that white Minnesotans treat them fairly, just as Sarah Wakefield had done.

Now what conclusions can be drawn from having examined Mary Renville's 56-page pamphlet. The first thing she makes reference to is the thievery of the hostile Indians in regards to the stealing of horses. She also describes the plundering of the settlers' homes, the stealing of per-sonal property, and the burning of homes, sometimes with live settlers and their children inside. Renville clearly describes the violent raping of young white girls. But as the evidence has shown, the academic Indian defenders and protectors, Westerman, Zeman, and Stodola, have presented the absurd concepts of "Rape Rhetoric" and "White Hysteria" to try to discredit the outrageous and heinous sexual crimes of their "Nobel Red Man." For them, white women have rarely experienced any sexual abuse by male Indians, especially in the numbers that they have reported, because, according to the Leftists and feminists, it is not part of their sacred religious culture.

The story of Mary Schwandt is another one that directly relates to the Great Sioux Uprising of 1862. The title of her book is *The Story of Mary Schwandt: Her Captivity during the Sioux "outbreak," 1862;* it was published in 1894. Mary was born near Berlin, Germany in 1848. Her family moved to the United States in 1858 and originally settled in Wisconsin. They remained there for four years before moving to the Minnesota River valley.

Her family was a large one by today's standards. She and her relatives com-prised a family of eight individuals and one hired man.

> Our family at this time consisted of my father and mother, my sister Karolina, aged nineteen, and her husband John Waltz; myself, aged fourteen; my brothers, August, Frederick and Christian, aged respectively, ten, six and four years old and a hired man, named John Fross. We all lived together...The greater part of the spring and summer was spent by the men in breaking the raw prairie and bottom lands so that the sod would be sufficiently rotted for the next season's planting...My father brought with him from Wisconsin some good horses and wagons and several head of cattle and other stock. He also brought a sum of money, the most of which was in gold. He had brought some money from Germany, and he added to it when in Wisconsin. Our situation in our new home was comfortable, and my father seemed well satisfied.[60]

One of the main problems that Mary and other young settlers had was that the neighbors and young people were isolated and lonely. It also shows the simple desires that the white settlers wanted, their own peaceful homestead on the western frontier. It was due to this loneliness that Mary Schwandt went to a neighbor's house, the Reynolds, to help them with their housework and chores. It was a good thing that she was not at home when the outbreak began. Both of Mary's parents, John and Christina, were at home at the time; and they were some of the first white settlers to suffer the outrages of the Sioux. The following scene is horrible beyond belief:

> As dawn broke on August 18, 1862, Shakopee, Red Middle Voice, and their warriors approached John Schwandt's cabin. Without any warning, they shot him dead as he repaired his roof. The Indians tomahawked and slashed Christina to death. Her body was discovered in a nearby field, but her head was never found. John Waltz, Karolina, Christian, Frederick, and John Fross, were similarly dispatched. August, a third brother, was tomahawked and believed dead, but survived. August saw the Indians slice open his sister, remove the fetus of her unborn child, and nail it to a tree.[61]

Schwandt tried to escape from the Reynolds' home but was unsuccessful. Mary and two other girls, Mary Anderson and Mattie Williams, were taken to a Chief Wacouta's home and kept there.

> Several Indians came to the house and pestered Mary with unwelcome attentions. One Indian forcibly touched her. When she screamed in protest he hit her in the mouth, causing it to bleed profusely. Mary said, "They

then took me out by force, to an unoccupied teepee, near the house, and perpetrated the most horrible and nameless outrages upon my person. These outrages were repeated at different times during my captivity."[62]

To further substantiate the charges of rape by the Sioux, one has to present the ordeal of Mattie Williams. Mattie was with Mary Schwandt during her stay in captivity. "She was one of the few women who agreed to testify about being raped. She named Tazoo as the one who tied her arms behind her and raped her repeatedly. Tazoo said, 'I ravished her.' He was later hanged."[63]

An interesting fact about the treatment of white women captives is that in some cases the Indian women went out of their way to protect and take care of them. In many instances protecting them from rude, obnoxious and sinister male Indians. In the case of Mary Schwandt, she was adopted by an old Indian woman by the name of Wam-nu-ka-win. The old woman had purchased her for one pony and gave her to her daughter, Snana. Mary was given to Snana (Maggie) because one of her own daughters had died. Mag-gie stated:

About eight days before the massacre, my oldest daughter had died, and hence my heart was still aching when the outbreak occurred. Two of my uncles went out to see the outbreak, and I told them that if they should hap-pen to see any girl I wished them not to hurt her but bring her to me that I might keep her for a length of time. One evening one of my uncles came to me and said that he had not found any girl, but there was a young man who brought a nice-looking girl. I asked my mother to go and bring this girl to me…When she brought this girl, whose name was Mary Schwandt, she was much larger than the one I had lost, who was only seven years old; but my heart was so sad that I was willing to take any girl at that time. The reason why I wished to keep this girl was to have her in place of the one I lost. So, I loved her and pitied her, and she was dear to me just the same as my own daughter.[64]

This is an interesting point because many white captives were often adopted into one of the families and, therefore, into the tribe itself, especially young women and children. This is the basic relationship that began between Maggie and Mary and became an endearing friendship that helped protect Mary while she was in captivity. Mary stated: "Maggie and her mother were both very kind to me, and Maggie could not have treated me more tenderly if I had been her daughter."[65]

Mary went on to state, "wherever you are, I want you to know that the little captive German girl you so often befriended and shielded from harm loves you still for your kindness and care, and she prays God to bless you and reward you in this life and that to come."[66] Mary and Maggie had separated and would not see each other for 32 years. Maggie said "until the autumn of 1894; when I learned that she lives in St. Paul, being the wife of Mr. William Schmidt. Soon I went to visit her, and I was respected and treated well. It was just as if I went to visit my own child."[67]

Mary Schwandt-Schmidt offers the following touching conclusion to her book:

> Life is made up of shadow and shine. I sometimes think I have had more than my share of sorrow and suffering, but I bear in mind that I have seen much of the agreeable side of life, too. A third of a century almost has passed since the period of my great bereavement and of my captivity. The memory of that period, with all its hideous features, often rises before me, but I put it down... my experience is a part of a leading incident in the history of Minnesota that ought to be given to the world. In the hope that what I have written may serve to inform the present and future generations what some of the pioneers of Minnesota underwent in their efforts to settle and civilize our great state, I submit my plain and imperfect story.[68]

The final captivity story we will examine is that of Fanny Kelly. Fanny was born in 1845 and lived to 1904; a total of 59 years. The name of her book is *Narrative of My Captivity Among the Sioux Indians,* originally published in 1871. Her maiden name was Wiggins and she married Josiah Kelly. While moving from Canada to what was to become Kansas, her father fell victim in 1867 to the infectious and deadly scourge of the western wagon trains, cholera. For those of you not familiar with cholera, it is defined as "an acute infectious disease of the small intestine caused by a bacteria that is characterized by profuse watery diarrhea, vomiting, and severe dehydration."[69] It is primarily caused by poor sanitation and contaminated drinking water. It has been suggested that cholera probably killed more settlers than the hostile warfare between the two groups. There certainly were an extensive number of headstones along the Oregon Trail marking the graves of the brave and determined settlers.

Fanny and her family had been joined on their journey by four other wagons. The size of their combined party was 11 individuals, which included two colored servants. Their unfortunate occurrence happened on the 12th of July, 1864. Fanny at that time was 19 years-old. Their combined group had the misfortune of being discovered by a large Indian war party of about 250 Sioux warriors. As was generally the case, the immigrants tried to appease the hostile Indians by providing food and other goods. Fanny wrote:

First, they said they would like to change one of their horses for the one Mr. Kelly was riding, a favorite race horse. Very much against his will, he gave into their request...The Indians asked for flour, and we gave them what they wanted. The flour they emptied upon the ground, only saving the sack...we allowed them to take whatever they desired, and offered them many pre-sents besides...They grew bolder and more insolent in their advances. One of them laid hold of my husband's gun, but, being repulsed, desisted...they requested that we should prepare supper, which they said they would share with us, and then go into the hills to sleep. The men of our party concluded it best to give them a feast and Mr. Kelly gave orders to our two servants to prepare a large meal immediately for the Indians...

The two black men had been slaves among the Cherokees, and knew the Indian character by experience. Their fear and horror of them was unbounded, and their terror seemed pitiable to us, as they had worked for us a long time, and were most faithful, trustworthy servants...Supper, that they had asked for, was in rapid progress of preparation, when suddenly our terrible enemies threw off their masks and displayed their truly demoniac character. There was a simultaneous discharge of arms...Mr. Taylor—I never can forget his face as I saw him shot through the forehead with a rifle ball. He looked at me as he fell backward to the ground, a corpse. I was the last object that met his eyes dying gaze...I had but little time for thought, for the Indians quickly sprang into our wagons, tearing off covers, breaking, crush-ing, and smashing all hindrances to blunder, breaking open locks, trunks, and boxes, and distributing or destroying our goods with great rapidity, using their tomahawks to pry open boxes, which they split up in savage reckless-ness. Oh, what horrible sights met my view![70]

The Indians surprised and viciously attacked the innocent setters with-out any warning. This surprise attack ended with the murder of three set-tlers, the wounding of one, and the escape of three, one of which was Fanny's husband, Josiah. Two women, Fanny and Sarah Larimer and two children were taken prisoner. And as usual, the Indians proved that not only were they murderers, mutilators and kidnappers, but also thieves; as stated before, they plundered the wagons. As the Indians broke up their camp, the women and children were allowed to take some clothing with them. Dur-ing the ride, Fanny developed a plan to set her step-daughter, Mary, free. She was to follow the path back to the main trail. This plan involved allowing little Mary to slip off the horse they both rode, during the night, and hide in the grass. Fanny tried the same deception but was noticed and caught by the Indians who beat her.

Mary's body was found by two different groups of people. The first was a group of soldiers led by Josiah Kelly, Fanny's husband. Mary's mutilated body was found on the 14th of July. Her remains were again discovered by another wagon train led by Julius Merrill on the 17th of July. "The body of the 'harmless child' was 'lying upon its face, both arms were thrown forward as if to prevent falling,' and it had been shot with arrows, tomahawked and scalped by 'the savage inhuman brutes.' Merrill now realized why those liv-ing on the frontier had developed 'so universal and a deadly hatred' against the Indians."[71] It is interesting that Merrill having seen the dead body of a 'harmless' and innocent child could comprehend the justified hatred of the frontiersmen against the Indians. But our left-wing apologists having not seen a butchered white child could not.

Fanny made many interesting observations of the Indian society during her captivity. One often hears that the Indians live in harmony with nature and extensively used the buffalo for all their needs. They never wasted any part of the buffalo and used every part to enhance their "natural" lives. "The buffalo, or bison, provided the economic basis for the Plains Indians' way of life. Its flesh was their principal source of food, and its skin supplied materi-als for clothing, shoes, tepees, blankets, robes, and utensils. 'Buffalo chips'— dried manure—provided fuel; buffalo bones became knives and arrow tips; buffalo tendons formed the strings of bows."[72] However, Fanny notes that there were glaring challenges to some of these Indian myths. "Fanny was subjected to numerous cruelties. She narrowly escaped death when she carelessly discarded a chief's pipe (that she had mistakenly broken)... They were wasteful of the buffalo they killed for food, with each Indian taking only a little part that he liked best and leaving the rest to decay. She also saw many mixed-blood (half-breeds) children treated cruelly by the full-blood boys and girls."[73]

Here we have Fanny's real world observations establishing two incon-trovertible facts. One of them being that the Indians did waste parts of the buffalo. There are also sources that state the Indians would readily kill the buffalo of their enemy when on their territory and let it rot. So much for our environmental heroes. After the Civil War, due to an economic inter-est, the sale of buffalo robes increased. "Some Indian tribes (notably the Blackfeet) also began killing large numbers of buffalo to sell in the boom-ing market."[74] The second one that she noticed was that they also practiced bigotry and discrimination against the mixed-blood children. It would seem that the "sacred" Indians had racial prejudices as well.

To show the contrasting attitudes of some of the Indian women, we need only look at the kindness of one Indian woman. Fanny "was given a little girl named Yellow Bird, to replace her own dead daughter. Some Indian women threatened to kill her, but another took her in. Fanny realized that the 'dusky maidens of romance' she had read about were only fictional, 'in strange contrast with the flesh and blood realities into whose hands I had fallen.' How different, she lamented, were 'the stately Logan, the fearless Philip, the bold Black Hawk, and the gentle Pocahontas,' from 'the greedy, cunning and cruel savages who had so ruthlessly torn me from my friends!' The novels were all fantasy. 'The true red man, as I saw him,' Fanny says, 'does not exist between the pages of many volumes.'"[75]

One can generally assume that Fanny is referring to James Fenimore Cooper's books, especially *The Last of the Mohicans*. This book is nothing more than naive romantic fantasy which has been used as pro-Indian propa-ganda. It is very similar to the fictional movie, Dances with Wolves; nothing more than Hollywood's continuous yearly celebration of one of their many "oppressed" minorities.

Another interesting but ghastly custom, in my opinion, was the eating of dog meat. Fanny was taken to a special ceremony and feast. She wrote:

> The lids were raised from the kettles, which were all filled with dog's meat, made into a sort of stew. My dish was given to me, and the absolute neces-sity of eating it was painful to contemplate…By the looks and gestures the women told me that I should feel highly honored by being called to a feast with chiefs and great warriors and, seeing the spirit in which it was given, I could not but treat it respectfully.
>
> As far as I could understand, the dog feast seems to be a truly religious ceremony. In it the superstitious Indian sacrifices his faithful companion to bear testimony to the sacredness of his vows of friendship for the Great Spirit. He always offers up a portion of the meat to his deity.[76]

Kelly goes on to state that not only are the faithful dogs sacrificed but also their faithful horses. She says that this sacrifice "is invariably done by giving the best in the herd or the kennel."[77] She also describes the number of dogs in a village. "The number and utility of these faithful dogs is at times astonishing, as they total in the hundreds…" It is interesting to note that, in one case, a chief had a white woman as a captive; and she reported that he had at least 13 dogs, and they all slept in the tent with them. The captive complained about the enormous flea bites that she had to put up with.

For the entire five-month period that Fanny was a captive, her hus-band, Josiah, continually searched for her and offered several rewards for her return. In one case, he offered a reward of 19 horses for his wife's return, but to no avail. In another case, he outfitted an Indian, which cost him about four hundred dollars; but the Indian left and never returned. "According to Josiah Kelly, he spent $1,075 in attempting to rescue or ransom Fanny and in escorting her home."[78] We can see here how determined many husbands were to have the safe return of their loving wives. Not knowing of their wives and children's well-being must have been an excruciating and heart-wrenching experience. We never hear about the emotional impact of these kidnappings on white women or their families. According to our politically correct leftist Indian protectors, these emotions are only the "imagination" of the white women.

The following is an example of the misery and uncertainty of one young white girl, who upon being kidnapped, was befriended by Fanny. Her name was Mary Boyeau, and she had been captured near Spirit Lake during the Great Sioux Uprising of 1862. Fanny wrote:

> Her family was murdered and Mary, then 14 years old, was captured. She was treated as a child for one year, until a warrior traded a horse for her and, said Mary, "carried me to his tipi as his wife." She hated him and his other wife, who starved her and beat her, and despised everything about "this fearful bondage." She hoped her younger sister was dead, because, she said, "From a life like mine death is an escape."[79]

This is quite clearly a horrific example of the fear, anxiety, and hopelessness that all of the captives must have felt at one time or another. A horror that was seldom noted by the politically correct sympathizers. Their Indians could do no wrong!

In reference to Fanny's sexual abuse, she writes that she was taken into captivity "and was forced to become the squaw of one of the O-gal-lal-lah Chiefs, who treated her in a manner too horrible to mention, and during her captivity was passed from Chief to Chief and treated in a similar manner."[80] As Fanny's five-month captivity drew to an end, a very important part of her search for freedom involved the military forces of General Alfred Sully. Sully's troops had been pursuing and engaging the Indians who had Fanny from the late part of July and to the late part of October. Sully's troops had decidedly defeated the Indians and had pushed them farther west. On the 23rd of October, the Indians fearing the onset of the brutal western win-ter and the frustration of not being able to defeat Sully, began to consider negotiations. The infamous Chief Sitting Bull, of the Little Big Horn and Buffalo Bill's Traveling Wild West Show, also got involved in the negotiations for Fanny's release. Sitting Bull convinced the Blackfeet to negotiate with a Capt. Pell, who was in charge of the fort.

The Blackfeet and Oglalas argued amongst themselves as to what was the best plan and how to use their white captives to their advantage. The Oglalas decided that the Blackfeet should take Fanny to the fort and accompany her inside. Other bands of Indians would hide in the hills outside the fort, where about a thousand Indians would be ready to attack. Once inside the fort, they would begin the slaughter of the garrison and keep the gate open for the rest of the escort party and hidden Indians to enter. Her escort party consisted of the main chiefs and 50 warriors; they were to be the lead ele-ments of the attack.

There was only one thing to upset this well laid out plan. Several days before the plan would be put into effect, Fanny talked to an Indian friend by the name of Jumping Bear. She asked him to take a note to the "Big Chief" in the fort to prove his friendship to her. It seems that Jumping Bear felt romantically towards Fanny. "Trembling with fear, I listened to his avowal of more than ordinary feelings. He assured me that I had no cause to fear him—that he had always liked me and wished to be more than a friend to me."[81] Fanny was a very beautiful young girl and had already sparked some romantic competition between two of the other chiefs. After discussing it several times, Jumping Bear agreed to go. The letter contained a warning to the commanding officer about the Indian plan and a plea to rescue her if they could.

> Then the gate was opened and Major House appeared, accompanied by several officers and an interpreter, and received the chiefs, who rode in advance.
>
> Captain Logan (officer of the day) approached me. Now that I felt myself so close to safety my emotions overcame me. I had borne grief and terror and privation, but the delight of being once more among my people was overpowering. I almost lost the power of speech or motion.
>
> "Am I free, indeed free?" I murmured.
>
> As soon as the chiefs who accompanied me had entered the fort, the commandant's voice thundered the order for the gates to be closed. Jumping Bear had delivered my letter! The Blackfeet were shut out, and I was beyond their power to recapture. After a bondage lasting more than five months, during which I had endured every torture, I once more stood free, among people of my own race, all ready to assist me and restore me to my husband's arms.[82]

One would think that after all the tragedy that had befallen Fanny Kelly, fate would look upon her with a kind face. But fate can be indifferent and unkind! Fanny and her husband were united and moved back to Geneva and eventually to Ellsworth, Kansas. Fanny's husband, Josiah, died of cholera in 1867. She was then offered a residence with the family of Sarah Larimer in Cheyenne, Wyoming. However, Fanny and Sarah got into a disagreement that led to Fanny filing a lawsuit in 1870 against Sarah over a supposed agreement to prepare a record of their captivity experiences.

It seems that Sarah took a copy of the manuscript to Philadelphia and published it under her name only. "The case was bitterly contested, with the last hearings dragging on until 1876, and the women becoming enemies. Fanny Kelly published her own version of the story in 1871. She married a second time in 1880…She was moderately wealthy when she died in Washington in December 1904."[83] It was not an easy life for Fanny Kelly; but she readily proved that the white pioneer women had the courage, stamina and bravery to survive some of the most brutal experiences that confronted them.

In concluding this chapter, it is clearly obvious that the paramount force driving Indian society and culture was war and vengeance![84] Whether it was murdering, scalping, or capturing female slaves, these basic practices were brutal and horrific. As previously quoted, "The young male Indian from childhood is taught to regard 'killing' as the highest of values."

The female captives, in some cases, did have to submit to the sexual advances of their captors, especially the young warriors on raids to the settlements. However, in some few cases, the individual personality of the captor played a major role in the treatment of the captive. Also, some of the Indian family's values were a major determination in the treatment of the white captives. Older wives sometimes abused the white captives. But in some cases, the family actually adopted them and treated them well. In the case of Sarah Wakefield, there was clearly no sexual abuse. She and her phy-sician husband had made friends with many of the Indians. It is the example of Sarah Wakefield that the politically correct academics use to try to argue for their biased viewpoint.

On the other hand, we definitely have the sexual abuse of Mary Schwandt, Mary Boyeau, Mattie Williams, Mary Anderson and Fanny Kelly. Obviously, the fate of the white women captives and their children were simply based upon fate. They really had limited control of what their treatment would be. As always, fate can be an unkind and indifferent determinant. However, in regards to the captivity of white women, the evidence clearly supports the fact that sexual abuse was widely practiced, especially by the young bucks.

The conclusions that can be made from the narrative of Fanny Kelly clearly destroy many of the Leftist myths about the Indian. There was sexual abuse of white women. It was not a fabrication of "Rhetorical Rape" or of hysterical and imaginative white women. The male warriors treated their squaws like menial slaves. The Indians did not worship the buffalo as usu-ally stated but killed many of them just for the delicacy of the tongue and left the rest to rot. They also killed the buffalo of their enemies and also left them to decay. They participated in major buffalo hunts just to provide buffalo robes for white traders.They practiced bigotry and racial intolerance in that they treated the half-breed children with contempt and indifference. They also reveled in murdering and mutilating their enemies whether they be men, women or children and infants.

This chapter has revealed the paramount values of the Indian culture and how they treated women captives. They had an historical beginning that can be easily traced back to the Aztec culture of the 1500's that practiced mutilation, heart sacrifice and cannibalism. The fundamental value of the Plains Indians was that of a warrior society where "killing was the high-est of virtues." Killing and murder were the only way a young Indian male could climb the social hierarchy. A major factor of this warrior culture was the gruesome practice of scalping and mutilating their enemies. The Plains Indians clearly practiced polygamy, but one never hears any criticism by today's feminists or left-wing academics. They seem to just gloss over this extensive, almost misogynistic, marriage pattern. The "Noble Red Man" used the practice of kidnapping women and young girls turning them into wives or sex slaves who they treated as their personal property.

The Indian atrocities, based upon the historical record, not Leftist fabricated myths, were brutal and abhorrent. Unfortunately, our left-wing apologist historians and social scientists have completely turned history upside-down. They have formulated an extensive distortion of the real his-torical record by practicing politically correct historical-relativism.

Endnotes for Chapter 1:

[1] Bernal Diaz, *The True History of the Conquest of New Spain*, trans and intro. by J.M. Cohen, (Baltimore: Penguin Books, 1963. Hereafter cited as Diaz.

[2] J.H. Parry, *The Spanish Seaborne Empire,* (New York: Alfred A. Knopf, 1981) 85. Hereafter cited as Parry.

[3] Diaz, 203.

[4] William H. Prescott, *History of the Conquest of Mexico*, ed. James Lockhart, (New York: The Modern Library, 2001), 43. Hereafter cited as Prescott.

[5] Ibid.,153.

[6] Parry, 21. Maurice Collis, *Cortes and Montezuma*, (New York: Avon Books, 1978) 83. Hereafter cited as Collis.

[7] Parry, 37.

[8] Collis, 134.

[9] Ibid., 135

[10] Diaz, 229

[11] Collis, 224.

[12] Ibid., 137

[13] Prescott, 43.

[14] Isaac V.D. Heard. *History of the Sioux War and Massacre of 1862 and 1863,* (New York: Harper & Brothers, Publishers, 1863), 32. Hereafter cited as Heard.

[15] Diane E. Foulds, "Who Scalped Whom? Historians Suggest Indians Were As Much Victims as Perpetrators". Originally published in the *Boston Globe,* 31 December, 2000, B-10. (accessed, 20 April, 2015). http://hawthorneinsalem. org/ScholarsForum/MMD2263.html. 1, Hereafter cited as Foulds. Foulds' arti-cle clearly supports the innocence of the Indians. She offers 4 defenders of the Indians and only one, James Axtell, defender of the English colonists. Also see Colin F. Taylor, *The Plains Indians,* (New York: Barnes & Noble Books, 1997), 51.

[16] Ibid.

[17] Ibid., 2.

[18] Ibid.

[19] James Axtell, *The European and the Indian: Essays in the Ethnohistory of Colonial North America,* (Oxford: Oxford University Press, 1981), 22-23. Hereafter cited as Axtell.

[20] Ibid., 214

[21] Ibid., 22. Scott Weidensaul, *The First Frontier: The Forgotten History of Struggle, Savagery, and Endurance in Early America,* (Boston: Houghton Mifflin Harcourt, 2012) 83. Hereafter cited as Weidensaul. Also see George A. Bray, "The Delicate Art of Scalping," Muzzleloader Magazine, vol. 13, nr. 2, 1986; 1-5., available from the writer. http://www.mohicanppress.com/mo08018.html. (accessed April 20, 2015).

[22] Axtell, 23.

[23] Ibid.

[24] Paul Schneider, *Brutal Journey: The Epic Story of the First Crossing of North America,* (New York: Henry Holt and Company, 2006), 149-150. Hereafter cited as Schneider.

[25] Charles C., Mann, *1491: New Revelations of the Americas before Columbus,* (New York: Alfred A, Knopf, 2005), 398, fn. 46. Hereafter cited as Mann. Also see James Axtell and William C. Sturtevant, "The Unkindest Cut, or Who Invented Scalp-ing," *The William and Mary Quarterly,* Vol. 37, No. 3, (July 1980): 451-72.

[26] Weidensaul, 83, 398, fn 83.

[27] Dee Brown, *The Fetterman Massacre formerly Fort Phil Kearny: An American Saga,* (Lincoln: University of Nebraska Press, 1962), 198. Hereafter cited as Brown-*Fetterman.*

[28] James Donovan, *A Terrible Glory: Custer and the Little Bighorn,The Last Great Battle of the American West,* (New York: Little Brown and Company, 2008), 244. Here-after cited as Donovan.

[29] Robert Caverly, *Heroism of Hannah Duston,* (Boston: B.B. Russell & Co., Publish-ers, 1875). 19-20. Hereafter cited as Caverly.

[30] Robert M. Utley, *The Last Days of the Sioux Nation,* (New Haven:Yale University Press, 2004), 11. Hereafter cited as Utley-*Last Days.*

[31] Royal B. Hassrick, *The Sioux: Life and Customs of a Warrior Society*, (Norman: Uni-versity of Oklahoma Press, 1988), 130-31. Hereafter cited as Hassrick.

[32] Ibid., 132.

[33] Charles Larpenteur, *Forty Years a Fur Trader, The Personal Narrative of Charles Lar-penteur, 1833-1872*. eds. Milo Milton Quaife and Paul L. Hendren, (Lincoln: University of Nebraska Press, 1989.) 326-27. Hereafter cited as Larpenteur.

[34] J. P. Dunn, Jr. *Massacres of the Mountains: A History of the Indian Wars of the Far West*, (Mechanicsburg: Stackpole Books, 2002). 427. Hereafter cited as Dunn.

[35] Ibid., 428.

[36] Sarah Wakefield, *Six Weeks in the Sioux Tepees*, 1st ed. (Minneapolis: Atlas Print Co., 1863.) 86. Republished by, (Guilford: The Globe Press, 2004). Hereafter cited as Wakefield-1st, ed.

[37] Ibid., 7.

[38] Ibid., 13.

[39] Ibid., 12.

[40] Ibid., 28.

[41] Ibid., 30.

[42] Ibid., 53.

[43] Sarah Wakefield, ed. June Namais, *Six Weeks in the Sioux Tepee: A Narrative of Indian Captivity*, 2nd ed. (Norman: University of Oklahoma Press, 1997), 26. Hereafter cited as Namais- *Six Weeks*.

[44] Ibid.,28-30.

[45] Wakefield-1st, ed. 57-8.

[46] Ibid., 30. *German Pioneer Accounts of the Great Sioux Uprising of 1862*, ed. Don Heinrich Tolzmann, (Milford: Little Miami Publishing Co., 2002), 21. Hereafter cited as Tolzmann-*German.*

[47] Wakefield-1st., ed. 66.

[48] Ibid., 70.

[49] Ibid., 84.

[50] Ibid., 85. Namais-*Six Weeks*, 121-22. Kathryn Zabelle Derounian-Stodola, ed. with intro. and notes. *Women's Indian Captivity Narratives*, (New York: Penguin Books, 1998), 308. Herefater cited as Stodola-*Captivity.*

[51] Duane Schultz, *Over the Earth I Come: The Great Sioux Uprising of 1862*, (New York: St. Martin's Press, 1992), 245. Hereafter cited as Schultz-*Over.*

[52] Mary B. Reville, *A Thrilling Narrative of Indian Captivity: Dispacthes from the Dakota War*, ed. Carrie and Kathryn Derounian-Stodola, (Lincoln: University of Nebraska Press, 2012), 43. Hereafter cited as Renville.

[53] Ibid., 156.

[54] Ibid., 159.

[55] Ibid., 178.

[56] Ibid., 180-81.

[57] Wakefield-1st., ed. 24.

[58] Renville, 187-88.

[59] Ibid.

[60] Mary Schwandt, *The Story of Mary Schwandt: her captivity during the Sioux "out-break," 1862-Primary Source Edition*, Minnesota Historical Society Collection (St. Paul: no p.d.), 461. Hereafter cited as MHSC-*Schwandt*. Also Mary Schwandt, *The Captivity of Mary Schwandt, (*Fairfield: Ye Galleon Press, 1975), 5. Hereafter cited as Schwandt-*Ye Galleon*. Tolzmann-*German, 9*.

[61] Gregory and Susan Michno, *A Fate Worse than Death: Indian Captivities in the West, 1830-1885*. (Caldwell: Caxton Press, 2009), 200 Hereafter cited as Michno-*Fate*.

[62] Ibid. Able B. Murch and Charles S. Bryant, *A History of the Great Massacre by the Sioux Indians, In Minnesota, Including the Personal Narratives of Many Who Escaped,* (Cincinnati: Rickey & Carroll, Publishers, 1864,) 340. Hereafter cited as Murch & Bryant. [The details of this poor girl's awful treatment in our possession, are to revolting for publication—Editors]. Schultz-Over, 72.

[63] Michno-*Fate*, 241, fn. 28.

[64] Gary C. Anderson and Alan R. Woolworth, *Through Dakota Eyes: Narrative Accounts of the Minnesota Indian War of 1862*. (St. Paul: Minnesota Historical Soci-ety Press, 1988), 142-43. Hereafter cited as Anderson-*Dakota Eyes*.

[65] Tolzmann-*German-Pioneer*, 18. Michno-*Fate*, 201. Schultz, 172.

[66] Tolzmann-*German-Pioneer*, 19.

[67] Anderson-*Dakota Eyes*, 258.

[68] MHSC-*Schwandt*, 474. Schwandt-*Ye Galleon*, 26.

[69] AHCD, 4th ed., s. v., "cholera."

[70] Fanny Kelly, *Narrative of My Captivity Among the Sioux Indians*, eds. Clark and Mary Lee Spence, (New York: Konecky & Konecky, 1990), 15-17. Hereafter cited as Kelly. (Originally published in 1872 at Toronto). Frederick Drimmer, ed. *Captured by the Indians: 15 First Hand Accounts, 1750-1870*, (New York: Dover Publications, 1961), 334-35. Hereafter cited as Drimmer. Michno-Fate, 130.

[71] Kelly, xxxviii. Drimmer, 338-39. Michno-*Fate*, 131.

[72] Alan Brinkley, *American History: A Survey*, 12th ed. (Boston: McGraw Hill, 2007), 434. Hereafter cited as Brinkley.

[73] Drimmer, 346-47. Michno-*Fate*, 132.

[74] Brinkley, 454.

[75] Michno-*Fate*, 133.

[76] Drimmer, 348-49. Kelly, 84. Larpenteur, 177.

[77] Kelly, 85.

[78] Ibid., 216, fn. 4.

[79] Michno, *Fate*, 133-34.

[80] Kelly, 273.

[81] Drimmer, 365.

[82] Ibid., 368-69.

[83] Michno-*Fate*, 135.

[84] J.P. Dunn, 427.

ON THE LITTLE BLUE.

This drawing shows the heinous murder of a frontier husband and the kidnapping of his wife while the child tries to crawl away to safety.

TORTURE BY PRAIRIE INDIANS.

One must look closely at this drawing to see the type of torture that the Indians consistently used on captive settlers. It shows a naked man tied on the ground with a fire burning on his stomach and groin area.

Chapter 2

Mountain Men and Father De Smet

"What was my horror at discovering all the children, eight in number, from one to fourteen years of age, lying in various positions in the dooryard with their throats cut, their scalps torn off, and the warm blood still oozing from their gaping wounds!"

Jim Beckwourth.

"...the best way to negotiate and settle disputes with hostile Indians is with the rifle; for that is the only pen that can write a treaty which they will not forget." Osborne Russell.

"None so blind as those who won't see." "Liver-Eating" Johnston.

The fascinating American mountain men of the West are an integral part of the story about the depredations and heinous brutality of the Plains and Rocky Mountain Indians. They were some of the first to encounter the horrific deeds that became so well known to the soldiers and settlers of the American west. Mountain men were also important because they were the first ones who discovered and blazed the trails that made it possible to explore and immigrate through the American West. The famous Oregon Trail, the California Trail and the Bozeman Trail were all explored and established by these men. The most important of all was the South Pass which made it possible to cross the formidable Rocky Mountains. The clas-sic mountain man period is directly associated with the hunting and trap-ping of beaver in the American West between the 1820's and 1840's. After the demise of the fur trading period the trappers generally became buffalo hunters and scouts for the Army. They also became guides for the increasing number of immigrant wagon trains making their way to Oregon, California and the gold fields of Montana. A good generalization about the mountain men was that they were:

...a breed of heroes; yet not heroic by intention or profession, but only in the nature of the circumstances, and as part of their day's work. These mountain men, far more than the solders and the statesmen, were the real means of seizing, holding and settling our vast Far West. They were the men of destiny, whose skill and courage enabled those Americans who followed their trail to conquer a continent within half a hundred years.[1]

There were two important aspects of the mountain men's lives that assisted the settlement of the West. The first one, already stated, was their exploration and discovery of the various trails and passes that crossed the Rocky Mountains. Of fundamental importance was the discovery of South Pass by Jedediah Smith and Thomas Fitzpatrick. However, the original discovery of the South Pass was made in 1812 by Robert Stuart. Jim Bridger's discoveries were just as important in that he was the first white man to see the Great Salt Lake and explore the Yellowstone National Park region. John Bozeman was responsible for the development of the Bozeman Trail which directly led to the Fetterman Massacre of December 21, 1866. Another famous mountain man was Jim Beckwourth, a half-breed who was known as a fur trapper, frontiersman and scout. He is credited with discovering the Beckwourth Pass which went through the Nevada Sierra Mountains. He was captured by Crow Indians and lived with them for approximately 8 years and eventually became a crow chief. The second one was their interaction with the indigenous Indian tribes. This was generally accomplished by the trappers marrying or living with Indian women and raising families within the tribal social system. These marriages helped them learn the various tribal cultures, languages and the important trails through their territories.

The discovery of gold in California in 1848-1849 initiated one of the most massive migrations in the history of the world. Men with "gold-fever" left their homes in the East and Mississippi River valley to find their fortunes in the West. If you have an interest in a primary source book about the "Gold Rush," I highly recommend the book, *The World Rushed In: The California Gold Rush Experience,* (1981), written by J.S. Holliday; it is truly an outstanding book![2] One of the individuals bitten by the "gold fever" states that, "A frenzy seized my soul...Piles of gold rose up before me...castles of marble, thousands of slaves...myriads of fair virgins contending with each other for my love...were among the fancies of my fevered imagination. The Rothschilds, Girard's, and Astor's appeared to be but poor people; in short, I had a very violent attack of the gold fever."[3]

It is estimated that approximately 300,000 people migrated to California from all over the world, including men from Latin America, Asia and

Europe; as many as 150,000 came from the eastern areas of the United States. Most of the overland American travelers used the Great Platte River Road which began at Fort Kearney, Nebraska, and ran to Fort Laramie, Wyoming. The Great Platte River Road would later become part of the famous Oregon Trail. The starting place for these adventurous souls was usually Independence or St. Joseph's, Missouri, or Fort Leavenworth, Kan-sas. The Oregon Trail was the major wagon route from the Missouri River area to the fertile valleys of Oregon. The trail became a reality due to the wanderings and explorations of the mountain men between 1810 and 1840. The Oregon Trail was about 2,000 miles long; and at its peak, from 1846 thru 1869, it carried about 400,000 settlers, farmers, immigrants and gold miners to the far west.

In addition to the stimulus of the California Gold Rush of 1849, there were two other important gold strikes. One was the "Colorado Gold Rush" of 1858-1859, also known as the "Pike's Peak Gold Rush," and the Mon-tana gold strike of 1863. Both of these gold strikes, naturally, caused more immigrants to travel west to seek their fortunes. The Montana gold strike of 1863 is the one of most interest because it directly caused the development of the Bozeman trail to Virginia City, Montana. It was the Bozeman trail that led to the beginning of Red Cloud's War and eventually to the Fetter-man Massacre of December 21st, 1866; Red Cloud's War lasted from 1866 to 1868. The fighting began due to failed treaty negotiations between the Indians and the U.S. Government in 1866. As the treaty talks were taking place, a troop of U.S. soldiers led by Colonel Carrington, the soon to be commander of Fort Phil Kearney, arrived on the scene. Red Cloud became enraged and charged that the government was already occupying the Trail before the treaty had been signed. He angrily left the negotiations and so began Red Cloud's War.

The Bozeman Trail was really a northern extension of the Great Platte River Road and the Oregon Trail. The Great Platte River Road began at Fort Kearney, Nebraska, which is located in the southcentral part of the state. It was also known as the "Great Medicine Road of the Whites" by the Indians. The fort acted as a funnel for all of the other trails coming out of the east including the Oregon and California Trails, the Mormon Trail and the Pony Express routes. All of these trails now followed the Platte River northwest to Fort Laramie in Wyoming. About 60 miles north of Fort Lara-mie, the Oregon Trail took a left-hand turn and followed the Platte River to the west. The Bozeman Trail broke off near present day Casper, Wyo-ming, and headed northwest to the first fort built on the Trail, Fort Reno. Fort Phil Kearney was second on the Trail and in the middle, and Fort C.

F. Smith was at the northern end of the military road. The Bozeman Trail continued north to around the area of present day Billings and then headed west through the cities of Bozeman and Three Forks and then south to the gold fields of Virginia City, Montana.

Many of us have misconceptions about the size and magnitude of these Conestoga wagon trains. A visit to the Frontier Western Museum in Chey-enne has several of the original wagons. We have watched far too many Hollywood movies and T.V. shows to really understand the impact of these wagon trains on the Indian lands. This is an example of one of the larger wagon trains using the Bozeman Trail.

> During the month of July, 1864, one emigrant train consisting of one hun-dred and fifty wagons, three hundred and sixty-nine men, thirty-six women, fifty-six children, six hundred and thirty-four oxen, one hundred and ninety-four cows, seventy-nine horses and a dozen mules, of a valuation of one hun-dred and thirty thousand dollars, reached the gold-fields over this forbidden path. Invasion of even one caravan of this magnitude enraged the Indians to hostile activity, for the penetration of this, their land, meant the destruction of the wild game and the influx and control by the whites. If fight it must be, the country of the Powder River and its minor streams was an inviting battlefield.[4]

The main problem with the Bozeman Trail, even though it was better watered and more direct, was that it traveled through the Powder River country on the eastern edge of the Big Horn Mountains. This land was the primary hunting grounds of the Sioux, Shoshone, Arapahoe and Northern Cheyenne. This presented a major point of conflict between these tribes and the miners and settlers traveling through it. It would be asinine not to recognize that the Indians had a legitimate claim against the government and settlers. The major problem was that the "peaceful" Indians were will-ing to negotiate, but the warrior factions were not. The peaceful Indians readily signed several treaties that allowed for the building of forts and roads through their territory in return for government annuities. The hostile war-rior tribes not only vehemently opposed these treaties but generally com-pletely ignored them. This is the general background of the main issues leading up to Red Cloud's War and the deadly attack on Capt. Fetterman's 80 troops on December 21st, 1866 at Fort Phil Kearney.

I would like to examine the contributions of famous men of the American West: Jim Bridger, Liver-Eating Johnston, Hugh Glass, James Beckwourth, Jedediah Smith and the Catholic Priest Father Pierre-Jean (Peter-John) De Smet. If one were to make a list of other famous mountain men, it would include the likes of John Colter, Peter Skene Ogden, Thomas Fritzpatrick, William Sublette, and Osborne Russell. If one were to write a book about these men, it would fill many pages; and, in many cases, this has already been done. I selected Jim Bridger for closer examination because he was at Fort Phil Kearney when the Fetterman battle took place. Hugh Glass is another interesting person involved with Bridger's early life and an object of one of the most fascinating stories, in my opinion, of the American West. Father De Smet is probably the most famous Catholic priest doing missionary work in the West between 1837 and 1846. He directly participated in the treaty negotiations of 1851 and 1868. He was the one individual most responsible for getting Sitting Bull to accept the important 1868 Treaty of Fort Laramie. De Smet was also a very close friend of Jim Bridger. The selection of these individuals is solely of my own personal choice. I found them linked to the Fetterman battle or, as in the case of Hugh Glass and Father De Smet, just plain fascinating.

Jim Bridger, "Old Gabe," was one of the most famous mountain men of the West. He got his nickname "Old Gabe" from Jedediah Smith. Smith said: "Old Jim possessed the skills of the angel Gabriel." Thereafter, Jim Bridger, who was not very old and did not look angelic, became "Old Gabe" to a gen-eration of trappers; and he was the mountain man who young trappers tried to emulate.[5] He was born in Richmond,Virginia, in 1804.His family moved to St. Louis in 1812. Both of his parents died when he was about 12 years old and that was when he apprenticed himself to a blacksmith. He was born in the year that the Lewis and Clark expedition began their great exploration of the American northwest; their return in 1806 stimulated a great interest in the Mississippi and especially the Missouri rivers. Bridger's early experiences with canoes and river life stirred his sense of adventure for the West.

Jim Bridger traveled into and out of the Rocky Mountains for the next 30 years from about 1822 until the early 1850's. In 1843, Jim and Louis Vasquez established the famous Fort Bridger on the route of the Oregon Trail in the southwest corner of Wyoming. As stated previously, he is given credit for being the first white man to see the Great Salt Lake and exploring the geysers and beautiful country of the Yellowstone Park region. Bridger married three Indian women, one a Flathead and two Shoshone, having 5 children with them. He became quite knowledgeable in Indian languages and culture. His trapping days came to an end as the beaver population declined due to over-trapping in the late 1840's and early 1850's. Also, the fashionable beaver hats of Europe and the American East coast lost favor; it was a simple example of the economic law of supply and demand. Beaver trapping had become economically unprofitable.

In the 1850's, "Old Gabe" turned to being a scout, guide and interpreter for the Army and the many immigrant wagon trains heading west. It is in this occupation as interpreter and guide that he found himself at the Fort Laramie Treaty of 1851. The influential Father De Smet, "Black Robe," was also there to represent and defend the Indians' concerns. Bridger and De Smet renewed their long-term friendship while serving as negotiators at the treaty council.[6] This was one of the largest gathering of Indians of that time. There were approximately ten thousand warriors from the eight major tribes: Sioux, Cheyenne, Arapahos, Crows, Assiniboines, Mandans, Hidatsa and Rees. It also included a large number of Shoshone who were the tradi-tional enemies of the Sioux. Even the young warriors, Sitting Bull and Red Cloud, attended this treaty negotiation.[7] The major result of the treaty was that the "peace" Indians consented to allow the building of forts and roads in their territories for extensive annuities, $50,000 over a 50-year period.

It was also in the occupation of guide and scout that Bridger found himself working at Fort Phil Kearney in 1866 on the Bozeman Trail; he was at the fort during the Fetterman massacre. But before that he was also involved in scouting a shorter and safer route to the gold mines of Montana. To demonstrate the superiority of Bridger's route he offered to race John Bozeman to Virginia City, Montana.

> In the spring of '64, Bridger ran his great race with John M. Bozeman, who had laid out the Bozeman Trail on which Fort Laramie and Fort Phil Kear-ney were afterwards built. Bozeman's route crossed the Powder River above Pumpkin Buttes and kept along the eastern edge of the Big Horn Mountains to Montana. Bridger thought Bozeman's trail too much exposed to the hos-tiles. Bozeman had already brought wagons over his trail, but no wagon had ever passed over Bridger's proposed route west of the Big Horns. Bozeman, confident that his trail was the best, let Jim have a few days' start, and, going through Bozeman Pass into the Gallatin Valley, followed the route pointed out by Sacajawea to Captains Lewis and Clark, while Bridger reached the valley by following the creek now bearing his name. Both wagon trains arrived at Virginia City about the same time.[8]

The obvious advantage of Jim Bridger's route was that it went west of the Big Horn Mountains and, therefore, kept the emigrants further way from the hostile Indians, especially the Sioux. John Bozeman's trail led northwest along the eastern side of the Big Horn Mountains; it was much more dan-gerous because it ran directly through the Powder River country. Bridger's trail led from Casper, Wyoming, to the south end of the Big Horn Moun-tains, around the western side of the Big Horns, and joined the Bozeman trail west of Fort C.F. Smith at Rock Creek. It then proceeded northwest through Bridger's Pass into Virginia City, Montana. John Bozeman's trail, however, was shorter in distance and, therefore, shorter in time of travel. Due to these factors, even though it was more dangerous, it became the more favored route. Another factor that has to be kept in mind is that the standard wagon train averaged between 12 and 15 miles on a good day; any savings in travel was therefore very important. The Bozeman Trail became the major route for the transportation of miners, settlers and the teamster wagon trains carrying supplies to the mining towns of Montana and the forts along the trail.

We will now investigate the role of Jim Bridger, "Old Gabe," and the famous Hawken rifle which was the favorite gun of choice for many of the mountain men. The Hawken rifle can be considered one of the major tools that helped settle the West. He apprenticed himself to a blacksmith from 1818 to 1822 and learned the trade of blacksmithing and gun repair quite well. While he was an apprentice in the gun-repair section, "young Bridger affectionately handled many guns, testing them for heft, feel, and fitness, as companionable, all-purpose friendly weapons. A gun to him was as personal as a jacket, and should fit its owner's hands, arms, shoulder and sighting-eye naturally."[9] His ability as a gunsmith influenced his choice of weapons: and he chose the famous mountain-man rifle, the Hawken rifle, which he used for most of his years in the mountains. The Hawken rifle was built by the Hawken brothers, Samuel and Jacob, in their rifle shop in St. Louis, Missouri, between 1815 and 1858; the guns were precisely built and hand-made.

A typical Hawken Plains rifle of the late mountain-man period has a heavy 34-inch octagonal barrel, about .53 caliber (1/2-ounce round-ball, 214 grains), low sights, set trigger...ramrod carried under a metal rib, sturdy butt stock, crescent-shaped butt plate, and the total weight of the piece 10 1/2 to 12 pounds. Because of its special qualities as a frontiersman's arm it won the reputation as the *ne plus ultra* mountainman gun. "From William Ashley's first forays on the Missouri and beyond the Rockies to the last days of Kit Carson at Taos, the name Hawken on a rifle was one to swear by."[10]

Its major advantages were that it was a high-quality gun, very accurate, light weight, which could bring down a large target, such as an elk or buffalo, at a long range. It was a round-shot, muzzle loaded weapon and had an accurate range from 350 to 400 yards. I have gone into detail on the Hawken because it is probably the most famous mountain-man rifle used in the days of beaver hunting and trapping in the American West.[11] The wife of Colonel Carrington, Margaret, who we will visit later when we investi-gate the Fetterman Massacre of 1866, said in reference to the Hawken rifle: "Rifles, both English and American, abound. The 'Hawkins' is a favorite, carrying what is called the 'trade ball,' and requiring a patch; but many of the old guides, trappers, and half-breeds still cling to their use as in the days of the Pathfinder and other heroes of Cooper."[12] Although it was highly desired, due to the fact that they were hand-made, precision rifles, their numbers were very limited; and it is estimated that only about 200 were ever made. Other guns made in the East and in Europe were much more commonly found due to the price and availability.

Modern interest in the Hawken rifle came about, in my opinion, because of the production of the popular movie, *Jeremiah Johnson*, starring Robert Redford, in 1972. I cite this movie and others because they bring popular attention and interest to the many outstanding historical experiences of the West. The interesting thing about the movie was that it was based on many of the real-life adventures of John "Crow Killer-Liver Eating" Johnston. The spark of interest in the Hawken gun came from a scene in the movie when Redford (as Johnson) comes across the body of another mountain man, "Hatchet" Jack. Jack is dead, "kilt" by a bear and is found with a Hawken .54 rifle in his frozen hands. Jeremiah (Redford) pries the gun from his hands and remarks that "it is a genuine Hawken." With the acquisition of this Hawken gun, Jeremiah's hunting and food gathering take a turn for the better; and he uses the gun throughout the rest of the movie.

The fictional legend of how he acquired his name, "Crow-Killing-Liver Eating Johnston," comes from a story that took place in 1847. He suppos-edly married a Flathead Indian girl (named Swan in the movie) and had left her alone in a cabin and went hunting for the winter. When he returned home in the spring, he found his wife's bones and the bones of their unborn child in the cabin.[13] Jeremiah discovered evidence that the Indian raiding party that killed his wife and child were Crow. The murder of his family served as the motivation for his personal vendetta against the Crow tribe. He waged a one-man war against the Crow, and Crow warriors began to show up dead with their livers cut out. Every Crow he killed, he removed their liver and supposedly ate it. That's how he came to be known as "Liver-Eating" Johnston. The movie was based upon two historical fiction books, *Mountain Man,* by Vardis Fisher, published in 1965 and *Crow Killer: The Saga of Liver-Eating Johnson,* by Raymond W. Thorp and Robert Bunker pub-lished in 1958.[14]

The only problem with the above story is that it is overwhelmingly movie myth. Johnston never married nor was he a "squaw-man," and the Indian vendetta he had was with the Sioux, not the Crow. The Crows had been continually friendly with white men and even served as scouts with Custer at the Little Big Horn. The real "Crow-Killing, Liver-Eating, John-ston" was born in New Jersey in about 1824. His original name was John Garrison. His ancestry was believed to be Irish or possibly Scotch-German; all three of these groups known for having violent tempers. "It's quite obvi-ous that there was a grizzly bear size rage festering inside Johnston most of the time."[15] He ran away from home due to an alcoholic and abusive father who almost worked him to death by using him as a "bond-servant". His father, Isaac Garrison, "would send his young son to local farmers to work off his (Isaac's) debts."[16]

Johnston was a jack-of-all-trades. Young John had an extensive back-ground in numerous jobs and occupations. His first adventure began aboard a whaling ship after leaving home. His sailing career lasted between 1838 and 1858. He served in the U.S. Navy during the Mexican-American War, 1846 thru 1848. He remained in the Navy or aboard a merchant sailing ship until about 1858. It is suggested that John Garrison changed his name to John Johnston to prevent his capture for an impulsive act aboard a U.S. Navy vessel. "Johnston was clearly an impulsive, hardened man, who appar-ently had a short fuse."[17] The following example is thought to represent the circumstances of why he changed his name.

The only incident he (Johnston) related of his naval experience was an act of insubordination, which was to his credit. A lieutenant, son of a commodore, struck one of his comrades a bad blow with his sword, when young Johnston dealt the officer a stunning blow in the neck, stretching him senseless on the deck. The officer, when he came to, did not know whether he had been struck by lightning or one of the spars, but Johnston was suspected. None would testify against him, however, so he escaped the capital punishment that would have been his fate, but was regarded with such suspicion that for thirty days he got no shore leave. When he did finally go ashore for one day he never returned and drifted to the unknown west.[18]

Beginning in 1858, he began wandering about the West as a miner, trap-per, Indian fighter and teamster. In February of 1864, he joined the Union Army in the capacity of scout and remained in the Army until 1865. Dur-ing this time period, he was a member of the 1st Colorado Cavalry, the 2nd and eventually ended up in the 3rd Colorado Cavalry. During his military service, he was wounded twice, once in the shoulder and once in the leg. It is this military service that allowed him to move to a Veteran's hospital in Los Angeles in 1900 where he died. Between 1865 and 1881, he worked again as a teamster, a wood hawk (one who cuts wood for the steamboats on the Missouri and Musselshell rivers), a whiskey peddler, a government scout and guide, managed a stage coach line, a Justice of the Peace and a wolfer. A wolfer was one who hunted or poisoned wolves. "As a wolfer, it was customary to pour a poison called strychnine on the flesh of a dead buffalo or antelope. When the wolves feasted upon the dead beast, death would quickly occur. It would not be unusual to kill an average of sixty wolves per day. In 1879, wolf hides were worth $3.50, while buffalo hides sold for a mere $3.00. Vic Smith reported that he once earned $617.00 for one-weeks' worth of wolfing."[19]

His legal involvement with Montana began in 1881 as deputy sheriff in Coulson and Billings. Coulson was the first name of that area which later became Billings. Between 1884 and 1888, he toured with Hardwick's Wild West show and acted as a guide for hunting trips and tourists. Between 1888 and 1895, a seven-year time period, he worked as a Constable in Red Lodge, Montana. Due to his size and strength, he was over six feet tall and weighed about 220 pounds, he very seldom used a gun in his duties. There were some reports that Johnston was six feet six inches tall but that is prob-ably just another myth. "Now that Johnston was an officer of the law again, he reverted back to the only way he knew how to keep the peace. He either kicked lawbreakers in the pants or banged their heads together. There was no jail, only a little one room log building, 10' x 12', which Johnston rarely used to house troublemakers."[20]

In reference to his nickname of Liver-Eating Johnston, he never really ate the Indian's liver that he had supposedly killed. The latest book about Johnston is titled *The Avenging Fury of the Plains* published in 2008. The myth about eating liver is not substantiated by the evidence that McLel-land presents. As stated earlier, the book by Bunker and Thorp was the main source material for the movie and has Johnston seeking revenge for the death of his wife and unborn child. The authentic facts, based upon McLelland, state that Johnston and a party of 15 fellow wood hawkers were plying their trade at the junction of the Missouri and the Musselshell riv-ers for the passing steamers. Johnston's crew was attacked by more than 60 Sioux Indians, and the wood cutters were doing an excellent job of defend-ing themselves and killing Sioux warriors. The Sioux, taking the brunt of the fight, asked for a pow wow and wanted to "call the affair a draw." But Johnston and his men knew enough not to trust the treacherous Indians.

One warrior tried to make an escape and was shot by Johnston's men. "But Johnston would make no terms. The Sioux must be treated to a dose of their own medicine…There was no more pow wowing after that and the Indians understood that their own merciless cruelty was being meted out to them in the order of "no quarter."[21] One Indian who had been severely wounded tried to crawl away but Johnston quickly jumped on him.

Johnston dropped his rifle and pulled out his hunting knife and felt the edge on his nail. "I'm goin' to kill you," Johnston said to the Indian, for he spoke Sioux like a native. "I'm going to scalp you first and then cut your throat like a dog's"… Grabbing the scalp lock, Johnston pulled it tight with his knee against the Indian. With the other hand he gave quick slash with his knife around the base and then a sharp pull and the trophy of Indian valor came off with a report like a small pistol--frightful agony as it must have been…Seizing the Sioux by the big brass rings which he wore in his ears, with a quick movement Johnston threw the Indian over his bent knee, and twisted his head around until every cord and muscle of the neck was tense and taut, gave it one quick, ugly sweep of the knife and the painted head came off in his hand, dripping a crimson flood, while the blood spurted in gushes from the headless trunk, which slipped to the ground… When he reached the group, one of them, a pilgrim, noticed a little piece of flesh hanging on the knife's blade, and inquired what it was. "That," said Johnston, glancing at the knife, "is a piece of the Injun's liver. I just had a feast off of one and thought maybe some of you would like a taste--try it!" And he passed the knife with the lit-tle piece of flesh around the circle, none of the men appeared to be hungry for that particular cut. With apparent offense at having his tid-bit slighted, he said, "You don't know how good it is. I eat nothing else when I am out on the plains if I can get Indian livers. They taste best raw." With that he lifted the knife to his mouth, made a motion as if he was eating the stuff. In reality he had dropped it to the ground by a twist of the hand, but the broad red splatch across his black beard gave the spectators a contrary opinion. From that day on, he was known far and wide as "Liver-eating Johnston."[22]

Another source, the Lewiston Saturday Journal, June 2, 1900, in reference to his obituary, has a much less gruesome description.

His name of "Liver-Eating Johnston" was a misnomer, of course, but he came by it in a way which indicates the ferocity of the man. "We were attacked by Injuns," said he, "and we licked 'em, licked 'em good. There was fifteen of us and we killed thirty six of 'em and wounded sixty. It was toward the close of the fight that I got my name. I was just gettin' my blood up and feelin' like fighting…We had a 500-yard run to the bushes and I caught one Injun by the hair of the head and threw him down at the edge of the brush. I ran my knife into him and killed him. As I gave the blade a twist and pulled it out, a bit of the Injun's liver came out with it. That's the way I got my name.[23]

The first description addresses a point that I will be arguing throughout this book. The only way to fight Indians is by using their own tactics and cruelty against them. This includes the mutilation of the dead Indian warriors. Now, I know that that sounds brutal and appalling, but the Indians were brutal and horrible to the innocent white settlers; and the only way to defeat such an enemy is to show them no quarter. Of course, the reader is free to disagree with my conclusion. One of the Sioux Indian women at the Battle of Wounded Knee in 1890 asked a soldier of the 7th Calvary why they had killed Indian women and children. She said that Indian warriors never did that. After reading the chapter on the Great Sioux Uprising of 1862, you can answer that question yourself. I will be mentioning this woman's ridiculous question throughout the book for emphasis! The heinous Indians killed and mutilated innocent white women and children; but when the favor was returned, the Indians became extremely fearful and their defend-ers, the left-wing academics, bemoan the so-called cruelty of the whites.

If you visit the City of Red Lodge, they have the original house with his name on it. It was located in the middle of town next to a gas station and vacant lot with high grass that covered it up; it was not easy to locate. It has since been moved next door to the present Visitor's Office and the Local Area Chamber of Commerce located at 701 North Broadway. I had the good fortune of going into his house during our vacation in July of 2015. It sent chills up my spine. I was really in the house that Liver-Eating John-ston had lived in. Three kind women of the Visitor's Center, Lauren Larson, Sherry Weamer, and Lynda Beach, called around town to find the key that opened the lock on Liver-Eating's house. The key was located at the Car-bon County Historical Society and Museum located at 224 Broadway Ave., North. There were also three very helpful women at the Museum, Deb-bie Brown, Samantha (Sam) Long and Dana Wahlquist, who explained the museum's collection including one of the actual guns that he used; it was a Winchester rifle that was presented to him 1894 by one Ben Greenoueh. Samantha Long, who is the Preservation Officer, was kind enough to bring the key and open the house. She also showed us the collection of rare pho-tographs of him at the museum. They also have an excellent 20-minute video that helps correct many of the myths about him in reference to the movie and the two historical novels used to make it. I cannot thank them enough for their assistance.

Johnston had briefly been a member of the U.S. Army during the Civil War; and his final residence was a veterans' home in Santa Monica, Califor-nia.When he died at the Veteran's home, he was originally buried in Califor-nia. This is where it really gets interesting. Liver-Eating Johnston probably should have been buried in Red Lodge, Montana. However, a teacher, prob-ably a social studies teacher, and his seventh-grade students launched a cam-paign to get his body moved and reburied in Cody, Wyoming. It seems the people of Red Lodge didn't want him for some unknown reason or reacted to late. This was accomplished in 1974, and Robert Redford attended the reburial ceremony. He is now buried in Old Trail Town with a bronze statue above his grave.

General William Ashley was known as one of the most important found-ers of the fur trade in the American West. He was not a fur trapper or explorer as the likes of Jedediah Smith, Jim Bridger, Jim Beckwourth or Thomas Fitzpatrick. He was a business entrepreneur who organized one of the first major fur trading expeditions from St. Louis in 1822. St. Louis was the premier trading center and city for the hunters and Indians who brought their furs and skins in for sale and trading. He and a close friend, Andrew Henry, offered the following advertisement in the *Missouri Gazette & Publication Advertiser* on the 13th of February, 1822:

> To enterprising young men. The subscriber wishes to engage ONE HUN-DRED MEN to ascend the Missouri River to its source, there to be employed for one, two or three years---For the particulars enquire of Major Andrew Henry, near the lead mines in the county of Washington, (who will ascend with, and command the party) or to the subscriber near St. Louis.[24]

This expedition included Jim Bridger, the Sublette brothers, Hugh Glass, Thomas Fitzpatrick, Dave Jackson, Louis Vasquez, Edward Rose, Seth Grant and the extraordinary Jedediah Smith. They left St. Louis on the 3rd of April, 1822; and they came to be known as "Ashley's Hundred." This group of traders was a veritable who's who of American trappers; Bridger was in excellent company.[25] Two of these individuals, Thomas Fitzpatrick and Jedediah Smith, are given credit for discovering the immensely important South Pass in 1824. The only problem was there were several others who had used the pass prior to Jedediah and Fitzpatrick's "discovery." One of the least known was an explorer by the name of Robert Stuart. He had been a member of the North-West Company and John Astor's Pacific Fur Company. It is stated that Stuart passed through the South Pass in an easterly direction in 1812, some 12 years ahead of Jedediah and Fitzpatrick.

The South Pass became the most widely used trail through the Rocky Mountains and over the Continental Divide for settlers who traveled to the West. The discovery of "South Pass was a high moment in American history...To this wide depression along the continent's spine, missionaries followed the mountain men, settlers and gold seekers coming in their turn, thousands on thousands pursuing the vision or driven by the need."[26] But the rediscovery in 1824 by Smith and Fitzpatrick, with the assistance of Bridger, opened the most important and traveled main route of the Oregon and California Trails. Jedediah Smith was unlike the other mountain men because he was highly educated and very religious. He was:

> a man of energetic mind and a devout Christian, and early formed the determination to become an explorer. He ranks with Lewis and Clark: in fact, he surpassed them. They merely passed over from the Upper Missouri Basin to the Columbia Valley. They traced a single route to the Western Ocean; Smith found three. No man living in his time was his equal in first-hand knowledge of the Far West. In gaining this knowledge, so necessary to the expansion of the United States, Smith had adventures galore.[27]

Jedediah Smith had a short but adventurous life. He was born in Bainbridge, New York, in January of 1799 and was killed by a group of between 15 or 20 Comanche Indians on the 27th of May, 1831; he was 32 years old. Smith was a unique mountain man in that he was very well educated in the Methodist religion and could read and write; he also kept a diary and read the Bible. "Diah" was his nickname when he was young. The one person who most affected the youth of Jedediah was Dr. Titus Simons. The follow-ing quote clearly indicates the importance of Dr. Simons in motivating his wander lust:

> A tall, slender youth of about twelve, with a restless interest in the world and a thirst for knowledge. He found a mentor in Dr. Titus Gordon Vespasian Simons, whose memory as a pioneer physician lingers in several Pennsylva-nia counties... Dr. Simons won Jedediah's love and respect for what he was himself, and Jedediah's letters are never so glowing as when they speak of the old doctor.
>
> It is said that Dr. Simons presented the youth with a copy of the book published in 1814 which at last gave to the world the narrative of the journey Meriwether Lewis and William Clark had made to the Pacific, and that Jedediah carried this book on all his travels. Perhaps that is legend only, for the tides of American history were strong enough to pick Jedediah up and fling him westward.[28]

As an adult, Jedediah's religious training had a very major impact upon his life. He was known to be a very devout individual during his wanderings. He took his religion very seriously, which set him apart from the other trappers.

Some of the defining traits of the mountain man culture he did not share. Drunken high jinks never counted him a participant. He almost never drank intoxicants, never used tobacco, never boasted, rarely indulged humor or relaxed his austerity enough to edge into the hilarious antics of his compan-ions, and never (so far as known) crawled beneath the robes of a compliant Indian maiden. Dominating the character of this serious young man was a stern Methodism that immersed him in meditation, prayer, and constant study of the Bible and that tormented him with an abiding sense of unwor-thiness in the sight of God. Few mountain men troubled themselves with theology.

Yet Jedediah Smith excelled in those essential aspects of mountain man culture that enabled him to survive and thrive in the wilderness and thereby command the respect of his comrades. He not only, as he intended, made himself "a first-rate hunter" and "thoroughly acquainted with the character and habits of the Indians." He possessed the physical strength and endur-ance, reservoirs of energy and courage, the fortitude to bear privation and suffering with good cheer, coolness in crisis, and all the wilderness skills of his craft, fortified by native intelligence and more than the usual formal education. Valuing these qualities, together with a demonstrated capacity for leadership, mountain men could tolerate his piety and other eccentricities. [29]

His extensive travels took him to many uncharted parts of the West to include the membership in the Ashley expedition between 1822 and 1824. A major tragedy occurred in September of 1823 when he was attacked by a large grizzly bear which almost killed him. While searching for the Crow Indians to do some trading, Smith and his men were working their way through a heavy underbrush. Charging out of the underbrush came an immense female grizzly bear who attacked Jedediah. One of the eyewit-nesses wrote:

"...Grissly did not hesitate a moment but sprung on the capt[ain] taking him by the head first." The enraged bear hurled Smith to the ground, seiz-ing his upper body in a deadly hug while its fearsome jaws again enveloped Jedediah's head. The savage embrace alone could have been fatal... Still, the grizzly snapped several of his ribs. Far worse, the grizzly's teeth transformed Smith's head into a gruesome tangle of lacerations, dangling flesh, and flow-ing blood. But Jedediah was still conscious. [30]

The bear was killed by several members of the scouting party. His wounds included the bear having "'taken nearly all of his head in his captious [capacious] mouth close to his left eye on one side and clos[e] to his right ear on the other and laid the skull bare to near the crown of his head leaving a white streak whare his teeth passed [.] [O]ne of his ears was torn from his head to the outer rim.'"[31] Amazingly, Smith remained conscious dur-ing the difficult procedure of trying to put him back together. None of the party members had any medical skill, so Smith remained conscious and gave instructions to a man named Clyman on how to stitch him up. He used a needle and thread to put Smith back together as best he could. Such stamina and toleration for pain is truly amazing.

After surviving such a horrible attack, Jedediah returned to his trapping and wandering ways. Between 1826 and 1827, he made his first trip to Cali-fornia and ran into difficulty with the Mexican authorities for not having any legal passport. He was escorted to San Diego by Mexican authorities. On the way back to the rendezvous, they crossed the Sierra Nevada moun-tains and came across the Great Salt Lake. They made it to the rendezvous on the 3rd of July, 1827. He made a second trip to California between 1827 and 1828: this time traveling to the San Bernardino valley. Between 1829 and 1830, he organized a trading expedition to the Blackfeet country; the Blackfeet were noted for being excessively brutal.[32] In 1830, he returned to St. Louis with a substantial profit and helped out his family who resided there.[33]

The interesting thing about his return to St. Louis in October of 1830 was that he had with him ten wagons. "For the first time, wagons had gone to the mountains. 'The ease with which they did it and could have gone on to the mouth of the Columbia,' commented an editorialist, 'shows the folly and nonsense of those 'scientific' characters who talk of the Rocky Mountains as the barrier which is to stop the westward march of the American people.'"[34] In 1831, having not done any exploring or trading in the southwest, he involved himself in a commercial venture that took him there. "Smith, Jackson, and Sublette," all fellow mountain men, trappers, and entrepreneurs, "turned their interest to the 'commerce of the prairies' that linked Missouri and New Mexico over the Santa Fe Trail."[35] It was on this trip that Jedediah Smith was killed by Comanche Indians in May of 1831. Obviously, Jedediah Smith was truly a unique mountain man.

William H. Ashley's original party in 1822 numbered 100 men, and other trapping parties usually involved at least 10 to 50 men each. It was much safer to travel and trap with a large party rather than to trap alone, where one became an easy target for murdering and thieving hostile Indians.

Ashley continued in the fur trading business until 1826 when he sold his fur trading company to Jedediah Smith, David E. Jackson and William L. Sublette. Before he terminated his interests in the fur trading business, Ashley had organized the "rendezvous system" of exchange. He held the first "rendezvous" in 1825 at Henry's Fork, west of Green River, in today's Wyoming. His system replaced the old one which had the trappers meeting at a specific fort and trading their furs for money and supplies. This method caused all of the trappers to come out of the mountains and valleys to meet at a convenient location for the fur company owners, usually one on a river that was easily connected to St. Louis. His system called for a predetermined organized rendezvous to take place each year at a specific, convenient location in the mountains. This would make it much easier for the trappers to travel to and would keep them in the field longer. They would not waste time coming from and going back to the fur trapping areas; they would remain there and immediately go back to trapping after the rendezvous was completed. Beginning with the "Rendezvous of 1825," there were an additional 15 rendezvous held, with the last one being held in 1840 at the confluence of Green River and Horse Creek, also in Wyoming.[36]

Considering the importance of the Rendezvous of 1825, let us examine it in detail because it would serve as the basic model for all of the other rendezvous that would follow.[37] Ashley left Fort Atkinson, Nebraska, on the 4th of November of 1824. He and his company arrived in the general area of the rendezvous around the 29th of June, 1825 near the intersec-tion of Henry's Fork and the Green River. This location is provided by Harvey L. Carter (a contributor to Leroy R. Hafen's book, *Mountain & Fur Traders*, see endnote) and is about 25 miles southeast of Fort Bridger near present day Burnt Fork, Wyoming.[38] This rendezvous lasted only one day, but the following meetings lasted for days and sometimes even weeks. All of the future rendezvous were held during the summer months because of the brutal weather conditions of the Rocky Mountain winters. Here are several descriptions of these wild meetings:

> As soon as everyone expected had arrived, the business began. The parties belonging to the company turned over their furs, and received their wages and new equipment. The free trappers and the Indians trafficked their furs on the best attainable terms and purchased their equipment for the ensuing year. While all of this business was going on, and while the cargoes were being made ready for the homeward journey, the heterogeneous assemblage went in for a good time. The flat alcohol kegs were broached, liquor flowed like water, and the wildest tumult at length ensued, ending not infrequently

with fatal results. The debauch extended likewise to the Indians, many of whom were presently reduced to a state of the most abhorrent and revolting intoxication. Gambling was actively rushed during the whole time, and few were the trappers who did not pay a heavy tribute upon the altar of chance. In fact, with gaming, treating, and feasting, most of the hard earnings of a year's toil found their way directly back to the pockets of the company at the enormous profit which their prices secured.[39]

This one is Jim Beckwourth's brief account of a rendezvous:

> ...General Ashley and Mr. Sublette came in, accompanied with three hundred pack mules, well laden with goods and all things necessary for the mountaineers and the Indian trade. It may well be supposed that the arrival of such a vast amount of luxuries from the East did not pass off without a general celebration. Mirth, songs, dancing, shouting, trading, running, jump-ing, singing, racing, target-shooting, yarns, frolic, with all sorts of extrava-gances that white men or Indian could invent, were freely indulged in. The unpacking of the medicine water contributed not a little to the heightening of our festivities.[40]

Here is another colorful description of one:

> The rendezvous was unlike anything before or since, a gathering of unin-hibited men down from the mountains. Camped nearby were perhaps ten times as many Indians, who brought their families, lodges, dogs and horses. Amusement ranged from horse racing to dalliance with Indian maidens. Wrestling matches, shooting contests, tomahawk throwing, and storytell-ing continued day and night, all the time stimulated by heavy drinking... "The rendezvous is one continued scene of drunkenness, gambling, brawl-ing and fighting, as long as the money and credit of the trappers lasts...of the gambling --one trapper even bet his scalp...These annual gatherings are often the scene of bloody duels, for over their cups and cards no men are more quarrelsome than your mountaineers. Rifles at twenty paces, settle all differences..."[41]

It can be seen from these three reports that the rendezvous became a raucous and hellacious celebration for men who had been in the mountains all year. In reference to the Indian attendees, one must consider that each Indian lodge generally contained at least 3-5 Indians. There were generally 4 horses per lodge and about 3 dogs per lodge. If we average 50 lodges to an Indian camp, some contained as many as 100 lodges, that would give us a minimum of 150 Indians, 200 horses and 150 dogs. That certainly makes, with the mountain men and whiskey thrown in, for a "wild and perilous" party.[42]

In reference to the economics of these gatherings, the individual beaver pelts or plews (the American nickname for beaver skins) were sold by the pound, usually selling for $2.50 to $3.00 per pound at the rendezvous. The interesting aspect of these sales was that the company bought it for $2.50 per pound from the trapper, but then sold it at a price of $6.00 per pound at St. Louis; that is a nice profit of $3.50 per pound. In one instance, Jedediah Smith sold his winter's trappings of 1,568 pounds at $2.50 per pound which earned him a total of $3,920.[43] However if you look at the profits of the company at $6.00 per pound that garners an interesting sum total of $9,408, a clear profit of $5,488 just on the sale of one trapper.

Obviously, the traders came out ahead on these transactions and the trappers lost. Not only did the trappers lose on the beaver skins, but they also lost on the purchase of goods and supplies from the trader who had an absolute monopoly on the sale of these goods to the trappers. The following are examples of the prices charged to the trappers for some of their basic needs by William Ashley at the Rendezvous of 1825:

Coffee-- $1.50 per pound
Sugar--- $1.50 per pound
Tobacco--$3.00 per pound
Powder---$2.00 per pound
Flints------$1.00 per dozen
Knives-----$2.50 each
Blue Cloth--$5.00 per yard
Scarlet Cloth--$6.00 per yard
Lead--$1.00 per pound
Buttons--$1.50 per dozen

Although there seemed to be a standard price for each item, often the prices would vary in dealings with different people. For example, sugar varied from $1.00 per pound to $2.00 per pound. Tobacco usually sold for $3.00 per pound, but sold to some for $2.00. Ashley usually paid $3.00 per pound for beaver as a standard amount, yet some mountain men received only $2.00. It appears from the account books that those who went to work for Ashely in 1822-23 were paid $2.00 per pound. Probably their agreement at that time specified that amount. A free trapper received $5.00 per pound.[44]

It is estimated that Ashley returned to St. Louis in early October of 1825 with between 80 to 100 packs of beaver fur worth approximately $50,000.

One source estimates that $17,000 of furs were worth $4 million dollars in today's money. That amount of profit would turn many a good man into a mountain man. The original packs weighed around 50 pounds each but they were repacked for shipping into 100 pound packs. A more accurate assessment stated that Ashley had 100 packs with a value of $48,000; that works out to be about $480 for a 100-pound pack. That weight and value became the standard unit for selling a pack of beaver skins.[45] The large profits described above clearly indicate the corrupt price fixing system that the company owners used to exploit the trappers. As the rendezvous sys-tem became more established, the prices paid by the trappers became more exploitive.

At the Rendezvous of 1837, the price of sugar was $4.00 per pint, coffee was $4.00 per pint, blankets cost $20.00 each, tobacco was $2.00 per pound, common cloth shirts were $5.00 each and watered-down alcohol $4.00 per pint.[46] One trapper, Johnson Gardner, openly complained that, "You have had these men already too long in your service and have most shamefully imposed on them, treating them like slaves, selling them goods at high prices and giving them nothing for their skins."[47] The only saving grace for many of the trappers was that they cared more for their freedom in the mountains than they did for the money. Many of them usually drank or gambled away their earnings at the yearly rendezvous; a mountain man's "saturnalia."

In August of 1822, Bridger is said to have been directly involved in the famous "Hugh Glass Grizzly Bear" story. Jim Bridger, Hugh Glass, Jedediah Smith, Major Andrew Henry and others were on their famous exploratory mission to map and hunt the Upper Missouri territory. Hugh Glass was something of a loner who "shrugged off orders and picked his own path through country he wished to inspect with no one in his hair. The man who did this had been shaped by forces which made it natural for him to be at once indifferent to the opinions of others and careless with his own skin."[48] Glass went off the river trail and made his way through the heavy underbrush on his own. His independence brought him into a confrontation with a mother grizzly bear and her two cubs; not a good situation. The bear pounced upon Glass, and his comrades describe the horrible scene:

> Our companion was literally torn in pieces. The flesh on his hip torn off, leaving the sinews bare, by the teeth of the bear. His side was so wounded in three places that his breath came through the openings; his head was dread-fully bruised, and his jaw was broken. His breath came out from both sides of his windpipe... No one supposed he would recover.[49]

Major Henry discovered himself in a quandary. He and his men were in dangerous Ree Indian country and now found themselves burdened with a seriously wounded comrade. Henry and his men deliberated on the difficult situation for a few days and then decided it was best to leave two men behind. These two men were Thomas Fitzpatrick and supposedly the young Jim Bridger.[50] Anyway, Major Henry got his other men to donate a dollar a day for the ones remaining, gathering 80 dollars for the two men. They were supposed to attend to his wounds and, when he finally transpired, give him a decent burial. Fitzpatrick and Bridger waited around for 3 days and then fearing prowling Ari-karas Indians decided to take Glass's rifle and equipment; they left him to die on his own.[51]

Glass came to find himself abandoned without his goods but, more importantly, without his rifle and ammunition. He then managed to crawl to a creek and remained there for 10 days recuperating. Upon regaining his strength, he began crawling and stumbling some 350 miles (some sources say 200 miles, others 350 miles) to Fort Kiowa (also known as Fort Lookout and Fort Brazeau). Some suggest that he fell in with a party of Sioux and that they helped him on his journey to Fort Kiowa. No matter what, he supposedly completed one of the most daring and arduous trips ever made by a lone mountain man without his gun or supplies. Glass had been driven by one of the most basic human motivations-- revenge upon the two men who had left him to die. After a long recuperation at Fort Kiowa, he went to find his two enemies, Fitzgerald and Bridger. Glass found Bridger up on the Yellowstone near the mouth of the Big Horn River. Glass confronted the apprehensive Bridger and said:

> Young man, it is Glass that is before you; the same that, not content with leav-ing, you thought, to a cruel death upon the prairie, you robbed, helpless as he was, of his rifle, his knife, of all, with which he could hope to defend or save himself...I swore an oath that I would be revenged on you, and the wretch who was with you, and I ever thought to have kept it. For this meeting I have braved the dangers of a long journey...But I cannot take your life; you have nothing to fear from me; go,-- you are free;--for your youth I forgive you.[52]

Glass continued to think of revenge on Fitzgerald, but he involved himself again in his hunting and trapping activities. However, in June of 1825, he heard that Fitzgerald was in the Council Bluffs area of Nebraska, specifically at Fort Atkinson. When he arrived, he found out that Fitzgerald had enlisted in the Army and was now a private. Realizing that killing a soldier would get him in serious trouble, he refrained from killing Fitzgerald; but he did get his favorite rifle back. Glass did confront Fitzgerald and told him, "Go false man & answer to your own conscience & to your God...You was well paid to have remained with me until I was able to walk--you promised to do so--or to wait to my death & bury my remains--I heard the bargain-- Your shameful perfidy & heartless cruelty--but enough--Again I say, settle the matter with your own conscience & your God."[53]

It is of interest to note that the author J. Cecil Alter who originally wrote his book, *Jim Bridger*, in 1925, presents a brief summary of four different versions of the Glass tale. He strongly suggests that the entire story might just be a "tall tale." The first version was written by James Clyman, in 1823. His version basically follows the Hugh Glass story as presented above. The second version was written by an anonymous author who wrote for the *Philadelphia Port Folio* in 1825. This author also follows the standard story but embellishes it with two additional Indian attacks on Glass and some associates, but only Glass survived these two attacks. The third interpretation is a recollection of the story as told by Glass to a George C. Young during the winter of 1828-29. It also follows the standard interpretation but uses an incorrect date for the attack, September 11, 1824, and also incorrectly identifies the place of the attack as southwestern Kansas. It was written by a writer "who had not known or seen Glass, being entirely hearsay and researched with several inconsistencies."[54] The fourth rendering was writ- ten by Edmund Flagg in 1839 and refers to one of the two betrayers as a "Bridges" not Bridger; an easy mistake to make.

Another mountain man, Moses "Black" Harris, was one of Major Henry "Ashley's 100" and had close personal contact with Glass and Bridger. "Moses (Black) Harris, 'who appears to be a correct and intelli-gent young man,' was interviewed that winter by down-river newspapers, but did not mention the bear fight, though one, and possibly both, of the caretakers were with him."[55] Since Moses Harris was with the original group that included Fitzpatrick and Bridger, he would have definitely been an eye-witness to the bear attack. However, he made no mention of the attack at all. J. Cecil Alter concludes that the "Hugh Glass story was nothing more than a frontier myth." He states that "Hugh Glass was not the only frontiersman who loved a joke and was a story in and of himself. The Glass bear story is clearly a product of the school of frontier braggarts, and its original author, Hugh Glass, far from meriting pity for being neglected, rightfully becomes instead a distinguished raconteur."[56] So ends the fascinating "true" story of the mountain-man tall tale of Hugh Glass. There is a Hollywood movie available that loosely follows the tale of Hugh Glass. It is titled *Man in the Wilderness.* It was released in 1971 and stars Richard Harris as the main character, Hugh Glass, and John Huston as Captain Henry. It is very well done. There is also a recent movie titled "Revenant" that stars Leonardo DiCaprio playing the part of Hugh Glass. The term revenant means "one that returns after a lengthy absence or one who returns after death."[57] The movie was released in December, 2016. It had some interesting scenes, especially the bear attack, but was a little slow and drawn out.[58]

One would assume, if the story was true, it would have served as a very instructional lesson for the young Jim Bridger. If it is a myth, it prepared Jim to make up some of his own whoppers, i.e., the "Petrified Forest" and the "Cheyenne Canyon." In reference to the "Petrified Forest," Jim told the novices that he had discovered a "petrified forest" which contained "petrified trees" which contained "petrified birds" who sang "petrified songs" in the Yellowstone region. Several sources give credit to Moses "Black" Harris for the tale about the "putrified forest."[59] It is the nature of these tellers of "tall tales," in many cases, to borrow and elaborate one another's stories. The Cheyenne Canyon story relates that Bridger was trapping in a valley when a Cheyenne war party attacked him, and he tried to make his getaway by high-tailing it down a canyon. The Cheyenne pursued him for several miles, and Jim found himself at the end of a box canyon where he was cornered by the Cheyenne. Supposedly, at this point in the story, Jim would make a long pause causing his listeners to inquire, "What happened then, Mr. Bridger?" and "Old Gabe" would respond, "They kilt me!"

Another famous mountain man who was at Fort Phil Kearney when the fort was under attack in 1866 was James Beckwourth. He was a mulatto American who had spent over 40 years exploring and trapping in the West. He was born about 1798 in Virginia as a slave. His father was white and his mother was a mulatto slave girl named "Miss Kill." His father, Sir Jen-nings Beckwith, was of English and Irish nobility. There is some confusion over the name Beckwith and Beckwourth. It is suggested that Thomas D. Booner, who interviewed Beckwourth, changed the spelling of his name from Beckwith to Beckwourth. "Nevertheless, it can now be stated with finality that Jim Beckwourth was technically a slave, although it is apparent that he was not so treated by his father, and that he enjoyed considerable freedom to come and go as he pleased."[60] Jim's father moved the entire family from Virginia to the wild country of St. Louis, Missouri, in 1806; the year that Lewis and Clark completed their famous "Expedition." He recalls that he was about nine years old when he had his first encounter with the hostile savages in the area where he lived. He stated:

One day my father called me to him, and inquired of me whether I thought myself man enough to carry a sack of corn to the mill. The idea of riding a horse, and visiting town, possessed attractions which I could not resist, and I replied with a hearty affirmative. A sack of corn was accordingly deposited on the back of a gentle horse selected for the purpose, and "Young Jim" (as I was called) was placed upon the sack and started for the mill two miles distant. About midway to the mill lived a neighbor having a large family of children, with whom I frequently joined in boyish sports. On my way I rode joyously up to the little fence which separated the house from the road, thinking to pass a word with my little playmates. What was my horror at discovering all the children, eight in number, from one to fourteen years of age, lying in various positions in the door-yard with their throats cut, their scalps torn off, and the warm lifeblood still oozing from their gaping wounds! In the door-way lay their father, and near him their mother, in the same condition; they had all shared the same fate. I found myself soon back at my father's house but without the sack of corn--how I managed to get it off I never discovered--and related the circumstances to my father. He imme-diately gave the alarm throughout the settlement, and a body of men started in pursuit of the savages who had perpetrated this fearful tragedy; my father, with ten of his own men, accompanying them. In two days the band had returned, bringing with them eighteen Indian scalps; for the backwoodsman fought the savage in Indian style, and it was scalp for scalp between them.

The day when I beheld the harrowing spectacle of my little murdered playmates is still fresh in my memory as at the time of its occurrence, and it will never fade from my mind. It was the first scene of Indian cruelty my young eyes had ever witnessed, and I wondered how even savages could pos-sess such relentless minds as to wish to bathe their hands in the blood of little innocents against whom they could have no quarrel.[61]

This incident further confirms the basic premise of this book because it clearly documents the horrendous savagery of the Indians in butchering innocent white men, and especially white women and children. These sav-age Indians not only killed innocent women and children but also brutally butchered them, just as the young Jim Beckwourth described. It must be noted here that Beckwourth changed his opinion of the Indians after living with the Crow for 8 years. He became very sympathetic to the Indian point of view. However, another well-known mountain man, Osborne Russell, sums it up best when he states, "that the best way to negotiate and settle disputes with hostile Indians is with the rifle; for that is the only pen that can write a treaty which they will not forget."[62]

In my opinion, one has to support the frontiersmen's Indian fighting methods, as mentioned above, "for the backwoodsman fought the savage in

Indian style, and it was scalp for scalp between them."You fight them Indian style just like they fight you for your own survival. I have mentioned this before in reference to fighting Indian battles. The east coast philanthropists and humanitarians hold to their idealistic misconceptions about the "Noble Red Man," whereas the white frontier farmer, settler and their families had to confront a much more horrible reality. Fighting the Indians with their own cruel tactics was the only way to gain respect from these detestable savages.

It has been stated that Beckwourth went to school for four years and also was apprenticed to a blacksmith by his father so he could learn a trade. His father set him free when he was 24. In the fall of 1824, he joined the third William Ashley expedition up the Missouri River and to the Rocky Mountains.[63] He states that, "Being possessed with a strong desire to see the celebrated Rocky Mountains, and the great Western wilderness so much talked about, I engaged in General's Ashley's Rocky Mountain Fur Com-pany. The company consisted of twentynine men, who were employed by the Fur Company as hunters and trappers. We started on the 11th of Octo-ber with horses and pack mules."[64]

After the completion of this famous trip, he continued to scout and trap in the mountains with many of his famous colleagues. In 1828, he was sup-posedly captured by the Crow and became one of the tribe. He married several Crow women and lived with the Crow tribe for approximately 8 years. While living with the Crow, he was supposed to have achieved the rank of Chief of the Crow Nation. Beckwourth stated: "We there built counsel-lodge, and all the prophets and medicine men in the village were assembled in it on its completion. The national records were read over, and, after a lengthy ceremony performed by the great men, it was unanimously declared that they had elected me First Counselor, and that, conjointly with Long Hair, I was head chief of the nation."[65] The problem with this state-ment is that Beckwourth had a reputation, just like Jim Bridger, of telling tall tales earning the nickname, "Gaudy Liar." Delmont R. Oswald, who wrote the introduction, notes and epilogue to the latest edition of Jim's autobiography *The Life and Adventures of James P. Beckwourth,* (1981), states that, "It is doubtful that Beckwourth was more than a subchief in the tribe. The Crows recognized two head chiefs only during the time of Arapooish and Long Hair. At the death of Arapooish, Long Hair, or Red-Feather-at-the-Temple, became the recognized head chief."[66] Obviously, there is a disagreement as to the accurate status of Beckwourth in reference to the Crow tribe and his chief's identification.

Much to my surprise, there also seems to be some disagreement as to how black Jim Beckwourth really was. In the classic picture of 1860, he definitely seems to be of a dark complexion. However, in Elinor Wilson's book, *Jim Beckwourth: Black Mountain Man and War Chief of the Crows,* she makes reference to the fact that, "Photographs do not indicate that he was darker than many swarthy frontiersmen and there is nothing Negroid about his features. His hair was wavy but not kinky, and in one photograph it appears heavy and almost straight. Moore's statement that there was nothing in Beckwourth's appearance to indicate Negro ancestry and the fact that several others did not remark that he was a mulatto (unless they wrote their memoirs years after they had already absorbed the legendary tales about him) are significant."[67] The reference to Meridith Moore's statement was taken from "What [Meridith T.] Moore saw of Beckwourth in California," Connelley Papers, *Kansas State Historical Society.*[68]

It is an undisputable fact that Beckwourth's father was Irish and white and his mother was a slave; that makes him a mulatto or a half-breed, or the P.C. term, "mixed-blood." Wilson also suggests that Beckwourth's mother, although a slave, was also a mulatto and could have been a light skinned quadroon. Another source states that, "With relatively light skin and European features, Beckwourth might have passed for white, but he went through life as a free black man."[69] An additional source states that, "Jim Beckwourth's handsome features led Francis Parkman to call him a French half-breed; others impressed by his black, gently waving hair, said that he resembled an Indian."[70] To cast more doubt on the Negro features of Beckwourth, one need only look at an early picture of Beckwourth that John Hope Franklin has in this classic book, *From Slavery to Freedom*, 8th edition. This exact same picture can be found in the book, *Black Indians: A Hidden Heritage*, by William L. Katz, published in 2012. I find it very interesting how many early black historians resort to calling mixed-blood, half-breed individuals as Negroes. It seems that many black historians have a practice of searching for famous historical blacks but; when a famous mixed-blood individual comes along, all of a sudden he, surprisingly, becomes "completely black." Many Afro-Centric historians like to make the charge that Cleopatra and Nefertiti are all black; a good look at facial features and accurate history dispel these myths.

Beckwourth had long wavy hair, a lightened complexion when he was young, and a somewhat Caucasian nose. One of the travelers and mountain men of the West, Rufus B. Sage, described a typical frontiersman as follows: "His skin, from constant exposure, assumes a hue almost as dark as that of the Aborigine, and his features and physical structure attain a rough and hardy cast."[71] In my opinion, he looks more like an Indian. That certainly makes the conversation a little bit more lively. The politically correct must be ranting and raving about racism as they usually do! Many of you say that history is boring; how wrong you are! You may draw your own conclusions! You research the sources and follow them where they lead.

Between 1828 and 1837, Beckwourth remained among the Crow tribe learning their culture and language and trapping throughout their tribal lands. During this time period, he also worked as a trapper for the Rocky Mountain Fur Company and the American Fur Company. In 1837, he returned to St. Louis; and he volunteered for service in the Second Semi-nole War, in Florida, as a civilian wagon master and mule handler. After his service in that war, he returned to Colorado; and between 1838 and 1840, he continued his activities as an Indian trader and helped establish a trading post near Pueblo, Colorado. He also became involved with Andrew Sublette as a trader on the Santa Fe Trail in New Mexico. He was also involved in the Mexican War of 1846-1848. As a result of the California gold rush of 1848-49, he found himself in California exploring and settling in the Sierra Nevada mountain region where he discovered what came to be known as Beckwourth Pass. Between 1854 and 1856, Beckwourth crossed paths with Thomas D. Booner who interviewed him and compiled his notes into the now famous book, *The Life and Adventures of James Beckwourth, Mountaineer, Scout, Pioneer, and Chief of the Crow Nation.*

The gold rush of 1858-59 in the Pikes Peak area of Colorado motivated Beckwourth to return to Colorado, and he ended up living in Denver. It was while he lived in Denver that he got involved, in 1864, with the so-called "Sand Creek Massacre," serving as an interpreter and guide for Colonel Chivington and his 3rd Colorado militia. There is something of a controversy over the status of Beckwourth as a guide for Chivington. Some suggest that he was a willing guide; others suggest that he was forced by Chivington to lead his militia to the Cheyenne-Arapaho camp of Black Kettle. Beckwourth's life comes to an end as he is negotiating with the Crow Indians at Fort Phil Kearney in the winter of 1866, just before the famous Fetterman Massacre. He supposedly died of a disease while at the Crow camp, but others believed that he was poisoned.

We will now examine another one of the most fascinating personali-ties of the American West, Father Pierre-Jean De Smet. One historian, I can't remember who, stated that De Smet was one of the least discussed figures of the American West, generally only mentioned in footnotes, but one of the most important. It is for this reason that I have chosen him for a more detailed investigation. He was a Jesuit priest who was considered by many to be the most influential Catholic priest that ministered to the Plains Indians during the mid-nineteenth century. His active ministry among the

Indians lasted from 1838 until 1846. He was born in Belgium in 1801 and immigrated to the United States in 1821. He was ordained a priest in 1827 and studied American Indian culture, customs and languages until 1830. Between 1833 and 1837, De Smet had to return to Belgium due to seri-ous health problems; health problems that would haunt his entire ministry in America. Father De Smet was also an active participant in the impor-tant treaty negotiations of 1851 and 1868. He wielded tremendous influ-ence among the Plains Indians, especially among the Potawatomi, Teton, Flathead, Crows and the Yankton Sioux. They considered him the only white man who never lied to them. Catholic priests were known as "Black Robes" to the Indians because of the obvious black religious garments they wore. Father De Smet came to be known as " Black Robe," and he wore this title proudly.

His first missionary work began when he left St. Louis in May of 1838. He landed at Council Bluffs, Iowa, and helped established the mission of St. Joseph's Church; its name was later changed to Saint Mary's Mission. He ministered to the Potawatomi Indians for the next two years, from 1838 until 1840. Much to his dismay, the Potawatomi had a severe problem with alcohol; and he became frustrated with his inability to change their behav-ior. De Smet agonized over this fact and stated that, "He could counsel them against idleness, gambling, polygamy and superstition, but when they were drunk, he said, 'all their good qualities vanish, they no longer resemble men; all must flee before them; their yells and howls are fearful; they hurl themselves upon each other, they bite off each others' noses and ears and mutilate each other horribly.'"[72] The problem became so severe that Father De Smet wrote several letters to the Secretary of War demanding an end to the illicit whiskey traffic on the Missouri River. But since the posting of mail took so long, and the fact that the Jesuit missions depended on a federal appropriation, the Jesuit's hierarchy censored and edited his letters. He was unable to get the needed reforms he wanted. The drinking problem became so onerous that he sometimes feared for his own safety. He describes these dangerous conditions as follows:

> The savages drink and gamble so long as there remains to them a half a far-thing. The love which they have for drink is truly inconceivable. It is neces-sary to see it to form any idea of it. It is to them a veritable tarantula. When they are soused all their blood is inflamed in their veins. They become lustful for more alcohol. Obtaining some, they continue to cry "More, more!" until consumed by firewater they fall dead drunk. No sooner have they regained their senses than their first and only exclamation is always: "Whisky, whisky, whisky," as if life and death depended on it.[73]

I go into detail about the Potawatomi problem with alcohol not only because of its importance to Father De Smet but because, as we shall see when we discuss the modern Sioux Indian Reservation at Pine Ridge, South Dakota (Wounded Knee), alcoholism is still a very destructive problem. The issues for today's Sioux are not only alcohol, but also drugs, internal tribal bickering and, of all things, urban gang activity. We will go into more detail on these modern problems when we discuss the Battle of Wounded Knee.

In addition to the Potawatomi, De Smet also considered the Blackfeet Indians unworthy of conversion. He said that the Blackfeet were "the only Indians of whose salvation we would have reason to despair...for they are murderers, thieves, traitors and all that is wicked." In addition, he stated: "'These are savages in the full sense of the word, accustomed to satiate their vengeance and to revel in blood and carnage. They are plunged in the grossest superstitions; they worship the sun and the moon, offering them sacrifices of propitiation and thanksgiving. They cut deep into their own flesh and even cut off the joints of their fingers. 'I offer you my blood,' they say to their divinity; 'now give me success in arms, and on my return I will offer you the homage of the scalps of my enemies.'" [74] The Blackfeet tribe had a reputation amongst the fur trappers, such as Osborne Russell, Jim Bridger, "Liver-Eating" Johnston, and Bill Sublette, for being the most vicious, feared and brutal tribe of the Rocky Mountain territory.

In addition to his concerns over the Potawatomi and Blackfeet, the St. Joseph's Mission, in the beginning of 1840, was not doing well. De Smet vol-unteered to travel to St. Louis during the winter to get additional instructions and supplies for the faltering mission. While in St. Louis, De Smet was fortu-nate enough to be assigned with two other priests to minister to the Rocky Mountain tribes. The Flathead Indians had previously made attempts to reach St. Louis to acquire "Black Robes" to minister to their people. As an example of his unique devotion to duty, he had promised to return for a second jour-ney to the Flathead Indians. This trip was going to be made based upon the Flatheads' desire for additional new missionaries. However, there was a lack of funding for making this return trip. In reference to this disappointment, Father De Smet states that, "The thought that the undertaking was doomed to failure, and that I could not keep the promise I had made to the poor Indi-ans, occasioned me much sorrow and regret. But I had been the recipient of direct help from on high too often to allow myself in this instance to yield to discouragement. My confidence in God remained unshaken."[75] At the com-pletion of his first two-year journey, 1840-1842, he had accomplished his mis-sion to make initial contact with not only the Flatheads but also the Crows.

The continual need for funds to operate the missions of the Upper Missouri and Oregon region were always a major worry for him, especially in reference to his desire to establish and build his new Indian Paraguayan Reduction program. The desire to establish new "Paraguayan Reductions" with the Plains Indians was one of his major goals as a Jesuit priest.The term "Paraguayan Reductions" refers to one of the most controversial conversion attempts on New World Indians. This idealistic, utopian experiment began with the Guarani Indians in Paraguay. It began in the early 1600's and lasted to the 1760's. In essence these "reductions" were an extensive indigenous Guarani tribal area which contained as many "as one hundred autonomous town like missions, which they called reductions, each containing from 350 to 7,000 native converts... Assisted by missionaries, natives administered the civil government, staffed an army, and managed the communal economy. European-style homes, workplaces, small hospitals, schools and farms made each community self-sufficient."[76] This utopian experiment ended in 1773 when the royal Spanish court became jealous of the power that the Jesuits wielded in the New World and suppressed their controversial experiments. (To vividly illustrate this experiment, I highly recommend the movie, *The Mission,* starring Robert De Niro and Jeremy Irons, made in 1986. This film directly discusses the Guarani missionary work, its organizational plan, and the establishment of "Reductions" in the 1750's. I consider it an outstand-ing movie.)

These "reductions" were what De Smet wanted to initially establish among the Flathead Indians of Montana. Between 1838 and 1841, he traveled extensively throughout the Pacific Northwest and established several small missions. But the first Jesuit mission to be based upon the "Paraguayan Reductions," which was organized by both De Smet and Father Nicolas Point, was the mission they called Saint Mary's Mission, the old St. Joseph's; it was established on September 24th, 1841. It was founded in the high mountains of the Bitterroot River valley and had as its primary target missionary work for the Flathead Indians. De Smet stated that, "we may draw this conclusion, that the nation of the Flatheads appears to be a chosen people--'the elect of God;' that it would be easy to make this tribe a model for other tribes."[77] The Bitterroot location was also advantageous because it had large numbers of other Indians close by, specifically the Pend Oreilles and Nez Perces. This location made it possible to administer to three tribes from one reduction. The importance of location was based upon the simple financial factor that the establishment, building and maintenance of reductions was an expensive investment.

De Smet envisioned a grand system of ten or more reductions for the Oregon country, each one branching out from the hub at St. Mary's. Natives would benefit from a full program of religious training and education in the European tradition. To obliterate paganism and replace it with the attributes of Christianity and western civilization was, after all, the measure of success for missionary activity in the nineteenth century. The Jesuit principle of accommodation provided a certain latitude in allowing the natives to maintain elements of their own culture, but the final goal would always be the conversion of the Indians to the twin principles of Christianity and civilization.[78]

In 1842, the second reduction was initially established at the northern end of Lake Coeur d'Alene. It was initially named the Saint Joseph Mission but was later moved and renamed the Coeur d'Alene Mission of the Sacred Heart. The moving and renaming of the various missions can cause some definite confusion but that was the way it was done. The third reduction was called Saint Michael's Mission and was located near the main tribe of the Kalispel Indians in Idaho; it was established in 1844.

To maintain and expand his reduction program, he traveled on numerous trips that included journeys from St. Louis back to the East coast and to Europe. He also made trips from Europe to San Francisco on the west coast by going around the dangerous southern tip of South America to get to the missions in the Northwest Territories. Here are two specific examples of his wide-ranging travels from his *Life, Letters and Travels of Father de Smet, s.j., 1801-1873, Volume 2,* Part III:

1843: For the purpose of soliciting funds for the missions, Father De Smet made a journey to New Orleans and back as far east as Boston and--He then went to Westport, Mo., with Father De Vos and companions--They left St. Louis for Europe--Embarked at New York (fourth voyage across the Atlantic)--In twenty-one days landed in Ireland---Visited Cork and Dublin--Crossed to Liverpool and London--Continued on to Antwerp-- Visited the principal cities in Belgium, France, Italy and Holland-- Embarked at Ant-werp with a father and a brother from Belgium, three Italian fathers, and six sisters of Notre Dame de Namur--Descended the Scheld to Flushing, where he was detained twenty-eight days by contrary winds. No dates given.
Distance traveled, 15,479 miles.

1844: Sailed January 9th with a favoring breeze (fifth voyage) -- Crossed the Equator February 14th - -Saw the Falkland Islands on the 16th of March-- Rounded Cape Horn on the 20th--Continued north ten days when a terrible tempest was encountered which drove the ship almost upon the coast of Patagonia--Ship driven south to the 66th degree south latitude among the icebergs...the coast of Chile in sight of the Cape of Tres Montes April 8th --Entered Valparaiso harbor April 11th --Made a journey to Santiago, arriving there April 25th...Visited Lima, the capital of Peru-- Sailed from Callao May 27th --Re-crossed the Equator in June and sighted the coast of Oregon July 28th --Crossed the bar July 31st and anchored in front of Astoria. August 2nd set out by skiff for Vancouver arriving there on the 4th --Started for the Willamette August 14th; reached St. Paul on the 17th and commenced the erection of St. Francis Xavier's residence--Was taken quite ill, and before he was entirely recovered, set out on horseback for the upper country... passed the winter among the Pend d'Oreilles. No dates given.

Distance traveled, 18,828 miles. [79]

This is a combined mileage for 1843 and 1844 of 34,307 miles. He seemed to be a man possessed with a wander lust for adventure. He had astonishing travels during his entire ministry; and it has been estimated that his travels covered about 200,000 total miles, many of them on foot. It is also believed that he made a combined number of 19 trips across the Atlantic Ocean and around the tip of South America.[80] To increase his fund rais-ing, he had written two books of his notes which he had published about his travels and used these to entice wealthy donors on the East Coast and in Europe to contribute to his mission. He had taken 15 of his own letters and issued them under the title, *Letters and Sketches with a Narrative of a Year's Residence among the Indian Tribes of the Rocky Mountains;* the second book was titled, *The Oregon Missions.* He had these books translated into French for his European contributors.

His amazing travels would involve trips to the east coast cities of New Orleans, Boston, Louisville, Cincinnati, Pittsburg, Baltimore, Washington, Philadelphia and New York. The sea trips he made to San Francisco went south around the Cape of Good Hope.When in Europe, he would return to Belgium and continue his "begging" activities with stops at Rome, Naples, Lyons, Spain, Germany, France, and Holland. The success of his fundraising can be seen when we look at the money he had raised in December of 1843. As he departed from Antwerp to return to the U. S., Father De Smet had "opened the pocketbooks of Europe...he carried with him a bank credit for more than 145,000 francs ($26,500), a princely sum for the times."[81]

Between the years 1843 and 1846, it is estimated that he traveled about 44,000 miles. "He crossed two oceans and the Columbia River bar; floated downstream on both the Columbia River and Missouri River; and in an effort to establish new reductions and make peace between the Flatheads and Blackfeet, rode across bleak desert landscapes and snow-shoed over steep mountain summits. And lest it be forgotten, De Smet also begged money on two continents, maintained a worldwide correspondence, and converted hundreds of Indians to Christianity."[82] In addition to these physi-cally exhausting travels, many of which he made by foot, he also had to concern himself with the Church's internal bureaucratic politics.

These internal politics initially concerned a difference of opinion between Father Nicolas Point and Father Peter De Vos, two Jesuits priests that served under De Smet. These two priests had disagreed over some unknown racial matters when they both served at a Jesuit college in Loui-siana. Point had written several formal letters to Father General Roothaan about this subject that were critical of De Vos. Roothaan was the Supe-rior-General of the Society of Jesus from 1829 until 1853 and was directly responsible for the administration and leadership of the Society. De Vos was also extremely critical of De Smet. In that opinion, "De Smet showed more interest in establishing a chain of reductions--building more buildings--than he did in mediating sensitive personnel matters for the society. De Smet loved to start missions, but he seldom remained in them for long. He sought glamour by planning, establishing, and publicizing the Indian missions."[83] In addition to this division, Father Point also disagreed with De Smet over the overall effectiveness of the reduction program for the Rocky Moun-tain Mission. Point thought that the reduction model was not a satisfactory method of dealing with specific Indians, especially the Flatheads. Another issue between Point and De Smet was over the reality of attempting to introduce a mission to the Blackfeet. Point, however, thought this reduction to be advisable, while De Smet had serious doubts due to their vicious rep-utation. There was also the fact that Father Point had a habit of writing to the Father General Roothaan, and De Smet didn't want any internal criti-cism of the administration of his reduction program forwarded to Rome. In reference to Father Point's criticisms of De Smet, De Vos had compiled a dossier on Point, and De Vos wanted De Smet to forward it to Roothaan. De Smet, again fearful of criticism, quashed this dossier and never deliv-ered it to Rome. This action caused De Vos to criticize De Smet and write letters to Roothaan critical of De Smet's organizational and management style. These letters were the basis for his dismissal ministering directly to the Rocky Mountain Mission Indians and his placement in a bureaucratic position in St. Louis.

With his completion of the journey of 1846, he returned to St. Louis in a state of poor health and exhaustion due to the fact that he completed most of that year's traveling by foot. Upon his arrival, he was surprised to find a letter addressed to him from Roothaan which had been mailed from Rome on August 6, 1845. "In the letter Father General Roothaan relieved De Smet of his responsibility for the Rocky Mountain Mission and named as his successor thirty-five-year-old Father Joseph Joset, S.J. Roothaan con-cluded his letter to De Smet with this terse statement: 'Your post, will be in Saint Louis. From there you will be in a position to serve your dear Indians from afar.'"[84] This letter came as a shock and disappointment to De Smet. Rather than minister to his beloved Indians, he was appointed as the treasurer of the university in St. Louis. The internal politics of the Church's bureaucracy had finally caught up with him.

Between 1847 and 1851, he had a variety of challenges that tested his strengths and convictions. At first, he was downtrodden about his removal from actual ministering to the Indians, but then he realized that he could still assist the missionary activities by using his time-tested ability as a fund raiser. Having previous success with the publication of one his books about the Indians, *Journeys to the Rocky Mountains*, he decided that he would use his writing ability to publish more of his adventures and travels. In 1847, he reorganized some more of his previous letters and observations and had them published as his second book, *Oregon Missions and Travels over the Rocky Mountains in 1845-46*. This edition was later published under the title, *The Oregon Missions.*[85] He returned to Europe in 1848 to see his family in Bel-gium and promote his books and solicit funds for his ministry. However, 1848 was a very volatile year in Europe as revolutions were breaking out all over the continent as well as in South America. The year 1848 was known as the "Year of Revolution" as some 50 nations were disrupted by vio-lent turmoil. During his stay in Europe, he visited Paris and Rome. While in Rome, he met with Father General Roothaan, but nothing was ever divulged about this meeting. Father De Smet left Europe in April of 1848 and returned to St. Louis in July of 1848. He was successful in that he had raised an estimated $5,500 in donations for his ministry.

The politics of the St. Louis offices of the Church changed in early 1849 for the better when Father Elet was appointed vice-provincial of the Missouri Jesuits. Elet and De Smet were friends; and this was beneficial to De Smet in that, although he was banned from ministering to the Rocky Mountain tribes, nothing was said about the Missouri River tribes. Elet allowed himself to be persuaded by De Smet to go up the Missouri River in search of tribes to Christianize, especially the Sioux. During the early part of 1848 and 1849, De Smet went up river and made contact, not only with the Sioux but also with the Ponca Indians. De Smet was surprised to discover the extreme warlike nature of the Sioux.

When Father De Smet came upon the Sioux, he found them reveling in all the horrors of their primitive savagery. Several warriors had just returned from an expedition against the Omahas, carrying thirty-two scalps dangling from their lances and horses' bits. At the sight of these hideous trophies the whole tribe jumped and shouted with joy. The "scalp dance and feast" was celebrated with the most discordant yells and horrible contortions. They planted a post daubed with vermilion in the middle of the camp; the warriors danced around it, the scalps swaying with each movement. To the deafening accompaniment of drums, each man howled his war-song, then, striking the pole with his tomahawk, proclaimed the victims it had immolated, exhibit-ing ostentatiously the scars of the wounds he had received. These depraved customs were the natural consequence of their barbarous instincts.[86]

The time he spent among the Sioux was a major factor in his being able to convince the Sioux to participate in the treaty negotiations of 1851 and 1868.

The year 1849 was a momentous year for the United States and the world as gold was discovered in California. Actually, gold was discovered in January of 1848 by James W. Marshall at Sutter's Mill in Coloma, California, a small settlement east of Sacramento. The news wasn't really widely known until the *New York Herald* first published it on the east coast in August of 1848. This was soon followed by a speech made in December of 1848 by President John Polk which confirmed the reality of gold being found in California. The really massive immigration to the west coast didn't begin until 1849, therefore the nickname, "forty-niners." As stated previously, the gold rush encouraged immigrants from all over the world to head for Cali-fornia. This, of course, caused a tremendous surge in the immigration to the state, primarily along the Oregon and California trails. This tremendous influx of immigrants had a devastating impact on the Indian tribes that lived along these trails; the "gold madness" had just begun. The 1849 gold rush was a prelude to the gold fever in Colorado in 1858, in Montana in 1862, and in South Dakota with Custer's Expedition of the Black Hills in 1874.

As for Father De Smet, he spent the years from 1849 to 1851 primarily performing his "administrative and bookkeeping duties, De Smet followed a busy schedule…He even found enjoyment by rewriting a series of five letters he originally penned during his 1848 excursion to the Great Plains and sending them to the publishing arm of the Association for the Propa-gation of the Faith…Black Robe distinguished himself from all others by his ability to play up missionary work in a variety of Catholic newspapers, magazines, and books. Moreover, the intuitive way in which he satisfied the public's curiosity, plus his natural ability to tell anecdotes, made De Smet the most recognized Catholic missionary in the nineteenth century."[87]

In addition to Father De Smet's duties as a treaty advisor, he still had his major obligations in ministering to the Indians. A disturbing dilemma in De Smet's missionary work was that he initially thought the Flatheads and other Indians really wanted to convert to Catholicism. There were many funda-mental similarities between the two cultures that seemed to blend them together. There were fundamental similarities between the Indian "Great Spirit" and the Catholic Supreme Being, "God." There were also similarities between the "Happy Hunting Ground" and the "Christian Heaven." Some of the other crucial similarities were:

> Baptism, marriage, the Mass, and other Catholic liturgy appealed to the Flatheads' sense of drama and color. Jesuits talked about miracles from the hand of the Blessed Mother and a lexicon of saints; the Indians sought their favors from the natural spirit helpers. The crucifix, holy medals, and rosaries paralleled sacred charms and other "medicines" used by the Indians. Grego-rian chants sung by the priests resembled tribal prophesy songs. The incense burned at the Mass seemed closely related to the smoke sage and tobacco that carried the Indians' own prayers skyward.[88]

The basic problem was that the Indians, especially the Flatheads, were really looking for protections against their tribal enemies, not redemption. What the Flatheads really desired was for the black robes to save them from their enemies. "The Jesuits, the Flatheads assumed, would protect them from raids and attacks, bullets and arrows. If the Black Robe wished them to learn prayers, sing hymns, and partake in Christian rituals, they considered it a small price to pay for invincibility."[89]

The following conversation took place between an Indian Chief and Father De Smet; it clearly shows the misunderstandings between the Indi-ans and missionaries. The great chief professed undying friendship. "'Black Robe,' he said, 'to you I owe my success at arms,' and taking from his neck a little bag, he displayed the remainder of the matches which Father De Smet had given him. 'I take them with me whenever I go to war, and if the match lights the first time I strike it, I fall upon my enemies, sure of vic-tory.' The missionary had the utmost difficulty in abolishing this ridiculous superstition. 'You see,' he said, in conclusion, 'with what trifles man wins renown with the Indians. The possessor of a few matches passes for a great man and receives distinguished honors!'"[90] Clearly, the Indians were more concerned with using the supposed superior powers of De Smet and the

Black Robes for their own hostile motivations; it had very little to do with saving souls.

Let me now introduce one of the most important duties that Father De Smet accomplished. It involves Father De Smet in his advisor's role at the Treaty of Fort Laramie in 1851. Both Jim Bridger and Father De Smet served as advisors for the Treaty of 1851. As part of the negotiations in 1851, there were mandatory Indian meals and feasts that the members had to attend. Father De Smet describes these fascinating feasts as follows:

> Notwithstanding the scarcity of provisions felt in the camp before the wag-ons came, the feasts were numerous and well attended. No epoch in Indian annals, probably, shows a greater massacre of the canine race. Among the Indians the flesh of the dog is most honorable and esteemed of all viands, especially in the absence of buffalo and other animals. On the present occa-sion it was a last resource. The carnage then may be conceived. I was invited to several of the banquets; a great chief, in particular, wished to give me a special mark of his friendship and respect for me. He had filled his great ket-tle with little fat dogs, skins and all. He presented me, on a wooden platter, the fattest, well boiled. I found the meat really delicate, and I can vouch that it is preferable to suckling-pig, which it nearly resembles in taste.[91]

The Indians definitely had some very unique and esoteric eating habits in comparison to their white companions. These same Indian eating habits were reported by Lewis and Clark on their famous "Expedition of Discovery" to the Pacific coast between 1804 and 1806. In addition to eating dogs, they sometimes killed and ate skunks. Father De Smet stated, "The strong odor of this animal is intolerable to the whites; the savages, on the contrary, appear to like it, and deem its flesh exquisite. How true is the proverb: *De gustibus non disputandum*!--there is no accounting for tastes."[92] We will encounter Father De Smet again later in the book when we examine his role in the Treaty of 1868 and his missionary role with the Indians. Let us leave De Smet and the unique eating habits of the Indians with a "bon appetit."

In addition to the treaty of 1851, there also was another important treaty signed with the southern tribes on October 14, 1865. This treaty took place on the Little Arkansas River in Kansas and surprisingly came to be known as the Little Arkansas Treaty or the Treaty of Fort Wise. The following chiefs and tribes negotiated the treaty: Chief Black Kettle of the Southern Chey-enne, Chief Little Raven of the Southern Arapahoe, Chief Satanta of the Kiowa, and other chiefs from the Comanche and Plains Apache. The main members of the government negotiating team were John Sanborn, William Harney, Kit Carson and William Bent. Bent was one of the most famous original frontier traders and entrepreneurs of the West. He began a trading empire with his three brothers and Ceram St. Vrain. Bent promoted the treaty of 1865 because it would give him a virtual monopoly on the fur, horse and mule trade in the area; he was a very shrewd businessman. The Treaty of 1865 was signed by the government and only the Cheyenne and Arapahoe Indians: and, as all future treaties would do, it abrogated all the previous treaties that the Indians had signed. This treaty would have cost the other Indians dearly had they agreed to it because it would have forced them to:

> ...cede all lands guaranteed to them by the Treaty of Fort Laramie in exchange for a small reservation along the Arkansas River centered, not sur-prisingly on Bent's New Fort. Only government employees and licensed traders would be allowed there, providing a secure trading monopoly for Bent. However, the treaty was doomed from the beginning, for no more than six chiefs signed it and they represented only Black Kettle's band of Wutapiu and a part of the Ridge People under White Antelope. The Council of Forty-four absolutely refused authority for a treaty or to give away any of their lands or compromise on the way they lived their lives. Black Ket-tle and the other five signers, who had no authority to commit the tribe, were viewed with contempt by the rest of the southern bands, and both the treaty and the reservation were ignored. The government, however, deemed it binding and designated five of the signers the five principal and ruling chiefs of the Cheyenne, even though they represented only a small part of the tribe.[93]

Even though this treaty was officially recognized by the U.S. government, the overwhelming number of the southern bands refused to sign the treaty and rejected all of its fundamental premises. Again, for an overwhelming majority of the Indian tribes this treaty simply did not exist.

You will have to bear with me, but I believe that the language of these treaties is very important because it clearly illustrates the devious method-ology of the Bureau of Indian Affairs, the Department of the Interior, and Congress when dealing with the Indian land problem. This treaty consisted of nine articles, but I will only discuss those articles that I think are impor-tant in understanding the impact of it.

The Treaty of 1865 and all of the other treaties began, as we shall see later, with the same naive foolish language.

Article 1 stated that "...hereafter perpetual peace shall be maintained between the people and Government of the United States and the Indian parties hereto, and that the Indian parties hereto, shall forever remain at peace with each other...."[94]

Perpetual peace between the U.S. government with its continuous land-stealing policies and the savage nomadic tribes; what wishful thinking.

Article 2 specifies the exact lands that the Indians will be restricted to and also addresses their placement and location on reservations. "The Indi-ans parties hereto... expressly agree to remove to and accept as their perma-nent home the country embraced within said limits whenever directed so to do by the President of the United States... and that they will not go from said country for hunting or other purposes without the consent in writing of their agent or other authorized person..."[95]

Article 4 is directly related to the treaty negotiations of 1851 in that it again gives the U.S. government the right to build roads and forts on Indian land. "It is further agreed by the parties hereto that the United States my lay off (mark off) and build through the reservation, provided for by Article 2 of this treaty, such roads or highways as may be deemed necessary; and may also establish such military posts within the same as may be found necessary in order to preserve peace among the Indians..."

This is the very idea, the building of roads and forts through the Powder River country, which caused Red Cloud to heatedly leave the 1866 nego-tiations. This is the stipulation that began Red Cloud's War and caused his raids on Fort Phil Kearney and the Bozeman Trail.

Article 6 discusses the government's acknowledgement of the "massacre" at Sand Creek with a reparations agreement to sooth the "savage soul". It states: "The United States being desirous to express its condemnation of, and, as far as may be, repudiate the gross and wanton outrages perpetuated against certain bands of Cheyenne and Arapahoe Indians...at Sand Creek, in Colorado Territory, while said Indians were at peace with the United States, and under its flag, whose protection they had by lawful authority been promised and induced to seek, and the Government being desirous to make some suitable reparation for the injuries done..."

Article 9 is the final coup de grace in that it states: "upon the ratification of this treaty all former treaties are hereby abrogated."

Obviously, that means any other treaties made in reference to lands that had been granted or allocated to the Indians, such as the right to hunt on certain sacred grounds and the Powder River, no longer were in force. A further note requires that one mention the obvious question: Did the American Plains Indians really comprehend a treaty made up of such legalized gobbledygook? The understanding of the Indians ulti-mately depended on the accuracy and ability of the translator; in many cases, the ability of the translator left much to be desired. In some cases, the Indians specifically requested individual translators that they knew and trusted.

This treaty, the treaty of 1851, the Medicine Lodge Treaty of 1867 and the Treaty of 1868 would all be similarly organized. Article 2 would usually be the most important part of each treaty as it precisely described the land allotments and geographical territories provided for the Indians. Also, some of the later treaties would require the signing of the treaty by three-fourths of all male members of the tribe or it would be illegal. The reality of the treaty process was that the U.S. government never followed the tenets of its own treaties. They never gathered the necessary three-fourth votes; and, therefore, most of the treaties were illegal. Also, the Government very rarely fulfilled the annuity requirements of the treaties. The Indian agents were notorious for exploiting the annuity programs for their own benefit.

As we proceed through the book, I will be introducing the exact wording of some of the specific articles of these treaties, as done above, to concretely demonstrate the incomprehensible bureaucratic and lawyer gobbledygook that was supposedly interpreted to the Indians for their understanding. The paramount factor in all these treaties, the treaty of 1851, 1865, the attempted treaty of 1866, 1867 and 1868, is the government's continuing demands to reduce the lands available to the Indian tribes. The government continually requested the right to establish roads and protective forts on Indian lands, especially the Bozeman Trail. The most profound changes to Indian culture would come out of the Treaty of Medicine Lodge in 1867 because it estab-lished a system of tribal reservations and it was:

> ...charged with negotiating treaties with the Plains Indians to remove them from the path of white settlements and to "establish a system of civilizing the tribes"... The tribes were required to move immediately to these reserva-tions, and the Indians were to be provided with schools and resident farm-ers to teach them white cultural practices and agricultural techniques...the principals of Indian assimilation and cultural elimination, first embodied in the Treaty of Medicine Lodge, continued as the foundation of Indian policy for nearly three quarters of a century to come.[96]

The bureaucratic specificity of the language of these treaties is frightening. One of them, the Treaty of Medicine Lodge of 1867, lists each of the buildings to be built on the reservation and its cost as follows: "a warehouse or storeroom for the use of the agent in storing goods for the residence of the agent, to cost not exceeding three thousand dollars, a residence for the physician, to cost not more than three thousand dollars; and five other buildings, for a carpenter, farmer, blacksmith, miller and engineer..."[97] The Medicine Lodge Treaty also included exact specifications as to what kind of clothes the Indians would receive and wear. "Each male person over fourteen years of age, a suit of good, substantial wool clothing, consisting of pan-taloons, a flannel shirt, hat, and a pair of home-made socks. For each female over twelve years of age, a flannel skirt, or the goods necessary to make it, a pair of woolen hose, twelve yards of calico and yards of cotton domestic."[98] The specifics of the Treaty of Medicine Lodge will be discussed in detail in the chapter on the battle of the Washita. However, the total control over the Indians that this treaty and the others gave to the U. S. government was truly "Orwellian."

Endnotes for Chapter 2

[1] Stanley Vestal, *Mountain Men*, (Boston: Houghton Mifflin Company, 1937). viii. Hereafter cited as Vestal-*Mountain.*

[2] J.S. Holliday, *The World Rushed In: The California Gold Rush Experience*, (NewYork, Simon and Schuster, 1981). Hereafter cited as Holliday. This is an absolutely out-standing eye witness account based on the diary and letters of William Swan. He leaves his family, home and peach orchard in Youngstown, New York, north of Buf-falo. He travels across the Great Lakes and overland using the Oregon and Califor-nia Trails. He describes his travel experiences and time in the gold fields between the spring of 1849 and February of 1851. Many consider this book a "Classic" of American western literature.

[3] Ibid, 34-35.

[4] Ibid, 220--221.

[5] George Laycock, *The Mountain Men*, (Guilford: The Lyons, Press, 1996), 83. Here-after cited as Laycock.

[6] Utley-*A Life Wild*, 277.

[7] Vestal-*Bridger*, 170-171.

[8] Ibid, 218-219

[9] J. Cecil Alter, *Jim Bridger*, (Norman: University of Oklahoma Press, 1962), 7. Here-after cited as Alter.

[10] Carl P. Russell, *Firearms, Traps, & Tools of the Mountain Men*, (Albuquerque, Univer-sity of New Mexico Press, 1998), 60-62. Hereafter cited as Russell. I also recom-mend Charles E. Hanson, Jr.'s book, *The Hawken Rifle: It's Place in History*, (Crawford, The Fur Press, 1994).

[11] Laycock, 103-104.

[12] Margaret I. Carrington, *Absaraka: Home of the Crows, Being the Experience of an Officer's Wife on the Plains*, (Lincoln, University of Nebraska Press, 1983), 189. Ab-sa-ra-ka: Home of the Crows was originally published in 1868 by J.B. Lippincott and Co., Philadelphia.

[13] Raymond W. Thorp and Robert Bunker, *Crow Killer: The Saga of Liver-Eating Johnson*. (Bloomington, Indiana University Press, 1983), 65. Hereafter cited as Thorp and Bunker. The other book that served as a source for the movie was the fictional book by Vardis Fisher, *Mountain Man*, (Moscow, University of Idaho Press, 2000). Also see, Matthew P. Mayo, *Cowboys, Mountain Men & Grizzly Bears*, (Helena: TWODOT-Globe Pequot Press, 2009), 63-67. Hereafter cited as Mayo.

[14] Vardis Fisher, Mountain Man: A Novel of Male and Female in the Early American West, (Moscow, Idaho: University of Idaho Press, 1965). Here after cited as Fisher. Also, Raymond W. Thorp and Robert Bunker, *Crow Killer: The Saga of Liver-Eating Johnson*, (Bloomington: Indiana University Press, 1958). Hereafter cited as Thorp and Bunker.

[15] Dennis J. McLelland, The Avenging Fury of the Plains: John "Liver-Eating" John-ston, Exploding the Myths-Discovering the Man, (West Conshohocken: Infinity Publishing, 2008). 23. Hereafter cited as McLelland.

[16] Ibid.

[17] Ibid., 26.

[18] Ibid., 26-27.

[19] Ibid., 111.

[20] Ibid., 173.

[21] Ibid., 92-95.

[22] Ibid., 97.

[23] "Living-Eating Johnston," *The Lewiston Saturday Journal*, 2 June, 1900, 17. Mon-tana Online Historical Newspapers, Goggle News Archive. Hereafter cited as Lewiston Journal.

[24] Eric Jay Dolin, *Fur, Fortune, and Empire: The Epic History of the Fur Trade in America*, (New York, W. W. Norton & Company, 2010), 224. Hereafter cited as Dolin. Also see Stanley Vestal, *Jim Bridger: Mountain Man: A Biography*, (Lincoln, University of Nebraska, 1970), 8. Hereafter cited as Vestal-Bridger. It must be noted here that there is disagreement on the date of the advertisement, J. Cecil Alter gives the date, of "March 20, 1822," Eric Jay Dolan provides, "February 13, 1822," Dale L. Mor-gan provides a date of Feb. 13.1822, and Stanley Vestal gives a date of "March 20, 1822." You can take your choice. This is the kind of madness that makes History fascinating.

[25] Vestal-*Mountain*, 47.

[26] Dale L. Morgan, *Jedediah Smith and the Opening of the West,* (Lincoln: University of Nebraska Press, 1964), 92. Hereafter cited as Morgan. Hafen, 95, fn. 10. Vestal-*Bridger*, 63.

[27] Vestal-*Mountain*, 62.

[28] Morgan., 25.

[29] Robert M. Utley, *After Lewis and Clark: Mountain Men and the Paths to the Pacific,* (Lincoln: University of Nebraska Press, 1997), 42. Hereafter cited as Utley, *Lewis and Clark.*

[30] Barton B. Barbour, *Jedediah Smith: No Ordinary Mountain Man,* (Norman: Uni-versity of Oklahoma Press, 2009), 50-51. Hereafter cited as Barton.

[31] Ibid.

[32] Utley, *Lewis and Clark,* 99.

[33] Ibid.

[34] Ibid,. 98.

[35] Ibid., 99.

[36] *Mountain Men and Life in the Rocky Mountain West, "Rendezvous."* http://www. mman.us/rendezvous.htm, 3-4 (accessed 10 March, 2015).

[37] Hiram Martin Chittenden, *The American Fur Trade of the Far West, Volume 1,* (Lin-coln, University of Nebraska Press, 1986), 171. Hereafter cited as Chittenden. Also, Harrison Clifford Dale, *The Explorations of William H. Ashely and Jedediah Smith, 1822-1829,* (Lincoln: University of Nebraska Press, 1991), 108. Hereafter cited as Dale. Dale argues that the real credit for organizing the first rendezvous should go to Andrew Henry. He argues the following: "It would, however, seem more reason-able, *a priori*, to assume that it was Andrew Henry's idea. He alone knew the trans mountain country from his winter on Henry's Fork in 1810-1811. It had been his intention, furthermore, to cross to that region to trade with the Indians "within and west of the Rocky Mountains." See "Licenses to trade with the Indians," in U.S. House, Executive documents, 18 cong., I sess., I, 33. See footnote 208 on page 108. Interesting argument!

[38] Leroy R. Hafen, *Mountain Men & Fur Traders of the Far West*, (Lincoln: University of Nebraska Press, 1965), 85, fn.18. Here after cited as Hafen.

[39] Chittenden, 39.

[40] Thomas D. Bonner, *The Life and Adventures of James P. Beckwourth as told to Thomas D. Bonner: Introduced and with notes and epilogue by Delmont R. Oswald.,* (Lincoln: University of Nebraska Press, 1972), 107. Hereafter cited as Bonner. Also, Fred R. Gowans, *Rocky Mountain Rendezvous: A History of the Fur Trade Rendezvous, 1825-1840,* (Layton: UT, Gibbs M. Smith Publisher, 1985), 18. Hereafter cited as Gow-ans. Also, Robert M. Utley, *A Life Wild and Perilous: Mountain Men and the Paths to the Pacific*, (New York: Henry Holt and Company, 1997), 81. Hereafter cited as Utley-*A Life Wild.*

[41] Laycock, 81.

[42] Utley, *A Life Wild*. Inside Jacket cover, quoted by Francis Parkman, Jr., "I defy the annals of chivalry to furnish the record of a life more wild and perilous than that of a Rocky Mountain trapper."

[43] Hafen, 103.

[44] Dale l. Morgan, *Jedediah Smith and the Opening of the West* (Lincoln: University of Nebraska Press, 1964), 171-72, and 232. Hereafter cited as Morgan. Gowans, 19-20.

[45] Gowans, 21, 31.

[46] Ibid., 152.

[47] Morgan, 149.

[48] John Myers Myers, *The Saga of Hugh Glass: Pirate, Pawnee, and Mountain Man*, (Lincoln: University of Nebraska Press, 1976), 114. Hereafter cited as Myers, Myers.

[49] Alter, 41. Myers, Myers, 117. Vestal-*Bridger*, 42.

[50] Vestal-*Mountain*, 53.

[51] Hafen, 253-54. Mayo, 21-26.

[52] Morgan, 102.

[53] Ibid., 108.

[54] Alter, 38-40.

[55] Ibid., 42-43.

[56] Ibid., 43. There are three well-known Western authors, Stanley Vestal, Dale E. Morgan and John Myers Myers who seem to accept the "Hugh Glass Tale" as factual. Here we have a classical case of conflicting historical interpretations. We will confront many of these conflicts and it is up to the reader to decide which interpretation seems to be the most accurate and reasonable. There is a Hollywood movie available that is loosely based on the Glass story is the "Revenant." It does a good job in addressing the problems of the early fur trappers.

[57] *American Heritage College dictionary*, 4th ed., s. v. "Revenant." Hereafter cited as *AHCD*.

[58] I consider Hollywood movies a very important source of general information on many topics of the American West. They are outstanding on presenting the fantastic and colorful scenery of such places as Monument Valley. If you have never heard of "Liver-Eating" Johnston, a must movie is "Jeremiah Johnson," starring Robert Redford, released in 1972. Johnston was a real historical person who is now bur-ied in Cody Wyoming. Another movie starring Richard Harris, that I consider very well done is, *"A Man Called Horse,"* it was released in 1970. It compares both cultures in an interesting manner and also has a very realistic scene depicting the famous Indian initiation ritual, the "Sun Dance." In the example provided in the movie the person initiated has to walk around the sacred center pole pierced through both sides of his chest with wooden spikes and suspended off the ground. The pain from this ritual is supposed to provide the individual with an important religious vision. The only book that I have found with a picture of the "Sundance" is in Paul l. Wellman's book, *Death on the Prairie: Thirty Years' Struggle of the Western Plains*, (Lincoln. University of Nebraska Press, 1962), 132. The most famous "Sun

Dance" is probably the one done by Sitting Bull several days before the battle of the Little Big Horn. He supposedly had 100 pieces of skin removed from his arms, 50 pieces on each arm, and predicted the fall of Custer. I also recommend the movie, *"Black Robe,"* made in 1991, *"Black Robe"* portrays the 1,500-mile journey of a young Jesuit priest in an attempt to minister to the Huron Indians on the east coast of the U.S. in the 1630's. It is a powerful movie that is dark, haunting and starkly realistic. Another movie dealing with the attempts of the Catholic Church to Christianize the New World Indians takes place in the 1750's is, *"The Mission,"* starring Robert De Niro and Jeremy Irons. It discusses the trials and tribulations of a Jesuit priest who attempts to minister to the Guarani Indians of South America.

[59] http://trapperswildwest.wordpress.com/tag/moses-harris/2. "While Harris survived his time as a mountain man and fur trader, circumnavigating the Great Salt Lake and visiting Yellowstone, later becoming a guide for wagon trains heading to Oregon, he was also given credit for the story of the petrified birds, sitting in petrified trees singing petrified songs in Yellowstone." (accessed October 12,2015). Also seen http://www.mman.us/harrismoses.htm. *Mountain Men and Life in the Rocky Mountain West: Moses "Black" Harris.* pages 2–3. "George Ruxton (Mountain Man and Author) says "... and the darndest liar was Black Harris for the lies tumbled out of his mouth like boudins out of a buffler's stomach. He was the child as saw the putrified forest..." Also see http://www.mman.us/putrifiedforest.htm. *Moses Black Harris and the Putrified Forest,* pages 1–3. " I've fout the 'Blackfoot' (and damnded bad I njuns they are); I've 'raised the hair' of more than one Apache, and made a Rapaho 'come' afore now; I've trapped in heav'n, in airth, and hell, and scalp my old head, marm, but I've seen a putrified forest".

[60] Elinor Wilson, *Jim Beckwourth, Black Mountain Man and War Chief of the Crows,* (Norman: University of Oklahoma Press, 1972), 19. Hereafter cited as Wilson.

[61] Bonner, 31-32. The Life and Adventures of James P. Beckwourth as told to Thomas Bonner, intro, notes and epilogue by Delmont R. Oswald,16. Hereafter cited as Oswald. Wilson, 22. http://www.mtmen.org/mtman/html/beckwourth/, *The Life and Adventures of James P. Beckwourth: Mountaineer, Scout, and Pioneer and Chief of the Crow Indians,* 4. (accessed October 18, 2015).

[62] Aubrey L Haines, ed., *Osborne Russell: Journal of a Trapper,* (New York: MJF Books, 1955), 60. Hereafter cited as Haines. Gowans, 152.

[63] LeRoy R. Hafen, ed. in an article written by Delmont R. Oswald, *Trappers of the Far west: Sixteen Biographical Sketches,* (Lincoln: University of Nebraska, 1983), 162-63. Hereafter cited as Hafen, *Trappers.*

[64] Bonner, 23.

[65] Ibid., 267.

[66] Ibid., 570, fn.267,17.

[67] Wilson, 18.

[68] Ibid., 198, fn. 2, and fn. 4. "Moore says that there was no appearance whatever of the negro in Beckwourth, yet all the old trappers and plainsmen called him a "nigger" according to William E. Connelly in "What Moore Saw of Beckwourth in

California." I was unable to locate the original article in the Connelley Papers. But it certainly makes for an interesting interpretation. See an early picture of Beck-wourth inside cover of Wilson's book and also see in John Hope Franklin's, *From Slavery To Freedom: A History of African Americans,* 8th edition, (New York: Alfred A. Knopf, 2000), 121.

[69] Dolin, 379-380, fn. 18.

[70] Gordon B. Dobbs article in Lamar ed., *The New Encyclopedia of the American West,* (New Haven: Yale University Press, 1998), 89-90. Hereafter cited as Dobbs

[71] Laycock, 4. Rufus B. Sage was an American writer, speaker, anti-slavery activist and mountain man who became famous for publishing his recollections in a book titled, *Rocky Mountain life: or, startling scenes and perilous adventures in the far west, during an expedition of three years,* (Boston: Wentworth & Company, 1857), 38. Reprinted by Kessinger Publishing, LLC.

[72] Robert C. Carriker, *Father Peter-John De Smet: Jesuit in the West,* (Norman: The University of Oklahoma Press, 1995), 23-24. Hereafter cited as Carriker.

[73] Ibid., 28.

[74] Fr. E. Laveille, *The Life of FATHER DE SMET, S.J.: Apostle of the Rocky Mountains, 1801-1873,* (Norman, TAN Books, 1981), 198-199. Hereafter cited as E. Laveille.

[75] Ibid., 119.

[76] Carriker, 48. REV. P.J. De Smet,108-109. Laveille, 126, fn. 13, 127. Also see Jacqueline Peterson and Laura Peer, *Sacred Encounters: Father De Smet and the Indians of the Rocky Mountain West,* Norman: University of Oklahoma Press, 1993), 28, 84 and 92. Hereafter cited as Peterson and Peers. This book is basically a picture and sketch book of De Smet and Father Nicolas Point's Rocky Mountain travels, their clothing, and Indian paraphernalia in the 1840's. Two of the most interesting sketches are one on the cover which is titled, " Altar in a Tepee," and "St, Mary's among the Flatheads," both done by Nicholas Pointe, S.J. The sketch of "St. Mary's" is especially interesting because it shows the building of Paraguay Reduction for the Flatheads. The book provides only brief biographical information on De Smet, but it has excellent illustrations and pictures.

[77] Carriker, 49.

[78] Ibid., 50.

[79] Hiram Martin Chittenden, Alfred Talbot Richardson, *Pierre Jean De Smet: Life, Letters and travels of Father Pierre de Smet, s. j. 1801-1873: missionary labors and adven-tures among the wild tribes of the North American Indians...[etc.] Volume 2-Primary Source Edition,* (New York: Francis P. Harper, 1905), 403-404. Hereafter cited as Chit-tenden and Richardson, Smet.

[80] Carriker, 240.

[81] Ibid., 67.

[82] Ibid., 106.

[83] Ibid., 78.

[84] Ibid., 107.

[85] Laveille, 203.

[86] Ibid., 209.

[87] Carriker, 126.

[88] Carriker, 55.

[89] Ibid., 54.

[90] Laveille, 294.

[91] Chittenden and Richardson, 682. Vestal-*Bridger*, 175. Henry B. Carrington, *The Indian Question*, (New York: Sol Lewis, 1973), 10.

[92] Chittenden and Richardson, 656.

[93] WilliamY. Chalfant, *Cheyenne and Horse Soldiers: The 1857 Expedition and the Bat-tle of Solomon's Fork,* (Norman: University of Oklahoma Press, 1989), 288. Hereafter cited as Chalfant.

[94] The Avalon Project: *Treaty with the Cheyenne and Arapahoe: October 14, 1865.* Found on line at, http://Avalon.law.yale.edu/19th_century/char65.asp, 1 Hereafter cited as Avalon. (accessed October 23, 2015).

[95] Ibid., 1-2.

[96] P. Richard Metcalf, article in Lamar, ed., The New Encyclopedia of the American West. 689-690. Hereafter cited as Metcalf.

[97] *Indian Affairs: Laws and Treaties. Vol. 2, Treaties*, Treaty with the Cheyenne and Arapaho, October 28th, 1867. Article 4. 986. http://digital.library.okstate.edu/kap-pler/Vol2/treaties/che0984.htm. Hereafter cited as Indian Treaties, Vol.2. (accessed October 17, 2015).

[98] Ibid., Article 10, 987.

This drawing shows the brutal indifference of the Plains Indians to the murder of innocent women and children.

SCALPING OF JOSIAH WILBARGER.

Josiah P. Wilbarger was scalped in August of 1833. He supposedly lived for 12 years after his scalping, dying in 1845. He was on a surveying party when it was attacked by a band of Comanche Indians close to present day Austin Texas.

Chapter 3

The Great Sioux Uprising of 1862

"Oh treachery, thy name is Dakota.

Isaac Heard, Military Court

Recorder. "If they are hungry, let them eat grass"

Andrew J. Myrick, Indian Trader.

"I, Taoyateduta, am not a coward. I will die with you."

Sioux Chief, Little Crow.

The Minnesota Great Sioux Uprising of August, 1862 is considered to be the greatest massacre of whites by Indians in American history. The fighting began on the 17th of August and lasted until Camp Release on the 26th of September. It is considered by many to be the largest massacre of whites by Indians in American history. The most horrific butchery lasted from the 18th of August until the 24th of August, 1862. Estimates of white Ameri-cans murdered began at about 500 and climbed as high as 1,000. President Lincoln put the number at around 800. C.M. Oehler, author of the book, *The Great Sioux Uprising,* stated that "Agent Thomas Galbraith made an area-by-area tally and reached a total of six hundred forty-four civilians and ninety-three soldiers, or a grand total of seven hundred thirty-seven. More there may be...and I think there are."[1] The round number of 800 seems to be the easiest to remember and probably most accurate.

There were several contributing factors which helped inflame the outbreak of the Great Uprising; it was a complicated multi-causal affair. One of them was the fact that the year 1862 was the second year of the Civil War, which had begun in April of 1861 with the firing at Fort Sumter. The war caused a reduction and redirection of men from the frontier to the battlegrounds of the east and south; there were less seasoned troops to defend the settlements in the west. The second one was that the new Indian agent, Major Thomas J. Galbraith, had just recently called for a new group of volunteers to go south and fight the Confederacy. This region had origi-nally been protected by 900 seasoned troops between 1860-61. But the war reduced this number and; at the time of the attacks, there were only 600 untrained raw recruits to protect the entire region. The largest fort con-tingent was 295 men stationed at Fort Randall, but Fort Randall was over 200 miles from Fort Ridgely where the original fighting broke out. Fort Ridgely reported 77 troops ready for duty.[2]

Thomas Galbraith supposedly did not have a very good reputation for being a responsible administrator or competent Indian agent. There are different points of view on his abilities. The Indians at both agencies, how-ever, were suffering similarly from hunger and from the trickery of the traders and the incompetence of the current administrator, Maj. Thomas J. Galbraith. He was not really a major of anything. This was an honorary title given to all agents to enhance their authority among Indians and their prestige among whites. Galbraith, who arrived in 1861, lived at the Upper Agency. It is interesting to note that many of the eye-witnesses from the primary sources had a more favorable opinion of him. Many of the sec-ondary source authors present an unfavorable view of him. They report:

> Like all agents, Galbraith was a political appointee; and like far too many of them, he knew nothing about Indians. In addition, he supposedly lacked the commitment or dedication to fair treatment for the Indians that some of his predecessors had demonstrated. Those who knew Galbraith described him as a man "supremely confident of his own rectitude, scornful of advice, inclined to oversimplify situations, and doggedly determined to cling to his interpre-tation of a situation and to justify his course of action afterward, regardless of the consequences." He was considered to be "arrogant, stubborn, emotion-ally unstable and a hard drinker." Little Crow would later charge that Gal-braith was entirely to blame for the Sioux uprising. He was the wrong man in the wrong place at the wrong time."[3]

In addition to Galbraith's supposed incompetence and the manpower problem, there was the serious shortage of gold caused by the Civil War. It was gold that the Indians preferred their payments to be made in, not worthless paper money. The Sioux were supposed to get their annual annu-ity payment in late June or early July, but it hadn't arrived on time. They were supposed to receive $71,000 in kegs of gold coins.

> This delay was probably the most important cause of the Sioux Uprising. There were two reasons why the money did not reach the Indians on sched-ule--one was the tardy action of Congress in appropriating the funds; the

other was a month-long discussion in the treasury department over whether to pay the Indians in paper currency instead of scarce gold. It was not until August 16 that the $71,000 in the customary gold coin arrived in St. Paul.[4]

The payment was to leave St. Paul and arrive at Fort Ridgely at noon on the 18th of August. As the old saying goes, "A day late, and in this case, many dollars short!" The money convoy "traveled throughout the night, making the 125 miles between St. Paul and Fort Ridgely and arriving exhausted at the fort at noon on Monday, August 18. They were only 13 miles from the Lower Sioux Agency. The Indians began the massacre earlier that same morning. The gold shipment was six hours late." [5] It is amazing how little things like being six hours late could have such horrible consequences. Had the payment arrived on time, or even one day earlier, there might not have been a Great Uprising.

Another cause of the Uprising was the harsh weather conditions of the winter of 1861-1862 and the loss of the previous year's corn crop. The corn crop from the previous year was almost a total loss due to the infestation of cutworms and previous drought conditions.[6] However, as you will see later, it is stated that the Indians did have a good summer crops of wheat and corn in 1862, but chose not to harvest them or eat them. They chose to wait for the summer distribution of annuities and food supplies and not take advantage of a plentiful crop of vegetables. One source has suggested that the Indians had a predilection for animal meat rather than planted crops.

The majority of settlers where recent immigrants from Germany and Scandinavia who were simply crop farmers, and they generally did not come armed. They were completely unprepared for an Indian uprising. Those who did have guns usually carried double-barreled shotguns as did many of the Indians. And if perchance they did have a gun, ammunition was very scarce. In one case, a settler had only four shotgun shells to defend himself and his family; one attempted to use his pitchfork. Another compli-cating problem was the difference in language between the Germans and the Scandinavians; many of them could not speak English.

In looking at the causes of the Great Sioux Uprising of 1862, it must be noted that a Dr. Thomas S. Williamson, a long-time veteran mission-ary for the Sioux, stated that "the primary cause" of the 1862 uprising was the failure of the "Great White Father to punish Inkpaduta's small band of butchers... the Spirit Lake affair further decreased the Indians' respect for the white man."[7] The Spirit Lake Massacre took place in 1857. The Indi-ans, based upon the fact that the Army could not find, confront or defeat Inkpaduta's band, concluded that they had nothing to fear from such an incompetent opponent.

Additional complaints by the Indians involved the widespread invasion of new settlements throughout the region. Improvements were not made on the reservations, and the federal government continually failed to make annuity payments on time. The federal government in Washington D.C., especially the Congress, failed to pass adequate budgets for the Department of the Interior. This failure to meet annuity payments and provide suppos-edly adequate food provisions led to further Indian grievances and seri-ous problems of hunger and starvation. The previous severe winter weather conditions and the failures of the government exacerbated the hunger problem for the Indians and caused some of the Indians to go begging for food at American settler homes and cabins. The plains Indians had a notori-ous reputation for being beggars and thieves.

Another factor that impacted the Uprising was the fundamental divi-sion within the tribe; there were two separate factions. One, the "blanket Indians," who were the traditional Sioux, and the other faction, "farmer Indians," also known as "Cut-Hairs." Many of the "farmer Indians" were also Christians; they were more sympathetic to the settlers and helped them to escape or hide. The farmer Indians "had moved to their allotted farms, worked the soil, cut their hair, discarded their blankets, and wore white men's clothing."[8] It must also be stated that many of the "farmer" Indians helped the settlers during the Uprising warning them about the impending attacks. It was the "blanket Indians" who did most of the murdering, raping, butchering and plundering under the leadership of Chief Little Crow.

The Superintendent and some of the Agents, such as Galbraith, favored the farmer Indians and provided them with more supplies than they did the blanket Indians. The government agents wanted to give the farmer Indians "two pairs of pants, two coats, two shirts, a yoke of oxen, and a cow to every male who would cut his hair and join the farmers, which was more than ten times the annual annuity of $10 to $20 each Indian would normally receive. The "blanket Indians" saw this as unfair and actually allied with the traders, who naturally opposed civilization efforts that ruined the lucrative business."[9] This special treatment angered the "blanket Indians" and caused them to envy and harass the farmer Indians. The "blanket Indians," then:

> teased and tormented the farmers, condemned them for being white "toad-ies," and tried to sabotage their efforts. For the traditional Indians the farmer [Indians] were nothing more than "Dutchmen," no better than the meek Germans who were crowding them off their lands. They stole the farmers' pigs, drove off their cattle, and raided their cornfields. The Dakota medicine men were particularly bitter in their denunciation.[10]

This internal division of the Sioux led to numerous confrontations between the two groups. The farmer Indians tended to be concentrated at the Upper Agency at Yellow Medicine while the "blanket Indians," or traditionalists," were more numerous at the Lower Agency at Redwood. There was a combined population of about 7,000 Sioux. It was the "blanket Indians" that helped launch the Uprising attacks at the Lower Agency on the 18th of August. The farmer Indians were the group that primarily assisted Sarah Wakefield, already discussed in the first chapter, and some of the other settlers.

The initial circumstances of the Great Sioux Uprising can be found in the two previous treaties which were made in 1851. The first treaty was the Treaty of Traverse des Sioux which was signed on July 23, 1851. The second treaty was known as the Treaty of Mendota and was signed on August 5, 1851. The fundamental goal of these first two treaties was to acquire large amounts of agricultural land for American settlers. The first treaty, Traverse des Sioux, involved two of the bands who resided at the Upper Dakota Agency located near Granite Falls, Minnesota. The Sisseton's and Wahpe-ton's Dakota sold their lands in:

> The state of Iowa and western Minnesota for $1,665,000 in cash and annuities and agreed to move to a 20-mile wide reservation stretching along both banks of the Western Minnesota River. Out of the money, $275,000 was to be paid to the chiefs to relocate their people, and $30,000 was earmarked for the building of mills, schools, blacksmith shops and farms. Of the remaining $1,360,000, they were to be paid five percent interest, or $68,000, annually. From that, $28,000 was subtracted to pay for agricultural improvement, education, and purchase of goods and provisions. Thirty-five Indians signed the agreement... Missionary Stephen R. Riggs interpreted, read and explained each article to the chiefs several times. The bottom line was that the two bands would only get $40,000 a year.[11]

It is obvious from the above statement that the $275,000 that was being paid to the chiefs was probably nothing more than a bribe which they will-ingly took. This $275,000 was to be divided between the chiefs of both tribes.[12] No one ever knew how much of this $275,000 was used to relo-cate the tribes or went into the private pockets of the chiefs. Our sympa-thetic Indian friends never address these kind of things because it clearly shows the greed and corruption that was also exhibited amongst the Indian leadership. This type of leadership is still practiced today and they still have the same divisions, traditionalists and secularists.

One of the devious aspects of this first treaty, Traverse des Sioux, was that the U.S. representatives, Territorial Governor Alexander Ramsey, and Commissioner of Indian Affairs, Luke Lea, had personal interests in the settlement of the treaty. These two corrupt governmental representatives got the Upper Dakota Agency Indians to sign a traders' agreement which "directed the government to first pay debts claimed by traders using the money promised to the Upper bands."[13] The infamous "Traders' Paper" required that the Indians pay off the top the various claims made by the white and half-breed fur traders before the Indians could get their share. This traders' paper was not read aloud or translated to the Indians, and this fact further inflamed the Dakota.

I am a firm believer that several of the actual Articles should be included in the chapter which deals with it. This allows the reader to decide as to the devious and corrupt nature of the U.S. governmental representatives, the agents of the Bureau of Indian Affairs, and other dishonest traders. I will do this for every important Treaty that will be discussed. This will also allow the reader to actually experience the "lawyered" gobbledygook that char-acterizes all these "legal" documents. The following are excerpts from the first treaty, the Treaty of Traverse des Sioux, signed on the 23rd of July, 1851:

ARTICLE 1. It is stipulated and solemnly agreed that the peace and friend-ship now so happily existing between the United States and the aforesaid bands of Indians, shall be perpetual. [14]

ARTICLE 2. The said See-see-ton and Wahl-pay-ton bands of Dakota or Sioux Indians, agree to cede, and do hereby cede, sell, and relinquish to the United States, all their lands in the State of Iowa; and, also all the lands in the Territory of Minnesota...

The rest of the article gives the specific geographical limitations and land-marks of their reservation. To cede, sell, and relinquish all their lands is quite a monumental sale, but the Indian leaders felt it was better to get annual annuities and food provisions then take a chance on the changing hunting environment and possibly starve.

ARTICLE 3. [Stricken out. See below.]

Article 4. Dealt with the various exact payments made to the Indians and other payments held in trust. "In further and full compensation of said ces-sion, the United States agree to pay said Indians the sum of one million six hundred and sixty-five thousand dollars (1,665,000) at the several times, in the manner and for the purpose following to wit:

1st. To the chiefs of the said bands, to enable them to settle their affairs...and in consideration of their removing themselves to the country set apart for them as above...the sum of two hundred and seventy-five thousand dollars ($275,000): Provided, that said sum shall be paid to the chiefs in such manner as they, hereafter, in open council shall request...

2d. To be laid out under the direction of the President for the establishment of manual-labor schools; the erection of mills and blacksmith shop, opening farms, fencing and breaking land, and for such other beneficial objects as may be deemed most conducive to the prosperity and happiness of said Indians, thirty thousand dollars, ($30,000.)

The balance of said sum of one million six hundred and sixty-five thou-sand dollars, ($1,665,000,) to wit: one million three hundred and sixty thou-sand dollars ($1,360,000) to remain in trust with the United States, and five percent interest thereon to be paid annually, to said Indians for the period of fifty years...the said payment to be applied under the direction of the President, as follows to wit:

3d. For a general agricultural improvement and civilization fund, the sum of twelve thousand dollars, ($12,000.)

4th. For educational purposes, the sum of six thousand dollars, ($6,000.)

5th. For the purchase of goods and provisions, the sum of ten thousand dol-lars, ($10,000).

6th. For money annuity, the sum of forty thousand dollars, ($40,000.)

Article 5.

The laws of the United States, prohibiting the introduction and sale of spirit-uous liquors in the Indian country shall be in full force and effect throughout the territory hereby ceded and lying in Minnesota until otherwise directed by Congress or the President of the United States.

Article 6. Rules and regulations to protect the rights of persons and prop-erty among the Indians, parties to this treaty, adapted to their condition and wants, may be prescribed and enforced in such manner as the President or the Congress of the United States, from time to time, shall direct.

In testimony whereof, the said Commissioners, Luke Lea and Alexander Ramsey, and the undersigned Chiefs and Headmen of the aforesaid See-see-toan and Wah-pay-toan bands of Dakota or Sioux Indians, have hereunto subscribed their names and affixed *seals, in duplicate, at Traverse des Sioux, Ter-ritory of Minnesota, this twenty-third day of July, one thousand eight hundred and fifty-one.*

L. Lea, [SEAL]
Alex. Ramsey, [SEAL]
Een-yang-ma-nee (Running Walker or "the Gun,")...[and the marks of thirty-four other Indians]
Signed in the presence of Thomas Foster, Secretary. Nathaniel McLean, Indian Agent. Alexander Faribault, Stephen R. Riggs... [and nine other white signatories.]

To the Indian names are subjoined marks.

SUPPLEMENTAL ARTICLE.

1st. The United States do hereby stipulate to pay the Sioux bands of Indians, parties to this treaty, at the rate of ten cents per acre, for the lands included in the reservation provided for in the third article of the treaty as originally agreed upon in the following words:

"ARTICLE 3. In part consideration of the foregoing cession, the United States do hereby set apart for the future occupancy and home of the Dakota Indians, parties to this treaty, to be held by them as Indian lands are held, all that tract of country on either side of the Minnesota River, from the western boundary of the lands herein ceded, east, to the Tchay-tam-bay River on the north, and to the Yellow Medicine River on the south side, to extend, on each side, a distance of not less than ten miles from the general course of said river; the boundaries of said tract to be marked out by as straight lines as practicable, whenever deemed expedient by the President, and in such manner as shall direct:" which article has been stricken out of the treaty by the Senate, and said payment to be in lieu of said reservation: the amount ascertained under instructions from the Department of the Interior, to be added to the trust-fund provided for in the fourth article.

2d. It is further stipulated, that the President be authorized, with the assent of the said Indians, parties to this treaty, and as soon after they shall have been given their assent to the foregoing article, as may be convenient, to cause to be set apart by appropriate landmarks and boundaries, such tracts of country without the limits of the cession made by the first [2d] article of the treaty as may be satisfactory for their future occupancy and home. *Provided,*

That the President may, with the consent of these Indians, vary the conditions aforesaid if deemed expedient.[15]

This exasperating example of "lawyered gobbledygook" confusingly took away the reservations' permanent location and thereby made their res-ervations temporary and subject to the whims of the President and Senate. The deleted Article 3 struck out the provisions for reservations and thus left the Indians without a permanent home.[16]

The written treaty sounds like a pretty good deal for the Indians "IF" the government would have fulfilled all of its responsibilities and the "traders' paper" had not been deviously forced upon the Indians. "At Traverse des Sioux, they asserted, the whites had tricked them into signing a " traders paper" which had not been explained to them. It gave to the traders and mixed-bloods claims against the Indians for some $400,000, "which would otherwise have been paid to the tribes"[17] "Greed and self-interest took over, as it usually did."[18] It should also be noted that the government bought this land for about ten cents an acre and sold it to the settlers for $1.25 cents per acre. Several sources estimated that it was worth at least $5.00 an acre. Not a bad profit for the U.S. Government's corrupt agencies.

Another dishonest aspect of the Government's treaty was the "$1,360,000 that was to remain in trust with the United States, and five percent to be paid annually…under the direction of the President…[19] One can readily see that far too much of the treaty enforcement relied upon the power and direction of the President and Congress. Both the Executive and Legislative branches have been notorious for not meeting their stated obligations for quite some time, obviously also including today!

At the time that the annuities or funds were to be distributed, "a yelling swarm of traders, fur company representatives, half-breeds, lobbyists, advis-ers, ex-agents, and petty opportunists appeared, demanding part or all of the money. 'You owe me nine dollars for sugar,' 'Eighteen for pork,' 'Ten for lard,' they would shout, and nobody, least of all the Indians, could produce any records to prove otherwise."[20]

The second treaty of 1851 was known as the Treaty of Mendota. It involved the two other Dakota bands of the Mdewakanton and the Wahpakota; they were also known as the Lower Dakota Agency Indians. It was signed on the 5th of August, 1851 about two weeks after the Treaty of Traverse des Sioux. Their two leaders, Little Crow and Wabasha, were wiser negotiators than the Upper Agency leaders. There was an issue over a previous treaty signed in 1837 wherein an annuity was never paid, and there was also an issue wanting the boundaries of the proposed reservation changed.

These two concerns caused the negotiations to stall; but with the $30,000 from the previous treaty of 1837 being paid, the treaty was culminated.

The treaty of Mendota was almost a verbatim copy of the Traverse treaty; it contained seven Articles and had the same Article 3 deleted by the U.S. Senate. A similar fact of this treaty was that the government was also going to pay the Lower Agency Indians ten cents an acre for the remaining land. Again, the Lower Agency Indians ceded "all their lands in the Territory of Minnesota, or in the state of Iowa," but their agreed upon total amount was $1,410,000. The chiefs of these two tribes were to get $220,000 for settling their affairs and removing their tribes; $30,000 for establishing schools and a blacksmith shop; $12,000 for agricultural and civilization funds, $6,000 for educational purposes; $10,000 for goods and provisions and $30,000 for money annuity. Their $1,410,000 minus the $220,000 and the $30,000 left them with $1,160,000 to remain in the trust of the United States at five percent interest to be paid annually for 50 years.[21] These chiefs also signed a "traders' paper," with the Mdewakanton band paying $70,000 to the traders and the Wahpakota tribe paying $90,000.[22]

In addition to the two treaties of 1851, there was another important treaty, The Treaty of 1858. The Sioux Indians "agreed to give up the strip of land along the north side of the Minnesota River--nearly a million acres--for a price to be fixed by the United States Senate, but it was two years before Congress appropriated thirty cents an acre in payment."[23]

The first two treaties were of paramount importance in bringing about the Spirit Lake massacre of 1857 and the Great Sioux Uprising of 1862. The combined total land ceded by the Sioux Indians was an astonishing 24 million acres; land that became open to land speculators, white settlers and immigrant farmers. It left the Indians with temporary reservations. The U.S. Government was to pay these 4 tribes a combined total of $3,075,000 ($1,665,000 plus $1,410,000). However, that was the total before the corrupt, dishonest traders, agents of the Bureau of Indian Affairs and the Department of the Interior got to claim their falsified debts. One should also reflect on the reality that some 7,000 Indians were claiming ownership of about 24 million acres. Common sense would cause one to think that this is a ridiculous amount of land for such a small tribe to claim. Another example of this insanity are the land claims of the Acoma Pueblo Indians who reside in western New Mexico. They had historically claimed 5 million acres of land. Today only 10% of this land, 500,000 acres is claimed by a tribe of 4,800 Indians.[24] These absurdly large land claims have become a basic feature of most of the future Indian treaties.

In reference to the dishonest monetary rewards of the first treaty, Traverse des Sioux, the "traders' paper" guaranteed the fur-traders and half-breeds claims of $400,000. This was before the Indians got any of their annuities.[25] One of the government agents, Alexander Ramsey, who would later become Governor, took $50,000 for "negotiating" the first treaty. The second treaty, Mendota, caused the Wahpekutes to pay $90,000 and the Mdewakanton to pay $70,000 to the traders.[26] That is a staggering $610,000 in phony debts skimmed right off the top of the Indian payments. No wonder the Indians were dissatisfied and angry with the treaties and the government agents; they had every reason to be. C.M. Oehler stated:

Probably there was nothing inherently evil or unfair about the treaties of 1851 and 1858, if one accepted the inevitability that North America someday would be occupied by Europeans and their descendants. But the manner in which the terms of the treaties were fulfilled was an altogether different matter. It was this that caused Indian indignation and gave the whites no reason for pride.[27]

The major results of these three treaties were:

(1) that the four Sioux tribes who signed the two treaties, The Treaty of Traverse des Sioux and the Treaty of Mendota, ceded and sold their land, some 24,000,000 combined acres to the U.S. Government for a total of $3,075,000 in annuities and payments over a 50-year period;

(2) The Traverse treaty Indians received $1,665,000 while the Mendota Indi-ans received $1,410,000. The four combined tribes sold their land for ten cents an acre.

(3) The Treaty of 1858, which occurred after Spirit Lake, acquired approximately 900,000 acres of land for the U. S. Government. The Indians were initially offered 10 cents an acre but that was later revised to 30 cents an acre by the time the Senate ratified it on the 27th of July, 1860.[28] The government paid about $268,000 for this piece of land.[29] Some members of the government administration thought the land was worth at least $5.00 an acre.[30] One must keep in mind that the government was going to sell all of the combined land to the settlers for $1.25 an acre.

(4) the Upper and Lower Agency tribes were given two separate reservations, each one twenty miles wide, ten miles on each side of the Minnesota River. The length of the combined reservation was approximately 150 miles.

(5) It is very interesting to note that the chiefs of these three treaties were awarded staggering amounts of money on the approval of each treaty. The Sisseton and Wahpeton chiefs were given $275,000 to split between them.[31] The Mdewakantyon and the Wahpakota chiefs received $220,000.[32] The chiefs of the third, the Treaty of 1858, which only sold 900,000 acres, received an amount of $70,000 to divide amongst themselves.[33]

(6) the corrupt and dishonest way the treaties were negotiated and administrated by the government agents, especially the "traders papers," were one of the fundamental underlying causes for the Spirit Lake and Great Sioux Uprising massacres.

The three following incidents took place prior to the Spirit Lake Massacre which occurred in March of 1857. The Spirit Lake Massacre is considered to be another major incident that lead to the Great Uprising in 1862. The first occurence was that the Indians found settlers homes built around their sacred lake. The second involved the murder of the Sioux Indian Sidmonadota, and the third involved an ill-fated elk hunt. These reasons have been cited by some as the main causes of the attack. As you can see, there are as many causes as there are authors. To say that the causes of the Great Uprising was a complicated affair would obviously be an understatement.

The first was the discovery that the settlers, during the summer of 1856, had built some of their homesteads close to and around two sacred lakes; Lake Okoboji and Spirit Lake. Micheal Clodfelter, describes in his book, *The Dakota War* (1998), the religious importance of the lakes to the Sioux. He wrote:

the fuel that drove their frenzy from one of pilferage and destruction to one of bloodlust and butchery was probably provided by the sight that offended their deepest senses and concentrated their rage when they reached the Okoboji lakes on the evening of March 7. The three lakes there were holy to the pantheistic Santee, and for a long time they had been set aside as a place to revere the spirits that united man to nature...Now, on those sacred shores, white men had built their log cabins and erected their split rail fences to lay claim to the land and lakes that no one but the spirits were ever to possess. The breaking point had been breached. The raiders now became killers.[34]

The actual attack on Spirit Lake took place on Sunday, the 8th of March 1857; and this attack was conducted by a renegade Wahpekute chief, Inkpaduta (Scarlet Point). Chief Inkpaduta led a band of 14 Indian renegades on a raid of the settlements around Lake Okoboji and Spirit Lake, Iowa. By the end of the attack on March 13, 1857, 39 settlers had been killed and four young white women had been taken as captives. The "Dakotas consid-ered the lakes as sacred dwelling places for the spirits. The Indians were not permitted to fish from these lakes or even place a canoe in the waters.[35] The sight of the log cabins and fences incensed the Indians to "bloodlust and butchery," for this was viewed as an invasion of their sacred shores."[36] This band of Indians were considered outcasts by the other tribes "on account of its peculiarly ferocious and quarrelsome character. It was, in short, a band of Indian outlaws."[37] Inkpaduta was a member of one of the southern tribes who signed the Mendota treaty of 1851 and lived in the northwest area of Iowa on the Minnesota border. Inkpaduta's raid on the Spirit Lake settle-ments were seen as one of the many causes of the Great Uprising.

The second was the supposed murder of Chief Inkpaduta's brother, Sid-ominadota, and his family. It was carried out in January of 1854 by Henry Lott, a white outcast and fugitive. "Lott is almost always described as being notoriously lawless, a horse thief, a vender of bad whiskey, a criminal, half-civilized, a desperado, and outlaw and a murderer."[38] It is ironic that one of the reasons for the massacre was the murder of one Indian criminal by one white criminal. The Indians reported the murder to the governmental authorities at Fort Ridgley and Fort Dodge but became very angry because of the inaction and lack of enthusiasm of the governmental authorities in pursuing and arresting Lott. The failure to catch Lott led the Indians to believe that the soldiers were not strong enough or smart enough to catch him. The soldiers' weaknesses were seen to be an advantage for the Indians.

The third related incident, which occurred earlier in February, 1856, involved an Indian hunting party that was in pursuit of an elk. The Indians complained that a group of whites had interfered in the chase. "One cause was said to be the murder of an Indian by a white man; another reason was that a white man's dog bit an Indian who then shot the dog, and the enraged owner beat the Indian senseless. This same Indian then claimed to converse with the "Great Spirit," who apparently approved the destruction of the bad white people who were responsible for all the Indians' suffering."[39] There was another minor incident where Indian squaws were caught stealing a settler's corn and hay, an example of continued Indian thievery. The settler whipped the squaws and drove them away. One has to challenge the hunger problem in light of the fact that the Indians, during the period of raiding, did not eat any of the settlers' stock that they killed. They killed the settlers' stock out of sheer vengeance; and considering the extent of their so-called hunger, that was outright stupidity! One must also consider the abundance of food crops and vegetables that the Indians had planted, but refused to harvest or eat. All of these incidents caused a great deal of animosity, tension and suspicion between the Indians and the white settlers.

In examining the many causes of the Great Uprising, I will be emphasizing the use of 5 primary sources and two secondary sources. The primary sources are those of Abigail Gardner, Sarah Wakefield, Abel B. Murch and Charles S. Bryant, Isaac V. D. Heard and Lavina Day Eastlick. The secondary authors will be Gary C. Anderson and Gregory F. Michno.

The first primary source book we shall examine is *History of the Spirit Lake Massacre and Captivity of Miss Abbie Gardner.* She was an eyewitness and captive who published her book 28 years after the massacre, in 1885. The Spirit Lake massacre began on Sunday, March 8th, 1857 and ended on the 12th of March, 1857. The raid began at the home of Roland and Francis Gardner. There were 7 other members of the family in the home when the attack began; two other adults and five children ranging in age from 16 years old to a child, Amanda, one-year old. The Gardner family included Abigail Gardner, their 13-year-old daughter, who was taken captive by Inkpaduta's renegade band. Abigail is famous because she wrote one of the most accurate captivity books about American women held by the Indians. She reports that the father of her family, Mr. Roland Gardner:

> ...stepped out of the cabin and saw nine Indians fast approaching. He called "We are all doomed to die!" Roland did not want to give up without a fight, but Frances Gardner (Abigail's mother) said, "If we have to die, let us die innocent of shedding blood." Honoring his wife's wish, Roland did not resist as the Indians entered his home and demanded flour. As he went to grab the barrel they shot him in the heart. The Indians than grabbed Frances Gard-ner and Mary Luce [Frances's oldest married daughter] and held their arms tight, while others took rifles, bashed in their heads and dragged the bodies outside. Abigail [Frances's 13-year-old daughter] sat in a chair in a state of shock. The Indians tore her sister's baby from her arms, dragged Roland Jr., and Mary's toddler outside, beat them with stove wood, and left them for dead. Seeing her family dead or dying around her, she begged the Indians to kill her too. They grabbed her by the arms and indicated she would not be killed, but would be taken prisoner. "All the terrible tortures and indignities," she said, "I had ever read or heard of being inflicted upon their captives now arose in horrid vividness before me."[40]

Obviously, Mrs. Gardner was a religious person, and religious people tend to be that way. Abigail pondered her hideous fate and reflected upon her family's horrid murder and butchery. She stated:

With a naturally sensitive nature, tenderly and affectionately reared, shuddering at the very thought of cruelty, you can, my dear reader, imagine, but only imagine, the agony I endured, when so suddenly plunged into scenes from which no element of the terrible or revolting seemed wanting. Behind me I left my heroic father, murdered in a cowardly manner, in the very act of extreme hospitality; shot down at my feet, and I had not the privilege of impressing one farewell kiss upon his lips, yet warm with life and affection. Just outside the door lay the three children--so dear to me--bruised, man-gled, and bleeding, while their moans and groans pierced my years, and called in vain for one loving caress which I was prevented from giving.[41]

This is a reflection of the unbearable pain and heartache that was felt by every one of the survivors of this brutal attack. Far too often we only read that there were many American victims of Indian "raids". But one has to recall that every single American settler who lived through the heinous crimes committed on their relatives by these savage Indians had the same wrenching heartache and agony.

Too many of the politically correct Indian apologists seem to ignore the settlers unbearable torment and just slough it off as "that's what Indians do"; it's just their culture. That's right; it is a culture of murder, rape, thievery, and butchery that had to be defeated and quarantined. The Indian wars of the 1850's and Wounded Knee of 1890 were simply a conflict between savagery and civilization!

Later in the book we will read about a Sioux Indian woman, at Wounded Knee, who made the ridiculous statement that Indian warriors never killed white children. Well where was she when the Spirit Lake massacre took place or the Great Uprising? We also have the other count-less examples of Indian butchery inflicted on American settlers through-out the 1700 and 1800's. Whenever one reads a contemporary book on the American West, one usually gets only the pro-Indian propaganda of American soldiers committing atrocities against the poor innocent Indi-ans. Does Inkadputa and his band of savages seem like innocent Indians? Abigail's heart-wrenching memories of the depraved murders of her fam-ily members must be remembered as an example of the horror that many American settlers experienced.

The Sioux took Abigail Gardner captive and continued with their hor-rendous raiding. Abigail passed a house that was on fire and could hear the horrible screams of two settlers who were being burned alive. They continued to murder settlers; one house had 7 adults and 4 children killed; another man had been shot and had the top half of his head chopped off with a broad-ax. Twenty-one innocent settlers were the victims of this first day's raid.[42]

Abigail spent her first night in captivity about a mile from her home. The next day the heinous butchery continued; one man was shot and had his head hacked off; they stopped at another house and murdered they entire family, 2 adult women, 5 sons, another young woman and a grandmother, the husband having already been killed. They broke into another home and shot the two males dead. They then took Lydia Noble's child and Elizabeth Thatcher's infant and "bashed their brains out on a nearby oak tree. They killed all of the livestock, plundered the house and took Lydia Noble and Elizabeth Thatcher prisoner."[43]

Between the 9th of March and the 13th, Indians moved further west with their captives and ended up on the west side of Spirit Lake. On the 13th of March, they entered the cabin of Mr. and Mrs. Marble, who were unaware that there were hostile Indians in the area.

> The Marbles welcomed the braves into their home and fed them. Then they traded for Mr. Marbles rifle and challenged him to a target shoot. After several shots the target fell over. As Mr. Marble turned to replace it, war-riors shot him in the back and stole his money belt containing $1,000 in gold. Margaret Ann Marble viewed the contest from the cabin. She saw her husband murdered and attempted to escape, but the Indians nabbed her and took her to the tipi containing Lydia Noble, Elizabeth Thatcher and Abigail Gardner. The warriors concluded another bloody day with a festive war dance.[44]

They continued to randomly commit murder and heinous crimes against innocent white families. The child of Lydia Noble and infant of Elizabeth Thatcher are but one of countless examples of the atrocities the Indians were capable of committing.

Another confrontation took place on the 26th of March when Ink-paduta's band attacked the town of Springfield. The town had been warned by a Mr. Markham who had earlier come across the massacre victims of the Noble and Thatcher families. The town members defended themselves; but the Indians killed three men, one woman and three children, one of which was an 8-year old boy named Willie Thomas who was shot in the head. The Indians "stole twelve horses, dry goods, food, powder, lead, clothing and quilts."[45]

Here is yet another example of the thievery and plundering that the Indians always included on their "raids" against white settlers. There has been no mention of sexual assault, but here is an agonizing description of what Abigail Gardner and her fellow captives had to go through.

> Abigail and Lydia Noble carried packs that weighed about seventy pounds. Margaret Marble carried a pack and a pudgy Indian toddler. The Indians had snow shoes to make their trek easier and the captives had none. Elizabeth Thatcher was in great physical distress, suffering from phlebitis, what Abbie called a "broken breast," and a combination of other maladies. She had to trudge through deep snow, cross frigid rivers, chop and carry wood, cut poles for tents, and perform other forms of drudgery, yet she displayed great perseverance throughout her suffering, but a medicine man did relieve her pain for a short time.[46]

In reference to the women captives' eating habits, they survived on the leftover animal parts from the master's meals and "subsisted mostly on digging roots, and roasting bones and feathers, to keep body and soul together."[47]

Attesting to the extreme savagery of the Sioux Indians, Abbie reported on the sadistic murder of Mrs. Elizabeth Thatcher and the hideous death of Mrs. Lydia Noble. The death of Elizabeth was especially brutal because they caused a weak and helpless woman to drown. Her death took place about the 6th week of her captivity after the massacre. Mrs. Thatcher had a weak constitution due the illnesses she had contracted while being a prisoner. She and the other captives were riding across a bridge when one of the young warriors, about 16 years old, pushed Elizabeth into the ice-cold river after removing her pack.

Mrs. Thatcher attempted to reach the shore, "by what seemed super-natural strength she breasted the dreadful torrent, and making a last struggle for life reached the shore which had just been left, and was clinging to the root of a tree, at the bank. She was met by some of the other Indians, who were just coming upon the scene; they commenced throwing clubs at her, and with long poles shoved her back again into the angry stream."[48] She continued to struggle against her tormentors who were throwing rocks and sticks at her and the rushing river. She finally reached another bridge only to be shot and put out of her misery. These "brave" Indian warriors had just brutally murdered, in a most inhumane manner, a young woman of 19 years of age, just in the morning of her life.[49]

The other murder is even more heinous due to the mutilation of the dead body of the victim, Mrs. Lydia Noble. Mrs. Noble and Abbie were sold to a Yankton Indian who planned to offer them up for ransom to the whites. Lydia and Abbie were sleeping in the same teepee when a son of Inkpaduta, Roaring Cloud, burst into the tent demanding that Lydia come with him. Lydia's first response was to say no even though Abbie advised her to obey his commands. "Mrs. Noble was the only one of us whoever dared to refuse obedience to our masters. Naturally of an independent nature, and conscious of her superiority to her masters in everything except brute force, it was hard for her to submit to their arbitrary and inhumane mandates."[50] Lydia Noble continued to refuse, and Roaring Cloud took her outside and beat her to death with a large piece of wood. "The piteous groans from my murdered companion continued for half an hour so--deep, sorrowful, and terrible; then all was silent. No one went out to administer relief or sym-pathy, or even out of curiosity. She was left to die alone, within a few feet of those she had faithfully served, and of one by whom she was tenderly loved."[51] The next day the warriors, savages that they were, used Lydia's dead body for target practice and for their own amusement. After they were done with their target practice, they continued using their knives to cut off her hair and mutilate her body. [52] When they got ready to leave, "They scalped her and tied her hair to the end of a stick. When they left, a young warrior walked next to Abbie, repeatedly whipping her in the face with the bloody scalp. "Such was the sympathy a lonely, brokenhearted girl got at the hands of the 'Noble Red Man,' she said."[53]

Again, the "brave and powerful warriors" of the Sioux nation had shown their prowess against two innocent, unarmed peaceful women, Mrs. Thatcher and Mrs. Noble. The Indians are nothing more than unmanly cowards! These two women did not deserve such an inhumane death. In reviewing the hideous conditions that these captives had to survive, it is certainly a tribute to the strength, courage and tenacity of every American woman who helped settled the West. They certainly deserve our everlasting recognition, praise and heartfelt thanks.

There were two military expeditions sent out to capture Inkpaduta's band after the raid; one was sent from Fort Dodge but arrived too late to defend the city of Springfield. The other was sent from Fort Ridgely but was unable to locate or engage this band; both of these expeditions had to confront severe winter conditions and deep snow which made traveling extremely difficult. These government expeditions were unsuccessful and caused the Indians to doubt the fighting ability of the white soldiers.

Abigail Gardner and Mrs. Margaret Marble were both eventually ransomed in the summer of 1857; Abbie was the last woman captive, and she was released on the 23rd of June, 1857.[54]

The second primary source we will examine is that of Sarah F. Wakefield. The title is *Six Weeks in the Sioux Teepee: A Narrative of Indian Captivity*, first written in 1863. This book has conflicting trains of thought. In many cases, she describes the brutality of the Indians and then she praises the friendly Indians who protected her from harm, especially one named Chaska and his family. Chaska and his relationship with Sarah were thoroughly discussed in chapter one. However, we will begin by examining an example of one of the horrible attacks described by Sarah:

> I know that many Indians now paid by the Government are murderers, but being connected with the officers by blood are saved, while the true-hearted full blood savage has been hung for these men's crimes. I know of one who came into a tepee one night. He had not seen me in a squaw dress, and did not know but that I was a squaw. He then and there related scenes that made my very blood curl in my veins. He then told of meeting a mother and three children, and after violating the oldest daughter, who was about fourteen years old, he beat them all to death with a club. When the Indians asked why he did it, he said they were only Dutch, and it was just like killing hogs. He now calls himself a friendly Indian, or a white man, as he is three-fourths white. Most of the half-breeds are treacherous like him. I would sooner trust a full blood than any of them.[55]

This atrocity again proves the point that many of the Indians were truly savages. The rest of the book deals with the escape of Sarah's husband and Gen. Sibley's expedition in June and July of 1863.

The second edition, published in 1864, contains the additional 3 pages that basically address the negative activities of the half-breeds and her regret over the death of Chaska. This section also relates the reunion with her hus-band and children. She also defends her previous positive comments of the harsh living conditions the Indians had to put up with and the failure of the government to treat them fairly. Sarah reported:

> The land is very poor.The Indians cannot raise any thing only on the bottom lands. The water is all alkali, causing the deaths of many after they reached there. The Indians are all dissatisfied...The have no good hunting grounds unless they cross the Missouri River, and they are in danger of being killed by the Brules and Tetons, who are at war with them. So this poor down-trodden race is in a dreadful condition. They must starve unless food is sent them by Government.[56]

June Namias, a committed advocate, edited, annotated and wrote an extensive 39-page introduction to the 1864 copy of the book which was published in 1997. An additional analysis of June Namias and other will be examined now, especially their concepts of "White Hysteria," "White Imagination" and "Rape Rhetoric." A brief summary will help you understand that Namias' ideas discuss the fact that previous scholarly analysis had interpreted the captivity narratives as "propaganda used to encourage land grabbing and the displacement of the Indian."[57] Namias further states that Wakefield's book "documents notions of family, religion, race, propriety, cleanliness, sexuality, and gender roles along with the actual responses of whites and Indians..."[58] I am sure Sarah Wakefield personally set out with these academic objectives in mind when she wrote her book.

Namias also introduces the concept that the academic community had viewed the captivity narratives as one-sided and had approached them as "myth and literature...and the works were seen only as creations of the white imagination—as propaganda rather than as potential history..."[59] The interesting thing about these two concepts is that they are still used by the Left to analyze white captivity narratives. In addition, they use the bizarre concept of "Rape Rhetoric."[60] They use these three biased concepts, white imagination, white hysteria and rape rhetoric, to challenge and criticize the rape numbers of the white victims in the Uprising. According to the politically correct liberals, now called "Progressives," only two white women were ever raped by the sacred, "Noble Red Man." It is all just the hallucinations of hysterical white women. The red warrior was innocent of these brutal crimes because they were nothing more than the imagination of hysterical white women captives. We have between 800 and 1,000 white people murdered and yet only two raped.

Namias refers to two other propagandist writers, one, Roy H. Pearce, who stated that the early captive narratives changed "as a form of Puritan religious writing... to a more sensational and sentimental genre in the nineteenth century, when the tales often became 'wild and woolly.'"[61] Pearce suggests that the more sensual and exciting the story, the more attention would be attracted to it. Another of these writers is Richard Slotkin, who found these "master narratives that created a mythic conception of the frontier, justifying violence as a way to regenerate American society."[62] Namias refers to herself and another author as deliberately writing books that "display more sympathetic and detailed accounts of native life."[63] Isn't it refresh-ing for the liberals to be so forthcoming with their scholarly fabrications. They can just manufacture their scholarship to fit their academic agenda, to be more sympathetic to the Indians.

June Namias states that one Neal Salisbury pointed to "the rather one-sided viewing captivity narratives received from the scholarly community.

With few exceptions, approach to the narratives as myth and literature dominated discussions, and the works were seen only as creations of the white imagination--as propaganda rather than as potential historical or eth-nographic sources."[64] The objectives of the so-called politically correct cap-tivity narrative scholars leave us with their analytical tools, mythology, white imagination, white hysteria, propaganda and rape rhetoric. What contrived tools they are!

Another continuous idea that feminists always propound is the "supe-riority of women's moral force." Namias, as all feminists, always have to prove their superiority to men in all and every endeavor. She reports that: "In our own time, an argument regarding the nature of female moral-ity is in the forefront of contemporary moral philosophy and feminist theory and has something to say about the Dakota case." Namias reports on another female author, Carol Gilligan, and writes she "has presented an argument for women's equal if not superior moral reasoning..."[65] Namias goes on to report that Gilligan's model "goes even farther, implying that the 'different voice' of women is actuality superior to men's."[66] Now the reader must be asking, what does this have to do with a white female's captivity narrative written in 1863/64? This clearly proves that these femi-nist writers distort what is essentially a good old-fashioned history book into a politically correct propaganda thesis that praises both the Indians and their moralistic female captives. The only reason Wakefield's book was chosen is because it defends the Indians and condemns the whites, based upon the feminists' analysis, as morally inferior. The feminists especially condemn white women for creating an imaginary hysterical rape mythol-ogy and a rhetoric of rape to falsely inflate the number of white women who were really molested.

In a similar propagandistic vein, we have a journal article written by Janet Dean titled, *Nameless Outrages: Narrative Authority, Rape Rhetoric, and the Dakota Conflict of 1862*, published in American Literature in 2005. She writes that her "essay will mark instances of narrative appropriation, that compromise the authorized history of the Dakota Conflict."[67] Ah yes, "nar-rative appropriation," and the words used which include "Rape Rhetoric," "discursive possibilities," and "metonymic drift of the paradigm of rape," that are utilized to confuse and distort their academic methodology. There is no attempt at clarity because that would make their work understand-able and that would break the intellectual monopoly of their academic discipline. Considering the academic gobbledygook they generate amongst themselves, it's a wonder they know what they're talking about! Dean goes on to say:

As Sabine Sielke puts it, "[R]ape narratives relate to real rape incidents in highly mediated ways only." Within the context of the struggle for narrative authority over the Dakota uprising, the dominant discourse displaces and silences individual witnesses by generalizing the crime of rape. Claims of universal rape are prominent in accounts of the conflict not just because they sensationalize but because they shift control of the story of racial conflict from witnesses to authorities. Rape Rhetoric enables historians, politicians, and journalists to take control of the story of the Dakota Conflict, displacing actual witnesses, like Wakefield, whose testimonies may not be contained easily within the official narrative…Sandra Gunning, for instance, exam-ines "discursive possibilities" of rape rhetoric and finds women's texts about rape engaged "with the problem of establishing female subjectivity with a public debate whose terms are universally established by men… Likewise, Sielke identifies a "metonymic drift of the paradigm of rape… in which "the objects of violations are left behind in the debris of displacement."[68]

According to our feminist friends and their historical, journalistic col-leagues, rapes during the Dakota Uprising were kept to a minimum. Many of them were not real but only the imagination, hysteria and rhetorical rape of the white female victims. This is a classic case of politically correct propaganda; the Indians are innocent and the white women are victims of their own imaginary hysteria. What foolishness!

Sarah Wakefield also addresses the "let them eat grass" controversy. This quote is considered by many to be the "spark" that ignited the Uprising. The main culprit in this enterprise is always identified as Andrew Myrick. Andrew J. Myrick is supposed to have said, "So far as I am concerned, if they are hungry, let them eat grass."[69] This has also been more harshly rendered as, "So far as I am concerned, if they are hungry, let them eat grass or their own dung."[70] But Sarah makes a vague reference to the possibilities that it could have been Agent Thomas J. Galbraith. She stated that "The traders said to them they would not get more money; that the Agent was going away to fight, and they would have to eat grass like cattle, etc."[71] If Wake-field is correct in her statement that the only agent who was going away to fight was Agent Galbraith, then he might have been the one. But it does not specifically identify him as the one; he just becomes one of the primary agents who might have said it. Round up the usual suspects!

Myrick was a trader and store owner at the Lower Agency. Many histori-cal researchers concentrate on who made the quote, when was it made and where. Most sources state that the quote was probably made just before the massacre broke out between the dates 15th-17th of August. If that is true, then the quote could definitely be viewed as inflammatory language or "the spark" that helped cause the massacre. However, as the evidence suggests, this is not the case. It could have been another individual, or there could have been a combination of more serious and deep-rooted reasons for the attack.

The third primary source describing the massacre is that of Abel B. Murch and Charles S. Bryant and in their book, *Indian Massacre in Minnesota*. It was originally published in 1864; it was republished in September of 2001.[72] These authors offer two underlying factors that they see as influencing the massacre. The first one is the impact and implementation of the two treaties signed in 1851, the treaty of Traverse des Sioux signed on the 23rd of July, 1851 and the treaty of Mendota, signed on the 5th of August, 1851. The second factor is the impact of the Spirit Lake Massacre of 1857 led by Inkpaduta. These two factors have been identified by many other authors. They initially discuss that the failure of the Government to honestly implement the stipulations of these two treaties was a constant source of anger, dissatisfaction and frustration for the Indians.

In 1857, the U.S. Government's Indian Department sent out an individual to investigate the complaints of the Indians in reference to these two treaties. The agent sent was Major Pritchette; and he stated in his report, after a year of investigation:

> The complaint which runs through all their councils points to the imperfect performance, or the non-fulfillment of treaty stipulations. Whether these were well or ill founded, it is not my province to discuss. That such a belief prevails among them, impairing their confidence and good faith in the Gov-ernment, cannot be questioned.[73]

Another investigation was made about the corruption of Governor of the Minnesota Territory, Alexander Ramsey. The U.S. Government appointed a Judge, John M. Young, and the newly appointed territorial Governor Willis A. Gorman to conduct this investigation. Young's report said:

> Governor Ramsey is next charged with having paid over the greater part of the money, appropriated under the fourth articles of the treaties of July 23 and August 5, 1851, to one Hugh Tyler, for payments or distribution to the "traders" and "half-breeds," contrary to the wishes and remonstrations of the Indians, and in violation of the law and the stipulations contained in said treaties; and also in violation of his own solemn pledges, previously made to them, in regard to said payments.
>
> Of the two hundred and seventy-five thousand dollars ($275,000) stipulated to be paid under the first clause of the fourth article of the treaty of Traverse des Sioux, of July 23, 1851, the sum of two hundred and fifty

thousand dollars ($250,000) was delivered over to Hugh Tyler by Governor Ramsey, for distribution among the "traders and half-breeds," according to the arrangement made by the schedule of the Traders' Paper. This payment or delivery of the money to the said Tyler was made on two powers of attor-ney, executed to him by the "traders" and "half-breeds"--the first at Traverse des Sioux, on December 1, 1852, and the second at Mendota, December 11, 1852, both of which were predicated upon the authority of the *Traders' Paper*, dated at Traverse des Sioux, July 23, 1851.

For this large sum of money Hugh Tyler executed two receipts to Gover-nor Ramsey, as the attorney for the "traders" and "half-breeds;" the one for two hundred and ten thousand dollars ($210,000) on account of the "trad-ers," and the other for forty thousand dollars ($40,000) on account of the "half-breeds;" the first dated at St. Paul, December 8, 1852, and the second at Mendota, December 11, 1852, both of which were predicated upon the authority of the *Traders' Paper*, dated at Traverse des Sioux, July 23, 1851.

The treaty stipulations required the money to be paid, for the several purposes specified, "to the chiefs," in such a manner as they hereafter, in "open council," shall request, and as soon after the removal of said Indians to the homes set apart for them as the necessary appropriation therefor shall be made by Congress...

But, in these matters, they have not been consulted at all in "open coun-cil," after the ratification of the treaties, as was intended; but, on the contrary, arbitrary divisions and distributions have been made of the entire funds, and their right denied to direct the manner in which they should be appropri-ated. The appropriations for the fulfillment of these treaty stipulations will be found in the acts of Congress of August 30, 1852...

And, finally, it is evident, from the testimony and the circumstances, that the money was not paid to the chiefs, either of the Sisseton and Wapeton or Medawakonton bands, "as they, in open council, requested," according to the stipulations of the treaties and the law making the appropriations; but that Governor Ramsey steadily refused so to pay it and threatened, if they would not consent to its payments to the traders, to take or send it back to Washing-ton. That, by the withholding of their "annuities," and the use of other appli-ances, mentioned in the testimony, the Indians were, in the end, compelled to submit to the arrangements as they were made by him, although contrary to their wishes." [74]

It becomes obvious that, according to Young and Gorman, Governor Ramsey and trader Hugh Tyler were disrespectable swindlers and thieves. The continued use of these blatantly dishonest tactics caused the Indians to distrust and hate the government officials in charge of the distribution of the annuities. It is truly astonishing that the "Senate of the United States fully exculpated Governor Ramsey from any censure in the manner of dispos-ing of these large amounts of moneys belonging to the Indians, the Indians themselves were never satisfied with the treatment they had received from the Government at the hands of its accredited agents."[75] It is no wonder that the Indians were angered and upset when their annuities were again not delivered on time. The Indians distinctly argued that the traders must be kept away from the annuity dispersal tables because of their corrupt prac-tices associated with their false claims against the Indians.

One of the more obvious reasons for the Uprising was the delayed pay-ment of the annuity distribution for that year. It was due in late June or early July, $71,000 in gold coin. It arrived 6 hours too late on the 18th of August, just after the Uprising began. It was late because the Federal Gov-ernment was involved in monetary machinations by attempting to switch the Indians gold payment to payment in paper money which was worth less than the gold. It is no wonder that the Indians, after 10 years of constant swindling, became enraged when the spring annuities were late again and they feared another mendacious deception. I believe that I must clarify my views in reference to the government's deceptive treatment of the Indians. I would, and could not, defend the government or completely blame the Indians. But I cannot accept the wholesale murder, rape and butchery that the Indians used against the honest, unarmed and innocent white settlers; they are nothing more than crimes against humanity!

As mentioned above, another of the primary reasons for the Uprising was the impact of the Spirit Lake massacre which took place in March of 1857. The Spirit Lake massacre began over the placement of settler homes around the sacred lake and the hunger problem among the Indians. The territorial government's attempt to capture the rogue band led by Ink-paduta was a failure. This caused the Little Crow band to doubt the fighting ability of the white soldiers. Murch and Bryant present their view of the Spirit Lake massacre and the failure of the government to capture Ink-paduta. They write:

> The Indians construed it either as an evidence of weakness, or that the whites were afraid to pursue the matter further, lest it terminate in still more disastrous results to the infant settlements of the state bordering upon the Indian country. The result was, Little Crow and his adherents had found capital out of which to foment future difficulties in which the two races should become involved. He reasoned, that if one outlawed Indian, with eleven of his followers, could massacre whole white settlements, and cre-ate a panic that should drive thousands from their homes, and thus, for a

time, depopulate vast portions of the State, and escape unpunished, that, by a concerted movement of the Sioux nation, numbering its warriors in the thousands, the whole white population of the border counties could be massacred, and the other portions, by the panic that such a catastrophe would create, could, by one grand effort, be driven beyond the Mississippi. And it is now believed, and subsequent circumstances have greatly strengthened that belief, that Little Crow, from the time the Government ceased its efforts to punish Inkpaduta, began to agitate his great scheme of driving the whites from the State of Minnesota, which finally culminated in the ever-to-be-remembered massacre of August A.D. 1862.[76]

Now, let us look at three of the distinguishing factors that make Murch and Bryant's book stand out from the others. One of the interesting facts about this book is that it praises Agent Thomas J. Galbraith, whereas most of the other sources criticize him. Not only that, it presents data on the food crops available suggesting that the Indians weren't really starving, but failed to harvest an abundant supply of vegetable foods before the massacre. Murch and Bryant also argue that there definitely was a conspiracy planned by the Indians, particularly Little Crow. A secret meeting took place several weeks before the attack began on August 18th. These are the provocative factors that stand in contrast to most of the other sources. Very few of the other leading authors agree with this point.

Beginning with Agent Galbraith, our authors state that in reference to the incompetence of the departing agent, the crop of 1861 was inadequately prepared.

> The late day on which Major Galbraith entered upon the duties of his office rendered the getting in of a large crop for the Indians that year [1861] impossible, as the outgoing officials had done next to nothing toward it. The new Agent went energetically to work, and as much ground as it was possible, under these disadvantageous circumstances were planted in corn, potatoes, and other crops; but the lateness of the planting, and the havoc of the cutworm among the corn, rendered the crop in the fall a meager one. Want, in the coming winter, stared the Indians in the face.[77]

Obviously, the previous agent, in their opinion, Major Joseph R. Brown, hadn't done his job; and the "energetic" Thomas Galbraith was a definite improvement. The authors take many direct and extensive quotes from Gal-braith's Official Report which was made on January 27th, 1863. However, Murch and Bryant take Galbraith's report and comments as fact and do not challenge his veracity. In his report, Galbraith stated:

Early in the autumn, in view of the necessitous situation...I made a requisi-tion on the Department for the sum $5,000 out of the special fund for the relief of "poor and destitute Indians;" and in anticipation of receiving this money, I made arrangement to feed the old and infirm men, and the women and children of these people. I directed the Rev. S.R. Riggs to make the selection, and furnish me a list.

He carefully did this, and we fed, in an economical, yea, even parsimonious way about 1,500 of these people from the middle of December until nearly the first of April. We had hoped to get them off on their spring hunt earlier, but a tremendous and unprecedented snow-storm during the last days of February prevented it. In response to my requisition, I received $3,000 and expended nearly $5,000 leaving a deficiency not properly chargeable to the regular fund of about $2,000. These people, it is believed, must have perished had it not been for this scanty assistance. In addition to this, the regular issues were made to the farmer Indians in payment for their labor...[78]

Murch and Bryant use this kind of information from Galbraith to reinforce their conclusion that, "We give these extracts for the purpose, also, of show-ing what efforts were being made by the Agents of the Government for the elevation and comfort of these tribes. In showing this it will, we think, clearly appear how utterly causeless was their terrible and bloody raid upon the innocent and defenseless settlers on the border."[79] Galbraith continues and states, "Thus it will be seen that, in the spring of 1862, there was on hand supplies and material sufficient to carry us through the coming year... Thus, to all appearances, the spring season opened propitiously...[80]

To further support their contentions of a beneficial agent, the use of Galbraith's data on acres planted is provided to prove that the Indians were not starving just before the outbreak of the uprising. He suggests that the "blanket Indians" refused to do women's work, it was below their status as warriors. One source also stated that the warriors didn't like vegetables and preferred animal meat. Galbraith breaks down the data of acres for each individual Agency, both the Lower and Upper reservations. He reports that on the lower Agency, "one thousand and twenty-five acres of corn, two hundred and sixty acres of potatoes, sixty acres of turnips and ruta-bagas, and twelve acres of wheat."[81] He estimated that this total number of planted acres would have provided something in the neighborhood of 74,865 bush-els of food harvested by the Indians for their fall crop. He then states the number of Indians on the Lower Agency, about 3,000 Indians and this har-vested crop, "would have yielded a full twenty-five bushels to each man, woman and child, including the blanket as well as the farmer Indians."[82]

Galbraith provides that same information for the Upper Agency and esti-mates a total harvested crop of 85,740 bushels. This included "one thousand one hundred acres of corn, three hundred acres of potatoes, ninety acres of turnips and ruta-bagas. It also included twelve acres of wheat and field and garden vegetables in due proportion."[83] His estimate for the total Indian population for the Upper Agency was about 4,000. He again provides the estimated bushel yield per person as, "twenty-one bushels for each man, woman and child, including, also, the blanket Indians."[84] Based upon this information, again provided by Galbraith, in his own report, after the attack had taken place, causes Murch and Bryant to reach the following conclusion:

> The sagacity and wise forethought of their Agent, and the unusually favora-ble seasons, had amply provided against the possibility of recurring want. The coming winter would have found their granaries full to overflowing. Add to this fact that they had a large cash annuity coming from the Government, as well as large amounts of goods, consisting of blankets, cloths, groceries, flour and meats, powder, shot, lead, etc., and we confidently submit to the enlightened reader the whole question of their alleged grievances, confident that there can be but one verdict at their hands, and that, the paternal care of the Government over them was good and just; nay, generous, and that those having the immediate supervision of their interests were performing their whole duty, honestly and nobly.[85]

The information provided above, which is extremely contrary to the con-sensus view about Galbraith and the food supply, makes reading their book very enlightening. They certainly have come up with a uniquely different interpretation.

The final controversial opinion that they argue was that the Uprising was definitely a planned conspiracy and not a spontaneous event. The begin-nings of the conspiracy theory are associated with founding of the "Soldiers' Lodge," in June of 1862. Greg Michno, author of *Dakota Dawn*, describes the soldiers' lodge organizational framework as follows:

> The old quasi-military society was organized primarily for hunters, but by the 1860s it was becoming a militant institution where the young men could gather to discuss tribal matters, protest conditions, and seek options--options which often included violent solutions. Galbraith viewed the soldiers' lodge at Yellow Medicine [Upper Agency] as particularly dangerous. Farmer Indi-ans privately informed him that the soldiers' lodge had the power to kill anyone who failed to follow their wishes, and many farmers were becoming targets.[86]

Galbraith states that he believed that the primary reason for the Lodges' organization was, "as far as I was able to learn through spies and informers, preventing the 'traders' from going to the pay-tables, as had been their custom. Since the outbreak, I have become satisfied that the real object of the 'Lodge' was to adopt measures to 'clean out' all the white people at the time of the payment."[87] However, Murch and Bryant argue that:

> Whatever may have been the cause of the fearful and bloody tragedy, it is certain that the manner of the execution of the infernal deed was a deep-laid conspiracy, long cherished by Little Crow, taking form under the guise of the "Soldiers' Lodge," and matured in secret Indian councils. In all these secret movements Little Crow was the moving spirit. He was the counselor, orator, and acknowledged chief.[88]

The main problem with this analysis is that our authors never give dates for these secret councils, except for the one on Sunday night, August the 3rd.The only members there were obviously the Indians. Murch and Bryant reported:

> Little Crow was the master-spirit of this council, and molded all of its delib-erations, exactly suited to the execution of his long-cherished purpose, to expel all the whites from the valley of the Minnesota...Here was a theme worthy of all the cunning of the fox, the wisdom of the serpent, the elo-quence of an accredited orator, and the highest anticipations of the sav-age heart, thirsting for human blood...The council matured the details of a conspiracy, which, for atrocity, has hitherto never found a place in recorded history, not excepting that of Cawnpore.[89]

Clearly, these three new important ideas: (1) that Agent Thomas Galbraith, was a man of integrity and honor, and he treated the Indians in a professional and honest manner; (2) that the crops that had been planted in the previous season were more than enough to feed the reservation Indians; and (3) that there was a definite conspiracy, led by Little Crow and the Soldiers' Lodge warriors. These ideas stand in interesting contrast to the views of many of the consensus writers. It must also be noted that neither of these two authors makes any reference to the infamous quote, "let them eat grass." We will deal with this infamous quote later in the chapter.

The fourth primary source author is Isaac V. D. Heard. The title to his book is *History of the Sioux war and Massacres of 1862 and 1863*. It was pub-lished in 1863 by Harper & Brothers. In the preface, Heard describes his background credentials for writing this book. He states that he was a resi-dent of Minnesota for twelve years before the war. He also writes:

He was a member of General Sibley's expedition against the savages in 1862, from its arrival at St. Peter's in August until its return in November, and acted as the Recorder of the Military Commission which tried some four hundred participants in the outbreak. During that time and since, he devoted particu-lar attention to obtaining from Indians, half-breeds, traders, white captives, fugitives from massacres, and others, particulars of the various outrages and the causes of the massacre. He has also carefully read the public treaties and other documents connected with Indian affairs, and the various newspaper articles pertinent thereto.[90]

Obviously, Mr. Heard was well prepared to examine and analyze his sub-ject matter. Heard has some very interesting comments to make about the trial of the Indian prisoners after the Uprising was over. He acted as the recorder for the Military Commission and there had a unique opportunity to observe and analyze the operations and conclusions of the Commission. In describing the procedures of the Commission Heard stated:

The prisoners were arraigned upon written charges specifying the crimina-tion acts. These charges were signed by Colonel Sibley or his adjutant, and were, with but few exceptions, based upon information furnished by the Rev. S.R. Riggs. He obtained it by assembling the half-breeds, and others possessed of means of knowledge, in a tent, and interrogating them con-cerning suspected parties. The names of the witnesses were appended to the charge. He was, in effect, the Grand Jury of the court. His long residence in the country, and extensive acquaintance with the Indians, his knowledge of the character and habits of most of them, enabling him to tell almost with certainty what Indians would be implicated and what ones not, either from their disposition or their relatives being engaged, and his familiarity with their language qualified him for the position.

Major Forbes, of General Sibley's staff, a trader of long standing among the Indians, acted as provost marshal, and Antoine Frenier as interpreter. The charges were first read to the accused, and, unless he admitted them, evidence on oath introduced.[91]

Reverend Stephen R. Riggs, who acted as the Grand Jury, had exten-sive experience with the Indians and had lived among them as a mission-ary from 1837 to 1862; 25 years. Riggs could interpret, read and explain government documents to the Sioux Indians.[92] "Following the uprising, Riggs, Williamson, and other clergy argued on behalf of fair trials for Indi-ans charged with capital crimes."[93] One could conclude, from the above information, that Rev. Riggs was openly a supporter and sympathizer of the Indians. It is readily apparent that having Riggs sitting as the Grand

Jury, with his knowledge of their language, was a major advantage for the Sioux.

Riggs was also friends with another important Presbyterian mission-ary, a medical doctor, Dr. Thomas S. Williamson. Williamson established a religious mission in the Lac qui Parle area in 1835. "Riggs went to the Minnesota country in 1837 to aid Williamson...The two men were friends for over forty years, and both helped to translate the Bible into the Dakota language."[94] In addition to translating the Bible, Riggs, after working 15 years on it with the assistance of others, edited and published the enormous Grammar and Dictionary of the Dakota Language, "which to a considerable degree fixed the written form of the language."[95] This prodigious achieve-ment was one of the most significant contributions of the missionaries in that it allowed the use of the Dakota Dictionary to produce books in their own language.[96] Both of them, Riggs and Williamson, opened missionaries, churches, schools and agricultural experimental farms for the Dakota Sioux. With this extensive knowledge of both the Indian language and culture, it was not unusual for both of them to be biased in favor of the Indians.

Heard mentions, as other writers have, the fact that the Sioux falsely proclaimed to be starving when they had an extensive harvest available to them if only they had taken advantage of it. He states that the "reservation was fertile and well adapted to farming purposes... About three thousand acres had been plowed, fenced, and planted, and which, as the afterward estimated, would have yielded, had the Indians remained and made a proper harvesting, over one hundred thousand bushels of corn, potatoes, and tur-nips, besides five hundred bushels of wheat, and large quantities of beans, peas, pumpkins, and other vegetables."[97]

So, the argument that the Indians were starving is false. It seems the "Blanket" and "Farmer" Indians didn't like to eat corn and potatoes; they preferred the traditional food of animal meat. They failed to harvest the crop that they had planted, and it would have provided them with the nec-essary food before the annuities were distributed. One must speculate as to why this wasn't done by the "Farmer" Indians. It might have been that they were threatened and frightened by the "Blanket" Indians who had not yet accepted the white man's agricultural techniques. The "Blanket" Indians believed that planting and harvesting crops was women's work and not worthy of a warrior's labor. He also mentioned a little unknown fact about the "Farmer" Indians and the planting of their crops. Heard stated:

> Then the wild Indians were very much incensed at the abandonment by
> the Farmer Indian of their ancient customs, their assumption of the white

dress, and adhesion to the Christian religion. They styled them opprobri-ously "whitewashed Indians" and "Dutchmen," whom they designated as "ea seicha" (the bad language). These "Farmer" Indians did very little work, had their lands plowed for them by the whites, and were much better supplied with food and clothing than the others, and the extra expense was deducted out of the common fund. This the latter thought very unjust, especially as they engaged themselves in hunting, and did much more than the others toward earning their living. Every favor that was granted the "Farmers" they looked upon with jealous eyes, and accused the agent and missionaries with gross injustice in making any distinction between them.[98]

The incomprehensible reality was that the "Farmer" Indians did not plow their own lands; no wonder they didn't harvest the large crop of corn and other vegetables that would have staved off starvation. They were probably too lazy or frightened and terrorized by the "Blanket" Indians. The above statement also clearly indicates the fundamental divisions that divided the "Farmer" Indians from the "Blanket" Indians and was one of the basic causes that directly influenced the Uprising.

We have already had the testimony of two individuals who openly praised Agent Galbraith and with Mr. Heard, we have a third. Heard writes that, "The agent, Mr. Galbraith, who was energetic and faithful, visited the whole reservation shortly before the outbreak, and congratulated himself on the thriving appearance of affairs."[99] As a matter of fact, Galbraith had just recently had a meeting with Little Crow and promised to build him a stone house. Galbraith was aware of the influence that Little Crow had over the "Blanket" Indians and was trying to win his confidence. So now we have eyewitnesses who have a favorable view of Galbraith but, obviously, they do not have the benefit of modern research. After all they were only eyewitnesses to the actual historic event. How can we possibly rely upon them?

Mr. Heard provides an excellent description of the "Blanket" Indians who would end up being the major perpetrators of the murder and butch-ery. He writes that the blanket Indians, "left their hair unshorn, wore the breechcloth, blanket, and leggings, married as many wives as they pleased, after their own fashion… made themselves brave with paint and with the feathers of the eagle, went upon the war-path against the Chippewas, and tortured, killed, scalped, and mutilated men, women and children."[100]

Heard presents two of the major factors of the Plains' Indian culture. One is the fact that they openly practiced polygamy and the other that inter-tribal warfare was quite a common activity which involved savage tor-ture, murder and the mutilation of enemy men, women and children. Heard lists the following complaints that the Indians had against the government.

The Sioux complained about the obvious hypocrisy of the white men tell-ing them that the wars against their historical enemy the Chippewa's should be prohibited. This hypocrisy, the Indians argued, was due to the American Civil War, wherein the white men were fighting their own people and kill-ing each other in large numbers. Heard wrote:

> Just before the massacre took place we had met great reverses in Virginia, [Antietam and second Bull Run] and half-breed and others who could read kept telling them all kinds of exaggerated stories about the war: some that the "niggers" had taken over, or were about to take Washington; that the Great Father and the agents were friends to these "niggers;" that the Father was "whipped out;" that the Indians would get no more money; that the "niggers" would take it, or that it would be used for the war. [101]

Their hostilities, "increased by the enormous prices charged by the trad-ers for goods, by their debauchery of their women, and the sale of liquors, which were attended by drunken brawls that often resulted fatally to the participants." [102]

I would argue that the use of alcohol is a free choice item; and if you know it does injurious things to you, you just do not use it. But the Indian sympathizers always use this as an excuse to blame it on the white traders. I believe that both the Indians and the white traders are to blame. This is an argument that you never hear. It is always the fault of the evil, devious and greedy white traders. No responsibility is ever placed on the Indians. But we never hear anything about the free choices that the Indians make because their protectors always view them as innocent children who can do no wrong. They also see their choices as a simple reflection of their "natural culture."

When the Indians saw that large numbers of white soldiers had left to fight in the Civil War, they concluded that the whites were weaker and more vulnerable to Indian attacks. Just before the Uprising began, on the 15th of August, Galbraith led a group of 50 men who had volunteered for service in the Union Army to Fort Ridgely. They were then supposed to go to Fort Snelling, which was quite some distance to the northeast of Fort Ridgely. This further reduced the fighting force at the Lower agency. The first act of the hostilities broke out on the 4th of August and was known as the "Bread Raid." The Indians had gotten tired of waiting for their food annuities and attacked the agency warehouse removing about 100 bags of flour. There were only 100 soldiers for defense of the agency while there were 800 angry Indians surrounding the warehouse. A council was held between the two groups: and after a substantial amount of provisions were distributed, the Indians returned home peaceably.[103]

Heard also presents an excellent analysis of Indian culture. It is very useful in understanding the motivations and factors that make an Indian an Indian. It substantiates the point I have made earlier in the book. He explains:

> The young Indian from childhood is taught to regard "killing" as the highest of virtues. In the dance and at the feasts, the warriors recite their deeds of theft, pillage, and slaughter as precious things, and, indeed, the only ambition of the young Indian is to secure the "feather," which is but the record of his having murdered, or participated in the murder of some human being--whether man, woman, or child is immaterial; and after he has secured his first feather, his appetite is whetted to increase the number in his hair, as an Indian brave is estimated by the number of his feathers. Without the feather the young Indian is regarded as a squaw, and, as a gen-eral rule, cannot get a wife, and is despised, derided, and treated with con-tumely by all. The head-dress filled with these feathers and other insignia of blood is regarded as 'wakan' (sacred), and no unhallowed hand of man or woman dare touch it.[104]

It becomes readily discernable to me that the Indian culture is based entirely on murder, mutilation, rape, savagery and thievery. I believe that this fun-damental fact explains many of the violent aspects of the savage Indian culture. I still cannot and will not accept the fact that the Indians were just following their natural culture; this could never be an excuse for their heinous behavior. Just like I stated before, I can't accept the rationale that the culture of today's terrorists is based on the Koran and therefore accept-able. Decapitating heads, slitting throats, kidnapping young girls, and raping them, treating them like slaves and burning individuals alive sounds just like our Sioux Indian friends.

Heard also makes reference to the infamous quote, "Let them eat grass," which was supposedly made by Indian Agent Andrew J. Myrick. He says in the following statement:

> On one occasion they appeared in large numbers before Myrick's store, and one made a speech, saying, "You have told us that you will give us no more credit, and that we might starve this winter, or eat hay or dirt. Now, since you will not give us credit, when you want wood or water don't get it on our reservation." To this Myrick replied, "Ho! All right! When you are cold this winter, and want to warm yourselves by my stove, I will put you

out of doors." Then they made the same speech to the other traders, and received about the same reply. Some of the more violent were ready for a general War.[105]

Again, we see no mention of the Indians eating their own dung, just hay, dirt or grass. We also note that the Indians were very angry about the fact that the traders would not grant them credit. This seems to be another of the critical factors for the beginning of the Uprising.

The initial killings began on the 17th of August, about six miles from the town of Acton. An unsuccessful hunting party of four young Indians came upon a nest of chicken eggs. It seems that one of the warriors, being hungry, wanted to take the eggs and eat them. But another Indian warned him not to take them as they belonged to a white man. An argument then ensued between these two which became very heated. The one who wanted to take the eggs and eat them said:

"You Rice Creek Indians talk a great deal against the whites, and yet you dare not take a few paltry eggs. I am not afraid of the miserable fools." "Don't abuse the white man," said the other; "he is absent. Abuse me. I am here, and am not frightened at your loud talk." "To the devil with you and the eggs," exclaimed the first, and he dashed them to the ground. "That's a very bold act," said the other, sneeringly, "to destroy a few hens eggs! You are a coward."[106]

Now, we know where this is going; to accuse a young warrior of being a coward, brings in that uncontrollable factor, male pride. The insulting of one's male pride is probably one of the most explosive of human emotions. To accuse a young man of being a coward, especially a young warrior, can only lead to one thing, a proving that he is not a coward. And that will always lead to some type of aggressive or violent behavior. The Indians continued with their heated discussion and came upon an ox.

...the one who had broken the eggs cried out, "I am a coward, am I? I am so brave, and so little afraid of the whites as to dare to kill one of their oxen. There!" and he drew up his gun and shot the ox. "You call that brave too do you?" said his former disputant; "I call it the act of a coward. You break eggs and kill an ox. You are a woman. I am a brave man, and know what is brave. I have been on war parties against the Chippeways, and have taken scalps."[107]

The hunting party continued on its way, arguing heatedly amongst themselves. One group had stated that to prove their prowess they would go and kill a white man. The first house they came to was unoccupied so that they had to continue on their way. The second house was the residence of a Mr. Robinson Jones, but Jones forced them to leave his house; they wanted whiskey and he wouldn't give it to him. They now went to a third house belonging to a Mr. Howard Baker. There were five people in the house, Mr. and Mrs. Baker, Mr. and Mrs. Jones and a young lady, Miss Wilson.

When they asked for some water and tobacco, Mr. Baker readily gave it to them. "They acted perfectly friendly until Jones came over with his wife and began talking with them. Jones accused the Indian of having taken his gun to shoot deer, and never having returned it, and again the Indian denied it. Mrs. Baker asked Mrs. Jones if she had given them any whiskey, and she said "No, we don't keep whiskey for such black devils as they. The Indians appeared to understand what she was saying, for they became very savage in their appearance, and Mrs. Baker begged Mrs. Jones to desist"[108]

The Indians then initiated their deadly plan of murder. They asked Mr. Jones to have a shooting contest with both of them using double-barreled shot guns. The Indians tricked Jones into firing his gun first which left him with an unloaded gun. The Indians then reloaded their guns and acted as if they going away, but then fired on the settlers and mortally wounded Mr. Jones and Mr. Baker. Mrs. Baker fell down into the cellar; and Mrs. Jones hid in the wagon, both being luckily spared for the moment. But Miss Wilson was shot after the Indians broke into the house.[109]

Heard does make reference to a courageously brave man, Mr. Jones, who having been seriously and painfully wounded by the Indians, "crammed handfuls of dirt into his mouth in his agony, and dug great holes with his heals in the hard ground. He did this to prevent himself from making any noise that might attract the Indians. He ordered his wife to fly and save her child, but she insisted on remaining until he died, and then went into the woods."[110] And so began the horrific and brutal butchery of unarmed white settlers. I say unarmed because the overwhelming majority of the set-tlers, German and Scandinavian traditional crop farmers, did not have many guns in their homes except shotguns and a limited amount of ammunition.

On the 18th of August, Andrew J. Myrick was one of the first killed. When he heard Indians outside his store, they were discussing burning the store down. Myrick ran up the stairs and then he went out a second story window and came down a lightning rod or a lean-to and attempted to escape. However, the Indians saw him and killed him, some say with a gun, while others say with arrows. He was found by his younger brother several days after "with a scythe and many arrows sticking in his body."[111] Heard does mention a quote about the Indians eating hay or grass; but he does not make any reference to Myrick having his mouth stuffed with "dirt and grass" at all.

In reference to some of the heinous butchery that took place, Heard describes an incident that occurred to a brave ferryman named Jacob Mau-ley. The settlers had run to the ferry station at Fort Ridgely and, upon getting across, they fled in every direction seeking safety. "The ferryman, Mauley, who resolutely ferried across the river at the agency all who desired to cross, was killed on the other side just as he had passed the last man over. He was disemboweled; his head, hands, and feet cut off, and thrust into his cavity. Obscure Frenchman though he was, the blood of no nobler hero died on the battle-fields of Thermopylae or Marathon."[112] The following are despicable illustrations of the extensive savagery practiced by the Sioux Indians during the Uprising:

A gentleman living near New Ulm with his family went to town without apprehending any danger. While he was gone the Indians came and killed two of his children before their mother's eyes, and were quickly dispatching her infant son, when she seized it and fled to her mother's house...They killed her mother, her sister, and servant-girl, but she escaped with her infant. When the father returned, he found one of his boys, aged twelve years, who had been left for dead, still living and he dragged him from the field. While doing so five bullets whizzed about his ears. He brought him safely to St. Peter's, though cut and bruised in every limb, his face horribly mangled and his skull fractured. An eyewitness of his suffering says, "He was asleep, but occasionally a low, heart-piercing moan would escape his lips. At times he would attempt to turn over, and then, in the agony occasioned by the effort, he would groan most piteously. At length he awoke, his lips quivered with pain, and the meaningless expression of his eyes added new horrors to the dreadful scene, until, sickened to my soul, I left the room."

Another little boy, whom they had left for dead, was brought into the settlements badly wounded. They had driven a knife into his right eye, and it had fallen from its socket and decayed upon his cheek.

A farmer and his two sons were engaged in stacking wheat. Twelve Indi-ans approached unseen to a fence, and from behind it shot the three. Then they entered the farmer's house and killed two of his young children in the presence of their mother, who was ill with consumption, and dragged the mother and a daughter aged thirteen years miles away to their camp. There in the presence of her dying mother, they stripped off her clothes, fastened her upon her back to the ground, and one by one violated her person until death came to her relief.

One Indian went into a house where a woman was making bread. Her small child was in the cradle. He split the mother's head open with his tomahawk, then placed the babe in the hot oven, where he kept it until it was almost dead, when he took it out and beat out its brains against the wall.

Children were nailed living to tables and doors, and knives and tomahawks thrown at them until they perished from fright and physical pain. The womb of the pregnant mother was ripped open, the palpitating infant torn forth, cut into bits, and thrown into the face of the dying women. The hands and heads of the victims were cut off, their hearts ripped out, and other disgusting mutilations inflicted. Whole families were burned alive in their homes. [113]

My God, what unspeakable horrors. But if we were to believe the politically correct academic elites, these are nothing more than the exaggerations and hysteria of the white settlers to portray the innocent Indians in the standard negative stereotypes. The problem for the sympathizers is that the negative stereotypes are accurate and true! Heard has an entire chapter, chapter VI, devoted to the extensive narratives of these atrocities; the chapter is 20 pages long and it is entitled "Farther Outrages During the Outbreak." It is interesting how many of these types of stories are reported and how similar they all are, yet we are supposed to dismiss these stories and relegate them to "white hysteria." I consider every one of them to be empirical evidence of Indian brutality and academic proof of my fundamental premise.

In reference to the actual functioning of the tribunal courts, Heard presents the following description:

The trials were elaborately conducted until the commission became acquainted with the details of the different outrages and battles, and then, the only point being the connection of the prisoner with them, five minutes would dispose of the case. If witnesses testified, or the prisoner admitted he was a participant, sufficient was established. As many as forty were sometimes tried in a day. Those convicted of plundering were condemned to imprisonment; those engaged in individual massacres and in battles, to death.

If you think that participation in battles did justify such a sentence, please reflect that any judicial tribunal in the state would have been compelled to pass it, and that the retaliatory laws of war, as recognized by all civilized nations, and also the code of the Indian, which takes life for life, justified it. The battles were not ordinary battles. The attacks upon New Ulm were directed against a village filled with frightened fugitives from the sur-rounding neighborhood, and the place was defended by civilians, hastily and indifferently armed, and were accompanied by the wanton burning of a large portion of the town, and by the slaughter of horses and cattle, and the destruction of all property which came within the power of the enemy. A number of persons from the country, who endeavored, while the attack was progressing, to make their way into town, where alone was possible safety, were shot down and horribly mutilated.[114]

Heard provides the description of one incidence to add a little levity to the tedious proceedings of the horrors of the trial.

An innocent-looking youth was tried on a charge of robbery. The following examination took place:
Ques. "What goods, if any, did you take from Forbes's store?"
Ans. "Some blankets."
Q. "Anything else?"
A. "Yes; some calico and cloth."
Q. "Anything else?"
A. "Yes; some flour, and some pork, and some coffee, and some rice, and some sugar, and some beans, and some tin cups, and some raisins, and some twine, and some fish hooks, and some needles, and some thread."
Q. "Was you going to set up a grocery store on your own account?"[115]

The humor was quite welcomed, but it didn't last long.

There had to be the testimony that described the hideous butchery that had taken place on such a large scale. The estimates of those murdered were from 500 to 800. In some cases, witnesses suggested a total of 1,000 innocent white victims. Agent Galbraith offered a total figure of 767 killed during the Uprising. The figure of 800 killed originated with Bishop Whipple. In a discussion with one Bishop Potter, Whipple stated that, "My diocese is desolated by Indian War; eight hundred of our people are dead, and I have just come from a hospital of wounded and dying."[116] He was the state's first Episcopal Bishop of Minnesota. As a religious man, he was also known as a humanitarian, and a champion and defender of Indian rights. For him to use the number of 800 as the total of white victims is very significant. He, being an Indian advocate, added his prestige to the accuracy of the number murdered. This is the number, 800, that he used in his face-to-face meeting with President Lincoln in Washington D.C.

A record of the testimony of the trials was sent to Lincoln who in turn gave the records to " two young attorneys, George Whiting and Francis Ruggles, and asked them to prepare an abstract of their findings. Based on his reading of their analysis, Lincoln concluded that only thirty-nine Indians were guilty of individual murders and atrocious abuse of female captives."[117] Lincoln based his opinion on the examination of the two inexperienced lawyers who were over two thousand miles from the uprising and had prob-ably never even seen an Indian, no less the atrocities they were capable of committing. One of the factors that might have influenced Lincoln was the recent battle of Antietam which took place on the 17th of September, 1862; only some three weeks after the Great Uprising. To utilize formal constitu-tional court procedures against heinous savages is, in my humble opinion, utterly ridiculous and unjust to the innocent victims of this horrendously cruel uprising.

Let's keep in mind that our politically correct Indian advocates always like to cite that only two Indians were convicted of rape during the tribu-nal testimony at the trial. However, most of the white female victims were probably butchered by the Sioux, and it is very difficult to get answers from the dead! Another fundamental factor related to the correct number of rapes had to do with the simple fact that Little Crow and his band of blood-thirsty warriors had all escaped after the last battle. It is, obviously, impossible to identify someone who is not there! After the war was over, the conditions of the returned prisoners were heartbreaking. Sibley's lieutenants had gathered "107 whites and 162 half-breeds. Some were demented by all they had undergone, most of the 107 were white women and children. Many were naked. They were a sight to make strong men weep. Many of the soldiers cried when they saw them."[118]

Again, we must consider the influence of Mr. Riggs on the tribunal testimony and the impact of Dr. Thomas Williamson and Bishop Henry B. Whipple. The most important individual was Whipple. He was paramount in influencing President Lincoln in reducing the number of Indians con-victed for death, from 303 to 38. We shall discuss the importance of Bishop Whipple later on in the chapter. In discussing the conclusion of the trials, Heard reported:

> The number of prisoners tried was over four hundred. Of these, three hun-dred and three were sentenced to death, eighteen to imprisonment...Some people have thought that the haste with which the accused were tried must have prevented any accuracy as to the ascertainment of their complicity. I have already shown one, viz., and participation in battles and massacres which had before been proven, and many of the prisoners confessing the fact, each case need only occupy a few minutes. It was completed when you asked him if he was in the battles of New Ulm and the forts, or either, and fired at the whites, and he said "yes..."

No one was sentenced to death for the mere robbery of goods, and not to exceed half a dozen for mere presence in the battle, although the prisoner had gone many miles to it, or on a general raid against the settlements. It was required that it should be proven by the testimony of witnesses, unless the prisoner admitted the fact, that he had fired in the battles, or brought ammunitions, or acted as commissary in supplying provisions to the combatants, or committed some separate murder. Some have criticized the action of the court because of the great number of the condemned... Great also was the number of crimes of which they were accused.[119]

In reference to the fairness of the Indians' representation, Heard offers that the court was made up of some of the most respectable and fair-minded men of the community. These individuals were not members of the settlements that had family members murdered nor had their homes been plundered or destroyed. These men had no ax to grind against the Indians due to the fact that they had not sustained any personal losses. "Before entering upon the trials they were solemnly sworn to a fair and impartial discharge of their duties. It would scarcely be supposed that men such as these, after such an oath, would take away human life without the accused were guilty."[120]

It must also be noted that a predominant role during the trial was played by the individuals, the Rev. Riggs and the trader William H. Forbes, who both knew the Indians language thoroughly. Heard wrote:

Mr. Riggs, their missionary, who furnished the grounds for the charges, had free intercourse with them, as he was well known to all of them personally or by reputation for his friendship and sympathy...and a gentleman of such kind impulses, and who took such a deep interest in their welfare, would not have hesitated to have had the defensive or excusatory fact be brought to the attention of the court, and he did not.

It is the height of improbability to believe that any Indian would be accused, especially by Mr. Riggs, and the subject of his guilt or innocence canvassed among the half-breed witnesses who had been present through the whole affair, and be conducted by Provost Marshall Forbes, who under-stood the Indian language, and was well acquainted with them... and in no instance was there suggestion made of any defensive testimony but what the court had produced, and gave to it due weight and consideration...[121]

How could one make the charge that the Sioux Indians who participated in this butchery did not get a fair trial? It was not a classical constitutional trial; but, in my opinion, it was fair enough for savages. But there are always some individuals out there who formulate falsehood to promote their own political agendas. Most of them are the Indian sympathizers and east coast pseudo-intellectuals who must protect their chosen minority from any kind of honest empirical analysis. Even Heard, in 1863, was aware of these con-trived criticisms. He stated: "Many of the presses in the East condemned the demands of the people of Minnesota for their execution as barbarous in the extreme."[122]

Bishop Whipple is mentioned in the back of Heard's book in the Appendix, wherein Whipple writes a nine-page letter titled,"An Appeal for the Red Man."[123] Within this Appendix is another letter written to President Lincoln with the heading, "To his Excellency the President of the United States." It contains six specific reforms that he believes would dramatically improve the government's Indian policy. This important letter states as follows:

Sir: We respectfully call your attention to the recent Indian outbreak, which has devastated one of the fairest portions of our country, as demanding the careful investigation of the Government.

The history of our relations with the Indian tribes of North America shows that after they enter into treaty stipulations with the United States a rapid deterioration always takes place. They become degraded, are liable to savage outbreaks, and are often incited to war. It is believed that much of this record has been the result of fundamental errors of policy that thwart the Government's fine intentions toward this helpless race. We therefore respect-fully call your attention to the following suggestions:

First, That it is impolitic for our Government to treat a heathen commu-nity living within our borders as an independent nation, instead of regarding them as our wards...

Second, That it is dangerous to ourselves and to them to leave these Indi-ans tribes without a Government, not subject to our laws, and where every corrupt influence of the border must inevitably foster a spirit of revenge leading to murder and war.

Third, That the solemn responsibility of the care of a heathen race requires that the agents and servants of the Government who have them in charge shall be men of eminent fitness, and in no case should such offices be regarded as a reward for political service.

Fourth, That every telling of honor and justice demands that the Indian funds, which we hold for them as a trust, shall be carefully expended under some well-devised system which will encourage their efforts toward civilization.

Fifth, That the present system of Indian trade is mischievous and demoral-izing, and ought to be so amended as to protect the Indian and prevent the possibility of the sale of patrimony of the tribe to satisfy individual debts.

Sixth, That it is believed that the history of our dealings with the Indians has been marked by gross acts of injustice and robbery, such as could not be prevented under the present system of management, and that these wrongs have often proved the prolific cause of war and bloodshed. It is due to the helpless red men that these evils shall be redressed, and without this we can-not hope for the blessing of Almighty God in our efforts to secure perma-nent peace and tranquility on our Western border.[124]

The reform plan that Whipple developed and presented to President Lincoln, if followed, would have solved many of the problems that existed between the Government and the Indians. However, it completely absolves the Indians of any individual responsibility for their actions; actions of mur-der, rape, kidnapping, plundering and butchery. That is where I totally disa-gree with Bishop Whipple. His identification of the Indians as a "helpless race" tries to exempt them from confronting the results of their own chosen behavior; savagery!

Another fundamental mistake that Whipple and all other missionaries make is to consider them as "our wards." Under this definition the Indi-ans, in the viewpoint of the missionaries, become children that have to be nurtured, cared for, and protected from the evils of the white world. And guess who these paternalistic protectors are going to be, who else but the missionaries. I cannot ever recall one missionary who ever asked an Indian if he or she wanted to become a Christian; it was just understood that this was the natural sequence of events for Indians to become part of the white world. But did anyone ask them if they wanted to be whit? However, in reality, they didn't really have any other choice because the fundamental conflict was between savagery and civilization.

Two of the major historical occurrences that I believe influenced both Lincoln and Bishop Whipple, especially Lincoln, were the recent causality reports of the battles of Second Bull Run and Antietam. The combined Union casualties at Second Bull Run, August 28-30, were approximately 1,700 killed and 8,200 wounded. In reference to the Battle of Antietam, which took place on September 17, 1862, it is considered a pyrrhic victory for the North. The total for the Union was estimated to be between 6,300 to 6,500 killed and mortally wounded. It was the single bloodiest day of American history.[125] These enormous casualties could have weighed heav-ily on Lincoln's decision.

Having considered the interesting reform plan presented to President Lincoln by Whipple and having considered the startling losses at Second Bull Run and Antietam, let us now examine the background forces that affected the decision-making process of Bishop Whipple. Whipple was born in New York State in 1822 and passed away in 1901 when he was

79. Whipple attended a private boarding school and the Jefferson County Institute in upstate New York. He also attended Oberlin Collegiate Institute between 1838 and 1839. He was admitted to holy orders in 1848, and he was elected Minnesota's first Episcopal Bishop in 1859. Bishop Henry Whipple was a very famous and influential man in the state of Minne-sota and in the nation. Whipple was the "descendant of Revolutionary War veterans, relative of luminaries, and friend to the great, protector of the downtrodden, indefatigable traveler, trailblazing educator, mentor, husband and father."[126]

Between 1859 and 1901, Whipple, for 42 years, continued his advocacy for the improvement of Indian conditions. Due to the fact that he always spoke honestly and truthfully to the Indians, in many cases, they called him "Straight Tongue."[127]

Whipple's papers reveal that he was no dilettante in Indian affairs, especially during the 1860s and 1870s. Policy-reform schemes, the appointment and behavior of federal Indian agents, questions about removal, treaty analyses, land cessions, annuities, timber and water resources, alcohol, "civilization" and education proposals, and, of course, missionary work are just some of the topics within the scope of his enormous correspondence. Whipple corresponded with sympathetic people of the reform scene--members of the Indian Rights Association, the Board of Indian Commissioners, the Indian Commission of the Protestant Episcopal Church, and like-minded do-gooders, as well as Sioux and Chippewas themselves. Moreover, he constantly lobbied with those who could directly influence the course of Indian policy, that is, the commissioners of Indian Affairs, army officers, secretaries of the interior, congressmen, the president, and Minnesota political leaders.

Whipple's published writings and letters reiterated his twin concerns for the physical and spiritual well-being of the Indians of Minnesota. He relent-lessly sought justice and honesty in Indian affairs, frequently decrying the degraded conditions of the reservation of his state. He was outraged by the injustices suffered from those who would profit from the "Indian business" and by the indifference, incompetence, and even the malevolence of govern-ment officials.[128]

Now, he is a political power elite who readily moved in influential circles. In reference to the basic facts that Heard discusses, we can come to the following conclusions: He introduces the idea that the universal concept of ethnocentrism applies to both the white and Indian societies. He provides a comprehensive explanation of the uncivilized Indian society which is founded on a warrior culture that worships murder, kidnapping, rape and thievery. He does address the origination of the famous quote, but he only reports that the quote refers to the Indians "eating hay or dirt." There is no reference to eating dung. He supports the already stated idea that there were many friendly and Christian Indians who helped the white settlers. He states that the "farmer" Indians did not suffer from starvation because they had several thousand bushels of corn and potatoes. They also had access to cattle, pigs and sheep but refused to eat them. They refused to eat them, especially the "blanket" Indians, because it was not the traditional source of animal protein that they were used to eating.

The next primary source that must be taken into consideration is that of Harriet E. Bishop McConkey. Her book, titled *Dakota War Whoop: Indian Massacre and War in Minnesota*, was originally published in 1863. It has recently been edited by Dale L. Morgan and republished by LAKESIDE Classics in 1965. Harriet was not a true eyewitness in that she was not directly involved in or captured during the period of the Uprising. She was, however, a noted student of the Uprising and knew many of the survivors; she lived in St. Paul at the time of the massacre.

She originally landed at the village of Little Crow at Kaposia in 1847. She lived and taught in the area for 15 years before the Uprising occurred and that explains her knowledge of the area and the people who lived there.[129] Mrs. McConkey does not make any reference to the infamous quote supposedly made by Andrew Myrick, she only describes his death on August 18, 1862. She stated:

> Andrew Myrick, formerly of Westport, N.Y., when the first gun was fired, ran upstairs, where for a long time he lay concealed under a dry goods box. The Indians, with all their daring, are errant cowards, and no one dare to be the first up for fear of being a victim to whatever weapons he might have. To bring him down, they in a loud voice proposed to fire the store, he climbed through the scuttle to the roof, let himself down by the lightening rod to a low addition, and jumped to the ground and ran towards the brush where he might have been safe. Unfortunately, [he was seen] and a shower of arrows pierced him through. He was dragged back to the store, and pelted the with gold coins they had found in his safe, while the vilest imprecations fell from his lips.[130]

One may ask the question: Why did the Indians use profanity, swearing and cursing when they were celebrating his death? It was more than likely in reaction to his offensive quote, "let them eat grass."

Dale Morgan, the editor of the 1965 edition, says: "The Sioux did not pelt Myrick with gold coins, but stuffed his mouth with grass, ironic response to Myrick's reported remark a few days earlier, 'So far as I am concerned, if they are hungry, let them eat grass.'"[131] So Morgan repeats the stand-ard statement; but Harriet McConkey, writing in 1863, describes Myrick's death and makes absolutely no reference to the quote or any description of his mouth being stuffed with grass. When one is examining these classic primary sources, you always have to be careful of the editor's additions. Not only that but one has to also be aware of discrepancies between primary eye-witnesses. They have to deal with the time when they witnessed the incident and their physical location.

McConkey makes an interesting suggestion in explaining the initial cir-cumstances that led to the famous "Bread Raid" that took place on August 4, 1862, some 13 days before the major Uprising. What McConkey describes below suggests that the Indians might have caused their own problems by reporting to the Agent earlier then they should have. The annuity process involved the Indians awaiting the call from the Agent and then coming into the Agency to complete the distributions of goods. McConkey reported:

> Choosing their own time to assemble, or instigated by a secret foe, the upper bands, numbering nearly 7,000 men, women and children, had come to their Agency demanding annuities, the arrival of which was delayed, and in regard to which the Agent, Thomas J. Galbraith, was not advised. They had brought little or no provisions with them, and the small amount of game, with the fish they caught, hardly served to satisfy so many stomachs. They demanded flour, for which orders of distribution had not yet been given—shot an ox belonging to the Agent, which was scarcely a mouthful, among so many… besides, the Government had not provided boarding accommodations at this point, on so grand a scale. But the spirit of unrest became more and more apparent, indicative of hostilities. The tents of their encampment were struck, and removed two miles to the rear. A consultation of the Government offi-cials resulted in sending to Fort Ridgley for an armed force.[132]

Several other sources have suggested the same thing, that someone or some group, possibly renegade white men, half-breeds or greedy traders had taken on the role of agents' provocateurs. Greg Michno, author of *Dakota Dawn* (2011), states: "They [the Indians] said they feared something was wrong and they would not get their money because white men had been tell-ing them so."[133] They manipulated the Indians with stories that the annui-ties would not be paid due to the Civil War. There were even rumors that negroes had taken over Washington D.C. and would prevent the money from being delivered. Duane Schultz refers to the same fear: "The "niggers," said the traders, were special friends of President Lincoln, the Great Father, and would get all the Indians' money that year—and maybe forever. There would be nothing left for the Sioux."[134] "Half-breeds who could read kept the leading Indians informed of the progress of the Civil War...The Great Father, they were told, was whipped—'cleaned out'— and 'niggers' would get the money due to the Indians."[135]

Again, our gruesome Indian "friends" would not let us down when it comes to examples of heinous crimes. McConkey cites the two following examples. The first has to do with the Indians atrocious behavior to white children. "One Indian boasted of going to a house where a woman was baking bread—the mother of a child which lay in the cradle—that he split the woman's head open with a tomahawk, and then placed the babe into the hot oven, keeping it there till it baked to death, when he beat its brains against the wall. This is corroborated by whites who have been at the house where it happened. When we reflect that these women and children fell into the hands of such monsters, we wonder at their...enduring powers."[136]

The second incident is truly hideous and totally refutes the Indian warrior value system expounded by the academic sympathizers.They argue that this type of butchery was nothing more than a natural reflection of Indian cultural behavior. Again, the concept of the "Noble Red Man" often offered up by the Indian defenders is completely refuted by the empirical evidence. McConkey wrote:

One man, evidently surprised at his meal, had fallen forward on the table. A woman was lying across a wagon-rack, near the body of a man, doubtless her husband, with his head cut off and several bullet-holes in his body. A child was found nailed through its hands and feet to a tree. Another literally skinned! O, the horrors of savage butchery![137]

Think for one moment. We must take a moment from our busy lives to reflect upon the psychological horror, heartache and nightmares that these families had to endure for the rest of their lives. To inflict these heinous crimes upon innocent men, women and children is beyond my comprehension. These atrocities are committed by the so-called "brave warri-ors" of the Sioux tribes. There is no excuse possible that could ever justify this inhumane butchery! Our Indian "friends" certainly do not qualify as "brave warriors." In summarization, Harriet McConkey does not offer any reference to Myrick's infamous quote, only the editor Morgan does. Her lack of reference to the quote casts doubt upon his responsibility for it. She does, however, offer two horrible examples of Indian butchery. She does introduce the idea that some or a group of individuals acted as provocateurs. She states that the 7,000 Indians who came in early to the Agency, which did not have enough food or supplies to meet their needs, caused the Indians further desperation. She also suggests that if the Indians had waited for the call of the Agent to come in, there might not have been a problem with the distribution of food supplies and there might not have been a massacre.

The final primary source book to be discussed is that of Lavina Day Eastlick. It is entitled, *A Personal Narrative of Indian Massacres, 1862*. It was first published in 1864. There are no numbered chapters. Eastlick offers a half page preface and then begins the narrative which begins on page 1 and continues to page 59, the end of her narrative. The remainder of the book, pages 60 thru 64, the Appendix, is a very brief biographical sketch of her existence from the summer of 1863 to 1885. On page 65, we will find a surprising standard apology for the vicious Indians without a signature. I assume it was one of the unknown politically correct editors or librarians who had republished the book in 1959 or 1967. Just another sympathetic, protective defense of the heinous crimes of the "Noble Red Man."

Lavina was born in New York State in 1833. She lived with her parents until 1848, when she moved in with her brother's family. She met her husband and married in 1850 and continued to move about the middle of the country. Her family moved to Indiana in 1854, Illinois in 1856, and Minnesota in 1857. The family originally settled in Olmstead County, Minnesota. It is located in the southeast corner of Minnesota about 45 miles west of La Crosse, Wisconsin, which is on the Mississippi River. The Eastlicks remained there until 1861. In 1861, John Eastlick decided to move his family to Murray County on Lake Shetek, the distance being about 200 miles due west of Olmstead County. Lake Shetek is about 65 miles southwest of New Ulm. These are all straight line distances as "the Crow flies." It must be remembered that the average distance covered by a wagon train was usu-ally 12 to 15 miles a day. It would have taken the Eastlick family between 14 to 16 days to make the trip from Olmsted to Lake Shetek. Their reason for moving west was an attempt to find a reasonable and inexpensive place to build a homestead where John could support his family. The standard American dream for many of the immigrants entering the nation and traveling West. Lavina stated:

> My husband was a poor man, and seeing a little family growing up around him, he began to feel keenly the need of a home. Thinking he could obtain a homestead cheaper by going further west, we removed to Illinois in the spring of 1856. But here it was entirely out of our power to purchase, as

the price of land was still higher than in the place we had left. My husband now began to talk of going to Minnesota. In the year 1857, our wagon was loaded once more, and we emigrated to Minnesota, accompanied by one our neighbors, named Thomas Ireland…

I was willing to accompany my husband wherever he thought he could best provide for his family. We started on our journey in the fall, taking nothing with us but our clothing, bedding, cattle, etc…My husband chose to settle by a small lake, called Lake Shetek, where we arrived on the 5th of November. We found that there was already a small settlement here; but, after our arrival there were only eleven settlers in all…

My husband chose a beautiful spot for our home, situated about midway between the two ends of the lake. In the spring of 1862 he built a house and put in crops, and we began to feel quite happy and contented in our new home. I no longer felt any fear of the Indians; quite a number of them had lived by the lake all winter, and had been accustomed to come to our house every day. Whenever any of them came, they invariably begged for something to eat, which was never refused them. We never turned them away… and in return they appeared to be very friendly, and playing with our children and taught them to speak the Indian language a little. In the spring, they left the lake, and we saw no more of them for two or three months.[138]

The above description clearly illustrates the basic viewpoint of a typical American homesteader searching for a better life. The sincerity and simplic-ity of Lavina's desire for a better life for her family exemplifies the heartfelt love that many settler women had for their husbands and families. "I was will-ing to accompany my husband wherever he thought he could best provide for his family."[139] The only problem for Lavina was the fact that the Indian uprising completely destroyed her vision of a new beginning for her family. The Sioux Indians murdered her husband and three of her five male chil-dren. Lavina had the horrible experience of seeing her husband die before her very eyes and the same fate awaited three of her sons. In reference to the death of her husband, she mournfully describes the event. She reported:

I could not go without seeing my husband. I went to him and found him fallen over upon his side, probably having died with a struggle. One hand was lying on his face, and the other still grasped his trusty rifle; his hat was on his head, and his dog lay by his side, watching over his lifeless remains. I could see no blood about him. I kneeled down beside him, and there in the tall grass, alone with the dead, but surrounded by cruel enemies, seeking my life, and dead and dying friends, I took my last farewell of poor John, expect-ing soon to follow him. I took his cold hand in mine, leaned over and kissed his brow, and looked, for the last time, on him who had been my companion for twelve years, and now had laid down his life in trying to protect his wife and little ones. [140]

Now you will forgive my sentimental reflections, but how could anyone read that sad and mournful description without having sorrowful tears well up in their eyes. A remorseful feeling envelopes one as a dark foggy cloud descends over one's very presence on a rainy day. What a painful and heart-broken experience for any woman to suffer. But there is more sor-row to follow for Mrs. Eastlick. She now describes the most horrific scene a mother could ever envision, the death of two of her children before her very eyes. She reports this gruesome sight as follows:

Little Freddy, one of my boys, aged five years, arose out of the grass, at my call, and started to come. Then, for the first time, I observed a hideous old squaw, who had joined the Indians; she ran after him, and felled him to the ground, with a blow upon the head, from something she carried in her hand. Weak, wounded, and tightly held by my captor, as I was, I could only stand and look on the scene which followed, while such anguish racked my soul as, I pray God, that you, ye mothers who read this, may never feel. The old hag beat him for some minutes upon the back part of the head, till I thought she had killed him. She stepped back a few paces, when the little innocent arose, and again started for me; but oh! What a hideous sight for a mother to behold! The blood was streaming from his nose, mouth, and ears. The old squaw, not yet satisfied, again knocked him down, and pounded him awhile; then took him by the clothes, raised him as high as she could, and with all her force, dashed him upon the ground. She then took a knife and stabbed him several times. I could not stop or return, for my captor was by this time dragging me away, but my eyes riveted upon the cruel murder of my defenseless little ones. I heard someone call out, "Mother! Mother!" I looked, and there stood little Frank, my next oldest child, on his knees, with hands raised towards heaven, calling "Mother!" while the blood was stream-ing from his mouth. O! Who could witness such a sight, and not feel their hearts melt with pity! None but the brutal Indians could. He had been shot in the mouth, knocking out four of his teeth--once through the thigh, and once through the bowels. But what could I do? Nothing, but gaze in silent horror on my children while they were being murdered by savages. [141]

What more is there to say about the excruciating heartache that this woman had to suffer and live through. It is this one horrendous experi-ence that serves as an example of the countless ghastly atrocities that the other 800 or more victims had to suffer through. It truly amazes me that our academic Left-wing elites cannot show any concern for these helpless victims. The indifference that these do-gooders and Indian sympathizers have towards these unarmed and innocent white settlers utterly confounds me! They can only concentrate on the supposed white crimes and the "Rhetoric of Rape" and "White-Hysteria" committed against their cho-sen minority. They are intellectually blinded to the obvious reality of the empirical world. I am sure that Mrs. Eastlick would have quite a different response.

One always hears about the poor innocent Indian women and children who were butchered by our "blood thirsty" soldiers at Sand Creek, the Washita, and Wounded Knee. Many making reference to the children suck-ling at their mother's breasts. Well, Lavina reports that "I also discovered the youngest child of Mrs. Ireland, lying upon the breast that had ever nour-ished it. I bent down my head and listened; the soft, low breathing showed me how sweetly she slept, upon that cold, cold bosom."[142] The remainder of her book discusses her terrible plight of escaping and hiding in the thorn-filled grasses, the cold water of the river, the incessant mosquitoes and the lack of drinking water and food. These hardships were not only for herself but also the other survivors, women and children, who accompanied her. She also had the misfortune of coming upon the body of her third child. She further stated:

> My eyes had become accustomed to the darkness, so that I could see indis-tinctly. I found that it was my poor little boy, Giles, shot through the breast by the Indians. He appeared to have died without a struggle; I seemed to see a smile wreath his cold lips and a dimple on his cheeks, and I fancied the angel spirit was watching me as I bent over that little house of clay. I could not wish him back, for he had gone to the land where suffering is unknown.[143]

These are the sorrowful reflections of a primary source eye-witness. They let the reader "feel down into their bone marrow" the pain, anguish, the heartache that these victims had truly experienced by the death of their family members in front of their very eyes. All the traveling she did was at night, so as not to be discovered by the Indians. The only problem with traveling at night is rather obvious, you can easily get lost. On one occasion, Lavina traveled for two nights, only to find that she had ended up where she had started out. "I cannot describe my grief and despair, at finding myself back there (Lake Shetek), after wandering two long nights, with feet bleed-ing and torn by briers and rough weeds, and with nothing to eat for three nights and two days."[144] One must recall that Lavina was traveling with four wounds in her. The worst one was an excruciating shot in her heel that made it almost impossible to walk; she also had no shoes. The first wound was a shot in the heel; the second wound had struck her in the side. The third wound hit her in the head with the bullet lodging between her skull and scalp. The fourth and final wound struck her:

> in the small of the back, entering at the left side of the spine, and coming out at the right side, just above my hip--also passing through my right arm...I heard the step of an Indian, and held my breath, thinking that he would pass me supposing me dead...He came up close beside me...then commenced beating me on the head with the butt of a gun. He struck me a great many times, so hard that my head bounded up from the sod, at every stroke, and then gave me three severe blows across the right shoulder.[145]

Dare I state that there were hundreds, probably thousands, of determined and courageous women, who through their own courage and perseverance, helped settle the American West. In my opinion, these determined ladies never get their due respect! After having escaped her captives during the night, she spent the next several days and nights searching for food, water and other survivors. Considering Lavina's loss of her husband and three of her five children, one is hard pressed to state that there was one bright ray of sunshine left for this weary soul. While hiding in the brush, she was discovered by a mail-carrier who traveled the route from Sioux Falls to New Ulm. The mail carrier and Lavina went to a nearby house. Here they found Tommy Ireland who had also escaped the massacre at Lake Shetek. "While the mail-carrier cared for his horse, we entered a house, and he told me that Merton had left the scene of the massacre on the same day, carrying little Johnny..." I was filled with hope and joy, to think that, perhaps, two of my children were spared."[146] Mr. Ireland related that he warned Merton not to leave him and that he would probably die on the prairie of starvation. 'No,' bravely replied Merton, 'Mother told me to carry Johnny as long as I live, and I am going to do it.'"[147]

While trying to continue her escape, she encountered a friend, Mrs. Hurd:

> She was unable to speak, for some time, but shook hands with us all, and finally told me that my Merton was a short distance ahead, just out of sight, and was carrying Johnny. I could stay to hear no more, and urging the horse along I soon came up with them. Merton stopped, gazed upon me, but spoke not a word. The mail-carrier took Johnny, who was sleeping, in his arms, and gave him to me; I clasped him to my breast, and, with tears of joy, I thanked God--Oh! how fervently--for sparing my children thus far. How I longed to press to my bosom my poor Merton, but could not, I was unable

to get off the sulky; (an open two-wheeled vehicle accommodating only the driver and drawn by one horse) all I could do was to press his wasted hand, and call him my brave boy. He, though only eleven years old, had carried the child, who was fifteen-months old, fifty miles, but now he could hardly stand alone; for he felt no fear now, and had nothing to excite him or keep up his strength. He was the poorest person I ever saw, able to stand alone. Two weeks of hard sickness could not have altered his looks more. And little Johnny, too, was sadly changed; his face was entirely covered with scab, where the mosquitos had bitten him and he had scratched off the skin; he lay stupid in my arms, and seemed not to notice anything; and he had pulled the hair all out of the back of his head. They had both been two days without food. After Merton had left Mr. Ireland… and reached Buffalo Lake before dark, on the day of the massacre, he stopped there all night. He laid his little brother on the ground, and bent over him to protect him from the cold rain. The wolves came around in the night, and he was obliged to halloo at them with all his power of voice to scare them away. Think of it, mothers, and fancy your own cherished darlings sleeping thus![148]

Merton's fifty-mile journey carrying his fifteen-month old brother to protection and safety has become a legend in that part of Minnesota. This fascinating story is also found in most, if not all, of the books on the Great Uprising. Lavina and some other captives, having reached safety, headed east from New Ulm to Mankato. When they got there, they were surrounded by people asking who they were and where they came from. When Lavina stated her name, several in the crowd asked about her famous son's adven-ture: "'Is this the little hero that traveled from Lake Shetek, carrying his little baby brother? We had heard about him, but supposed they had starved to death upon the prairie before this.' They became quite excited about the boy, and crowded each other hither and thither to get a sight of him."[149] Another man came up to Lavina and asked, "'Is this the boy that ran away from the Indians, and carried his brother?'" "'Yes,' said I. 'Give me your hand, my brave little man,' said he shaking his hand warmly; 'and is this the child he carried so far?' On being told it was, he took Johnny in his arms, and kissed him several times; then, after we had started on, he walked half a mile beside our wagon, talking to Mrs. Hurd and myself."[150] This is the ray of sunshine that I mentioned earlier that possibly helped Lavina ease her pain. She then describes her journey from Mankato to Winona to St. Charles.

The conflict being over, the Indians surrendered to Colonel Sibley on the 26th of September, 1862 at Camp Release. Col. Sibley was a very famous businessman and politician of Minnesota and served as its first Democratic governor from May 1858 until January of 1860. In 1862, he was appointed by Governor Ramsey, to be Colonel of the Minnesota militia, to engage and defeat the Sioux Uprising that had begun in Acton on August 18th, 1862. He led the last decisive battle against the Sioux at Wood Lake on September 23rd of 1862 and captured between 1,700 and 2,000 Indians. Camp Release is located near the present-day city of Montevideo, which is approximately 75 miles northwest of New Ulm. At Camp Release, the Sioux Indians brought in and released approximately 270 white and half-breed captives. Mrs. Eastlick returned to Mankato where Col. Sibley's camp housed about 380 Indian captives; she had been advised to go back and see if should could identify any of the hostiles. When she got there she reported:

> We found the prisoners seemingly enjoying life much better than they deserved; some sleeping, some smoking, some eating, and some playing cards. It made my blood boil, to see them so merry, after their hellish deeds. I felt as if I could see them butchered, one and all; and no one, who has suffered what we settlers have, from their ferocity, can entertain any milder feelings towards them. [151]

In the afterward at the end of her book, someone has written a standard pro-Indian diatribe designed to protect and defend his/her favorite minority, the American Indian. I will present it in its entirety so I will not be charged with quoting things out of context. This little bit of propaganda states:

> Although the foregoing account is a true one, based upon the personal expe-riences of the author, it reflects the bitter, one-sided viewpoint of the early settlers. Accounts such as this one generally speaks very critically of the Indi-ans, accusing them of vicious and unprovoked atrocities against the whites while ignoring the long series of abuses which had driven the Indians to desperation. Later scholars, viewing the incidents with greater historical per-spective, have of course recognized the fact that extreme provocations was seldom lacking.
>
> The reader is reminded that the natives had been cheated, deprived of their land, and driven even farther westward before the advancement tide of white settlement.
>
> Broken treaties, white treachery, and the extermination of the buffalo from which they derived their living ultimately pushed the Indians to such brutal retaliation as is recorded in this chronicle of the Indian War of "62".
>
> In all fairness it should also be noted that some of the Indians opposed the massacres of this period. Among them was Chief Red Iron, mentioned by the author, who freed white prisoners from their Indian captors and deliv-ered them safely to General Sibley. [152]

Here comes a common-sense question for you. If you had seen, before your very eyes, the murder and mutilation of your family, wouldn't you have had a very bitter and one-sided view of the Indians? Of course, you would! Lavina and the other settlers accused the Indians of vicious and unprovoked atrocities because that is exactly what the Indians did! Lavina also explained how the settlers provided food, drink and tobacco for the Indians earlier, only to have them turn on the very settlers who had helped them. Mrs. Eastlick also raises the issue of Indian cowardice. Lavina stated: "The Indians only showed themselves one or two at a time, they would skulk behind the hills, crawl up to the top, rise up, fire on us, and drop out of sight instantly, thus proving themselves to be great cowards. The odds were fearfully against us; two hundred Indians against six white men."[153]

Having examined the brief propagandist afterward, now let us examine the preface that Lavina wrote as the introduction to her book.

PREFACE

In presenting this pamphlet to the public, I have given merely a plain, unvarnished statement of all facts that came under my observation, during the dread-ful massacre of the settlers of Minnesota. Mine only was a single case among hundreds of similar instances. It is only from explicit and minute accounts from the pens of the sufferers themselves, that people living at this distance from the scene of the atrocities can arrive at any just and adequate conception of the fiendishness of the Indian character, or the extremities of pain, terror and distress endured by the victims. It can hardly be decided which were the least unfortunate, those who met an immediate death at the hands of the sav-ages, or the survivors who, after enduring the tortures worse than death, from hunger, fear, fatigue, and wounds, at last escaped barely with life.

Mrs. L. Eastlick [154]

When we compare both of these written documents there is a vast difference, obviously, in the descriptions of the Uprising. The first one, made by Lavina, presents specific acts of viciousness and mutilations that she observed as an eyewitness. The one at the end of the book defends the Indians based upon a generalized series of Indian grievances.

An additional incident, causing overwhelming grief, involved a settler, Joe Coursolle. He had to confront one of the most heartbreaking and sorrowful experiences a man could deal with, the killing of his own dog. Coursolle went searching for his two daughters who he had told to hide in the brushes. He searched up and down the bank, then headed inland toward his house, hoping they would find their way home. The house had been burned to the ground. Everything was gone except Duta, the red setter, who leaped on him, barking with joy. Coursolle was terrified that the barks would attract Indians. "'I was forced to do the cruelest task of my life,' he said. 'I slipped off my belt and pulled it tight around Duta's neck.' Tears ran from my eyes as I felt him struggle for breath. Finally he was dead. I knelt down, took his head in my lap and whispered 'Forgive me, Duta, forgive me.'"[155]

This is one of the saddest and most excruciating experiences that a person can suffer. It was a sacrifice that Joe Coursolle had to make. Many people just "read" a book but they never "feel" a book and, in my opinion, that is the "only" way you can really internalize the true meaning of a book. It must be done slowly, thoughtfully and with serious reflection.

The secondary sources we will examine are the three books written by Gary Anderson. The first book is *Kinsmen of Another Kind;* it was published in 1984. This book primarily deals with the general relations between Dakotas and the white men entering their tribal lands. Besides this topic, it also has an excellent chapter, chapter 12, dealing specifically with the Great Uprising. Anderson has written two other excellent secondary books and one journal article on the topic of the Great Uprising.

His next two books go into greater detail about Chief Little Crow and the views of the Indian witnesses to the war. The book about Chief Little Crow, the leader of the hostile Sioux Indians, is not surprisingly called *Lit-tle Crow*. It was published in 1986. The title of the second book is *Through Dakota Eyes: Narrative Accounts of the Minnesota Indian War of 1862*. Again, the title of the book identifies its topic. Anderson also wrote an excellent earlier journal article in the "Minnesota Historical Society" titled "Myrick's Insult: A Fresh Look at Myth and Reality," which was published in 1983. It is in this journal article that Anderson mentions Myrick's quote and the relationship between authors Winifred W. Barton and W. Folwell. Barton is the daughter of John P. Williamson who did the translating at the meeting between the Indians and the traders. William Watts Folwell is the famous Minnesota historian who used Barton's quote information to suggest the dates of the meeting as between the 14th and 15th of August. It is Folwell's use of the later dates that legitimizes the use of these inaccurate dates.[156]

Anderson argues that the quote was probably made sometime between August 4th and the 8th. It was at a specific council meeting in early August that Myrick supposedly made the infamous quote. Anderson writes:

> Most white observers felt that Sioux discontent had peaked at Yellow Medicine during the first week of August. War seemed imminent on several

occasions, especially after Dakota leaders, prompted by Little Crow, asked the traders for credits and supposedly were told by Andrew Myrick: "So far as I am concerned if they are hungry, let them eat grass." Although histori-ans, following the lead of William W. Folwell, have generally described this exchange as taking place at the lower agency on the 14 or 15 of August and have seen it as the trigger for the war that began on the seventeenth, the sequence of events and the people involved make that impossible. Winifred W. Barton first reported the incident in a biography of her father, John P. Williamson. She notes that after the regular interpreter refused to translate the comment, Galbraith asked Williamson to repeat it in Dakota for the Sioux. Williamson complied, whereupon Dakota representatives "broke into weird and savage war-whoops."[157]

Anderson, in reference to the quote, identifies the biography written by Winifred Barton, *John P. Williamson: A Brother to the* Sioux (1919), as the first one who made reference to the quote. Anderson states that "Barton responded that she had heard her Father repeat the account more than once, but that he did so mainly in his later years when 'his mind seemed to revert to the past.'"[158]

The fact that Barton used the unreliable comments of her elderly father, arguing that she had heard him repeat it numerous times, plants the seeds of doubt about its accuracy. Anderson's investigation makes the argument that the quote was not an immediate cause to the Uprising because it was stated ten days before it began. That does not remove the possibility of it still having a lingering impact on the Uprising. Little Crow made a specific ref-erence to the Indians' dire food situation around August 5th or 6th. Winifred Barton reported that the chief [Little Crow] "told the assemblage that when Indians get hungry, 'they help themselves.'"[159] So the failure of the agents to distribute food and the insulting statement about eating grass further inflamed the Indians. All they needed was one incident to initiate a conflict. It is interesting to note that one of the authors does state that Little Crow did make reference the quote, "let them eat grass." This statement would substantiate that the quote was made between August 4th or 5th.

The attack on Acton initiated by the famous "Egg Nest" argument occurred on August 17th. The most intensive fighting took place between the 17th and 24th of August. One source, C.M. Oehler, reported that as many as 400 whites were killed on the first day of serious fighting on Mon-day, the 18th of August.[160] Michno, on the other hand, reports about 225 killed on that first day. His number seems much more realistic. The first days were exceedingly bloody. The entire number of 800 would be from the date of 17th August to the 24th of September. Between the 18th of August and 24th of September there were 23 separate battles.[161]

We will now discuss the specific actions of the conflict to get a realistic look at how Little Crow participated in the war. It must be recalled that initially Little Crow disagreed with the idea of fighting the whites; but once his manhood was challenged, he became a dedicated and brutal murderer. On the 1st of September, Little Crow and Gray Bird were planning two different attacks, one led by Gray Bird on Birch Coulee and another led by Little Crow on Big Woods. A coulee is a "deep gulch or a ravine with slop-ing sides, often dry in summer."[162]

Between the battle of Birch Coulee on the 2nd of September and the decisive battle of Wood Lake on the 23rd of September, there were three additional battles. Gray Bird led a group of 350 warriors towards Birch Coulee, and Little Crow took 110 warriors towards Big Woods.

> Little Crow's forces intended to do some plundering and, if possible, threaten the rear of Sibley's army at Fort Ridgely and perhaps capture its provisions as they came in. Eventually, if all went as planned, Gray Bird's warriors were to cross the river and join Little Crow for further moves against the settlements further down the valley.[163]

The division of Little Crow's forces into two different war parties was not a brilliant military idea. Had he kept all of the warriors together, he would have had 460 total Indians and probably defeated the troops gathered at Birch Coulee. With this division, Joseph R. Brown, a former agent, did not have to face the combined Indian force.

While the battle of Birch Coulee was being fought, Little Crow had taken his 110 warriors to raid Big Woods. A further division occurred again wherein there was an argument as to whether to continue the raiding party into Big Woods or attack Hutchinson and Forest City. Little Crow argued that the two towns would be difficult to attack because they had built strong stockades. Of the 110 that originally went with Little Crow only 40 war-riors stayed with him. But upon breaking camp, they came across a Min-nesota militia led by a Capt. Richard Strout and a battle ensued that caused Capt. Strout's troops to withdraw back to Hutchinson. Anderson reports that another fifty Indians joined Little Crow's band and the combined war party of 90 Indians proceeded to plunder and burn the two towns.

> The Big Woods campaign had not altered the course of the war, but it pro-duced a second exodus from several Minnesota counties. Whereas the Big

Woods raids and the Birch Coulee battle must have strengthened the Mde-wakanton soldiers' basic belief that they could defeat the whites, this optimism quickly faded when Little Crow returned to Hazelwood on September 7.[164]

An additional council was held at Hazelwood, and Little Crow was disappointed to find that a large number of upper agency and "friendly" Indians argued against the war and wanted peace with the white man. "Present in the councils were partisans of war, advocates of peace, soldiers' lodge spokesmen, a Christian bloc, a combination of traditionalist and conservatives, Lower Indians, Upper Indians tribesmen some clamoring for instantaneous flight, and others denouncing all talk of a departure, one faction urging immediate surrender of the captives, and another demanding the prisoners be killed at once."[165] Obviously Little Crow's coalition had fallen apart, and this fragmentation led to peace overtures to Col. Sibley. The interesting thing was that Col. Sibley had already initiated a peace proposal. He asked why the war had been started. He posted this note on a tree trunk knowing it would get back to Little Crow. These peace negotiations lasted from the 7th of September until the 21st of September; one of the main sticking points being the treatment of the white prisoners.

On the morning of the 22nd, a decision had been made by the soldiers' lodge to attack Sibley's troops which now numbered about 1,600 men and were camped on what came to be known as Wood Lake. In reality, Sibley had marched his troops on the night of the 22nd of September to the shore of Battle Lake. "The guide mistook this small body of water for Wood Lake (actually located three and a half miles to the west), and thus the battle that ensued is incorrectly named."[166]

Little Crow organized his 740 braves for a carefully laid plan to ambush Sibley's forces on the morning of the 23rd. The battle was hard fought, but Little Crow and his warriors were defeated after two hours of fighting. There were about 25 Indians killed and about 30 to 50 wounded; Sibley lost 7 dead and 34 wounded. "Several of the Santee dead left behind were scalped by vengeful soldiers, but Sibley made clear his objections to such practices with his general order the next day, 'The bodies of the dead, even of a savage enemy, shall not be subjected to indignities by civilized Christian men.'"[167]

Vengeance is a very natural and human emotion. In my opinion and that of Jim Bridger, the only way to fight Indians is to fight them the way they fight you, viciously and brutally. The only fear Indians know is the fear of unbridled power; they see humane treatment as weakness. Revenge is all they understand. Turning the other cheek will just get you murdered, scalped and mutilated in the American West.

As a matter of fact, many male warriors accused the white men of being weak because they did not kill Indian women and children. J.P. Dunn, Jr., states: "They took advantage of the white man by killing his helpless people, while for the safety of their own, they relied on the white man's ideas of warfare...There is not a bit of doubt that killing women and children has a very dampening effect of the ardor of the Indian."[168] The only way to successfully fight the Indians was to use their own tactics against them.

After the battle of Wood Lake was over, there were some minor attempts at negotiations between Col. Sibley and Little Crow. But Little Crow knew that his major role in instigating the war would not go easy with Sibley. Anderson cites Little Crow who stated: "The long merchant Sibley would like to put the rope around my neck, but he won't get the chance."[169] Schultz quotes Little Crow as having said "anything else but to give myself up to hang by the neck like a woman. If they would shoot me like a man I would, but otherwise they will never get my live body."[170] After the defeat at Wood Lake:

On Wednesday, the 24th, Little Crow called all his warriors together and told them to pack up and leave for the plains and save the women and children, the troops would soon be upon them and no time should be lost. "But," he said, "the captives must all be killed before we leave. They seek to defy us," he went on, "and dug trenches while we were away. They must die."

The camp of the friendlies, where trenches were dug and earth works thrown up, and where the captives had been secreted, was pitched a little way from the main or hostile camp...[171]

The number of captives he was willing to kill was roughly about 108. However, he later rescinded this order. On the 24th of September, Little Crow and approximately two to three hundred Indians who wanted to continue the war followed him to Devil's Lake in northern Dakota.[172] Lit-tle Crow was hoping to find other Indian allies to continue the fight. Also on the 24th, "as a bright sun arose, foreordaining the end of the struggle and drying the rain-drenched Minnesota prairie, Little Crow rode out of the valley of the Minnesota River, stopping for a few moments on a hilltop to look out over his old home. 'We shall never go back there,' he said loudly to his few companions, and then he turned to the plains beyond."[173]

The Indians who had escaped with Little Crow were considered "the shrewdest, most cautious, or most guilty ones...they took Little Crow's advice to 'scatter over the plains like wolves.' "[174] Another source, Duane

Schultz states that, "Most of the Indians who had committed the murders and atrocities during the uprising had, indeed, gotten away, some heading north with Little Crow and still on the move."[175] This information is very important because it illustrates the reason why there were only two convicted rape cases. More than likely, the perpetrators of these heinous crimes were never captured and escaped with Little Crow. "Except for the half-breeds, George Spencer was the only adult male among the prison-ers. 'The female captives,' wrote Spencer, 'were, with few exceptions, sub-jected to the most horrible treatment. In some cases, a woman would be taken out into the woods, and her person violated by six, seven, and as many as ten or twelve of these fiends.'" "'The night before the troops came,' reported Nancy Faribault, 'twenty or thirty Indians came in with a young white girl of sixteen or seventeen. She was nearly heart-broken, and quite in despair.'"[176]

This is a classic example of the value of a primary source eye-witness account. George Spencer and many other whites who had been victims of the uprising testified to the rapes and brutality of the Sioux. The most heart-breaking scene of this entire tragedy was when the captives were released and returned to their loved ones.

> At last, the speeches came to an end and it was time for the prisoners to be formally set free. They numbered 269 in all, 162 mixed-bloods and 107 whites. They walked and ran and stumbled, laughed, cried, and shouted as they made their way from the Indian camp to the soldiers'.
>
> "The woe written on the faces of the half-starved and nearly naked women and children would have melted the hardest heart," wrote one officer. "Some seemed stolid," Sibley recorded, "as if their minds had been strained to madness and reaction had brought vacant gloom, indifference, and despair. They gazed with a sad stare. Others acted differently. The great body of the poor creatures rushed wildly to the spot where I was standing with my brave officers, pressing as close to us as possible, grasping our hands and clinging to our limbs, as if fearful that the Red Devils might yet reclaim their victims.
>
> For a few of the whites and the Indians, there were heart-felt and tearful farewells.[177]

This is the information that should have been sent to President Lincoln. Not the nonsense that Bishop Whipple had been allowed to fabricate to keep the east coast philanthropists happy in their own little delusional world. The horrible truth is that fantasy replaced reality, and a grave injustice had been done to the 800 innocent white settlers and soldiers who fought against the depraved Indians.

The final and excellent secondary source book I highly recommend is Gregory Michno's *Dakota Dawn: The Decisive First Week of the Sioux Uprising, August 17-24, 1862,* published in 2011. It goes into extensive detail that describes the day-to-day brutal actions of the Indian slaughter. Michno also makes a very interesting comment about the impact of the ethnocentric beliefs of the Sioux Indians. He stated that the Indians had much of the same negative stereotypes against whites as the whites had against the Indi-ans. Michno writes in reference to Heard's interpretation as follows:

> Indians' ethnocentrism had a great deal to do with the war but would be looked at with disfavor in the 21st Century, when historians appear more comfortable ascribing racist arrogance as solely an Anglo provenance. Heard, however, was not far off the mark. The whites' attitude of superiority was hard for the Indians to stomach, because they owned a similar mind-set. Philander Prescott, who married into the tribe and lived with the Dakotas for four decades, said that the Dakotas thought they were "wiser and better than the others." In council with the whites they acted humble, but "by them-selves they would say whites were the greatest fools they ever saw." Big Eagle affirmed the sentiment: "The Dakotas did not believe there were better men in the world than they." When two ethnocentric peoples try to co-exist there is little chance for compromise.[178]

I would contend that every culture suffers from ethnocentrism; but as Michno states above, our recent politically correct historians can only see one side of their delusional agenda. He also describes the honest complaints that the Indians had against the white agents and traders, but "the main problem was all about land."[179] To say that the Indians did not have any legitimate complaints about the government's handling of the treaties would be ridiculous; they certainly had! But I cannot accept that as an excuse to murder, rape, butcher and plunder innocent unarmed white set-tlers and their families. If you have justifiable grievances, which they did, against the government's agents and traders, then those are the individuals you fight.

He also wrote an article in *True West Magazine*, which was published in 2012. The article is titled, "10 Myths of the Dakota Uprising."[180] He offers up ten questions about the Uprising and then provides true and false responses with explanations. It is a very good brief summary. As an example, let's read one of the questions and the answer to it. Question 2: "Trader Andrew Myrick's infamous statement, 'Let them eat grass,' was the key insult to the Dakotas that caused them to revolt. False. Only the Indians witnessed Myrick making the 'grass' statement. An interpreter's daughter first mentioned it 57 years after the event. Since then, however, the claim that this incited the Dakotas to revolt has proliferated as truth in virtually every subsequent retelling. Like so much of our history, unfortunately, rep-etition is equated with accuracy."[181] The other nine questions are presented in the same format and answer some very fundamental questions about the Great Uprising.

An example of the disingenuous concept of "white hallucination" is also presented by Michno in this book. He references the work, *History of the Santee Sioux,* by Roy W. Meyer. Michno states that Meyer "likens the set-tlers' experiences to a type of Falstaffian farce that crumbles upon close examination. According to Meyer, instances of torture and mutilation were rare, and that the hundreds of people who were captured, wounded, or escaped from the rampaging Dakotas were exaggerating or hallucinating... Meyer calls these atrocities 'isolated instances' that 'were multiplied in the imagination of refugees.'"[182] In order, again, to dispel the charge of contex-tual dishonesty, here are Meyer's exact words:

> Much of our information about the uprising comes from the stories told by these captives. In addition to a good deal of brutality; these accounts frequently tell of the kindness and even heroism on the part of individual Indians towards their white prisoners. Early accounts of the uprising seized upon the occasional instances of torture and mutilation, exaggerated them, and conjured up a picture of wholesale atrocities unparalleled in the history of Indian warfare. Some of the stories revel in details of babies nailed to walls, of unborn infants torn from the maternal womb and flung in the faces of dying mothers, of bodies hacked up beyond all recognition. Like Falstaff's story of the men he battled, however, the closer these stories are scrutinized, the less foundation there seems to be for them...Atrocities there no doubt were, as there have been in every war since the beginning of time, and they were all not committed by the Indians. But these isolated instances were multiplied in the imagination of refugees and their details were detail exag-gerated to such a degree that the early accounts can no longer by accepted by sober scholarship.[183]

As I have previously argued and will continue to, the modern-day polit-ically correct Indian sympathizers have developed a unique way of dis-crediting the white victims of these horrible Indian atrocities. They have developed a deceptive vocabulary and insidious theories that they prom-ulgate as an excuse to protect the villainous "Noble Red Man." These two theories, as mentioned above, are related to the fraudulent and fabricated concepts of the "Rhetoric of Rape" and "White Hallucinations."

You can compare Lavina Eastlick's innumerable examples of eye-witness evidence against the deductive machinations of Meyer. Meyer provides only one single reference citation for his "imagination and exaggeration" state-ments. He references a letter written by Governor Ramsey which "gave official sanction to the atrocity stories by repeating some of the most lurid in his special message to the legislature, September 9, 1862, printed in Min-nesota Executive Documents, 1862, pp. 3–15 (extra session)."[184] One would assume that some 12 pages, written by Governor Ramsey of Minnesota, would provide a plethora of citations to substantiate Meyer's charges; but alas, only one is presented.

Michno also presents another author with the same views as Meyer. In this case, it is a female author named Ellen Farrell who published an article in the *Journal of the Indian Wars* titled " The Most Terrible Stories: Dakota Conflict and White Imagination." Farrell states the Dakota "did not engage in 'indiscriminate rampage.' Michno argues, "that 'even though they were provoked, which is true, but when she contends that much of the supposed Indian barbarism was the result of self-serving white imagination, she belit-tles the white settlers' experience. It is easy for authors writing 150 years after the fact to be cavalier about the ordeal they did not live through."[185] I have and will continue to argue against the anti-white bias, bigotry and obvious discrimination by today's Leftist, academic elites. Michno hits it right on the head when he writes:

> It is not politically correct today to portray white settlers as victims, but dur-ing the opening week of the Dakota uprising they certainly were victims. The hundreds who were killed and wounded and thousands more driven from their homes, many of them peaceful Scandinavian and German emi-grants, did not deserve their fates. At the same time, the Dakotas did not deserve the years of poor treatment they had received that pushed them over the edge into violence. Innocent people of both sides were victims. The Western Indian Wars were essentially guerrilla wars, and the losers were not the warriors and soldiers. It is in the Indian villages and the frontier settle-ments where the tragedy of the Indian Wars is found.[186]

In my opinion, I consider the following, written by Roy W. Meyer, to be a classic example of the cunning and contrived allegations that the Left presents:

> Although the evidence would not support the contentions that the Sioux Uprising was deliberately provoked by the whites as an excuse for extermi-nating the Sioux or driving them out of the state and opening their lands

to settlement, there were undoubtedly plenty of Minnesotans who felt, and perhaps pressed the view privately, that the cloud had a silver lining, that though the murder of hundreds of settlers was a high price to pay to be rid of the Indians, yet one could not be blind to their advantage it now offered in terms of the opportunity to satisfy the greed of those safely behind the lines. And what better way was there to mask this greed than to wave the bloody shirt and call righteously for the extermination of the "inhuman fiends" who had heretofore stood in the way of Manifest Destiny, Minnesota brand?[187]

Meyer's first sentence correctly states that there is no evidence to support his deceitful charge, but he continues on anyway to directly blame the whites for starting the uprising. What a dishonest allegation. That the whites would knowingly provoke a slaughter and butchery to over eight hundred to a thousand men, women and children, of their own people, is incomprehensible! The empirical evidence overwhelmingly proves that Meyer's speculation is completely incorrect. "Have you no sense of dignity, sir?"

When it comes to a "fate worse than death," supposedly only two women out of hundreds were raped. They were not raped according to our feminist friends because the taking off of their clothes was only a cultural practice meant to offend their men folk rather than to gratify sexual deviance. It is really incomprehensible to believe the lies that these people fabricate all under the name of political correctness and white guilt! I read somewhere that the Left in America really hate this country. You know what, I com-pletely believe it.

If you really want to read the truth about rape in the American West, I highly recommend the book titled, *A Fate Worse Than Death: Indian Captives in the West, 1830-1885,* written by Gregory and Susan Michno, and pub-lished in 2009. I highly recommend that you read it in conjunction with *Dakota Dawn.*[188] In this book, they devote an entire chapter to the captured victims of the Great Uprising, Mary Schwandt, August Busse, Sarah Wakefield, and Lavina Eastlick. They also discuss Abigail Gardner of the Spirit Lake incident. In reference to Myrick's quote, Michno argues, as stated above, that his quote was not one of the immediate causes of the Uprising.

As to the fundamental question, what was the major cause of the Great Uprising? Michno believes that there were two main causes:

greed and land hunger---from both the white and Indian. There is no ques-tion that Indian tribes coveted land and the stronger tribes took it from the weaker tribes whenever it suited their needs. If they had no concept of legal ownership as did the white man, they certainly understood ownership by conquest. The white man coveted land also, and although he may have used more subtle "legal" measures, if they failed, physical conquest was a tried and true option. To paraphrase an American folk song, "some men will rob you with a six-gun, while others will rob you with a fountain pen." White Americans were practiced at both.[189]

Two factors that the politically correct crowd very seldom bother to dis-cuss are the extensive begging and plundering of the Indians. In reference to the begging problem, Michno describes a German schoolteacher, named Leonhart, who lived near New Ulm.

"Don't think the settlers never saw any Indians before the uprising," Leon-hart wrote in his reminiscences. "On the contrary almost every day they were on our backs, as they surpass even the slickest Caucasian tramps as beg-gars. They practice the business with dignity, as if it were the most honorable profession on earth."[190]

One Indian and his "half-grown" son visited the Leonhart home during the winter. When they indicated they were hungry and the boy was sick, Mrs. Leonhart prepared a meal. The pair consumed six pounds of beef and took with them the bones, two loaves of bread, and three gallons of coffee. "We hoped to see if the stomachs of these gourmet lovers might be filled," wrote Leonhart, "Vain expectations!" When they asked for a third serving, Rudolf declared supper over and it was time for them to leave.[191]

An additional characteristic, as stated previously, of the Sioux Indians was that they were accomplished thieves. After they had killed the initial five settlers in Acton, they continued on their treacherous ways. They came to a Peter Wicklund's home and stole two of his horses: and as they contin-ued south, they stole an additional two more horses. One settler who was heading for Henderson, Minnesota, managed to escape the Indians; but they stole his wagon, his blankets and other property. There were numerous instances of the Indians not bothering to kill settlers. They instead headed directly towards the corrals and stables to steal horses, also to plunder houses. Michno gives an excellent summary when he states: "The Dakotas may have harbored an intense hatred for the people they believed had cheated them, but for many it was not murder, but booty that was their first object. The Dakotas near Nairn (one of the settlers) ran to get as many horses as they could as the carpenter broke for his house to get his family. 'A few persons only escaped because of the eagerness of the Indians for their share of the plunder,' he said."[192]

As an illustration of the Indian savagery, I will offer another example pro-vided by Michno. He describes the horrendous mental anguish that seven abandoned children went through while waiting for a hopeful change in their circumstances. A man by the name of Antoine Frenier observed that, "The youngsters were so traumatized, hungry, and exhausted that they 'appeared to be stupid and unconscious of their condition.'"[193] These are the kinds of incomprehensible feelings and heartaches that the settler fami-lies, in this case young children, had to confront during the Uprising. The children's fate is described below:

> The Indians had returned...and burned the cabin to the ground with the wounded children still inside. The horrendous act killed Tille's one-and two-year old sons, Grundmann's one-year-old son and four-year-old daughter, Heining's one-and three-year-old sons, and one other child...[194]

This example of the burning alive of seven innocent children is beyond human belief. On February 7th, 2015, newspapers and TV news reported the burning alive of one Jordanian pilot by ISSI. This horrible act by the ISSI terrorist group ignited a storm of world-wide protest. What do you think would be the world's response to the burning alive of seven innocent young children? This is the context that we must put this cruel murderous action in today. We must reflect on the individual, horrible experiences that those seven young children had to endure with the burning of their flesh while they were still alive before dying. In addition, we have to review the heinous and blood thirsty butchery of the Sioux Indians that took place against the estimated 800 victims of the Great Uprising. In addition, at the end of the conflict, the Sioux turned over 269 captives, 162 half-breeds and 107 whites, who were mostly women and children. One must never forget the rape of the women captives and treatment of the innocent children. The most accurate and damning quote about the Sioux Indians during this war was made by Isaac V. D. Heard, who was the Recorder of the Military Com-mission, "Oh treachery, thy name is Dakota."

End Notes for Chapter 3.

[1] C. M. Oehler, *The Great Sioux Uprising*, (New York: Da Capo Press, 1997), 235. Hereafter cited as Oehler.

[2] Micheal Clodfelter, *The Dakota War: The United States Army Versus the Sioux, 1862-1865,* (Jefferson: McFarland & Company, Inc., 1998), 40. Hereafter cited as Clodfelter.

[3] Duane Schultz, *Over the Earth I Come: The Great Sioux Uprising of 1862,* (St. Martin's Griffin: Thomas Dunne Books, 1992), 10-11. Hereafter cited as Schultz-*Over*. *German Pioneer Accounts of the Great Sioux Uprising of 186*2, ed. Don Heinrich Tolzmann, (Milford: Littler Miami Publishing CO. 2002), 82, fn.13. Hereafter cited as Tolzmann-*German Pioneer*.

[4] Kenneth Carley, *The Dakota War of 1862: Minnesota's Other Civil War,* (St. Paul: Minnesota Historical Society Press, 1976), 5. Hereafter cited as Carley.

[5] Gregory and Susan Michno, *A Fate Worse than Death: Indian Captives in the West, 1830-1885*, (Caldwell: Caxton Press, 2009). 2. Hereafter cited a Michno-*A Fate.*

[6] Gregory F. Michno, *Dakota Dawn: The Decisive First Week of the Sioux Uprising, August 17-24, 1862,* (New York: Savas Beatie, 2011), 25. Hereafter cited as Michno-*Dakota-Dawn.* Roy W. Meyer, *History of the Santee Sioux: United States Indian Policy onTrial,* (Lincoln: University of Nebraska Press, 1993) 111. Hereafter cited as Meyer.

[7] Carley, 5. Clodfelter, 34.

[8] Michno, *Dakota-Dawn*, 16.

[9] Ibid., 17.

[10] Ibid.

[11] Michno, *Dakota-Dawn*, 3.

[12] Ibid.

[13] Thomas Teakle and R. A. Smith, *The Sioux Massacre: Two Accounts of the Santee Sioux Attack on the Iowa Settlements,* (Leonar: Oakpast Ltd., 2013), 15. Hereafter cited as Teakle. http://www.mnopedia.org/event/treaty-mendota. 1. (accessed Novem-ber 3, 2015).

[14] Charles J. Kappler, Indian Affairs: Laws and Treaties, Vol. 2, Treaties, Treaty with the Sisseton and Wahpeton Bands, 1851. 588-589. http://digital.library.okstate. edu/kappler/Vol2/treaties/sio0588.html... 2. (accessed November 4, 2015).

[15] Ibid., 5 of 6.

[16] Meyer, 85. Kappler, *Indian Affairs,* 593.

[17] Carley, 3. Schultz-*Over* 9.

[18] Michno, *Dakota-Dawn*, 7.

[19] okstate.edu, page 2 and 3 of 6.

[20] Oehler, 13.

[21] http://digital.library.okstate.edu/kappler/vol2/treaties/sio0591.htm. 2. Hereafter cited as okstate.edu. 0591. Also known as Charles J. Kappler, *Indian Affairs: Laws and Treaties.* Vol. 2, Treaties, Treaty with the Sioux-Mdewakanton and Wahpakoota Bands, 1851. (accessed November 6, 2015).

[22] http://www.minnpost.com/mnopedias/2013/07/when-dakota-mo... 3 Here-after cited as minnpost, 2.

[23] Carley, 4.

[24] " Acoma Indian Reservation." 1-6. https://aaanativearts.com/american-indian-reservation-a-to-c/acoma-indian-reservation. (accessed November 16, 2015).

[25] Ibid., 12.

[26] minnpost. page 3 of 4.

[27] Oehler, 13.

[28] Carley, 4.

[29] Oehler, 12. Schultz-*Over*, 25.

[30] Michno, *Dakota-Dawn*, 9. Meyer, 104.

[31] okstate.edu.0591, Kappler, page 2 of 6. Also noted as page 589.

[32] okstate.edu.0588. Kappler, page 2 of 6. Also noted as page 590.

[33] Ibid., page 4 of 9. Also noted as page 786.

[34] Ibid., 29.

[35] Teakel, 45.

[36] Michno, *A-Fate.* 190. Clodfelter, 28.

[37] Teakle, 36.

[38] Teakle, 38. Clodfelter, 27.

[39] Michno, *A-Fate*, 190.

[40] Michno-*A Fate*, 191-192.

[41] Abbie Gardner-Sharp, *History of the Spirit Lake Massacre & Captivity of Miss Abbie Gardner: The Raid of the Santee Sioux Against the Iowa Frontier Settlements, 1857*, (Leonaur is an imprint of Oakpast Ltd., 2011), 41. Hereafter cited as Gardner-*Sharp.*

[42] Michno-*Fate,* 192.

[43] Ibid. Gardner-*Sharp*, 45.

[44] Michno-*Fate,* 193. Gardner-*Sharp,* 47.

[45] Michno-*Fate,* 193-194.

[46] Ibid.

[47] Ibid., 195.

[48] Gardner-*Sharp,* 101.

[49] Ibid. Clodfelter, 31.

[50] Gardner-*Sharp,* 127. Teakle, 181.

[51] Gardner-*Sharp*, 129.

[52] Ibid, 130. Teakle, 181. Clodfelter, 32.

[53] Michno, *A-Fate,* 196.

[54] Teakle, 186.

[55] Wakefield-*Namias,* 123-124.

[56] Ibid., 126-127.

[57] Ibid., 24.

[58] Ibid.

[59] Ibid., 25.

[60] Janet Dean, "Nameless Outrages: Narrative Authority, Rape Rhetoric, and the Dakota Conflict of 1862, *American Literature,* Vol. 77, no.1, (2005), 104-105. Hereafter cited as Dean. Kathryn Zabelle Derounian-Stodola, *Women's Indian Captivity Narratives*, (New York: Penguin Books, 1998), xvi. Hereafter cited as Stodola.

[61] Wakefield, 24.

[62] Ibid.

[63] Ibid.

[64] Ibid., 25.

[65] Ibid., 36.

[66] Ibid.

[67] Dean, 105

[68] Ibid.

[69] Meyer, 114. Michno,*Dakota-Dawn*, 31, 33. Clodfelter, 39. Oehler, 27.

[70] Schultz-*Over the Earth*, 28. Michno, *Dakota-Dawn,* 36. Wakefield-, 20, 134, fn. 35. In reference to the vulgar quote, Namias mistakenly and inaccurately identifies her own book, *White Captives,* 214-219 as a reference to it. But the quote is only mentioned on page 214, none of the other pages. I find this interesting since she is using her own book. She only makes one reference and it is to the regular quote, "A trader named Andrew Myrick laughed and told them that they could eat grass." Another incorrect reference to the quote made by Namias is to Gary Anderson's book, *Kinsmen of Another Kind,* pages 250–253. Again the only reference to the quote is on page 250-251 and it is to the regular quote, not the vulgar one.

[71] Wakefield-*Namias*, 65.

[72] Abel B. Murch & Charles S. Bryant, *A History of the Massacre by the Sioux Indi-ans, in Minnesota, Including the Personal Narratives of Many Who Escape*, (Cincinnati: Rickey & Carroll, Publishers, 1864). This is a reproduction of a library book that was digitized by Google books. Hereafter cited as Murch & Bryant. There is a newer hardback copy of this book produced by Digital Scanning, Inc, Sictuate, MA, 2001. All endnotes will be referencing the original 1864 digitized book by Google.

[73] Murch & Bryant, 34.

[74] Ibid., 35-37.

[75] Ibid., 38.

[76] Ibid., 45-46.

[77] Ibid., 65.

[78] Ibid., 66-67.

[79] Ibid.

[80] Ibid., 69.

[81] Ibid., 72.

[82] Ibid.

[83] Ibid.

[84] Ibid.

[85] Ibid., 74.

[86] Michno, *Dakota-Dawn*, 26.

[87] Murch & Bryant, 53.

[88] Ibid., 54.

[89] Ibid., 55. The city of Cawnpore was the sight of one of the most brutal mas-sacres to take place during the Indian [of India] rebellion of 1857. The British post contained 900 civilians and 300 soldiers for a total of 1,200. The British had made a bargain to surrender the post in exchange for safe passage out of the region. However, upon leaving the post, the evacuation turned into a massacre and of the 1,200 individuals at the post only 7 British subjects survived, 5 men and 2 women.

Once the British learned of the horrible massacre in which 120 British women and children were hacked to death and mutilated with meat cleavers, they initiated a revenge campaign which some have estimated as high as 7,000 Sepoy mutineers were killed.

[90] Isaac V. D. Heard, *History of the Sioux War and Massacres of 1862 and 1863*, (New York: Harper & Brothers, 1863), v. Hereafter cited as Heard.

[91] Ibid., 251-252.

[92] Michno, *Dakota-Dawn*, 3. Doane Robinson, A History of the Dakota or Sioux Indians, (Minneapolis: Ross & Haines, Inc. 1974. 213.

[93] Jerry Keenan, *The Great Sioux Uprising: Rebellion on the Plains, August-September 1862*, (Cambridge: Da Capo Press, 2003), 13. Hereafter cited as Keenan. Recently republished by the University of Michigan, University of Library in 2014.

[94] Carley, 18.

[95] Meyer, 53.

[96] Ibid.

[97] Ibid., 22.

[98] Ibid., 42-43.

[99] Ibid., 25.

[100] Ibid., 21-22.

[101] Ibid., 44.

[102] Heard, 31.

[103] Ibid., 47. Schultz-*Over*, 26. Michno-*Dakota Dawn*, 32.

[104] Heard, 32.

[105] Ibid., 49.

[106] Ibid., 53.

[107] Ibid.

[108] Ibid., 54-55.

[109] Ibid. Schultz-*Over*, 32. Michno-*Dakota-Dawn*, 50-51. Kenneth Carley, *The Dakota War of 1862: Minnesota's Other Civil War*, (St. Paul: Minnesota Historical Society Press, 1961), 8-9. Hereafter cited as Carley.

[110] Heard, 56.

[111] Ibid., 62. There is quite a controversy about whether or not Andrew Myrick actually had grass stuffed in his mouth. Michno, in *Dakota-Dawn*, mentions on page 58, footnote 4. Carley on page 6 states that Andrew J. Myrick, remarked brutally, "If they are hungry, let them eat grass"-- a statement widely regarded as another immediate cause of the 1862 uprising. Anderson in *Insults* states that the quote was made two weeks before the hostile outbreak, between August 4 and August 8.

[112] Ibid., 67.

[113] Ibid., 69-71.

[114] Heard, 254-255.

[115] Ibid., 260.

[116] Henry B. Whipple, *Lights and Shadows of a Long Episcopate,* (New York: Macmillan Co, 1899), 138. Hereafter cited as Whipple-*Lights and Shadows.*

[117] Schultz-*Over*, 259. Anderson, *Little-Crow*, 165. Oehler, 209, Carley, 72. Clod-felter, 58.

[118] Osgood, 163.

[119] Heard, 269-270.

[120] Ibid., 268.

[121] Ibid., 269.

[122] Ibid., 270.

[123] Milner and O'Neil, 343.

[124] Heard, 349-350. Whipple- *Lights and Shadows,* 138-140, Osgood, 174-175. Gustav Niebuhr, *Lincoln's Bishop,* (New York: HarperCollins Publisher, 2014), 132. Hereafter cited as Niebhur.

[125] Ibid., 129 and 177, fn. 56.

[126] Scott W. Berg, *38 Nooses: Lincoln, Little Crow, and the Beginning of the Frontier's End,* (New York: Pantheon Books, 2012), 40.

[127] Ibid., 41.

[128] Clyde A. Milner II, and Floyd A. O'Neil, *Churchmen and the Western Indians 1820*-1920, (Norman: University of Oklahoma Press, 1985), 181. Hereafter cited as Milner and O'Neil.

[129] Harriet E.B. McConkey, *Dakota War Whoop: Indian Massacres and War in Minne-sota, of 1862-3,* (St. Paul: W.J. Moses' Press, 1864) ed. Dale L. Morgan, republished (Chicago: R. R. Donnelley & Sons Company, 1965), xvii-xix. Hereafter cited as McConkey.

[130] Ibid., 27.

[131] Ibid. 27, fn. 15.

[132] Ibid., 6-7.

[133] Michno, *Dakota-Dawn*, 30. Meyer, 112.

[134] Schultz, 8.

[135] William Watts Folwell, *A History of Minnesota, Vol. II,* (St. Paul: The Minnesota Historical Society, 1961), 234. Hereafter cited as Folwell. Heard, 44.

[136] McConkey, 288.

[137] McConkey, 171.

[138] Lavina Day Eastlick, *A Personal Narrative of Indian Massacres, 1862,* (1st Print-ing-1864,) 2nd Printing-May 1959, Life Magazine; 3rd Printing, American Herit-age Magazine, April, 1962. 1-2. Hereafter cited as Eastlick.

[139] Ibid., 1.

[140] Ibid., 14.

[141] Ibid., 16-17.

[142] Ibid., 21.

[143] Ibid., 21-22.

[144] Ibid., 25.

[145] Ibid., 18.

[146] Ibid., 29.

[147] Ibid., 30.

[148] Ibid., 32-33.
[149] Ibid., 43.
[150] Ibid., 44.
[151] Ibid., 54.
[152] Ibid., 65.
[153] Ibid., 11-12
[154] Ibid., iii.
[155] Anderson-*Dakota Eyes* 57-60. Michno, *Dakota-Dawn,* 73. Schultz-*Over*, 50.
[156] Gary C. Anderson, "Myrick's Insult: A Fresh look at Myth and Reality," *Minne-sota Historical Society,* Spring 1983, 201. Hereafter cited as Anderson-*Myrick's Insult.*
[157] Gary C. Anderson, *Kinsmen of Another Kind,* (Lincoln: University of Nebraska Press, 1984), 250-51. Hereafter cited as Anderson-Kinsmen. Ibid., 200. Gary C. Anderson, *Little Crow: Spokesman for the Sioux*, (St. Paul: The Minnesota Historical Society Press, 1986.) 128. Hereafter cited as Anderson, *Little-Crow.*
[158] Anderson, *Myrick s'-Insult.* 201
[159] Ibid., 204.
[160] Oehler, xiii.
[161] Michno, *Dakota-Dawn* 399-403.
[162] AHCD, s.v. coulee.
[163] Carley, 43.
[164] Anderson, *Little-Crow,* 155. Carley, 48.
[165] Oehler, 185.
[166] Anderson, *Little-Crow*, 158. Carley, 52. Clodfelter, 55-56. Keenan, 71.
[167] Clodfelter, 57. Schultz-*Over,* 233.
[168] Dunn, 426.
[169] Schultz-*Over*, 236. Anderson, *Little-Crow*, 160-161.
[170] Ibid.
[171] Anderson, *Dakota-Eyes,* 223. Marion Satterlee, *Outbreak and Massacre by the Dakota Indians in Minnesota in 1862,* ed. Don Heinrich Tolzmann, (Westminster: Heritage Books, Inc., 2001), 77. Hereafter cited as Satterlee, Outbreak and Massacre.
[172] Clodfelter, 57. Anderson-, 223.
[173] Anderson, *Little-Crow*, 161.
[174] Oehler, 200.
[175] Schultz-*Over*, 245.
[176] Oehler, 199.
[177] Schultz-*Over*, 241.
[178] Michno, *Dakota-Dawn*, 24.
[179] Ibid., 25.
[180] Gregory F. Michno, "10 Myths on the Dakota Uprising, *True West*, December 2012, 46-47. Hereafter cited as Michno's -*10 Myths.*
[181] Ibid.
[182] Michno, *Dakota-Dawn*, 393.
[183] Meyer, 120.

[184] Ibid., f. n. 16.

[185] Michno, *Dakota-Dawn,* 393.

[186] Ibid., 393-94.

[187] Meyer, 125.

[188] Michno-*Fate, 189.*

[189] Michno, *Dakota-Dawn*, 2.

[190] Ibid., 44.

[191] Ibid.

[192] Ibid., 65.

[193] Ibid., 161.

[194] Ibid., 162.

Chapter 4

The Sand Creek Massacre of 1864

"Alongside of her [Mrs. Hungate] lie two small children, one at her right arm and one at her left, with their throats severed completely, so that their handsome little heads and pale innocent countenances had to be stuck on..." Rocky Mountain News, Denver.

"Remember our wives and children murdered on the Platte and Arkansas." Colonel John M. Chivington.

"Black Kettle had a large American flag...fluttering in the grey light of the winter dawn."

George Bent, half-breed Cheyenne warrior.

On November 29, 1864, the battle or "massacre" at Sand Creek took place. It involved the Cheyenne and Arapahoe Indians and the military forces of the Colorado territory. These two tribes of Indians had been conducting murderous raids and the stealing of stock and property during the entire year. These depredations also included the mutilation of the dead and the kidnapping of white women and children. It was these Indian activities that were the primary motivation for the attack at Sand Creek. I will be using two primary sources, three secondary sources and a number of internet sources. The first primary source will be Morse H. Coffin's book, *Battle of Sand Creek,* originally published in 1879 and republished in 1965. The second primary source is the book written by Irving Howbert, published in 1914 and titled *The Indians of the Pike's Peak Region*. The first second-ary source will be that of Stan Hoig, *The Sand Creek Massacre*, published 1961. The second secondary source will be the book written by Gregory F. Michno, *Battle of Sand Creek: The Military Perspective*, published in 2004. The final secondary book will be *The Three Battles of Sand Creek*, also by Michno, recently published in 2017.

The attack at Sand Creek took place during the winter because this was the best seasonal advantage for the army to attack the Indians. The basic Indian strategy was to carry out raids and depredations during the good weather months of the spring and summer, wherein the Indians could more easily escape the army's attempts to engage them. In comparing and con-trasting the cavalry horses and Indian ponies there were some stark differ-ences. The cavalry horses were:

> Large powerful cavalry mounts well suited for carrying a trooper with a full pack and fighting gear, but their energy needs were enormous—at least fourteen pounds of hay or grass and twelve pounds of grain every day. That demand could be supplied only with trains of large and ponderous wagons that slowed the march of an attack column. Cut loose from the wagons and fed only on native grass, [cavalry] horses quickly lost weight and stamina... The smaller Indian horses, by contrast, carried far lighter loads and were conditioned for rapid, far-ranging forays. Most important, they had been grass-fed since birth. During summer their fuel grew all around them. This of course was the key to their great remaining advantage—mobility. Cavalry might be lucky and find and destroy villages during the summer, but they could rarely catch the mounted warriors...But winter turned the tables. Grass, the fuel of movement, offered less nourishment as dropping tempera-tures required more energy.[1]

They did this primarily because their ponies were weak; the cold and snowy winter weather impaired their mobility and limited their raiding opportunities.They settled into their camp sites and tried to negotiate peace-ful terms for the duration of the winter. It was during the winter peace nego-tiations that they tried to acquire annuities, supplies, guns and ammunition for their spring and summer raids. This was done under the guise that they needed these supplies for their seasonable "buffalo hunts." The incompetents at the Indian Bureau readily provided their request for newer repeating rifles. The Indian agents did this without paying any attention to the army's and settlers' complaints. It seems the agents and bureau representatives could not comprehend the simple reality of their devious plan. Their "peaceful" Indian friends would use these very same guns to carry out their raids and depreda-tions during the spring and summer months. It was this very strategy that Chief Black Kettle, Chief of the Cheyenne, was attempting to use with the civilian and military officials of the Colorado territory in the winter of 1864.

The battle of Sand Creek took place in the southeastern corner of the Colorado Territory. The major players in this battle were Colonel

Chivington, who led the attack, and Chief Black Kettle of the Cheyenne. Other important players were Governor Evans, Major Anthony and Major Wynkoop, who negotiated the so-called peace agreement. The consensus interpretation portrays this attack as a vicious atrocity wherein the Colo-rado 3rd Territorial militia, led by Chivington, attacked a peaceful village of friendly Cheyenne and Arapahoe Indians killing and mutilating them without any provocation.[2] Was Chivington and the Colorado militia really unprovoked or was there a justifiable reason for their attack? And was Chief Black Kettle really the leader of a "friendly" tribe and did he really have a governmental guarantee of safe haven?

One must examine the circumstances that led up to the battle of Sand Creek and distill the accurate facts that caused this so-called "unprovoked" attack. The District of Colorado, the area within which Sand Creek was located, came under the supervision of Colonel Chivington and Gov. John Evans. Evans was the Governor of the Colorado territory. Chivington was the commander of the Military District of Colorado. One of the main problems facing the civilians and military personnel of Colorado was the Civil War. It was still going on, and the federal authorities had pulled most of the army troops out of the region to fight back east and on the Texas border area. These are the same circumstances that impacted the Great Sioux Uprising of 1862. "Most troops were being with drawn to the East in fear of a Confederate thrust into Kansas..."[3] This relocation of military forces caused the people of the District of Colorado to rely on the "hundred-day men" local militia troops known as the Third Colorado and a reduced number of federal troops for protection. It was the Third Colorado who were charged with committing most of the Indian mutilations. The other unit was the First Colorado, these soldiers were considered to be the more professional soldiers. These are the dire circumstances that confronted Colonel Chivington and Governor Evans and led to the vengeance attack at Sand Creek.

One of the major incidents which caused the Sand Creek attack was the Hungate murder and mutilations. This incident took place on June 11th, 1864, about 20 miles southeast of Denver. The Hungate family consisted of the father, Nathan Hungate, his wife, Ellen, and two young daughters. One girl was two-years old and the other was just an infant of 4 months. The contemporary family grave site is located in Fairmont Cemetery, Denver, Colorado.[4] It is believed that Arapahoe Indians initiated the attack bent on running off the horses on the ranch. Hungate and another worker named Miller worked at the Isaac Van Wormer ranch. Mr. Hungate saw smoke rising from the direction of his household and frantically returned in an attempt to save his family. It is suggested that as the attack took place the family took shelter in the house and put up a formidable fight, possibly wounding or killing one of the Indians. The Indians set the house on fire and killed Mr. and Mrs. Hungate and their two children as they fled the house. Mr. Hungate's body was found "riddled with more than eighty bullets."[5] In addition, "An arrow protruded from each breast, his heart was cut out, his scalp taken, throat cut, and was otherwise mutilated with the wounds all fly blown."[6]

> Mrs. Hungate and the children were cut down within a few hundred yards, and the angry warriors vented their rage upon their bodies, raping Mrs. Hungate before stabbing and scalping her. The two young girls, one an infant of three or four months and the other two years old, had their heads nearly severed while the infant was disemboweled.[7]

This horrible butchery clearly shows the fundamental cruelty that char-acterized Plains Indian culture. To murder defenseless civilian settlers, men, women, children and infants, is beyond human comprehension. "The bow-els of the younger one was ripped open, and its entrails scattered by the sides of the mother and children."[8] How much more empirical evidence does one need to gather to prove the point that the American Plains Indians were fiendish savages?

Their sympathizers would overlook this brutal massacre and say that this is just their Indian culture. George Bent accurately described this process when he referenced the raids of the early summer of 1864. He stated: "I do not intend to give a detailed account of the raids that were made during July and August. They were terrible affairs, but after all, the Indians were wild in those days; they had been attacked again and again by the troops without any cause, and they were retaliating in the only way they knew how."[9] "Wild" is their surreptitious term for heinous savagery. Their excuse being that they were retaliating in kind. Their inhumane behavior is gener-ally dismissed as ritual mutilations that needed no further explanation. This behavior certainly does need explanation, accurate description, and most importantly accountability.

What makes it so disturbing is that these mutilated bodies of four inno-cent human beings were brought to Denver on the 15th of June and dis-played in a wagon box. They were put on display for all the panic-ridden citizens to view. A Denver newspaper described the same scene as follows:

> A HORRIBLE SIGHT! The bodies of those four people who were massa-cred by the Cheyenne on Van Wormer's ranch, thirty miles down the Cut-off, were brought to town this morning, and a coroner's inquest held over them. It was a most solemn sight indeed, to see the mutilated corpses stretched in

the stiffness of death, upon that wagon bed, first the father, Nathan Hungate, about 30 years of age, with his head scalped and his either cheeks and eyes chopped in as with an axe or tomahawk. Next lay his wife, Ellen, with her head also scalped through from ear-to-ear. Along side of her lie two small children, one at her right arm and one at her left, with their throats severed completely, so that their handsome little heads and pale innocent countenances had to be stuck on, as it were, to preserve the humanity of form. Those that perpetuate such unnatural, brutal butchery as this ought to be hunted to the farthest bounds of these broad plains and burned at the stake alive, was the general remark of the hundreds of spectators this afternoon...[10]

The display of the four mutilated bodies for all the people to see inflamed the citizens, soldiers and the Colorado militia. "Everybody saw the four, and anger and revenge mounted all day long as the people filed past or remained to talk over Indian outrages and means of protection and reprisal."[11] Add to the extensive list of continuing depredations by the Indians, the Hungate incident, and the unauthorized peace negotiations with Major Wynkoop, I believe that these are the major causes for the attack. Just before Chivington began the attack, he yelled to his militia troops, "remember our wives and children murdered on the Platte and Arkansas."[12] Later research indicated that it was Arapahoe, not Cheyenne Indians.

Throughout the summer of 1864, "there was a virtual epidemic of raids on settlements and wagon trains through western Nebraska and eastern Colorado. Colonel Chivington's 1st and 3rd Colorado Cavalry undertook patrols aimed at apprehending the perpetrators. For the most part, the pickings were slim, as the Cheyenne meticulously avoided the troops."[13] The following is a brief summary of the Indian attacks made in the latter part of July: July 17th, the Cheyenne Dog Soldiers and Sioux carry out eight vicious attacks that leave six white settlers dead and several hundred horses and cattle stolen; on July 18th, two more Indian raids close to Denver with five settlers murdered and scalped; July 24th, Dog Soldiers and Sioux attack and burn four wagon trains in Kansas; July 30th, Kiowa warriors raided Fort Larned and kill one sentry and stole 250 horses and mules.[14] Any attempt to call these Indians "peaceful" is an obviously false statement. And this is just the month of July.

By the summer of 1864, there was a virtual epidemic of raids on settlements and wagon trains through western Nebraska and eastern Colorado. During the first week of August alone, there were fifty-one people killed and seven abducted by mainly Cheyenne raiders on the Little Blue River and in the Plum Creek area of Nebraska.[15]

As an example of the horrors that the Indians perpetrated on the captive frontier women and children during a raid, let us examine some of the events that occurred during the early days of August. These included Mrs. William Eubanks, her 4-year-old daughter, Isabelle, and her infant son. The rest of the unfortunate captives were Laura Wilbur, a 16-year-old girl, a 17-year-old, Lucinda Eubanks, Mrs. Roper and her daughter, Laurie Roper, and a Mrs. Snyder. There is some confusion on the individuals who were captured especially in reference to a Laurie Roper as to whether she was a mother or a young girl. Also on the 8th of August, ranches and settlements along the Little Blue River in Nebraska and Kansas were attacked. During the two-day period of the 9th and 10th of August, Cheyenne and Sioux warriors stole and destroyed $68,000 worth of property and livestock. They also attacked several wagon trains and killed 14 men and kidnapped another two women and 4 children.[16]

On the 29th of August, Black Kettle sent a message, based on a request from William Bent, about peace negotiations with the army. Bent was a well-known trapper, trader and entrepreneur. He built the famous per-manent trading post, Bent's Old Fort, in the early 1830's; it was built of adobe. The use of adobe was a very smart move by Bent. It was more fireproof than wood, and it was cooler in the summer and warmer in the winter. He brought in Mexican adobe builders to make sure the adobe bricks were made correctly.[17] William Bent, two of his brothers, and a French aristocrat, Ceran St. Vrain, were extensively involved in the Indian trade and with the travelers on the Santa Fe Trail. Bent was made a member of the Cheyenne tribe and eventually became a sub-chief. When he died of pneumonia in 1869, the Cheyenne regarded him as a trusted tribal advisor and the only white man who truly understood them.[18]

He also had several half-breed sons who were directly involved in the battle, George and Robert; George fought directly on the side of the Chey-enne. On behalf of Black Kettle, George and Ed Guerrier each wrote exact letters, one to Agent Colley and the other to Major Wynkoop, the com-manding officer at Fort Lyon. Black The letter stated:

Cheyenne Village, Aug. 29th/64
Major Colley.

Sir

We received a letter from Bent (William Bent) wishing us to make peace. We held a consel in regard to it & all came to the conclusion to make peace with you providing you make peace with the Kiowas, Commenches [sic],

Arrapahoes, Apaches and Siouxs. We are going to send a message to the Kiowas and to the other nations about our going to make [peace] with you. We heard that you [have] some prisoners in Denver. We have seven prisoners of you which we are willing to give up providing you give up yours.

There are three war parties out yet and two of Arrapahoes. They have been out some time and expect now soon.

When we held this counsel, there were few Arrapahoes and Siouxs pre-sent; we want true news from you in return, that is a letter.

Black Kettle & other Chieves [19]

This letter is important because it clearly states Black Kettle's conditions for peace. The army must also make peace with all the other nations before Black Kettle will consider making peace. He also clearly states that there are five raiding parties out and also that he has seven white captives. Later on, in the peace negotiations, we will see that Black Kettle does not meet his own conditions for peace and lies about trading the seven white captives. Having five raiding parties out does not sound like these are" friendly" Indians; it clearly makes them hostiles, who were at war with the U.S. Government!

War parties of the Cheyenne and Sioux continued their raids on innocent civilian settlements and wagon trains in September and October. In October, a Colorado unit attacked a Cheyenne camp in eastern Colorado and killed eleven Cheyenne. In the Indian camp "the scalp and personal property of an emigrant woman was found and recovered at the scene."[20] Between October 7th and October 28th there were seven separate Cheyenne and Sioux Indian attacks in Nebraska. In the month of November, just prior to the date of the battle, there were seven individual raids carried out by the Indians; the 6th, 12th, 15th, 17th, 19th and the 25th and 26th. The last two, on the 25th and 26th of November, the Cheyenne and Sioux attacked the Plum Creek Nebraska stage coach station twice, with two whites killed and three wounded.[21]

These attacks clearly prove that the Cheyenne and Sioux were not "friendly" Indians operating under a peace agreement. They were "hos-tiles" actively carrying out raids against innocent settlers and committing murders, rapes, kidnapping, mutilations and thievery. Clearly, this evidence justifies Col. Chivington's attack at Sand Creek. These were not friendly nor peaceful Indians. It was a revenge dawn surprise attack against openly hostile Indians. These extensive and continuous series of murderous Indian attacks and kidnapping raids, beginning in July and lasting throughout the month of November, had a devastating effect on the citizens of Colorado and Nebraska. Clearly, an atmosphere of anxiety and fear existed in reference to the Indian killings and depredations. This apprehension permeated the City of Denver, the District of Colorado, and western Nebraska. Den-ver was in danger of being completely cut off from contact with Nebraska, Kansas, and the rest of the United States. The Indians had stopped all supply trains, wagon trains, emigrant trains and mail service from traveling to the City. The price of basic foodstuffs had increased dramatically. The price of flour rose from "nine dollars per 100 pounds to 24 dollars."[22] During the month of August, from the 8th to the 28th, "more than fifty whites along the Platte River trail were murdered."[23] The citizens in Denver were in a panic; and in the middle of August, Governor Evans issued a dispatch to the U.S. Secretary of War Edwin Stanton in Washington stating:

> Extensive Indian depredations, with the murder of families, occurred yester-day thirty miles south of Denver. Our lines of communication are cut, and our crops, our sole dependence, are all in exposed localities, and cannot be gathered by our scattered population... we are in danger of destruction both from the attack of Indians and starvation. I earnestly request that Colonel Ford's regiment of 2d Colorado Volunteers be immediately sent to our relief. It is impossible to exaggerate our danger. We are doing all we can for our defense.[24]

It is obvious that Governor Evans saw the Indian threat as serious enough to call for federal troops to come to their rescue.[25] He would be in little sympathy to any calls for Indian immunity based on a spring, summer, and fall of continuous brutal depredations. "The residents of Denver felt them-selves under siege and isolated from the rest of the country. Martial law remained in effect throughout the summer. Men carried guns with them at all times."[26]

In addition to the attacks lasting from August through November, there had also been a complicated series of misleading and confusing peace negotiations begun in early September between Chief Black Kettle and Major Wynkoop. Wynkoop had been the commanding officer at Fort Lyon and had originated these negotiations on his own without approval from higher headquarters. He was relieved of duty on the 5th of November for hav-ing conducted these peace negotiations. He was replaced by Major Scott Anthony. Anthony became the commanding officer of Fort Lyon and later joined Chivington to participate in the attack. Anthony made a report on the 28th of November after the arrival of Chivington's force; it showed "that he fully approved the attack on the friendly camp."[27]

Higher headquarters consisted of Brig. Gen. James G. Blunt, one of Wynkoop's superior officers. He was commander of the newly created District of the Upper Arkansas. Maj. General Samuel H. Curtis, the other superior of Wynkoop's, had been appointed commanding officer of the Department of Kansas, which included the Colorado Territory. Both of these superior commanding officers strongly objected to Wynkoop's unap-proved negotiations. In addition to these two General Officers, the Gov-ernor of the Colorado Territory, John Evans, and Col. Chivington both vehemently disagreed with Wynkoop's individual peace initiative. Under his own direction, Wynkoop had negotiated with Black Kettle to move his tribe to Sand Creek and offered him his personal guarantee of safety from army attack. This was a promise that Wynkoop was not authorized to make. He was removed and relieved from duty on the 5th of November before the attack took place. He was not at the battle on the 29th of November. Obvi-ously, there was no peace agreement or guarantee of safety for Black Kettle's tribe between the 5th and the 29th of November.

Wynkoop had earlier arranged a meeting which came to be known as the Camp Weld Conference. It took place between Black Kettle, Neva, White Antelope, Governor Evans, Col. Chivington and several other Army officers and civilians in Denver. The meeting took place on the 28th of September.

> Evans began by asking what the chiefs had to say and Black Kettle said that they were there because of Evan's circular of 27 June, telling the friendly Indians to come to the forts. It was not the truth. Black Kettle contemplated coming in only after Bent wrote a personal message that was carried to him by One Eye in mid-August. He had the circular for about one and-a-half months without acting on it. He came in only after Wynkoop met him and suggested it. Evans said that he was sorry that the Indians did not respond to his appeal earlier, that they had allied themselves with the Sioux and had made war all summer.[28]

In a proposed meeting between Evans and Black Kettle, Black Kettle had refused to even meet with him. At the Camp Weld meeting, Evans went on to say:

> "Your young men are on the warpath," Evans said. "My soldiers are prepar-ing for the fight. You, so far, have had the advantage, but the time is near at hand when the plains will swarm with United States soldiers." Evans said he believed that the Indians only wanted peace for the winter, but would make war again when the grass was fresh in the spring. Then, he added a

dark, prophetic observation: "The time when you can make war best, is in the summer time; when I can make war best, is in the winter…my time is just coming."[29]

Evans stated that "whatever peace was made must be made with the soldiers and not him." This is an interesting statement. It is plausible that Black Kettle, having negotiated with the military, Major Wynkoop, believed that he had done what Evans asked. The nuances of these unauthorized negotiations could possibly be seen as evidence that Black Kettle could have believed that he had met Evans' requirements. However, Wynkoop was not one of the military authorities; General Blunt, General Curtis and Colo-nel Chivington were; and Black Kettle had no agreement with them. Also, on the previous date of the 10th of September, Wynkoop had directly told Black Kettle that "he was not authorized to make a peace agreement…"[30] The meeting ended up in a bizarre manner with the chiefs shaking hands with everyone, and Black Kettle embracing Governor Evans. But no peace arrangements were made, and no promises of immunity had been given.

Obviously, something might have been lost in the translation and talks that took place. Black Kettle seemed to believe that he had an agreement, but Evans and Chivington had no such thoughts. During the closing moments of the meeting, Col. Chivington made the following statement: "I am not a big war chief, but all the soldiers in this country are at my command. My rule of fighting white men or Indians is to fight them until they lay down their arms and submit to military authority."[31] Clearly, Governor Evans and Col. Chivington did not believe that a peace agreement had been made; any Indian village they came across would be a legitimate target for attack.

As for the Indian chiefs, several days after the Denver meeting enroute to Fort Lyon, they stopped and talked to John Powers. Powers was a former employee of William Bent who had worked as a clerk, freighter, rancher and interpreter in the area. He had married an Indian woman and was quite knowledgeable in reference to the Cheyenne. In a conversation between the chiefs and Powers, the chiefs told him "they had seen Governor Evans and Colonel Chivington and that they could not make any treaty of peace with them."[32] The Indians knew that no peace treaty had been made with the military authorities! So, Black Kettle clearly knew that he had no guar-antee of peace and was not under military protection at Sand Creek.

As stated earlier, Indian raids continued throughout the remainder of September, with seven raids taking place in October. In November, there were also seven raids. The raid on the 12th of November is an instructive example of the way the Indians conducted themselves:

On November 12, after Black Kettle had gone to Sand Creek, a party of Cheyennes and Arapahoes approached a government train on Walnut Creek, east of Fort Larned, and after protesting friendship and shaking hands, sud-denly fell upon the teamsters and killed fourteen of them, the only person who escaped alive being a boy who was scalped and left for dead. He recov-ered, but became an imbecile, and died from the effects of the injury…The Cheyennes never denied that they were hostiles…[33]

So much for the Indians being "peaceful" and innocent of conducting raids.

The last of these raids took place on the 25th and 26th of November, only days before the battle of Sand Creek on November 29th. These raids were made by 75 Cheyenne and Sioux warriors on a train at Plum Creek. They killed two and wounded one woman and two men.[34] Clearly, the Indians had not made any kind of peace agreement with the military authorities. Therefore, the Cheyenne and Arapahoe Indian camp at Sand Creek was a justified military target. An eye-witness soldier, Irving Howbert, who had inspected the Indian camp after the battle was over reported: "The camp was over-flowing with proof that these Indians were among those who had been raiding the settlements of Colorado during the previous summer, killing people, robbing wagon-trains, burning houses, running off stock, and com-mitting outrages of which only a savage could be guilty; this evidence only corroborated in the strongest possible manner what we already know."[35]

The standard interpretation of the battle, by the politically correct Indian apologists, who call it a massacre, states that the blood-thirsty Col-orado militia attack swept through the peaceful village without warning. An attack where Black Kettle displayed an American flag and a white flag over his tepee; and the militia murdered and mutilated innocent Indians, two-thirds of them women and children. The opposing explanation of the battle, not a massacre, is a far different and more complicated affair. The entire allegation that the attack at Sand Creek was a massacre is entirely based upon the testimony of several pro-Indian individuals who were critical of Col. Chivington. These individuals wanted to exact revenge against Chivington because of the personal and military grievances they had against him.

The first question which has already been challenged is the fact that the Indians were "friendly." They definitely committed atrocities throughout the spring, summer, and late fall. Much is made to differentiate between Black Kettle's camp and the raiding done by the Dog Soldiers. But the Dog Soldiers always returned to Black Kettle's camp, and he readily admitted that he had no control of his young warriors and several bands were still out on raids. In reference to the Dog Soldiers, "the Dog Soldiers were not a separate band, but were a separate department within the tribal government. Black Kettle and his band did not deny connection with them or responsi-bility for them; many of the band at Sand Creek were Dog Soldiers."[36] Sec-ondly, the Indians had no peace agreement with the U.S. Government; they only had a verbal agreement with Major Wynkoop. He was removed from his command in early November for not adhering to higher headquarters' directives which clearly prohibited any peace negotiations made by him. He was in Kansas when the attack took place; and he was, therefore, not even an eye-witness to the attack.

The accumulated evidence can be clearly seen to answer the two previ-ously asked questions: (1) Were the Indians friendly? No, they were definitely hostile! And (2) Were they living under government protection? No, they knew that no peace treaty had been made, and they were not living under government protection. The only guarantees made were those of one man, Major Wynkoop; and he had no authorization to negotiate with the Indians.

A third allegation made about the attack had to do with the questions about whether or not an American and a white flag had been seen dur-ing the attack. It is reported by Michno that of all the individual soldiers at the battle "only three persons said they saw Black Kettle display an American or a white flag."[37] A corrected count shows that only two eye-witness soldiers said they had seen any flags, one was Naman D. Snyder and the other was George M. Roan.[38] The fundamental problem with their testimony was that they only saw an American flag flying; they made no reference to a white flag. It is interesting in that there were at least 685 soldiers that participated in the battle; and, out of these 685 soldiers, only two soldiers said that they saw an American flag. Snyder testified to the question, "(Did you see an American flag?) Yes, at the lower end of the village. The west end..." Roan stated: "I saw a camp of Indians, and the stars and stripes waving over the camp."[39] One must also speculate that the American flag could have been difficult to see being located at the lower west end of the village in addition to the chaos, smoke and confu-sion of the battle.

In reference to the white flag that has been reported by Stan Hoig, only two out of his selected 31 witnesses made any reference to it. Stan Hoig, a professor of journalism, wrote a book titled *The Sand Creek Massacre,* which was published in 1961. Hoig's book is blatantly pro-Indian and contains extracts from only 31 witnesses provided to the Sanborn Commission. The Sanborn Commission held hearings to ascertain the guilt or innocence of

Chivington and his troops. George Bird Grinnell stated in his book, *The Fighting Cheyennes* (1915), the following: "At the council of 1860 Black Kettle had been given a large American flag, and now he ran it up on a long lodge pole before his lodge, with a small white flag underneath it as a sign that the camp was friendly."[40] No footnote or endnote citation to this quote is made by Grinnell. In George Hyde's book, *Life of George Bent: Written From His Letters,* (1968), there is no mention of a white flag, only an American flag. In the book of Halaas & Masich, *Halfbreed,* (2004), they attribute the following statement to George Bent, stating that he "looked toward Black Kettle's tipi and saw the garrison flag fluttering in the breeze over his lodge, a small white flag tied beneath it."[41] They also do not use any citations, none whatsoever, to identify their sources.

Michno reports in his book, *Battle at Sand Creek: The Military Perspective,* (2004), that soldier David Louderback, "placed a white handkerchief on a stick, and when they (he and John Smith) reached the edge of the camp he waved it…when the bullets began to fly, they retreated into the village."[42] Michno further states that, "…teamster Watson Clark also tried to signal the troops. "When the attack was made, I got up on a wagon and waved a white skin—a flag of truce,' he said. 'When I was waving it three or four bullets went through it. Then I got down and lay under a wagon, as I had nothing to fight with.'"[43] Michno does offer an extensive footnote to substantiate his information. He, in my opinion, is the only one that makes any sense. Another fact to take into consideration is that neither of Michno's refer-ences makes any mention of a white flag tied to the bottom of Black Ket-tle's lodge pole. These white flags were quickly raised and quickly retrieved by Louderback and Clark.

It must also be noted here that the soldiers, after the battle was over, deliberately killed John Smith's son, Jack. He was killed because there was a widespread belief among the soldiers that he had "participated in raids with the Cheyenne and that he ought to have been killed with the rest."[44] This fact plays a definite role in casting doubt on John Smith's later testimony against Chivington.

The extent of George and Robert Bent's extensive blood ties to the Cheyenne also play a role in their future testimony against Colonel Chivington. It should also be noted that George had fought for the Confederacy and had been a Union prisoner of war for a short time.[45] Both of them were half-breed (mixed-blood for the P. C. crowd) sons of William Bent, whose wife was a full-blooded Cheyenne. There was a third Bent brother in the camp, Charles Bent; he played no significant role in the battle. George and Robert Bent had been members of the Cheyenne Dog Soldiers. The

Dog Soldiers were the tribal law enforcers or police. The Dog Soldiers were one of seven soldier societies or bands:

> These soldier bands included a large number, but not all, of the able-bodied and ambitious men of the tribe, from youth to old age. They were the organized military force of the camp, and acted as its police force. To them was entrusted the enforcement of the orders of the chiefs. Since, in the Indian camp, public opinion was the ruling force, and since the soldiers constituted a majority of the bravest and most influential men in the tribe, the soldier bands were often consulted by the chiefs on important matters relating to peace or war. Sometimes one or more of these societies, acting unitedly, might force the tribe to adopt some certain course of action that it was not generally desired to take, or might even oblige some priest or important man to perform an act that he felt to be wrong or to threaten harm to the tribe.[46]

George was not only the son of a full-blooded Cheyenne mother, but he was also married to a full-blooded Cheyenne. His wife's name was Magpie, and she was the niece of Black Kettle.[47] Obviously, George had very close family ties to the Cheyenne tribe that was under attack.

During the battle, George fought on the side of the Cheyenne. He was fighting with the Cheyenne against the Colorado militia. The question now becomes, how objective and unbiased would his testimony be? Not unbi-ased at all!

George Bent stated: "Black Kettle had a large American flag tied to the end of a long lodge pole, holding the pole with the flag fluttering in the grey light of the winter dawn."[48] Robert Bent testified to the exact same thing.[49] What a vivid, colorful and poetic description! It is interesting to note that other eye-witnesses reported that the day was cold and calm; they reported no wind blowing through the camp. Robert, who was unwillingly pressed into service as a scout for the Colorado military, also stated that he "could clearly see a six-by-twelve-foot American flag above Black Kettle's lodge."[50]

Again, let us interject a little common sense into the argument. You must fully comprehend the size of a six-by-twelve-foot flag; that is one big flag. The standard tepee was estimated to be between 16 or 20 feet high; that flag would have basically covered the entire front of the tepee. The standard flag that most people fly in front of their houses is two feet six inches wide and four feet in length. The flag that Black Kettle supposedly had was about three times as big as the standard flag. It would have been impossible to miss it fluttering in the non-existent breeze. But only a total of six individuals claim to have seen this flag; and, of these six, four are, in my opinion, clearly unreliable, being John S. Smith, Samuel Colley, and the two Bent brothers. That leaves only two witnesses to the American flag, soldiers Naman Synder and George Roan. So, only two soldiers out of six hundred and eighty-five claimed to have seen the six foot by twelve foot flag waving over Black Kettle's lodge. Their conclusion seems somewhat tenuous to me!

Three military officers participating in the battle testified to seeing no flag at all. The first officer was Major Jacob Downing of the First Colorado Cavalry. He testified that," I did not see any flag over the village, but afterwards saw a man with a small flag who said he got it out of a lodge."[51] The second was Captain Presley Talbott of the Third Regiment, Colorado Cavalry. He testified that, "I did not see any flag displayed by the Indians."[52] The third officer was Dr. Caleb S. Burdsal, Assistant Surgeon, Third Regiment, Colorado Regiment. He testified that, "I did not see any kind of Indian flag in the Indian camp."[53] So again, it becomes quite evident that there are significant opposing testimonies to the "flying flag" controversy.

Another bit of common sense deals with the aftermath of the battle. The soldiers came back to the camp in the afternoon or early evening after the battle was over. They searched for contraband in the Indian camp; no flags were found. The only contraband found were buffalo robes, a Cheyenne war flag, trinkets, food stuffs, supplies and white people's scalps and pos-sessions. Now, if you know anything about military people, they have a very high regard for the flag of the United States. For no flag to be found after the battle is very significant. If a flag had been found, it would have been duly noted. This fact causes more serious doubt to be cast on the flag argument.

Further contradictory evidence on the flags and the motivations of John S. Smith is offered by the first-hand, eye-witness account of Morse H. Cof-fin. He was a member of Company D, Third Colorado Cavalry, a soldier directly involved in the battle.[54] Soldier Coffin stated:

> Now about the white flag so much talked about by the opponents of the fight.
>
> I am not unmindful of the fact that the testimony of one or two hundred men even, who did not see such a flag displayed at the Sand Creek village, is no positive proof that none was exhibited, but it does tend to make it improbable except that fact be proven by reliable witnesses.
>
> I am not aware that a white flag at Sand Creek was ever heard of, until the one-sided investigations of those old coveys (the "Committee on the Conduct of the War") took place in Colorado in the summer of 1865; nor

do I now know on whose evidence it rests, though most likely on that of the truthful (?) and impartial (?) John Smith. I will add, that I have never seen or heard of anything, either in conversations with comrades or otherwise, at the time of the battle, or since, which even made it appear to me probable that any white or truce flag was exhibited by any one at the above-named battle.[55]

Coffin further stated that the "flag story" rested on the testimony of the corrupt John S. Smith, the same Indian Agent who was trying to recover $25,000 in restitution from the Federal Government. This false bill was based on the fact that Smith and Colley claimed that they lost merchandise, 105 buffalo robes, two white ponies and a wagon full of supplies, probably worth about $6,000. The buffalo robes were worth an average of $35.00 for a total worth of $3,675.00.[56] Their claim of restitution surprisingly grew to be a bill of $25,000. Smith stated that "they would realize $25,000 out of it and damn Colonel Chivington."[57].

These facts must be considered when evaluating the testimony of Colley, Smith, and that of the Bent brothers. I believe that their testimony is totally unreliable. The only other references to white flags were by private David Louderback and a teamster, Watson Clark. Both were with the trading party in the Indian village during the heat of the battle.[58] Clark said that he attempted to alert the soldiers by a waving a flag made out of white animal skin. He stated, as reported above: "When I was waving it three or four bul-lets went through it. Then I got down and lay under the wagon, as I had nothing to fight with."[59] Both Louderback and Clark have to be considered unreliable because they were involved with the corrupt trading practices of Smith and Colley. Their testimony, if accurate, indicates that such white flags would have only been momentarily displayed and therefore difficult to see.

There was also mention made of a Cheyenne "war flag" reported by Lt. Cramer, who said he saw it later that night in the camp. He stated that this flag might have been the Cheyenne "war flag" presented to Lt. Colo-nel Bowen after the battle. Bowen testified: "The war flag of this band of Cheyennes is in my possession, presented by Stephan Decatur, commissary sergeant of company C, who acted as my battalion adjutant."[60] Hoig deals with this problem and stated: "Decatur said much of his seeing no white flag during the battle but avoids any mention of the 'war flag,' which evidently was the United States flag raised by Black Kettle."[61] Now to conclude that a seasoned Lt. Colonel Bowen could not differentiate between an Indian war flag and a sixby-twelve foot American Flag is beyond comprehension and defies common sense. One can conclude, after this detailed and thorough investigation of the issue of flags flying before and during the attack, that very few reliable witnesses agree on this issue.

The fourth charge under dispute is the total time of the battle and whether or not it was a lightening quick charge through the village with guns blazing and swords flashing. Most witnesses agree that the attack began at sunrise; some have suggested about 6 a.m. There seems to be little debate on that fact. But the length of the battle could determine whether or not it was a short, swift massacre, an easy victory, or a lengthy contested battle that lasted several hours, if not all day. Some sources have stated that the battle lasted until 10 or 11 a.m. Major Anthony, who was at the battle, said that the Indians "defended themselves for about four hours."[62] On another occasion he stated: "We fought them for about six hours along the creek for five miles."[63] That would make it a battle until about noon or so. Several other officers have stated that they terminated the battle just before sunset. These sources suggest a lengthy conflict with the Indians mounting a determined defense that caused the fighting to last for an extensive period of time. Another source stated:

> The Indians were surprised, but they were better armed than the soldiers and they put up a desperate fight.
>
> The Indians had excavated trenches under the bank of Sand Creek for several miles, and they took shelter in these trenches as soon as the attack began. Although they put up a stubborn resistance and contested every inch of ground, they were slowly driven back from one position to another for about four miles, and finally about two o'clock in the afternoon they dis-persed in all directions and were pursued by the troops until night.[64]

Obviously, the battle took a long time. It was stated by several of the officers and soldiers that the Indians put up a desperate and determined fight. "The enemy proved themselves to be possessed of the most daring courage, especially in emergencies. I believe the Sand Creek fight raised in the minds of many their estimation of Indian courage."[65]

In further reference to the length of the battle, Col. Chivington stated that the Indians put up a determined fight and "they 'finally abandoned resistance and dispersed in all direction, and were pursued by my troops until night fall.'"[66] Eye-witness Morse Coffin made the following statement about the time spent fighting the Indians: "I think it was about three or four o'clock in the afternoon (likely the latter hour) when company "I" came in and I know nothing of any fighting after this..."[67] The sources listed clearly show that the battle took a minimum of four hours to a maximum of ten hours or longer. That doesn't sound much like a massacre to me but instead a long, determined conflict in which the "enemy proved themselves to be possessed of the most daring courage ..."[68]

This battle was not a hell-bent-charge through the village with guns blazing and swords flashing. "The traditional, hell-for-leather charge of Colonel Chivington and his Coloradans did not happen."[69] "There was no furious charge on horseback. 'We proceeded through the village on a walk', said Coffin. 'I think the town at this time was entirely deserted by the Indians, as not one was to be seen thereabouts, though plenty were not far away...'"[70] This evidence clearly suggests that the fighting at Sand Creek was not a mas-sacre, nor was it a lightening charge through the village. It was a long drawn out, serious and contentious battle between two determined enemies.

A tangential and minor issue associated with the battle is whether or not the Indians used already dugout sand pits to defend themselves during the battle. George Bent states that in reference to the battle:

> Presently we came to a place where the main party had stopped, and were now hiding in pits that they had dug in the high bank of the stream. Just as we reached this place, I was struck by a ball in the hip and badly wounded, but I managed to get into one of the pits. About these pits nearly all of Chiv-ington's men had gathered and more were continually coming up, for they had given up the pursuit of the small bodies of Indians who had fled to the sand hills.[71]

A few sources stated that these trenches were dug out ahead of time as a preparation for defense. Supposedly, American Plains Indians have seldom been known to build defensive barriers around their camp sites. Several sources stated that the sand trenches were used in the battle by the Indians on the bluffs of the river, but they were hastily dug out as the battle pre-ceded up the river. The sand pits on the west side of the river allowed the Cheyenne to put up a withering fire that caused the soldiers a great number of wounded. This issue has several individuals defending both sides of the argument; no conclusion has yet been reached.

Another one of the major allegations is the number of women and children killed at the battle.The most frequent number reported was two-thirds. This number was reported by four individuals; soldier David Louderback, Major Wynkoop, Major Anthony and Scout Jim Beckwourth.[72] Louderback, Watson Clark, John S. Smith and Jack Jr., were in one of the tents. They were trading with the Indians at the time the battle began, and all of these men had a monetary stake in the outcome of the investigation.

One of the incidents of the raid was that John Smith's son, Jack Jr., had previously been noted raiding with the Indians; and some of the cavalry troops got together and purposely shot him after the battle was over.[73] To hide the reality of the shooting of Jack Jr., Major Anthony "told a different story. John Smith's son…was suddenly taken ill in the night and died before morning."[74]

Major Wynkoop was not even at the battle. He had been removed for making peace overtures to the Indians without the permission of higher headquarters. In his testimony, he stated: "Numerous eye-witnesses have described scenes to me…"[75] Wynkoop's testimony can be challenged as hearsay evidence. Major Anthony, prior to the battle and during it, was in full agreement with Col. Chivington but, during the various hearings after the battle, turned against Chivington. Jim Beckwourth was a mullatto born in Virginia. He was an ex-mountain man, trapper, trader and Crow Indian "chief."[76] Beckwourth was considered no friend of Col. Chivington but was made to scout for him. The cold temperature had kept the old scout from completing his tracking duties. Robert Bent was then ordered to take over the scouting.[77] A Sergeant Lucian Palmer said, "I think among the dead bodies one-third were women and children."[78] Major Jacob Down-ing, a member of the First Colorado Cavalry, reported that he had seen about twelve or fifteen women and a few children killed on the battlefield. It becomes readily apparent that there was no agreement as to the specific number of women or children that were killed at the battle. For the sake of argument, let's take the number of two-thirds as a correct assumption. One source, Greg Michno, offers an interesting explanation in reference to the two-thirds number being used:

> The two-thirds women and children figure is insisted upon in many eye-witness accounts, attested to as if it was an extraordinary proportion, apparently to place a greater stigma on the Colorado volunteers. However, if one couple had only two children, then fully three-fourths of the family would consist of women and children; if they had three children, then four-fifths of the camp would be woman and children. Families with several children were common, while some were very large, with eight or ten offspring. One old man named Half Bear had four wives and 30 children… Louderback said that there were not any more women and children in the village than are usually in any village…In addition, the Cheyennes were one of the few tribes to have a considerable number of female warriors.[79]

Another factor that explains the number of women and children killed at the battle is this description of a specific part of the battle: "The fight soon became general all up and down the valley, the Indians continuously firing from their places of defense along the banks, and a constant fusillade being kept up by the soldiers, who were shooting at every Indian that appeared. I think it was in this way that a good many squaws were killed. It was utterly impossible, at a distance of two hundred yards, to discern between the sexes, on account of their similarity of dress."[80] I would suggest that this also pertains to the teenage boys and other youth who could shoot a gun or a bow. This would definitely help explain the young men and boys who were killed in the battle.

Two privates of the 3rd Colorado, Shaw and Patterson, reported that "squaws would take their bow and arrows and at every opportunity would down a soldier."[81] Several other eyewitness reports further verified that squaws were shooting at the soldiers. One incidence involved a soldier named Joseph H. Connor. Connor had been having a duel with a certain warrior who he eventually shot. The men with Connor warned him not to stand up in the open. Almost immediately a squaw jumped up and shot an arrow at Connor that pierced his right lung.[82] In another instant, a soldier reported that he had been hit in the shoulder by an arrow shot by an Indian woman. "The squaws were fighting along with the men."[83] Clearly, the Indian squaws were actively involved in the battle and that explains the fact that they were casualties.

As for the children, a Cheyenne squaw said that, "all who were left to protect them (the Indians) were teenage boys...they bravely took on the job."[84] It is further stated that, "The oldest ones, armed only with bows and arrows, rode their ponies straight into Capt. Talbot's oncoming sol-diers. When they were scattered or killed, the younger boys went in, with the same result. Whether adult warriors or teenagers, they put up a good show."[85] From these eye-witness accounts it can be easily determined that the Cheyenne women and children took part in the battle as active partici-pants. Irving Howbert reported: "Some squaws and youth fought alongside the warriors and, consequently, became casualties."[86] He goes on to say, "I never saw anyone deliberately shoot a squaw, nor do I believe that any children were intentionally killed."[87] Another factor that would have made the shooting of women and children possible was the battlefield smoke and haze. However, Morse Coffin, another eyewitness, reported:

> Now I know a part of this is true, and many were unavoidably killed; that it was not easy to distinguish the sexes during the fight, and it would have been perfectly impossible to help killing many women and children; and I also know perfectly well (and nearly every other man who was in the Sand

Creek fight must be satisfied of it) that it was the purpose during that battle to kill old and young of both sexes. That is the fact of the case, and it is useless to shirk it, or pretend it was all accidental.[88]

Coffin's primary source statement clearly provides the evidence that there is no doubt that the 3rd Colorado Militia did brutally kill many of the Indian women and children. This historical fact can no longer be denied. One of the major motivations of this attack led by Col. Chivington was retaliation and vengeance. Chivington stated before the battle began, "Remember our wives and children murdered on the Platte and Arkansas."[89]

A problem associated with the killing of the women and children is the total number of victims involved. Just as we had the problem of conflicting testimony about women and children, we have the same problem with the number killed, both the total number of dead Indians and the number of dead women and children. There are as many different numbers as there are so-called witnesses to the event. The total number of Indians in the camp was estimated to be between 600 and 750 Indians, consisting of warriors, women and children. The camp itself was estimated to be about 120 Cheyenne lodges and 8 Arapahoe lodges. If one averages 5 Indians to each lodge that would make for 600 Cheyenne and 40 Arapahoe for a total of about 640 Indians.[90] I would consider this to be the accurate number of Indians in the village.

In reference to the number of Indians killed, some sources have suggested as few as 70 to a high of 125.[91] Some have even said, as Chivington did, that as many as 500 to 600; but Chivington's numbers are considered exagger-ated. If we use the number of 125 as valid, and we take two-thirds as a reliable figure, we end up with a maximum of 83 women and children killed at the battle. If we assume the total number in the camp to be 640, and the total number of Indians killed to be 125, we have about 500 Indians that survived. That can hardly be called a "massacre." Another interesting question is, where did these surviving Indians go? It is reported that the surviving Indians fled the village and headed north and east to escape the fight. Dare I be so bold to suggest that it was the Indians who were the cowards, not the soldiers of the Third Cavalry, as suggested by one of our upcoming critics. This fact reinforces the point already made that the Indians only fight when the num-bers are overwhelmingly in their favor. Are they smart or are they cowards?

An additional factor of interest that deals with the battle is the com-position of the men who made up the Colorado military forces during the attack. There has been a tendency to denigrate these militia men as drunken, blood thirsty misfits. One infamous source, Dee Brown, stated: "Lack of discipline, combined with heavy drinking of whiskey during the night ride, cowardice and poor marksmanship made it possible for many Indians to escape."[92] Another source critical of the Colorado Third Volunteers is Elliott West. He stated: "The third was composed of untrained locals and included a sizable portion of gutter-scrapings."[93] Schultz reported, in reference to the attack, that "Chivington's men were a mob—primitive, unrestrained, crude, barbaric—stripped for that time of even the thinnest veneer of civilization."[94] These three individuals provide no evidentiary footnotes or endnotes to prove their statements. Therefore, there is no historical evidence to back up these unjustifiable claims! Dee Brown wrote that some of Chivington's men were drunk and that many of the soldiers' casualties were due to friendly fire.[95] But neither of these claims is supported by Gregory F. Michno or Stan Hoig in their books devoted to the massacre. Both of these men are well-known experts in this field of study. The night being made reference to is the 28th of November. I could not find one piece of historical evidence to support these allegations. Isn't it fascinating how some Indian sympathizers can fabricate historical facts out of the blue without having anything to back it up, and they get away with it in today's politically correct environment!

There is direct evidence to dispute these allegations. It can be readily found in the eyewitness accounts of two of the Third Cavalry soldiers, Pvt. Irving Howbert and Pvt. Morse Coffin. Pvt. Howbert initially stated: "For the most part, the regiment had been enlisted from the ranchmen, miners and business men of the State..."[96] Further on in his diary, he says, "I wish to emphasize the fact that a large majority of the members of the Third Colorado Cavalry were high-class men, whatever may be said to the con-trary...These people were from every part of the United States, many of them farmers, merchants and professional men, and the men who enlisted in the Third Cavalry were largely of this class."[97] Michno also supports this premise when he writes:

> Ultimately, a total of 1,149 men enrolled. Of the approximately 800 men whose occupations were known, more than 500 were farmers and miners, and about 200 were laborers, clerks, teamsters, carpenters, engineers, printers and merchants. The men were not the dregs of society as some have claimed, but a typical cross-section of citizens.[98]

Howbert goes on to describe the activities that took place on the night of the 28th. "All night long it was walk, trot, gallop, dismount and lead. I had had very little sleep for two or three nights previously, and consequently, this all-night march was very exhausting. During the latter part of the night,

I would willingly have run the risk of being scalped by the Indians for a half-hour's sleep... During the night, in order to keep awake, we had been nibbling on our hardtack, which in the morning, much to our disgust, were found to be very much alive"(weevils).[99] This account clearly indicates that there was no drinking on the night of the 28th, just a long, tedious march to get to the Indian village before dawn.

The second eye-witness to this allegation was Pvt. Morse H. Coffin. He stated that on the night of the 28th, "Soon after we arrived in camp near the fort, an order was circulated to prepare three days' rations, and be ready to start at eight o'clock in the evening. We supposed this meant business; and the result was a lively camp. Some cooking was done, fire arms put in the best possible condition, and ammunition handed out."[100] He further stated: "It was likely 9 o'clock when we got well under way...Save tempo-rary halts of a few minutes each, we marched steadily all night, and to me it seemed a long one...But when a halt was made many would dismount and dropping on the ground fell asleep in a minute, to awake the instant the others moved. Thus, the night wore away, and the early dawn of the 29th found us still marching, and some miles from the Indian village."[101] Again, no mention of drinking on the night of the 28th. Let me interject another bit of common sense. If you were a soldier going into battle the next morning, would you want to suffer from a hangover when your very life might depend on your state of mind and physical condition? Let's also keep in mind that these soldiers had no idea how large this Indian camp would be. They had no idea whether or not the battle would be a victory or a defeat.

As for the allegation of poor marksmanship, Soldier Howbert said: "The guns were old, out of date Austrian muskets of large bore with paper car-tridges which we had to bite off the end when loading. These guns sent a bullet rather viciously, but one could never tell where it would hit."[102] One must also include the important fact that there was a significant halt made by Chivington and Anthony to rescue the four white men in the camp. The escape of so many Indians is due to these factors. If we summarize the evidence presented, we can readily discern that (1) there was no drinking of whiskey on the night of the 28th; the troops of the Third Cavalry were not drunk; (2) there is no evidence to back up the charge of cowardice; (3) the so-called lack of marksmanship can readily be blamed on the old, outdated guns that were used by the soldiers; and (4) there was a purposeful halt to rescue the white men in the camp.

Let us now take a brief look at the actual battle itself. As previously stated, the attack began about sunrise, on a cold, calm morning. There was two-feet of snow on the ground. There was no hell-bent charge through the village, and the fight lasted a minimum of four hours. The preponderance of evi-dence suggests that the battle lasted all day, until about 4:00 p. m. One of the first and most important steps in fighting Indians is to keep them separated from their pony herd. Indians on foot are at a major disadvantage in a battle. As has often been said, the Indians are considered "the best mounted horse soldiers in the world." Chivington's strategy was to first capture the pony herds, then rescue the white men in the camp, and finally attack the village from three sides.

An interesting incident occurred at the beginning of the battle that I believe clearly points out the extreme contradictions provided by both the Indian sympathizers and the defenders of Col. Chivington. It is in reference to the killing of White Antelope. According to one source, Hoig, an Indian sympathizer:

> White Antelope, meanwhile, had run out from the village towards the troops, holding his hands high in the air and yelling at them not to fire. The troops kept coming on, and White Antelope, one of the bravest and greatest of the Cheyenne warriors, stood in the middle of Sand Creek with his arms folded over his chest, hoping to signify by the gesture that the Cheyennes did not wish to fight the whites. The heroic act was wasted on the soldiers, and he was shot down in the bed of the creek.[103]

Major Wynkoop, a critic of Colonel Chivington, makes the same charge:

> White Antelope folded his arms stoically, and was shot down, refusing to leave the field... he chanted his death song:
> "Nothing lives long,
> Except the earth and the mountains."[104]

The major problem with this description is that, just like previously noted above, the authors do not provide any footnote citation. No identification of the historical sources are provided.

This same incident is also described by soldiers but in quite a differ-ent manner. Michno wrote: "The little resistance that the Indians made in the village was evidenced by White Antelope, Stand In The Water, and a few others...(Lieutenant) Wilson saw the Indians, 'who had approached me under a bank as if they were going to fight.'[105] Louderback saw them also, and believed that they tried to tell the soldiers they did not want to fight, but they were fired upon."[106] However, Louderback changed his testimony later on when he was cross-examined. He then stated that he had heard the story about White Antelope's death from John Smith.[107] Wilson is reported to have said: "The Indians returned our first fire almost instantaneously." Michno further wrote: "Black Kettle stayed back, but White Antelope and Stand-In-The-Water went to their lodges, 'got their guns, came back, and commenced firing at the troops. Both of them were killed within fifty yards of each other,' said Louderback…Private Safely, who knew White Antelope by sight, assisted in his demise… 'He came running directly towards Company H;' Safely said, 'he had a pistol in his left hand, and a bow with some arrows in his right. He got within about fifty yards of the company; he commenced shooting his pistol, still in his left hand.'"[108] Pvt. Safely wounded White Antelope and another soldier, Billy Henderson, killed him.

Now for the verification of the evidence. One offers the eye-witness testimony of Lt. Luther Wilson, Private Alexander F. Safely and a Lt. Andrew J. Templeton, all of the Third Colorado. Templeton says he "saw White Antelope lead in the fighting until he was killed."[109] Now you can certainly argue that White Antelope had every right to defend himself after he had been fired upon. In one report, we have White Antelope standing with his arms folded over his chest making a courageous stand; and in the other, we have a Cheyenne warrior attacking the soldiers with a gun and bow. It is a fact that White Antelope was one of the Indians who was viciously mutilated by Chivington's militia. Several sources stated that "The body of White Antelope…was a prime target. Besides scalping him the soldiers cut off his nose, ears and testicles--the last, for a tobacco pouch supposedly."[110]

In reference to the major geographical lay out of Sand Creek, it runs from the northwest to the southeast, with the creek taking an abrupt curve from the west to the east about half-way down, then continuing in a southeast direction.[111] There were two Indian pony herds located at the camp, one to the southwest and another on the northeast of the village. Two groups of soldiers were sent to drive the Indian pony herds away from the village so that they could not be effectively used by the Indians. Meanwhile, two other groups of soldiers attacked the main camp. One attacked the southern end of the camp, while Chivington and the main body attacked the eastern part of the camp.

The Indians seemed to have been forewarned about the attack, and it wasn't the surprise attack that Chivington had planned. Some of the Indian herders had run back to the camp as soon as they saw the soldiers advanc-ing on the pony herds and warned the village. Morse Coffin's comments about the beginning of the battle are most illuminating. He stated that as the column advanced toward the village:

About day-break the command was started, on a lively "double-quick," which continued for several miles, until we reached rather deep sand, about one half of a mile from the Indian village, and in full view of it. During this fast ride, (of perhaps an hour,) the Artillery were, if not in the advance, certainly near the head of the column, and going at the rate we were, they made an awful din and clatter, which must have been heard for several miles away, as the morning was clear, cool and calm. Some remarked at the time, that this was a queer way to surprise the Indians, and we wondered that we were not timed to reach the enemy's camp at dawn, provided we were to attack them.[112]

Coffin continued:

When we reached the sand, and in full view of the Indian camp, and distant from it about half a mile, the command was halted and ordered to throw off all superfluous luggage, such as blanket, overcoats, grub, & etc. Each man seemed to be making all possible haste, still each moment seemed to be counted by the officers, and Col. Chivington called to the boys to make hast. Also, during this two or three-minute halt, Col. Chivington, turning to the command, said: "Boys I shall not tell you what you are to kill, but remember our slaughtered women and children..."[113]

When it came time to attack the village, Coffin stated: "Now the command was fronted into line...we proceeded through the village on a walk. I think the town at this time was entirely deserted by the Indians, as not one was to be seen thereabouts, though plenty were not far away, as will appear presently."[114] Michno explains that Chivington's hesitation on immediately launch-ing the attack is revealed by an agreement made between Major Anthony and Col. Chivington. They made an agreement between themselves not to directly charge into the village. Anthony was concerned about the three white men (there were really four) in the village trading with the Indi-ans. Anthony also wanted to save Chief Black Kettle, One Eye and Left Hand. Chivington did not completely share Anthony's concerns but stated: "However, it is not my intention to attack without warning." He further informed Anthony "that the operation depends on the conditions they find upon arrival. If he could immobilize the Indians, he would offer surrender terms."[115] Chivington also said that the overall objective of the attack was to "surround the camp and take the stolen stock and kill the Indians who had been committing depredations during the last spring and summer."[116] This agreement between Anthony and Chivington was not known amongst the troops, but would help explain why the Indian village was deserted when Chivington got there. To repeat what Pvt. Coffin said, "we proceeded through the village on a walk. I think the town at this time was entirely deserted by the Indians..."[117] As we shall see later, this agreement would also explain how 500 or so "brave" Indians had escaped from the village, and the rest were able to flee up the creek to the safety of the sand pits and high bluffs. Chivington did manage to rescue the four white men in the camp, John Smith, his son "Jack" Smith, Pvt. David Louderback, and teamster R. Watson Clark. It must be noted that the soldiers later murdered Jack Smith. They believed that Jack had participated with the Indians on numerous raids throughout the territory.[118] Major Anthony, in a letter to his brother, attempted to cover up the shooting of Jack. Anthony stated: "We, of course, took no prisoners, except John Smith's son, and he was taken seriously ill in the night, and died before morning."[119] Another bogus story about Jack's death was made up by a Major Sayr. He "tried to say that Jack was killed accidently when looking at a gun..."[120]

As the battle began, the Indians, due to Chivington's brief halt to attempt a rescue of the white men, were able to withdraw northwest up Sand Creek and dig themselves in on the high bluffs and sand pits along the creek. The fighting continued along this four or five-mile front with casualties taken by both sides. The fighting terminated in the late afternoon or early even-ing, and the troops were recalled to search the village for property. What was found were primarily buffalo robes and other contraband gotten from the recent raids of the Indians, including white scalps of women and children. This finding inflamed the soldiers. It must also be noted that the famous six-by-twelve-foot American flag was not located; not one soldier reported finding that "famous" flag.

Another erroneous charge made against the soldiers was that they illegally stole a large number of Indian ponies and other Indian possessions, especially buffalo robes. This charge, however, entirely overlooked the fact that Governor Evans had announced a Proclamation on the 11th of August, 1864, referring to the payments that the soldiers would receive for their services. This Proclamation said: And further, as the only reward I am authorized to offer for such services, I hereby empower such citizens, or party of citizens, to take captive and hold to their own private use and benefit all the property of said hostile Indians that they may capture, and to receive for all stolen property recovered from said Indians such reward as may be deemed proper and just therefore."[121] Also the recruiting poster of the Third Colorado Volunteer Cavalry Regiment, published in Central City on August 13, 1864, clearly stated that, "The Company will also be entitled to all horses and other blunder taken from the Indians."[122] It is quite evident from these two documents that the charges made against the soldiers in reference to stolen buffalo robes, contraband, and horses is a complete fabrication. These charges were made by the two corrupt traders, John S. Smith and Samuel G. Colley, in testimony against Col. Chivington in later hearings.

As the soldiers were searching the Indian village, they came upon a num-ber of white scalps. Irving Howbert reported: "In many of the tents there were articles of wearing apparel and other things that had been taken from wagon-trains which the Indians had robbed during the previous summer." He went on the say, "In these same tents we found a dozen or more scalps of white people, some of them being from the heads of women and children, as was evidenced by the color and fineness of the hair, which could not be mistaken for that of any other race. One of the scalps showed plainly from its condition that it had been taken only recently."[123] One could readily suggest that the finding of these white scalps, especially those of women and children, might definitely have incited the young soldiers to commit scalpings against the dead Indians.

The most controversial charge made against Col. Chivington and his troops is that they brutally mutilated the Indian women and children. It has already been proven that the killing of the women and children were a result of both groups participating in the shooting. There was a great deal of confusion in the battle area. It has also been stated that, "It was utterly impossible, at a distance of two hundred yards, (that's twice the length of a football field) to discern between the sexes, on account of their similarity of dress."[124] As has been previously stated, the reliability and motivations of the witnesses, in this case to the mutilations, must be thoroughly examined. I will use the testimonies of five various individuals on each side of the argu-ment drawn from Professor Hoig's Appendix in his book, *The Sand Creek Massacre.*[125] I will only use the testimonies and affidavits of key personnel. Hoig uses a total of 30 individuals to support his charges of atrocities. It is of interest that out of these 30 individuals, 21 are anti-Chivington and only 9 are supportive. That in and of itself suggests a biased sampling of sources.

The comparative method of analysis is, in my opinion, the best by which the reader can fully evaluate the evidence themselves rather than trusting in the selection of the author. Obviously, it us up to the discretionary choice of each reader to select which testimony he or she believes. When it comes to selecting witnesses or sources, the process used by dishonest historians is known as "cherry picking." When one does this, one basically ONLY picks the sources that defend or supports one's own argument. Many writers use this process, but never openly admit it. I would argue that many of the so called "popular" and academic books on Sand Creek have suffered from this process, especially those of the Indian sympathizers.

My objective, as stated earlier, is to find accurate evidence that clarifies the role of Colonel Chivington and the 3rd Colorado militia. By presenting both sides of the issue, I hope to avoid the charge of "cherry picking." You have to decide which testimony sounds more relevant, honest and, above all else, logical. You have to decide if I have been successful or not. I report, you decide. The five individuals below all support the negative charges against Col. Chivington.

The first source used to make the case for the mutilations is the testimony of Samuel G. Colley, Indian Agent. Colley stated: "They were followed up (the creek) and pursued and killed and butchered...they were butchered in a brutal manner and mutilated as bad as an Indian ever did to a white man...The officers told me they killed and butchered all they came to. They saw little papooses killed by the soldiers."[126] The fundamental fal-lacy with this testimony is the introduction to his report. He clearly said "I can state according to the received version..." and then he goes on to say, that, "The officers told me they killed and butchered all..." I beg your pardon. Sam Colley's evidence is based on "the officers told me" and "I can state according to the received version." More importantly, Agent Colley was not even at the battle. His close relationship with Samuel S. Smith, as trading partners, has already been clearly established. Colley's evidence, in my opinion, is obviously hearsay evidence and influenced by his dislike of Chivington.

The next source I will use is that of James D. Cannon, First Lieutenant, First Infantry, New Mexico Volunteers. I am including his affidavit taken on the 16th of January, 1865, some 6 weeks after the battle, to illustrate the horrendous mutilations that were charged against Colonel Chiving-ton and his men. Cannon said: "...in going over the battle-ground the next day I did not see a body of man, woman, or child but was scalped, and in many instances their bodies were mutilated in the most horrible manner-- men, women, and children's privates cut out, &c; I heard one man say that he had cut out a woman's private parts and had them for exhibition on a stick; I heard another man say he had cut the fingers off an Indian to get the rings on the hand... I also heard of numerous instances in which men had cut out the private parts of females and stretched them over the saddle-bows, and wore them over their hats while riding in the ranks."[127]

There is no doubt that Cannon was directly involved in the fighting. He served as Major Anthony's adjutant and rode with him during the fight-ing on the north side of the creek.[128] The major problem with Cannon's testimony is that part of it is also hearsay evidence. He stated that "I heard one man say…" on two different occasions and on a third he said "I heard of numerous instances…" One must note that Cannon's evidence, although hearsay, is the most damning and hideous testimony to the atrocities charged against Colonel Chivington and his troops. If his testimony is accurate and reliable, then there can be no justification for defending Col. Chivington. But as stated previously, much of what he reports is primarily hearsay evi-dence; and Cannon was also one of the friends of Major Wynkoop.

The third testimony used against Chivington is made by John S. Smith, interpreter and Indian agent trader, who was at the battle. One must recall his dubious past when considering the reliability of his testimony. In refer-ence to his past activities, it is stated that, "When he located in the Bent's Fort area, he was well acquainted with the many ways an Indian agent could make money off the Indians and the government, and had acquired several nicknames: 'Blackfeet,' 'Gray Blanket,' and 'Lying John' Smith."[129] Smith testified: "All manner of depredations were inflicted on their persons: they were scalped, their brains knocked out; the men used their knives, ripped open women, clubbed little children, knocked them in the head with their guns, beat their brains out, mutilated their bodies in every sense of the word."[130] He went on to say, "I saw the bodies of those lying there cut all to pieces, worse mutilated than any I saw before, the women all cut to pieces;…children two or three months old; all ages lying there, from suck-ing infants up to warriors."[131] "Sucking infants," now isn't that a morbid piece of "Yellow Journalism!" Please keep in mind that the testimony of Sam Colley and John Smith have already been challenged, and their own personal monetary claim can be seen as a primary motivation to besmirch Col. Chivington.

The fourth witness is Major Edward W. Wynkoop of the First Colorado Cavalry. He was outraged when he heard of the attack. He stated: "Numer-ous eye-witnesses have described scenes to me, coming under the notice of Colonel Chivington, of the most disgusting and horrible character, the dead bodies of females profaned in such a manner that the recital is sickening… I have been informed by Captain Booth…he visited the field and counted sixty-nine bodies, and by others who were present, but that few, if any, over that number were killed, and that two-thirds of them were women and children."[132]

You will recall that Major Wynkoop was not at the battle. He had been removed from the command of Fort Lyons on the 2nd of November for disobeying orders. He was clearly a defender of the Indians and sympathetic to their cause. He was the primary architect of the false peace negotiations. The battle occurred on the 29th of November. He had negotiated with

Black Kettle and White Antelope completely on his own without commu-nicating his intentions to higher headquarters or getting their permission. At the time of the battle, he was at Fort Larned, in the middle of Kansas. His testimony is based on "numerous eye-witnesses have described to me" and by being informed by a Capt. Booth. His evidence is also nothing more than hearsay evidence, as is that of Samuel Colley.

The next testimony that I will now cite is that of Robert Bent, one of the half-breed sons of William Bent, who served as a "forced" guide for Colonel Chivington. I find his testimony of interest because it is an actu-ally sworn statement of omission. He reports nothing about the atrocities charged by the other individuals who were selected. With his blood ties to the Cheyenne tribe under attack at Sand Creek, and the fact that two of his brothers, Charles and George, were in the village, you would think that he would enthusiastically provide eye-witness proof of the atrocities charged against Chivington. However, he does not do so. Absolutely no mention is made of any mutilations to Indian bodies. An omission of any reference to mutilations, other than scalping, by an individual so obviously biased against Chivington, I believe is a very significant fact.

What Robert did testify to is the presence of the two flags, but we have already mentioned that.[133] He also stated, "I think there were six hun-dred Indians in all. I think there were thirty-five braves and some old men, about sixty in all... I visited the battleground one month afterwards, saw the remains of a good many; counted sixty-nine, but a number had been eaten by the wolves and dogs...Everyone I saw dead was scalped."[134] Let's analyze that statement! Sixty-nine total Indians dead and scalped. Not one men-tion of any atrocities committed against the Indians other than some were scalped. There is not one charge of mutilation brought against Chivington and his men. Considering the close family ties of Robert to his two broth-ers, George and Charles, who were in the camp, this testimony of omission actually casts doubt on the fact that mutilations took place.

The final negative comments we will examine are those made by George Bent, the Indian son of William Bent, and brother to Robert and Charles Bent. George Bent, as described before, was raised in the Cheyenne tradi-tion by his 100% Cheyenne mother, Owl Woman. In 1853, he was sent off to two English-speaking boarding schools. The first one was located in Kansas City, Missouri, and the second one, Webster College near St. Louis. This educational background allowed him, with the added influence of Americans around his father's fort, to learn to read, write and speak English. He was considered "husky, intelligent, and better educated than many of the whites flowing each day up the trail."[135] Having been raised in a Cheyenne family, he also spoke their language fluently. Interestingly, he joined and served in the Confederate Army from 1861 until 1863. He was captured by Union forces and served a brief term as a prisoner of war. After 1863, feeling unwelcome by the pro-Union people around his father's fort, he returned to his mother's Cheyenne people.

At the time of the Sand Creek battle, he was about twenty-one years old. As stated previously, he was in the Cheyenne camp as an Indian warrior at the time of the attack; he fought against Chivington's soldiers. During the attack, he was seriously wounded in the hip, but was rescued by other war-riors. George Bent described what he saw during the battle:

> From down the creek a large body of troops was advancing at a rapid trot, some to the east of the camp, and others on the opposite side of the creek, to the west. More soldiers could be seen making for the pony herds to the south of the camps; in the camps themselves all was confusion and noise— men, women and children rushing out of the lodges partly dressed; women and children screaming at the sight of the troops; men running back into the lodges for their arms, other men already armed, or with lassos and bridles in their hands, running for the herds to attempt to get some of the ponies before the troops could reach the animals and drive them off. I looked towards the chief's lodge and saw that Black Kettle had a large American flag tied to the end of a long lodgepole and was standing in front of his lodge, holding the pole, with the flag fluttering in the gray light of the winter dawn. I hear him call to the people not to be afraid, that the soldiers would not hurt them; then the troops opened fire from two sides of the camps. [136]

A main factor that must be taken into consideration is where was the location of Black Kettle's lodge? If one uses the map in George E. Hyde's book, which is cited as being taken from Grinnell's book, *The Fighting Cheyenne*, it confuses the locations. Hyde's book, *Life of George Bent: Written from His Letters,* was published in 1968. It was based on a series of letters exchanged between Bent and George Hyde between 1905 and 1918. [137] It provides the location of five different Indian tribes. War Bonnet's tribe was on the upper northwest corner of the camp. Next, we have White Antelope's located in the north central part of the camp, with Lone Bear directly next to White Antelope's camp. Next to Lone Bear, on the north-east side of Sand Creek, we have Black Kettle. Further east of Black Kettle, we have Left Hand's camp. Looking at the map it becomes readily discern-able that Black Kettle's camp is located directly in the middle of the camp site. If the soldiers are attacking from the southeast and the east, Black Ket-tle's lodge would not have been seen by the advancing troops even if he did have this infamous American flag "fluttering in the grey light of the winter dawn."

Only one eye-witness provided accurate information on the location of Black Kettle's lodge and that is N. D. Snyder, a soldier of Co. D, First Colorado Cavalry. He responded to the question, "Did you see an American flag?" He stated, "Yes, at the lower end of the village. The west end..."[138] Therefore, he did see a flag at the lower west end of the village. But we would need a much more accurate map than what Grinnell provides. One must recall that one important eye-witness, Morse H. Coffin, wrote that "the morning was clear, cool and calm..."[139] There was no fluttering breeze. Of the 30 witnesses that Hoig lists in his Appendix only four said they saw a flag; with George Bent's testimony added, that makes 5 out of 31. A total of 26 made absolutely no mention of seeing an American flag flying. Of the 650 odd soldiers of Chivington's command, only two, N. D. Snyder and George M. Roan, both of the 1st Colorado Cavalry, testified that they saw an American flag during the battle. An additional individual who said he saw a flag was Sam Colley, an Indian Agent, but he was not at the camp the day of the attack. His testimony, as stated earlier, is just hearsay evidence and false.

Let us now take a look at the testimony of Colonel Chivington and his supporters. In this testimony, he inflates the number of dead Indians found on the battlefield and refutes that the Indians at Sand Creek were under any government protection. One must stress the fact that this testimony has been pre-selected and edited by Hoig. And is, therefore, under suspicion in reference to content, accuracy and comprehensiveness. Let us remember that out of thirty testimonies selected, twenty-one present evidence against Chivington and only nine provide evidence in favor of Chivington.

Chivington states in testimony on the 29th of November that, "We killed chiefs Black Kettle, White Antelope and Little Robe, and between four and five hundred other Indians; captured between four and five hundred ponies and mules..."[140] Obviously, he is wrong about killing Black Kettle. He mentions that, "There was an unusual number of males among them [the Indians at Sand Creek] for the reason that the war chiefs of both nations were assembled there evidently for some special purpose..." In reference to his own inspection of the battlefield, he describes it as follows: "I myself passed over some portions of the field after the fight, and saw but one woman who had been killed, and one who hanged herself; I saw no dead children. From all I could learn, I arrived at the conclusion that but few women and children had been slain." He further reported that, "On my arrival at Fort Lyon, in all my conversations with Major Anthony commanding the post and Major Colley, Indian agent, I heard nothing of this recent statement that the Indians were under the protection of the government &c..." This selection of Chivington's testimony makes him look like a fool who is totally ignorant of the results of the battle. One should be suspicious of the motivations for this selection of Chivington's testimony.

The second source used to refute the charges of mutilation will be that of Jacob Downing, formerly Major, First Colorado Cavalry. Downing reported: "Indians were killed five to six miles from the village; but of the two hundred killed, I counted about twelve or fifteen women and a few children, who had been killed in the trenches."[141] He went on to say, "I saw no soldier scalping anybody, but saw one or two bodies which evidently had been scalped... I saw no mutilated bodies besides scalping, but heard that some bodies were mutilated. I don't know that I saw any squaw that had been scalped." This testimony clearly states that scalping had taken place, but this individual provides only hearsay evidence in reference to mutilations.

The next witness is Dr. Caleb S. Burdsal, formerly Assistant Surgeon, Third Regiment Colorado Cavalry. I consider Dr. Burdsal's statements to be very important due to his medical training as a surgeon. He stated that, "a soldier called my attention to some white scalps he held in his hand; my impression, after examination, was that two or three of them were quite fresh."[142] He continued and said: "I saw in the hands of soldiers silk dresses and other garments belonging to women; I saw some squaws that were dead, but did not go over the ground; I did not see any Indian scalped, but saw the bodies after they were scalped; I saw no other mutilations... I know of none being killed after being taken prisoner..."[143] So once again, we have testimony to the fact that there was scalping of the Indians that had taken place, but no other mutilations. Again, I consider this testimony to be important due to the medical expertise of the witness.

The fourth witness that was supportive of Col. Chivington was Leav-itt Bowen, formerly Lt. Colonel, Third Regiment Colorado Cavalry. There were only two of his statements included in the Appendix and both of them were very brief. In reference to the number of Indians killed, he stated: "From the most reliable information, from actual count and positions occupied, I have no doubt that at least one hundred and fifty Indians were killed by my battalion." The next comment he made was, "The war flag of this band of Cheyennes is in my possession, presented by Stephen Decatur, commissary sergeant of company C, who acted as my battalion adjutant."[144] This is a very brief testimony but does offer some insight to the flag con-troversy. It is possible that this Indian war flag was misidentified as one of those white surrender flags referred to by other individuals. But the brief testimony provided by Bowen suggests that the selection process of those testifying may have been "cherry picked" by the individual doing the picking! There are far too few witnesses presented who are in favor of Colonel Chivington. In my opinion, this is definitely not a fair and balanced trial.

The final witness is Stephen Decatur, formerly Sergeant in the Third Regiment Colorado Cavalry. He stated: "The next day after the battle I went over the battle-ground, in the capacity of clerk, for Lieutenant Colo-nel Bowen, and counted four hundred and fifty dead Indian warriors..."[145] He is incorrect in this statement. Most eye-witnesses use the number of approximately 125 total Indians killed. He continued, "I saw some of the men opening bundles or bales. I saw them take therefrom a number of white persons' scalps- men's, women's and children's; some daguerreotypes, ladies' wearing apparel and white children's and saw part of a lady's toilet and one box of rouge, also a box containing a powder puff. I saw one scalp of a white woman in particular...I saw, comparatively speaking, a small number of women killed." This testimony clearly indicates that there were white scalps of men, women and children and also quite a bit of apparel of white women. This evidence is provided to prove that the Cheyenne Indians in this village were obviously hostile and had recently committed scalpings of white people. This evidence alone would justify Chivington's attack on this supposed "peaceful" village. This reference to white scalps might have been one of the main motivations as to whatever mutilation did take place on the Indians, the other one being the atrocious mutilations of the Hungate family in June.

The summary of evidence presented indicates that scalping did take place. The most commonly supported mutilation is that of White Antelope and scalping of the male warriors. When it comes to the mutilation of White Antelope, many agree that it did take place. Michno says: "White Antelope was said to have his scalp taken, and his nose, ears and testicles were cut off."[146] The scout Jim Beckwourth, one of the pro-Indian advo-cates, stated: "White Antelope was the only one I saw that was otherwise mutilated."[147] One can conclude that White Antelope was definitely muti-lated, but there is doubt as to the extent of mutilations committed against women and children.

Michno wrote: "When the main fighting was over and the soldiers returned to camp, there occurred some of the ghoulish deeds that made the battle at Sand Creek infamous. A number of soldiers stopped to scalp and mutilate the dead. Stories circulated among the Indians and soldiers, of instances where fingers, ears, hearts, and genitals were mutilated or cut out, from both men and women."[148] There were other reports that the soldiers had cut off fingers to get at rings and scalped Indians to get trinkets and other jewelry out of their hair. This evidence clearly supports the fact that mutilations of the Indians did take place! MIchno went on to say: "Certainly there were atrocities committed by the soldiers, but dead and wounded soldiers who fell into Indian hands received the same treatment."[149] An example of this is the mutilation of Pvt. Robert McFarland, Company D. "They found it [his body] stripped of every thing except his drawers, his chest chopped open, and his broken gun jammed in the wound."[150] How-ever, this explanation of the mutilations committed by both sides does not clarify the issue of how widespread were the soldier's mutilations of women and children. The evidence so far investigated does not seem to be able to answer this question.

The following evidence about the mutilations helps explain what may have been the basic motivations of the soldiers to commit them. The testimony of these two men, Howbert and Coffin, is most enlightening. Private Irving Howbert said: "Among the members of our regiment, there were many who had had friends and relatives killed, scalped and mutilated by these Indians, and almost every man had sustained financial loss by reason of their raids; consequently it is not surprising they should be determined to inflict such punishment upon the savages as would deter them from further raids upon our settlements."[151] He went to say: "Notwithstanding the fact that this grim determination was firmly fixed in the mind of every one, I never saw any one deliberately shoot at a squaw, nor do I believe that any children were intentionally killed."[152] Howbert explains that the previous experiences of the soldiers in reference to atrocities committed by the Indians had not been forgotten. He does not present any solid evidence about mutilations, but he clearly hints that it did take place and explains why it "was firmly fixed in the mind of every one…"

Morse Coffin presented similar evidence when he stated that, "many were unavoidably killed; that it was not easy to distinguish the sexes during the fight, and that it would have been impossible to help killing many women and children; and I also know perfectly well (and every other man who was in the Sand Creek fight must be satisfied of it) that it was the pur-pose during that battle to kill old and young of both sexes."[153] He went on to say, "This is the fact of the case, and it is useless to shirk it, or to pretend it was all accidental." Coffin is stating that all the killings that did take place were not accidental, and the primary purpose of the battle was to kill all the Indians involved. Coffin, as a soldier who was at the battle and participated in it, seems to be one of the only men who honestly accepts responsibility for what took place.

Another gruesome incident one cannot forget is the impact of the shocking atrocities committed upon the Hungate family; there is no reason to repeat them here.[154] It is ironic that the Indian apologists are always so concerned with the mutilations of the Indians, but they don't give a damn about the atrocities committed on the white settlers. I find their disregard for the pain and brutal suffering of the white settlers to be an abomination against humanity! I offer these facts to clarify the motivations of Chivington's troops to mutilate the dead Indians, not to jus-tify them. One cannot condone the mutilation of women and children, whether they be white or red. But the charges about mutilated women and children are exclusively made by individuals known for their dislike of Chivington. You will forgive my callous belief that there should be no apology made for the battle at Sand Creek. It was a long overdue victory of vengeance and retribution for years of continuous raids of Indian murder, mutilation, kidnapping and rape carried out by the Plains Indians.

One should examine the impact of the mutilations at Sand Creek on the Indians involved, the Cheyenne and Arapaho. There always seems to add horror to the subject when the victims are women and children. Much ado is made when Indian women and children are badly treated or muti-lated. However, there is no outcry about the horrible treatment that white women and children experienced at the hands of the Indians. Again, the politically correct Indian sympathizers do not care one damn bit about how the white women and children suffered, in some cases being repeatedly raped and abused. Interesting, racial indifference to what happened to the white women by the Indian sympathizers.

In reference to the impact of Sand Creek on the Indians, J.P. Dunn argued the following:

> There is not a bit of doubt that killing women and children has a very dampening effect on the ardor of the Indian. In the very case of Sand Creek they said "they had always heard that the whites did not kill women and children, but now they had lost all confidence in them." Their "loss of confidence" grows a trifle amusing, when it is remembered that they had been killing women and children all summer long. Scalping and mutilation also strike terror to the Indian heart. Their religious belief is that the spirit in the body of the next world has the same injuries that are inflicted on the body here. For that reason, they almost invariably mutilate corpses, besides taking the scalp, which is almost an essential for entrance to the happy hunting grounds...That the Sand Creek affair inspired them with terror is beyond question. The Cheyennes and Arapahoes got over into Kansas and the Indian Territory as quickly as possible, and stayed there...[155]

The effect of Sand Creek on the Indians was they now feared the white man and what he would do to Indians involved in depredations against whites. Major Scott Anthony, who testified before the Joint Committee of the Conduct of the War on March 14, 1865, which was investigating the attack, clearly supported using Indian tactics against Indians. He stated: "It is the general impression among the people of that country that the only way to fight the Indians is to fight them as they fight us; if they scalp and mutilate the bodies we must do the same."[156]

The impact of the battle was accurately presented by Pvt. Howbert wherein he stated: "During the three years following the battle of Sand Creek there was little trouble with the Indians in El Paso County; consequently the people of that section of Colorado, while keeping a sharp look-out, felt fairly safe upon their ranches."[157] Another source that substantiates the fact that the Sand Creek battle did reduce the number of Indian raids in the area is that of Gregory Michno, in his book, *Encyclopedia of Indian Wars*. Michno states:

> Chivington's attack at Sand Creek brings us to another common assertion that is confounded by the numbers. Many histories hold that the Sand Creek massacre so infuriated the Indians that afterward the soldiers and settlers on the surrounding plains suffered a wrath greater than any seen before. Yet a contemporary, settler Elizabeth J. Tallman, wrote, "For a few years after the battle of Sand Creek, the Cheyenne and Arapahoe Indians were much quieter." The numbers support her statement. In Colorado in 1864, there were 69 white casualties. In 1865, after the supposed unprecedented Indian retaliation, there were only 41 white casualties, and in 1866 there were 4...Rather than causing new heights in bloodshed, it appears that Chivington accomplished his purpose: to drive the warring Indians out of the territory.[158]

The battle of Sand Creek did exactly what it was supposed to do--put at least a temporary end to the Indian raids against the white population of the Colorado territory.

Obviously, the Indian warriors did not like the reality of being brutalized and mutilated in the same manner as they brutalized the women and chil-dren of their white enemies. Using the same tactics and appalling behavior of the Indians against them seemed to be an excellent example of payback and vengeance. And make no mistake about it; numerous sources clearly indicate that vengeance was a primary motive of the Colorado soldiers in the battle at Sand Creek. All one has to do is "Remember the Hungate fam-ily" and the year-long depredations perpetrated against the citizens of the Colorado territory.

J.P. Dunn describes the horrible treatment of women kidnapped at the hands of the "Noble Red Man." He states:

> The treatment of women, by any Indians, is usually bad, but by the plains Indians especially so. When a woman is captured by a war-party she is the common property of all of them, each night, till they reach their village, when she becomes the special property of her individual captor, who may sell or gamble her away when he likes...She is also beaten, mutilated, or even killed, for resistance. [159]

What a grotesque horror, for any innocent woman, to be continually raped by murderous savages every night and then treated like a piece of second-hand property. Sold or gambled away to the highest bidder and then have to endure again the same vile sexual abuse. But our politically correct Indian sympathizers couldn't care less. What an injustice!

With the battle concluded, the initial results were applauded by the citizens of Denver and Col. Chivington was welcomed as a hero. There was a tumultuous parade for the returning soldiers who were waving their Indian scalp trophies for all to see. But the happy celebration did not last long. There were already plans being made by the detractors of Colonel Chivington to destroy his reputation and that of the Colorado Calvary's 3rd Regiment. The first rumblings of discontent came from Lt. Cramer and Major Wynkoop. Cramer stated, in late November, that Chivington "was working for a brigadier general's commission, and that he did not care how many lives he lost in getting it so that he got it."[160] Later on, in December, Cramer wrote a letter to Wynkoop and requested that, "for God's sake, Major, keep Chivington from being a Bri'g General." Obviously, Cram-er's main motivation was professional military jealousy. Wynkoop had two major disagreements with Chivington; the most obvious was the treat-ment of the Cheyenne Indians at Sand Creek. When Wynkoop heard about the massacre, he went "wild with rage."[161] The other reason was that he believed that Chivington was a major antagonist in reference to his self-appointed peace negotiations.

As for Samuel Colley, John Smith and David Louderback, one cannot overlook the monetary scheme they had devised for their $6,000 worth of merchandise that they wanted to fraudulently bill the federal government. You will recall that Smith had previously stated, "they would realize $25,000 out of it, and damn Colonel Chivington." Louderback had also previously stated that, "he would go to Washington City and present the same, and that he had friends who would help him get it."[162] Their motivation was driven by the desire for monetary gain. In addition to the fraudulent bill, they also feared a disruption in their lucrative and corrupt trading practices with the Indians.

The beginnings of the public campaign to discredit Col. Chivington began with a letter from a member of the 1st Colorado to a Judge Stephen S. Harding in Denver. He was a political enemy of both Governor Evans and Col. Chivington. This letter alleged that a brutal massacre had taken place at Sand Creek. The transmittal of the charge of this massacre was a classic case of contacting friends in "high places." Harding wrote to a John Wright who was a friend of the Colleys and Secretary of the Interior John. P. Usher.[163] To have a friend with contacts to the President's Cabinet was a fact that could obviously be used to great advantage.

Harding's letter first appeared in the *New York Herald* on the 26th of December. Other eastern newspapers followed: the *Washington Star*, the *Advertiser & Union* and the *National Intelligencer.* It should be noted here that there were other instigators in this "yellow" journalistic endeavor. John Smith, Indian agent, also bragged that "soon the eastern papers would be filled with letters from Ft. Lyon, blaming Chivington for the death of his son and 'that he would be avenged by using every effort with the depart-ment possible.'"[164] All of these individuals, Major Wynkoop, Lt. Cramer, John Smith, the Colleys and Louderback, readily admitted that they were going to wage a war of propaganda to destroy the reputation of Chivington and get what the government owed them.

The *Rocky Mountain News* wrote a brief article on the 29th of December that announced that there were problems brewing for Chivington and the Colorado 3rd. It stated that the recent battle at Sand Creek was to be the subject of a Congressional investigation. This article inflamed the citizens of Denver and the Colorado territory who had seen the battle as a great victory against hostile Indians, who had for the past several months com-mitted horrible depredations against them. The newspaper article stated: "Letters received from high officials in Colorado say that the Indians were killed after surrendering, and that a large proportion of them were women and children."[165] It was later determined that these high officials were Chief Justice of Colorado, Benjamin Hall, and also Colley who had written to Senator Doolittle of Wisconsin.[166]

Major Wynkoop, who had been reinstated at Fort Lyon as commander, was ordered to take testimony and make a detailed report on the incident. The testimony and affidavits he gathered came from John Smith, Lt. James D. Cannon, Lt. W. P. Minton, Pvt. David Louderback, teamster R. Watson Clark and Samuel Colley. All of these "witnesses" provided derogatory evidence against Chivington; not one of them spoke in his defense. Based upon this "evidence," Wynkoop sent a negative report to district headquarters on the 15th of January, "which was forwarded through channels to Washington, in which he called Chivington an 'inhuman monster.'"[167]

There were three investigations made of Sand Creek; all three of them heavily biased against Chivington. The first one was organized by the House of Representatives and was called the "Joint Committee on the Conduct of the War-1865," also known as the "Massacre of the Cheyenne Indians." The second one was the "Joint Special Committee Report on the Condition of the Indian Tribes." The third one was "The Sand Creek Massacre Report of the Secretary of War;" it was also known as the "Military Investigation of the Sand Creek Massacre." This third committee was supposed to be a military commission ordered to investigate "the conduct of the late Colonel Chivington...in his recent campaign against the Indians."[168]

Formation of the first committee, the Joint Committee on the Conduct of the War-1865, was made on the 10th of January, 1865. Testimony began on March 13th, 1865. The Commission initially met in Washington D.C. and called Governor Evans and Jesse Leavenworth. Evans spoke in defense of Chivington and stated that "the fuss about Sand Creek had a lot to do with the personalities and politics..."[169] The Committee also took testi-mony from individuals from Fort Lyon and Denver. Colonel Leavenworth's testimony was critical of Chivington. Leavenworth's motives can originally be traced to a promotion conflict between himself and Col. Chivington which took place in 1863. It began over the promotion of a generalship of the Colorado territory; Leavenworth was passed over for promotion to General. He believed that Chivington had something to do it. Also, Chivington did not have a very high regard for Leavenworth. He considered him to be a "worthless Democrat 'and the meanest old whore monger and drunkard in all the mountains.'"[170]

Promotion controversies also laid the foundation of the dislike between Chivington and a Lt. Col. Tappan. Chivington was promoted to full Colo-nel, and Lt. Col. Tappan was passed over for promotion as was Leaven-worth.[171] In addition to these promotion controversies, Chivington had both Leavenworth and Tappan previously removed from command. These occurrences generated a great deal of animosity between Leavenworth, Tappan and Chivington. The importance of Lt. Col. Tappan was that he was later made the presiding officer of the third committee, The Military Investigation of the Sand Creek Massacre, an appointment that dramatically affected the outcome of that investigation.

The purpose of the first committee, The Joint Committee on the Con-duct of the War, was to "inquire into and report all the facts connected with the late attack of the third regiment of Colorado volunteers, under Colonel Chivington, on a village of the Cheyenne tribe of Indians, near Fort Lyon."[172] This committee called a total of fifteen witnesses, twelve against Chivington and only three in defense, Chivington, Governor Evans, and Major Scott J. Anthony.[173] Chivington's evidence was provided to the committee only by deposition.[174] To say that the evidence was extensively skewed against Chivington is an understatement. The primary witnesses called against Chivington were Leavenworth, John S. Smith, Dexter Colley, Samuel Colley, Capt. Robbins, U.S. Marshall A.C. Hunt, and Major Scott Anthony. Anthony had changed his testimony from defending Chivingtion to that of criticizing him once he determined which way the political winds were blowing during this investigation. Later on, Pvt. Coffin stated that Anthony tried to resurrect his reputation and stand by Chivington.

The most interesting aspect of their testimony was that Leavenworth, Capt. Robbins, Dexter Colley and A.C. Hunt were not even at the battle.[175] All of their testimony was simply hearsay evidence. Leavenworth, whose past animosity against Chivington has already been discussed, stated: "I do not know anything positively, because I was not there..."[176] "Lying" John Smith, who was at the battle, was pressing his fraudulent bill for $25,000 and stated: "I saw the bodies of those lying there cut all to pieces, worse mutilated than any I ever saw before, the women cut all to pieces."[177] Let's not forget that the soldiers killed Jack Smith, his son. Dexter Colley, the son of Sam Colley, stated that at the time of the attack, "I was in St. Louis at the time."[178] Samuel Colley, close business partner of John Smith, said: "I was not at the fight."[179] Smith and the Colleys both had personal and monetary grievances against Chivington. Capt. Robbins stated that he was not with Col. Chivington at the time of the attack and that, "I have no personal knowledge of anything that transpired at Sand Creek."[180] Marshall Hunt of Denver responded to the question, "Do you know anything in connection with the killing of the Indians at Sand Creek, about the last of November, 1864?" "I do not suppose that I know anything that would be admissible as evidence. All I know is from general rumor, not being on the ground at all."[181] So much for the reliable evidence of these "stunning" witnesses.

If one carefully examines Major Anthony's initial testimony before this Committee, it was one of fundamental consistency. He only disagrees with Chivington on one occasion. He is asked the question, "Did you under the circumstances, approve of this attack upon those Indians?" He responded by saying, "I did not."[182] Chivington's charge of betrayal is based on the fact that, before the battle, Anthony supported killing the Indians at Sand Creek and, after the battle, he changed his testimony. This change of mind is based on the following facts: On the 28th of November, Anthony said to a Capt. Talbot that he was grateful for the reinforcements he had brought. He stated "that he would have attacked them before this time if he had had the force enough at his command."[183]

A Capt. Silas Soule stated: "I talked to Anthony about it [attack], and he said that some of those Indians ought to be killed; that he had only been waiting for a good chance to pitch into them."[184] Anthony also recom-mended to Chivington that, after the battle at Sand Creek was over, they should continue on and attack the Indian camp at Smoky Hill, a major Indian camp eighty miles north of Sand Creek. Clearly, before the battle, Anthony was all for attacking and killing the Indians, both at Sand Creek and Smoky Hill. Another source stated that Anthony wrote a letter after the attack which stated: "The massacre was a terrible one and such a one as each of the hostile tribes on the plains richly deserve. I think that one such visitation to each hostile tribe would forever put an end to Indian war on the plains..."[185]

Clearly, Anthony believed after the attack that it would have a devastating impact on the Indians, an attack that each Indian tribe richly deserves. Others have identified several instances after the attack where Anthony changed his mind. He had supposedly written a letter to his brother wherein he stated that Chivington "whipped the only peaceable Indians in the coun-try..."[186] Anthony knew this was a lie; he had continually identified these Indians as hostile. Another source reported that, "...on December 15, Anthony immediately reported to Fort Riley: 'I am of the (same) opinion that I was when reporting on the 25th of November. I then thought that it would not be policy to fight these Indians who were suing for peace until they were completely humbled.'"[187]

If one completely reads Anthony's detailed and duplicitous testimony before the Committee, Section 1, one can readily see that Anthony's comments before the attack and his testimony before this Committee, are basically inconsistent and inaccurate. He explained about the length of the attack, about 7 hours, and the number of Indian lodges, 130. He stated that after the battle, "...I think one such visitation to each hostile tribe would forever put an end to Indian war on the plains, and I regret exceedingly that this punishment could not have fallen upon some other band."[188]

Anthony discussed the negotiations he had and stated, "I told them I had no authority from department headquarters to make peace with them." He further stated: "It was the understanding that I was not in favor of peace with them." He described the hostilities that the Cheyenne and Arapahoe had committed during the year and said that the Indians were already at war with the whites and that "they were sending out their raiding parties." He stated that "the only way to fight Indians is to fight them as they as they fight us; if they scalp and mutilate bodies we must do the same. If they kill our women and children, kill their women and children and kill them." The only time he disagrees with Chivington is when he is asked: "Did you approve of this attack?" He responded, "I did not."[189]

Pvt. Coffin had an interesting statement about the testimony of Anthony before the Committee. He said, "...it seems that Major A. remains of the same opinion in regard to this as entertained at the time of the fight, though for years he has had the credit (or rather discredit) of having changed front, and which later I had supposed to be the case, until a recent letter from him-- in reply to one of inquiry from myself--makes all plain. It seems injus-tice has been done Major A. on account of the report of that notorious committee."[190] It is after the Committee's hearings that he is charged with changing his mind about the attack. Coffin's account suggests that Anthony, after some time had expired, changed his mind again and supports Chiving-ton's side of the argument. The passage of time and possibly the influence of one's conscience can have a fascinating impact on one's judgment.

The conclusion of the Committee, made by Senator Benjamin F. Wade of Ohio, was very critical of Anthony's testimony. The committee stated: "The testimony of Major Anthony, who succeeded an officer disposed to treat these Indians with justice and humanity, is sufficient of itself to show how unprovoked and unwarranted was this massacre... And when Colonel Chivington appeared at Fort Lyon, on his mission of murder and barbar-ity, Major Anthony made haste to accompany him with men and artillery, although Colonel Chivington had no authority whatever over him."[191] The Committee chastised Anthony but put the blame for the attack clearly on Colonel Chivington. Let us remember that the Committee had called a total of 15 individuals and only three of them supported Chivington: Chiv-ington himself, Governor Evans and, originally, Anthony. It is of interest to note that the chairman, Senator Benjamin Wade, "... a year later admitted that he had never even attended the hearings, nor did he understand the full import of the committee report."[192]

The following is another point of view in reference to an analysis of the Committee's conclusions. It is provided by Pvt. Morse Coffin, Company D, Third Colorado Cavalry, a soldier who fought in the battle. He stated:

> This battle is usually (especially in the east) referred to as the "Sand Creek Massacre" or "Chivington's Massacre;" and as such has it gone forth to the

world, and as such is it likely to be handed down to posterity. I think this is unjust. It merits no such infamous brand...

For this affair the commander of the expedition has been censured, lied about, and cursed generally beyond all reason. I am no special admirer of Col. Chivington, nor can I justify all that was done at Sand Creek; but I have a strong desire to see justice done him, as well as all others who have been and are under the ban of condemnation on account of the mistaken idea abroad in regard to the battle. In this connection I must record my contempt for the work of the "Committee on the Conduct of the War" in relation to this fight.

This committee consisted of Ben Wade, Doolittle, and I believe Foster. I suppose they were honest, but they were evidently imposed upon, and their so-called investigations and report have furnished authority for most of the untruths, misconceptions, and unjust censurings, connected with this affair, and which has moulded popular sentiment in the east regarding Sand Creek.

While Col. Chivington seems to have had many enemies who took this opportunity of venting their spite, the grand origin of the trouble appears to have been John Smith, Indian interpreter, and Major Colley, Indian agent...
...They--Smith & Colley—also said they would go in person to Wash-ington and represent the Sand Creek fight as a massacre, and they would do anything to damn Col. Chivington or Major Downing. [193]

Private Coffin's analysis completely disagrees with that of the Committee. He accurately points out the fundamental differences of opinion between the western Coloradans and east coast Indian sympathizers. He also plainly and directly puts the blame for the entire affair on the duplicitous activities of Smith and Colley. Coffin considers the congressmen on the Committee to be honest but sug\gests that they were duped.

Additional analysis of the Committee's conclusions is presented by a soldier who also fought at the battle. Private Irving Howbert's analysis also agreed with that of Coffin. He stated:

In the hearing before the Committee on the Conduct of the War, Colo-nel Shoup was not represented, and Colonel Chivington only by means of deposition...The accusation made at each hearing was that the Cheyenne and Arapahoe Indians attacked by Colonel Chivington's command at Sand Creek were not only friendly to the whites, but were under the protection of the military authorities at Fort Lyon. The battle was, by the consent, if not by the direction of Colonel Chivington, an indiscriminate massacre. All of this I believe is proved to be untrue, to the satisfaction of any reasonable person by the facts related in my account of the battle, and of the hostilities in El Paso County and elsewhere preceding. [194]

The choices are rather simple. Does one believe the testimonies of John Smith, Samuel Colley, Dexter Colley, Lt. Cramer or the testimonies of Gov-ernor Evans, Col. Chivington, Major Anthony, and the opinions of Pvt. Coffin and Pvt. Howbert.

The second committee to investigate the attack was the Joint Special Committee Report on the Condition of the Indian Tribes. The chairman of this committee was Senator James R. Doolittle of Wisconsin, who was also the chairman of the Senate Indian Affairs Committee. This is the same James Doolittle that Samuel Colley had previously contacted when he had written a letter to his cousin, William P. Dole, Commissioner of Indian Affairs. He also wrote to John P. Usher, the Secretary of the Inte-rior. In addition, he wrote "to the *Missouri Intelligencer* newspaper in which he declared the fight at Sand Creek to be a massacre of peaceable Indians who were under the protection of the United States Government, and laid the blame on Colonel Chivington and his Colorado troops. It was these letters, and Colley's accusations, which were supported by Lt. Colo-nel Tappan, Major Wynkoop, John Smith, and several others that brought about the Congressional and Army investigations into the affair."[195] Col-ley had previously been complaining about the hostile Indians for the past several months but now charged Chivington with making a surprise attack on an Indian village. He stated Col. Chivington "killed one half of them, all women and children..."[196] To have a cousin who is the Com-missioner of Indian Affairs, and other political contacts, such as senators in Washington, obviously interjects the issue of bias into the investigation.

This committee initially took the testimony in Washington from Samuel Colley, Leavenworth, John Smith and Governor Evans. The committee then traveled out west to take testimony from Major Wynkoop, and George and Robert Bent. We have already discussed the hatred that Wynkoop had for Chivington. And let us not forget the close family ties that both of the Bents had with the Cheyenne.[197] Both George and Charley were in the village when the attack took place. Robert served as the reluctant scout for Chivington at the battle. "The memory of Sand Creek, where he had been forced to lead the soldiers to Black Kettle's camp had haunted Bob all his life. But at great risk in 1865 he had testified about the horrors of the massa-cre before the congressional committee."[198] The reliability and motivations of Leavenworth, John Smith, Sam Colley, Wynkoop and the Bents have already been discussed at length. Considering their backgrounds, I consider their testimony to be unreliable and biased.

One of the most bizarre testimonies of this committee was the testimony of the famous "Kit" Carson. Christopher H. "Kit Carson" was a mountain man, fur trapper, guide, U. S. Army officer and Indian agent. He became famous due to his reputation for opening the West to American settlers. This committee had previously been organized to investigate the conditions of all the western Indian tribes and their treatment by civil and military authorities. The committee was divided by geographical regions. The group led by Senator Doolittle was directed to investigate the areas of Kansas, the Indian Nation, and the territories of Colorado, New Mexico and Utah.[199] This is how the committee ended up in Santa Fe interviewing Kit Carson. Carson had heard hearsay reports about the Sand Creek battle but was not an eyewitness in any sense of the imagination. Santa Fe is quite a long distance from Sand Creek. Yet his testimony was included in the report. He stated: "I have heard…that the authorities of Colorado, expecting that their troops would be sent to the Potomac, determined to get up an Indian war, so that the troops would be compelled to remain. I know of no acts of hostility on the part of the Cheyenne and Arapahoe committed previous to the attacks made upon them…"[200] Much was made of the famous Kit Car-son's testimony. What does this testimony, being nothing other than long-distance hearsay evidence heard in Santa Fe, have to do with Sand Creek? He had absolutely no knowledge of the raids carried out throughout the year of 1864. This included numerous raids in Nebraska and Colorado and also included the raids on the 19th, 25th and 26th of November. He was clueless. He was making reference to the rumor that the Colorado troops were going to be shipped east to fight the Rebels during the Civil War. But to suggest that this was the fundamental reason for the battle at Sand Creek is ludicrous and bizarre! It has no place as testimony before this committee, but it was included because of the celebrity status of Carson. Returning to the committee hearings. This committee reached the conclusion that:

> …the fact which gives such terrible force to the condemnation of the wholesale massacre of Arapahoes and Cheyennes, by the Colorado troops under Colonel Chivington, near Fort Lyon, was, that those Indians were there encamped under the direction of our own officers, and believed them-selves to be under the protection of our flag.[201]

It has already been argued that the only two officers who had directed the Indians to the camp at Sand Creek were Major Edward W. Wynkoop and Major Scott Anthony. It has already been stated that Major Wynkoop had disobeyed orders and initiated peace talks on his own without get-ting permission from higher headquarters. He had been removed from command at Fort Lyon for this very reason. And as for the Indians being peaceful, one need only recall the long and continuous raids they made throughout the spring, summer, and late fall of 1864. This included numerous raids throughout October and November. How anyone could conclude that these Indians were peaceful is beyond common sense and logic. As to the American flag controversy, it has also been argued to be in serious doubt. Out of approximately 680 soldiers at the battle, only two reported seeing an American flag. There were four other individuals who reported seeing the flag, Samuel Colley, John Smith and the Bent brothers, George and Robert. There were no comments made by Charles Bent. Having already argued the reliability of the corrupt Indian agents, Colley and Smith, and also dis-cussed the Cheyenne allegiances of the Bent brothers, it would be difficult to accept their testimony at face value. In reference to the validity and reli-ability of these congressional hearings, they should all be under doubt. Pvt. Howbert states that, "worst of all, it was given wide publicity through the two Congressional committees following unfair, one-sided and prejudiced investigations."[202]

The final committee to examine the battle was the Sand Creek Mas-sacre Report of the Secretary of War. It was also known as the Military Investigation of the Sand Creek Massacre. Testimony began on the 12th of February, 1865, and continued until the 30th of May, 1865. Its fundamental objective was to investigate "the conduct of the late [resigned] Colonel J.M. Chivington, first regiment Colorado cavalry in his recent campaign against the Indians."[203] In addition, the committee was charged under Spe-cial Orders No. 23 to "investigate and accumulate facts called for by the government, to fix the responsibility, if any, and to insure justice to all par-ties."[204] It is very important to emphasize those last six words, "to insure justice to all parties."

This commission was directed by Colonel Moonlight, who was then in command of the district which Chivington had commanded. Moonlight selected the three main presiding officers of the committee, Captain Ed Jacobs, Captain George Stilwell, and Lt. Colonel Samuel F. Tappan; all were officers of the 1st Colorado, not one from Chivington's 3rd Colorado Cav-alry. Tappan was selected as the president of the commission, but he was a long-standing enemy of Chivington. He was passed over for promotion to colonel and Chivington was selected instead of him. Not only was Tappan passed over for promotion, but Chivington had him removed from com-mand at Fort Lyon and "banished to Fort Garland in the Sangre Cristo Mountains of southern Colorado."[205]

This obviously caused Chivington great concern, and he attempted to have Tappan dismissed from the presidency. Chivington also asked to have the hearings held in public, but both requests were rejected. Naturally, Tappan refused to step down; and he overruled a majority of Chivington's objections. Tappan had previously condemned the attack. He stated: "A few days after the affair of Sand creek I remarked to Captain Maynard that from what I could hear, the attack on the Indians at Sand Creek was the greatest military blunder of the age, and fatal in its consequences. As to my alleged prejudice and alleged personal enmity, even if true, I should not consider them at all influencing me performing the duties assigned me in this commission..."[206] Obviously, with Tappan in charge along with his fellow offic-ers of the 1st Colorado, it was going to be impossible for Chivington to get a fair hearing and receive "justice to all parties."

The commission interviewed a total of 37 witnesses and produced 227 pages of testimony. It began its testimony in Denver, Colorado. The first two major witnesses were Captain Silas Soule and Second Lieutenant Joseph A. Cramer, both of the 1st Colorado Cavalry and both close friends of Major Wynkoop.

Capt. Soule was the first witness. He responded on the 16th of February to the question, "Were the women and children followed while attempting to escape, shot down and scalped, and otherwise mutilated, by any of Colo-nel Chivington's command?" He answered, "They were."[207] It has already been debated that the scalping and mutilation took place after the battle was over, at about five p.m. or sunset, not during the battle. In reference to the question, "Did you see any soldiers in the act of scalping or mutilating Indian children?" Soule responded, "I think not. I saw soldiers with chil-dren's scalps during the day, but did not see them cut them off."[208] "I think not," an interesting comment.

As an example of his false testimony was his answer to the question, "Had the Indians committed any depredations in the vicinity of Fort Lyon, and on the road to Larned, during the three months prior to the 29th of November?" His response was," not to my knowledge."[209] It has already been proven that the Cheyenne and Arapahoe had been carrying out raids throughout the spring, summer, and late fall and had even carried out raids on the 25th and 26th of November. It must also be remembered that a basic Indian strategy was to go out raiding during the fair-weather months but attempt to make peace during the winter. They did this because they knew they were most vulnerable during the winter. The testimony of Capt. Soule was critical of Chivington and supports the testimony of Major Wynkoop. His statement about the Indian depredations can easily been challenged.

The second testimony was that of 2nd Lieutenant Joseph Cramer. His initial testimony dealt with the Camp Weld Council that began on the 28th of September, 1864. This meeting was between the Cheyenne Indian chiefs, Black Kettle, White Antelope, and the Arapahoe Chief Neva. It must be noted that Neva admitted that Arapahoes under Chief Roman Nose had killed and mutilated the Hungate family.[210] Major Wynkoop, Capt. Soule, Lt. Cramer, Governor Evans, Colonel Chivington and several other individuals who represented the military and civilian leaders of the Colorado territory met with the Indians. As stated previously, this conference met with mixed signals, being understood by the Indians who thought they had a supposed peace agreement, at least with Major Wynkoop. Governor Evans, on the other hand, said that he had declined to make peace with them. That was the gist of his first testimony, two days, the 23rd and 24th of February. Cramer was then excused from the committee due to illness.

He was recalled to testify on the 28th of February. Lt. Cramer's testimony continued to support the role of Major Wynkoop as the major peace negotiator with the Indians. In reference to the battle, he was asked, "Did you have any further conversation with officers at Fort Lyon in reference to the contemplated attack on Black Kettle's Camp?" Cramer responded, "I had some conversation with Major Downing, Lt. Maynard, and Colonel Chivington. I stated to them my feelings in regard to the matter, that I believed it to be 'murder,' and stated the obligations that we of Major Wynkoop's command were under to those Indians."[211] Cramer further testified to the fact that an agreement had been made between Major Anthony and Col. Chivington to rescue the white men in the camp before the attack was begun.[212] That would explain the halt that took place before the attack. Cramer also said in reference to those killed at Sand Creek, "I should think two-thirds were women and children." His testimony fully supported Wynkoop and was very critical of Col. Chivington.

On March 20th, 1865, the commission moved from Denver to Fort Lyon and continued taking testimony. The first witness was Major Edward W. Wynkoop, the instigator of the infamous "peace" talks that led to the battle of Sand Creek. Wynkoop explained, in detail, the convoluted peace negotiations he had started on his own. Beginning with his first contacts made with the Indians on the 4th of September, through the Smoky Hill meeting, the Camp Weld Council, and ending with his being relieved from command at Fort Lyon. He stated that the Indian chiefs wanted to make peace and were friendly, and they were willing to follow his instructions. He had organized a separate peace council, the Camp Weld Council, and brought the chiefs into Denver to discuss peace negotiations with Gover-nor Evans.

Evans was not at all pleased with Wynkoop's actions. Governor Evans and higher headquarters had not given him any instructions to initiate or carry on any such negotiations. That was why he had been removed from command at Fort Lyon. Wynkoop made his removal as commander from Fort Lyon sound like a normal rotation of officers from one command to another. The truth was that he was purposely removed from command for acting on his own and disobeying orders. Wynkoop stated: "On the 5th day of November, 1864, Major Scott J. Anthony, First Cavalry of Colorado, relieved me from the command of Fort Lyon, in pursuance of an order from district headquarters..."[213] This statement was purposely innocuous and did not accurately reflect the seriousness of the charges brought against him. He completely left out the fact that he did not communicate or get permission from Gov. Evans, Maj. General Blunt or General Curtis, his commanding officers, who had "relieved" him of command.

In reference to the depredations of Indian raids taking place, Wynkoop was either completely uninformed or a downright liar. Wynkoop's response to the question of how long did they continue to commit depredations on the road was, "Up to within a couple of weeks of the 10th of September, 1864, the date of my consultation on the Smoky Hill. I heard of no depre-dations being committed between the 10th of September and the 29th of November, 1864, the date of Chivington's massacre at Sand Creek."[214] The only problem with this statement is that it is completely false. Several skir-mishes took place between Maj. General Blunt and the Cheyenne and Ara-pahoe Indians near Walnut Creek between the 22nd and 25th of September. Between the 10th of September and the 26th of November, 1864, there were 14 individual Indian raids and battles with the soldiers. There were six raids in November, November 9th, 16th, 17th, 19th, 25th, and November 26th; the last attack only three days before the battle. Wynkoop was relieved from command on the 5th of November. He left Fort Lyon on the 26th of November, 1864, the same date as the last Indian attack; three days before the Sand Creek battle.[215]

The fourth individual examined was James D. Cannon, 1st Lieutenant of the First Infantry, New Mexico Volunteers. He testified that the Indians who fought Colonel Chivington's command were "scalped and mutilated in various ways." He also said that the scalping and mutilation was done throughout the entire fight as soon as the battle began.[216] This testimony is at odds with that which states that most of the mutilations took place after finding the white scalps in the Indian village. He also stated: "I heard one man say that he had cut a squaw's heart out, and he had it stuck up on a stick."[217] Cannon also reported that "...Major Anthony adopted the same policy in regard to the Indians as Major Wynkoop had."[218] This is obviously a lie in that it has already been proven that Major Anthony, before the battle, had wanted to attack the Indians and fully supported Chivington's position about fighting them.

We shall now investigate one of the unusual circumstances that took place after the committee finished its deliberations. It is one that makes the investigation of the Sand Creek battle even more fascinating. It has to do with the killing of Capt. Soule and Lt. Cannon. They were among the first witnesses called to testify against Col. Chivington. Later on after their testimony, they were both killed and charges of "assassination" were made against the supporters of Chivington. The hearings of the court of military inquiry had been held behind closed doors, and the public citizens of Denver were not allowed to attend the commission hearings. Hearings behind closed doors mean one thing, questionable; they have something to hide. However, word got around that Soule had testified against Chivington; and some of the citizens of Denver supposedly exhibited open hostility towards Capt. Soule and others. Soule had reported that he had seen women and children scalped and mutilated while escaping the battle. In the interim, after the committee had closed its hearings, Soule had been promoted to Provost Marshal of Denver. A Provost Marshal is a "military officer in charge of military police and thus responsible for military discipline in a large camp, area or city."[219] Dare I suggest that his promotion might have had something to do with his testimony and friendship with Lt. Colonel Tappan and Major Wynkoop. They were both promoted after the hearings.

The story becomes intriguing when Capt. Soule took a wife. He mar-ried a woman named Theresa Coberly on the 1st of April, 1865. The only problem was that he was already married to another woman, one named Emma S. Bright. They had gotten married in Central City, Colorado, on November 28th, 1863. His first wife stated in an affidavit that she "lived and cohabited as man and wife up to the time she left Denver City, Colo. April 3rd 1865" to return to Iowa. Soule was a newly wedded, happy man. "He already hitched up to a second wife three days before the first one left town."[220] His good fortune took a turn for the worse on the 23rd of April when he was conducting his duties as provost marshal. He responded to gunshots in the street and confronted two drunken individuals, one Charles Squiers, and another man named Morrow. Shots were exchanged and Soule was killed.[221] It seems there had been previous hard feelings between Soule and Squiers. Squiers was arrested but escaped to New Mexico. Some indi-viduals suggested that Soule had been purposely "assassinated" for his role in the hearings. One Colorado newspaper, the *Black Hawk Journal,* made allegations that, "Soule was killed so that he wouldn't testify, but retracted when it learned that he had already testified."[222] The so-called newsmen at the *Black Hawk Journal* were not too swift.

Another bizarre occurrence took place in conjunction with the death of Soule. It was the puzzling death of Lieutenant Cannon of the New Mexico Volunteers. He was found dead in his room at a hotel in Denver on the 14th of July, 1865. Cannon had also provided damaging testimony against Colonel Chivington. It seems that someone in New Mexico recog-nized Squiers and Cannon arrested him. Cannon returned with Squiers to Denver but, "On July 14, Lieutenant Cannon was found mysteriously dead in his room at the Tremont House. It was suspected that that he had been poisoned, though no proof of this was ever established."[223] Squiers escaped and headed out west to California, never to be heard of again. Allegations were immediately made that the same individuals that had killed Soule had also killed Cannon. In reference to Cannon's death, the *Rocky Mountain News* reported that, "Cannon had been gambling and drinking heavily, plus he was a morphine user."[224] The doctors could not agree on the cause of death, so they said that he had died of "congestion of the brain."[225] What an interesting cause of death. This is the kind of complicated intrigue that makes history truly fascinating.

One must examine the testimony of the military court of inquiry led by Lt. Colonel Tappan. When one reviews the questioning of the anti-Chiv-ington witnesses before the military commission, one can see how these testimonies supported the brutal claims of scalping and mutilation of the Indians, including women and children. And this is just a sampling of the 37 individuals who testified before the committee. But as previously stated, one must always look at the motivations of those presenting evidence.

The testimony for the defenders of the battle at Sand Creek can be found in *The Sand Creek Massacre Report of the Secretary of War,* Sections 4 and 5. I will only be summarizing the testimony of the primary defenders of Col. Chivington, Colonel Shoup, Capt. Cree, Sergeant Decatur and Capt. Talbot. The interesting thing about comparing the two sets of testimonies, the "massacre" group versus the "battle" group, is the glaring lack of ques-tions asked of the defenders about the murder and mutilation of the Indian women and children. Some of the questions posed are downright stupid and ask about the number of horses in a command and who provided the forage for them; how many horses were provided by the quarter master and how much corn was provided. What this has to do with the investigation is beyond imagination. Many of the questions were of this nature; but then again, it was a "military" investigation!!

The first defender of Chivington is Colonel George L. Shoup, 3rd Colo-rado Cavalry, an eyewitness to the attack. He testified that he saw about three hundred Indians killed and, of that three hundred, there were some women and children. Based upon previous testimony, his estimation of Indians killed is incorrect; most sources suggest about 125. In reference to the question about seeing any scalping or mutilation being done by men from his command, he responded, "I saw one or two men who were in the act of scalping, but I am not positive."[226] One or two men in his command scalping, but no mention of mutilation. That doesn't sound like the blood thirsty soldiers previously identified.

In reference to a question about the comments of Major Colley (Samuel Colley-Indian Agent, who was not at the battle) about the disposition and policy that should be taken in reference to the Indians in the camp, Shoup responded: "I had an interview with Major Colley on the evening of the 28th November, in which he stated to me that these Indians had violated their treaty; that there were a few Indians that he would not like to see punished, but as long as they affiliated with the hostiles we could not discriminate; that no treaty could be made that would be lasting till they were all severely chastised..."[227] That is a contradiction to Colley's previous testimony. Samuel Colley was one of the main witnesses against Chivington.

The next pertinent witness was Theodore G. Cree, former Captain of the Third Colorado Cavalry. Cree testified in reference to a conversation he had with Lt. Cramer in regards to Colonel Chivington. Cree said: "I recollect of him saying (Cramer) that all Colonel Chivington was work-ing for was a brigadier general's commission, and that he did not care how many lives he lost in getting it so he got it; and that we (meaning himself and I don't know who else) were going to crush him if we could. He said he thought they could make a massacre out of the Sand Creek affair and crush him."[228] It seems obvious from his statement that the primary moti-vation of Cramer was to humiliate Chivington and prevent him from being promoted by falsifying charges about the attack at Sand Creek. This is a clear example of not having a *Voir Dire*, the Latin term meaning "to tell the truth." It is a legal term which describes the "process by which prospective jurors are questioned about their backgrounds and potential biases before being chosen to sit on a jury."[229] This commission's witnesses could have never withstood a *Voir Dire*. There was absolutely no attempt to honestly examine the background motivations and biases of the primary witnesses.

Another witness supporting Chivington was Stephen Decatur, formerly Sergeant of the 3rd Regiment of the Colorado Cavalry. Some of Decatur's testimony has already been discussed, especially those comments about finding scalps of white men, women and children and women's apparel in the village. He went on to say, "I saw one scalp of a white woman…It had been completely taken off; the head had been skinned, taking all the hair; the scalp had been tanned to preserve it; the hair was auburn and hung in ringlets; it was very long hair. There were two holes in the scalp in front, for the purpose of tying it on their heads when they appeared in the scalp dance."[230] This statement readily supports the basic premise that the Indians had carried out heinous mutilations on white women before the attack.

Decatur further stated: "I saw, comparatively speaking, a small number of women killed. They were in the rifle pits." In reference to a question about the controversial rifle pits, "Had the Indians prepared any rifle-pits or any other means of defence…?" He responded, "They must have done it, as there were holes longer and deeper than they could have dug after we attacked them in the morning. That is my honest opinion."[231] It must be noted here that supposedly the Plains Indians were very seldom, if ever, reported using pre-dug rifle pits. This is the basis for the controversy over them existing at the battle of Sand Creek.

The last supporter of Chivington was former Captain Presley Tal-bot of the 3rd Regiment, Colorado Cavalry. He reported that he, "Had several consultations with Major Colley, Indian agent, and John Smith, Indian interpreter; stated that they had considerable sympathy for me [Talbot had been wounded during the battle]…but they would do any-thing to damn Colonel John M. Chivington, or Major Downing…"[232] He further said that John Smith had a bill against the government for the buffalo robes and supplies he lost at the battle and "that he would go to Washington city and present the same, and that he had friends who would help him get it. Smith and Colley both told me they were equally interested in the trade with the Indians. "[233] This testimony further rein-forces the fact that Colley and Smith's interest in the battle was for the fraudulent bill they had made. The simple fact is that they wanted to continue their lucrative, corrupt trading practices with the Indians. In many cases, they were selling the Indians the supplies they were supposed to get for free.

Chivington then asked the following question of Talbot, "Did you hear Major Colley, Indian agent, and John Smith, Indian interpreter, say that they would swear to anything to ruin Colonel Chivington?" And to the question, "State any other conversation that you had with Major Colley and John Smith, if you remember any, pertaining to matters connected with Sand Creek." Talbot said that he overheard a conversation between

Smith, Colley and Olmstead "the purport of which was denouncing Colonel Chivington and the Sand Creek fight, addressed to the superintendent of Indian affairs, Washington city. I also heard Smith boastingly in my presence state that the eastern papers would be filled with let-ters from that post, (Fort Lyon,) denouncing the same, and that Colonel Chivington had murdered his boy, and that he would be avenged by using every effort with the department possible."[234] He continued and said, "Colley and Smith stated to me in person that they would go to Washington and represent the Sand Creek battle as nothing more than a massacre; and Smith said that he would realize twenty-five thousand dollars from his losses."[235] This is the most precise presentation of the motivations of Colley and Smith in reference to the battle at Sand Creek. It completely destroys the integrity of their testimony. The testimony of these four individuals clearly offers a different interpretation of the battle at Sand Creek. It fully supports the argument that Colley, Smith, Soule, Cramer, Wynkoop and Cannon were testifying to purposely make the battle into a massacre.

In reviewing the testimony of these witnesses before this committee, and the others, I think it can be reasonably argued that the fight at Sand Creek was not a massacre in any sense of the word. After examining the various negative and self-serving motivations of those testifying against Colonel Chivington, it should become clear that there is significant evidence to support an entirely different interpretation of Sand Creek; it was a battle. The standard interpretation is that the fight at Sand Creek was a "massacre" of innocent Indians. The very fact that the names of two of the committees had changed their titles; *The Joint Committee of the Conduct of the War-1865* became the "Massacre of the Cheyenne Indians." The military inquiry became *"The Sand Creek Massacre Report of the Secretary of War* (MRSW.)"

These very minor changes, sometimes even before testimony had been completed, clearly show the prejudice of both committees to prove the Sand Creek attack to be a "massacre." The fact that Lt. Colonel Tappan, the presiding officer, had personal military grudges against Chivington should cast doubt about the fairness of the hearings. The following fact is most illuminating: "Throughout the course of the inquiry 63 percent of Chiv-ington's objections were over ruled, while, not surprisingly, 93 percent of Tappan's objections were sustained."[236] The fairness of the committee's findings, based on the behavior of Lt. Col. Tappan, must be viewed with an extremely skeptical eye!

Therefore, there will be no doubt that if one accepts the evidence of the anti-Chivington witnesses, we have a "massacre." If, on the other hand, the motivations of these individuals have been successfully challenged and disputed, we clearly have a "battle." The pro-Chivington evidence indicates that the Indians were not peaceful, but clearly hostiles. They had been carrying out depredations, murders and kidnappings for an entire year. They were not under the protection of the govern-ment, only Major Wynkoop had proposed that and he did so without permission. The allegation that Black Kettle flew an American six-by-twelve-foot flag or a white flag over his tepee during the battle has been vigorously challenged, and I believe disproved. The criticism that there was a "hell-bent-for leather" charge through the Indian camp is also disproven; the battle took place from 6:00 a. m. until at least noon. It was also stated that the battle lasted until late afternoon, about 9 hours. The total amount of time taken for the battle refutes the allegation of a fast and furious massacre.

The accusation that Colonel Chivington's soldiers were drunken mis-fits on the night before the battle, by Dee Brown, has thoroughly been disproved by the eye-witness testimonies of Privates Coffin and Howbert. And this testimony has been clearly documented! The estimates, high estimates, of the total Indians killed were 125 and that would leave us with a number of 83 women and children killed. One cannot forget that about 500 Indians escaped from the battle out of an estimated 650 total Indians. How can these warriors be brave! What kind of massacre is that! The charge that two-thirds of those killed were women and children is NOT being questioned; it seems to be the agreed upon percentage. It was customary for two-thirds of the camp to be inhabited by women and children. The fact that women and children were killed is also NOT in dispute. Some were killed because they participated in the battle; and as stated previously by one of the eye-witnesses, "it was utterly impossible... to discern between the sexes, on account of their similarity of dress."[237]

In addition, the Cheyenne are one of the few tribes that have women war-riors. Both of these factors help explain the number of women and children killed. The charge that mutilations took place is NOT refuted; they obviously did, especially of the male warriors. The case of White Antelope is one repulsive example of that truth! The evidence provided by both Privates Coffin and Howbert support the charge of mutilations. And one renowned expert on the subject, Gregory Michno, also supports that charge: "When the fighting was over and the soldiers returned to the camp, there occurred some of the ghoulish deeds that made the battle infamous. A number of soldiers stopped to scalp and mutilate the dead."[238] While one cannot make excuses for these mutilations, one must recall that they took place after finding numerous scalps of white women and children in the camp. And one must also not forget the impact of the horrible Hungate mutilations. The acceptance of the limited pro-Chivington evidence, in my opinion, transforms the massacre into a jus-tifiable battle, not an unprovoked attack on "innocent" Indians.

We will find, when we investigate the battle of Wounded Knee in 1890, very similar circumstances to Sand Creek. A very important item not discussed in reference to Sand Creek is the impact of battlefield gun smoke on the Indian casualties. In the battle of Wounded Knee, the battlefield smoke played a very decisive role in increasing the numbers of Indian and soldier casualties and smoke probably played the same role at Sand Creek.[239]

There can be no doubt, in my opinion, that the Battle of Sand Creek was a vengeance motivated surprise attack made during the winter. The winter was the only time the white soldiers and volunteers could engage the Indians on terms favorable to them. The evidence that white soldiers and volunteers had mutilated some of the Indians is also true. The only question the evidence cannot answer is, how extensive was the mutilation of the Indian women and children? To that question, the evidence has yet to yield a satisfactory answer.

Today, the same controversies continue over the attack and the number of Indians killed. On the 7th of November, 2000, a Public Law was passed, Number 106-465, in order to "recognize the national significance of the massacres in American history, and its ongoing significance to the Cheyenne and Arapahoe people and the descendants of the massacre victims."[240] There is still a heated debate about the battle. When I visited Sand Creek in the summer of June, 2016, I asked a Park Ranger why there was not a lot of information on the Hungate murders and rape on the plaques around the park site? He said there was not any specific data identifying the tribe that committed this atrocity. He is completely wrong! Historian Gregory Michno identified that tribe as the Arapahoe. So we do have positive iden-tification of which tribe hideously butchered the family and raped Mrs. Hungate. One of the Arapahoe chiefs, Neva, was asked the question, "Who committed the murder of the Hungate family on Running Creek?" Neva answered, "The Arapahoe; a party of the northern band were passing north, it was Medicine Man or Roman Nose and three others."[241]

It has been my personal experience, after my many visits to National Parks and Battlefields, that many of the Park Rangers have a definite bias towards the Indians. I found this to be especially true of the rangers at Sand Creek, the Washita, and the Little Big Horn. Upon starting a conversa-tion with them about a specific battle, they readily noticed my different interpretation and became very defensive about the Indian side of the bat-tle. It is interesting to note that both the renowned Robert M. Utley and Jerome A. Greene have been associated with the National Park Service. In my opinion, both men are excellent writers. Mr. Utley was the Chief His-torian of the National Park Service, and Mr. Greene retired as a Research Historian for the National Park Service. Mr. Utley, in reference to Sand Creek, made the following statement: "In November 1864 Colorado militia under Colonel John M. Chivington had brutally massacred Black Kettle's band of Southern Cheyenne."[242] Greene readily reinforced the pro-Indian bias by stating, "a mounted U.S. volunteer force charged down on a peaceful Southern Cheyenne and Arapaho village in the cold dawn of November 29, 1864, unmercifully killing many of its inhabitants."[243] Clearly, the extensive evidence provided above shows that the politically correct biases of yester-day still continue to shape the contentious arguments of today!

Endnotes for Chapter 4

[1] Elliott West, *The Contested Plains: Indians, Goldseekers, and the Rush to Colorado,* (Lawrence: University Press of Kansas, 1998), 299-300. Hereafter cited as West.

[2] S.C. Gwynne, *Empire of the Summer Moon*, (New York: Scribner, 2010), p.220-221. Hereafter cited as Gwynne. James Donovan, *A Terrible Glory: Custer and the Little Big Horn—the Last Great Battle of the American West*, (New York: Little, Brown and Company, 2008), 23-24. Hereafter cited as Donovan.

[3] West, 288.

[4] Gregory F. Michno, *Battle at Sand Creek: The Military Perspective*. (El Segundo: Upton and Sons Publishers, 2004), 117. Hereafter cited as Michno-*MP*.

[5] Duane Schultz, *Month of the Freezing Moon: The Sand Creek Massacre, November 1864*, (New York: St. Martin's Press, 1990), 80. Hereafter cited as Schultz-*Freezing Moon*.

[6] Michno-*MP*, 116. Stan Hoig, *The Sand Creek Massacre*, (Norman: University of Oklahoma Press, 1974), 59. Hereafter cited as Hoig-*SC*. West, 290.

[7] Michno-*MP*, 117.

[8] Greg F. Michno, *The Three Battles of Sand Creek: In Blood, in Court, and as the End of History,* (El Dorado Hills: Savas Beatie LLC, 2017) 17-18. Hereafter cited as Michno-*Three Battles*. Jeff Broome, "Shedding New Light on the 1864 Hungate Family Massacre," *Wild West*, June 2006., 52. Hereafter cited as Broome.

[9] Michno-*MP*, 133. fn.46. Hyde, *Bent*, 139.

[10] Schultz-*Freezing Moon*. 80-81. Michno-*MP*, 118. Michno-*Three Battles*, 17-18. West, 290-291.

[11] Hoig-*SC,* 59.

[12] Ibid. 206. Thomas Goodrich, *Scalp Dance*, (Mechanicsburg: Stackpole Books, 1997) 3. Hereafter cited as Goodrich. Michno-*Three Battles*, 62. Hoig, 147.

[13] Bill Yenne, *Indian Wars: The Campaign for the American West*, (Yardely: Westholme Publishing, 2008), 104. Hereafter cited as Yenne.

[14] *Sand Creek Massacre Timeline-Summer 1864*. 2-3 Hereafter cited as *Timeline-Sum-mer, 1864, www.kclonewolf.com/History/SandCreek/sctime-04-1864.*

[15] Yenne, 104-105.

[16] *Sand Creek* Massacre, *Timeline-Summer,1864* page 3 of 4.

[17] George Bird Grinnell, *Bent's Old Fort and Its Builders*, (Kansas State Historical Collections, vol. 15, 1923), 5. Hereafter cited as *Grinnell-Bent*'s Old Fort. http://hdl.handle.net/2027/njp.32101107982 5426 (accessed October 16, 2015).

[18] Halaas & Masich, 264.

[19] David Fridtjof Halaas and Andrew E. Masich, *Halfbreed: The Remarkable True Story of George Bent*, (Perseus Books Group: De Capo Press, 2004), 132-133. Hereafter cited Halaas & Masich. David Lavender, *Bent's Fort*, (Garden City: Doubleday and Company, Inc., 1954), 356. Hereafter cited as Lavender. Berthrong, 207. Schultz, 95.

[20] Halaas & Masich, 106.

[21] *Sand Creek Massacre, Timeline-Winter 1864*, pages 1 and 2 of 3.

[22] Michno-*MP,* 151. J.P. Dunn, 410.

[23] Schultz-*Freezing Moon*, 86.

[24] J.P. Dunn, 410. Berthrong, 202-203.

[25] Michno-*Three Battles*, 19.

[26] Schultz-*Freezing Moon*, 86.

[27] George Bird Grinnell, *The Fighting Cheyenne*, (Norman: University of Oklahoma Press, 1955), 144. Hereafter cited as Grinnell-*Fighting.*

[28] Michno-*MP*, 164.

[29] Ibid. 165. Schultz-*Freezing Moon*, 111. Schultz-*Coming Through Fire*, (Chiving-ton), 91. Michno-*Three Battles*, 33-34.

[30] Michno-*MP,* 155-56

[31] J.P. Dunn, 420.

[32] Michno-*MP*, 167.

[33] J.P. Dunn, 412.

[34] Michno-*MP*, 189.

[35] Irving Howbert, *The Indians of the Pike's Peak Region*, (New York: The Knickerbocker Press, 1914) 110. Original source was http://archive.org/stream/indianspikespea00unkngoog. Hereafter cited as Howbert. (accessed November 5, 2016).

[36] J.P. Dunn, 431.

[37] Michno-*MP*, 210-211. Schultz-*Freezing Moon*, 134. Morse H. Coffin, T*he Battle of Sand Creek*, ed. Alan W. Farley, (Waco: W. M. Morrison-Publisher, 1965), 35 fn.25. Hereafter cited as Coffin. William R. Dunn, *I Stand by Sand Creek*, Fort Collins: The Old Army Press, 1985, 147. Hereafter cited as W.R. Dunn.

[38] Michno-*MP*, 210-211. Coffin, 35.

[39] Hoig-*SC*, 190

[40] Grinnell-*Fighting,* 145.

[41] Halaas & Masich, 141.

[42] Michno-*MP*, 210.

[43] Ibid.

[44] Michno-*MP,* 249.

[45] Halaas & Masich, 82. Hyde, 110-111.

[46] George Bird Grinnell, *The Cheyenne Indians: War, Ceremonies, and Religion,* Vol-ume II, (Lincoln: University of Nebraska Press, 1972), 48-49. Hereafter cited as Grinnell-*Cheyenne Wars.*

[47] Grinnell- *Fighting, 151.*

[48] Michno-*MP*, 217.

[49] *Joint Special Committee on the Report of the Condition of the Indian Tribes,* (Government Printing Office, Washington, 1867), 96. Hereafter cited as the *JSCRC of Indian Tribes.*

[50] Halaas, 145.

[51] Hoig-*SC,* 183

[52] Ibid.

[53] Ibid., 184.

[54] Coffin, 4.

[55] Ibid., 35-36.

[56] *Report of the Joint Committee on the Conduct of the War, Sand Creek Massacre,* section 1 page 45. www.kclonewolf.com/History/SandCreek/sc-documents/sc Hereafter cited as the RJCCW-*Sand Creek Massacre.* (accessed July 2, 2013).

[57] Michno-*MP*, 258.

[58] Ibid., 210.

[59] Ibid.

[60] Hoig-*SC*, 189.

[61] Ibid., 158.

[62] Grinnell-*Fighting,* 147.

[63] Berthrong, 219.

[64] T.J. Stiles, ed. *In Their Own Words: Warriors and Pioneers,* (New York: The Berkley Publishing Group, 1996), 86. Hereafter cited as Stiles. Berthrong, 219.

[65] Coffin., 31.

[66] Berthrong, 217.

[67] Coffin, 25.

[68] Ibid., 31. Michno-*MP*, 222.

[69] Michno-*MP*, 214.

[70] Coffin, 19. Michno-*MP*, 216.

[71] Grinnell-*Fighting*, 152.

[72] Hoig-SC, 180-189.

[73] Schultz-*Freezing Moon,* 141. Michno-*MP*, 249.

[74] Louis Kraft, *Ned Wynkoop and the Lonely Road from Sand Creek,* (Norman: Uni-versity of Oklahoma Press, 2011), 135-136. Hereafter cited as Kraft. Hoig, 155-156, fn. 12. Michno-*MP*, 249-250.

[75] Hoig-*SC*, 182.

[76] Michno-*MP,* 181.

[77] Berthrong, 217.

[78] Hoig-*SC*, 185.

[79] Michno-*MP,* 207.

[80] Howbert, 103-104.

[81] Michno-*MP,* 223-224.

[82] Ibid., 234.

[83] J.P. Dunn, 398.

[84] Michno-*MP,* 221.

[85] Ibid., 221-222.

[86] W. R. Dunn, 27.

[87] Ibid., 29.

[88] Coffin, 29.

[89] Michno- *Three Battles*, 62.

[90] Grinnell-*Fighting,* 145.

[91] Michno-*MP,* 241. Coffin, 34.

[92] Dee Brown, *Bury My Heart at Wounded Knee: An Indian History of the American West* (New York: Holt, Rinehart & Winston, 1970). 91. Hereafter cited as Brown-*Bury.*

[93] West, 293.

[94] Schultz-*Freezing Moon*, 137.

[95] Brown-*Bury*, 91.

[96] Howbert, 97-98.

[97] Ibid., 115.

[98] Michno-*Three Battles*, 25.

[99] Ibid., 99. Michno-*MP,* 200-201.

[100] Coffin, 17.

[101] Ibid., 18. Michno-*MP*, 200-201.

[102] Howbert, 97.

[103] Hoig-*SC*, 150-151. Schultz-*Freezing Moon*, 135.

[104] Schultz, *Freezing-Moon*, 135. JSCR, 64. Hoig-*SC*, 150. Kraft, 131-132.

[105] Michno-*MP*, 214.

[106] Ibid.

[107] Ibid., 216, fn.50. I highly recommend reading the entire footnote. It gives an excellent explanation of the controversy surrounding White Antelope's death.

[108] Ibid., 215.

[109] Ibid., 214-215.

[110] Hoig-*SC,* 153, fn. 9. Michno-*MP*, 239. Kraft, 146. Schultz-*Freezing Moon*, 135.

[111] Grinnell-*Fighting*, 146. W.R. Dunn, 25.

[112] Coffin,18.

[113] Ibid., 19.

[114] Ibid., 18-19. Hoig-*SC*, 147. Schultz-*Freezing Moon*, 134.

[115] Michno-*MP*, 195-196.

[116] Ibid., 198. Schultz-*Freezing Moon*, 131.

[117] Coffin., 19.

[118] Schultz-*Freezing Moon*, 141. Hoig-*SC*, 155-157, fn.12. Michno-*MP*, 249.

[119] Schultz-*Freezing Moon*, 141. Hoig-*SC*, 156.

[120] Hoig, 156.

[121] RJCCW-*Sand Creek Massacre*, Governor Evans, Section 2, 47. Michno-*MP*, 241. W.R. Dunn, 86-87.

[122] W.R. Dunn, 19.

[123] Howbert, 110. J.P. Dunn, 416. Schultz-*Freezing Moon*, 144.

[124] Howbert, 104. Coffin, 29.

[125] Hoig-*SC*, 177-190.

[126] Ibid., 177-178.

[127] Ibid., 180.

[128] Michno-*MP*, 225.

[129] Ibid., 32.

[130] Hoig-*SC*, 179.

[131] Ibid.

[132] Ibid., 182.

[133] Ibid., 192.

[134] Ibid.

[135] Lavender, 349.

[136] George E. Hyde, *Life of George Bent; Written from his Letters*, ed. Savoie Lottinville (Norman: University of Oklahoma Press, 1968), 151-153. Michno-*MP*, 217. Hoig, 150. It is interesting to note that Hoig cites his reference with a footnote from Grinnell, *The Fighting Cheyenne*, 177-78. When one goes to Grinnell's book the cited information is not there. The pages 177–78 are discussing the Powder River Expedition, 1865. Hoig cites in his bibliography the Grinnell book he used as published in 1956. The book I'm using cites original publication 1915, assigned to the University of Oklahoma Press, 1955, I assumed published in 1956. So, we are both using the same book with dramatically different outcomes. Since I have both books in front of me, I have to conclude that Hoig is incorrect.

[137] Ibid., v.

[138] Hoig-*SC*, 189-190.

[139] Coffin, 18. Michno-*MP*, 217-218. Hyde, 152. Halaas & Masich, 141, state that George Bent said that, "Wind snapped at loose tipi flaps and, occasionally, a dog barked."

[140] Hoig-*SC*, 186.

[141] Ibid., 183.

[142] Ibid., 184.

[143] Ibid.

[144] Ibid., 189.

[145] Ibid., 191.

[146] Michno-*MP*, 239. Hoig-*SC*, fn. 9, 153.

[147] Michno-*MP,* 239.

[148] Ibid.

[149] Ibid., 240.

[150] Coffin, 27, 33. Michno-*MP,* 240.

[151] Howbert, 110.

[152] Ibid., 111.

[153] Coffin, 29.

[154] Michno-*MP*, 117-118. Hoig-*SC*, 59.

[155] J.P. Dunn, 426-427. Michno-*MP*, 279.

[156] RJCCW-*Sand Creek Massacre,* Major Anthony, Section 1, 26.

[157] Howbert, 187. Michno-*MP*, 278.

[158] Gregory F. Michno, *Encyclopedia of Indian Wars: Battles and Skirmishes, 1850-1890,* (Missoula: Mountain Press Publishing Company, 2005), 355. Hereafter cited as Michno-*Encyclopedia.*

[159] J.P. Dunn, 427.

[160] Michno-*MP*, 258.

[161] Hoig-*SC*, 164.

[162] Michno-*MP*, 258

[163] Ibid., 259.

[163] Ibid.

[164] Ibid., 258.

[165] Ibid., 256.

[166] Hoig-*SC,* 164, fn. 2.

[167] Ibid., 164.

[168] Ibid., 169.

[169] Michno-*MP*, 261.

[170] Ibid., 54.

[171] Ibid., 75.

[172] Hoig-*SC*, 165

[173] RJCCW-*Sand Creek Massacre,* Maj. Anthony, Section 1, 16-29; Evans, Sec. 1, 32-43, Chivington, Sec. 2, 101-108.

[174] Howbert, 122.

[175] Michno-*MP*, 262.

[176] RJCCW-*Sand Creek Massacre,* Leavenworth, Section 1, 4.

[177] Ibid, John S. Smith, Section 1, 9.

[178] Ibid, Dexter Colley, Section 1, 14.

[179] Ibid, Maj. Samuel Colley, Section 1, 29.

[180] Ibid, Capt. Samuel Robbins, Section 1, 12.

[181] Ibid U.S. Marshall Hunt, Section 1, 44.

[182] Ibid, Maj. Scott Anthony, Section 1, 27.

[183] Michno-*MP*, 195. W.R. Dunn, 145.

[184] Hoig-*SC*, 141.

[185] Berthrong, 223. Hoig-*SC*, 167, fn., 9.

[186] Michno-*MP, 260.

[187] Hoig-*SC, 167, fn., 9.

[188] Ibid.

[189] RJCCW-*Sand Creek Massacre*, Section 1, page 27.

[190] Coffin, 39.

[191] RJCCW-*Sand Creek Massacre,* iv-v. Hoig-*SC,* 167.

[192] Michno-*MP*, 263.

[193] Coffin, 38.

[194] Howbert, 122.

[195] W.R. Dunn, 138.

[196] Michno-*MP*, 259-260.

[197] Ibid., 238. Halaas & Masich, 62. Hoig-SC, 7, fn. 6.

[198] Halaas & Masich, 317.

[199] Hoig-*SC*, 168-169.

[200] Joint Special Committee Report, 96. Michno-*MP*, 264.

[201] Hoig-*SC*, 169.

[202] Howbert, 114.

[203] Hoig-*SC*, 169.

[204] Michno-*MP*, 270.

[205] Ibid., 74.

[206] *Sand Creek Massacre Report of the Secretary of War*, 8. www.kclonewolf.com/His-tory/SandCreek/sc-documents/sc-. Hereafter cited as *Sand Creek-Massacre, RSW.* Hoig, 170. (accessed June 6, 2013).

[207] *Sand Creek-Massacre, RSW*, 14. Michno-*MP*, 265.

[208] *Sand Creek-Massacre, RSW*, 23.

[209] Ibid., 15.

[210] Michno-*MP*,165.

[211] *Sand Creek-Massacre RSW,* 47.

[212] Ibid., 48.

[213] Ibid., 87. Louis Kraft, *Ned Wynkoop and the Lonely Road from Sand Creek,* (Nor-man: University of Oklahoma Press, 2011), 147. Hereafter cited as Kraft.

[214] Ibid., 88.

[215] *Sand Creek Massacre Timeline*, Fall-pages 2–4. Winter-pages 1 and 2.

[216] *Sand Creek-Massacre, RSW,* 112.

[217] Ibid., 113.

[218] Ibid.

[219] *AHCD*, 4th ed., s. v. "provost marshal."

[220] Michno-*MP*, 267.

[221] Hoig-*SC,* 172.

[222] Michno-*MP,* 268.

[223] Margaret Coel, *Chief Left Hand, Southern Arapaho,* (Norman: University of Okla-homa Press, 1981), 310. Hereafter cited as Coel. Hoig-*SC,* 172.

[224] Michno-*MP*, 268.

[225] Ibid.

[226] *Sand Creek-Massacre, RSW*, 176-177.

[227] Ibid., 178.

[228] Ibid., 190.

[229] *AHCD*, 4th ed., s. v. "Voir dire."

[230] *Sand Creek-Massacre, RSW,* 195.

[231] Ibid. Hoig, 191.

[232] Ibid., 208. Schultz-*Freezing Moon*, 173.

[233] Ibid.

[234] Ibid., 209.

[235] Ibid.

[236] Michno-*MP*, 270.

[237] Howbert, 104.

[238] Michno-*MP*, 239. Grinnell-*Fighting*, 152. Berthrong, 221.

[239] Ibid.

[240] Public Law 105-243. "Sand Creek Massacre National Historic Site of 1998." https://www.congress.gov/105/publ243/PLAWS-105publ243. (accessed August 25, 2016)

[241] J. P. Dune, 412-415. Michno-MP, 165.

[242] Robert M. Utley, *The Lance and the Shield: The Life and Times of Sitting Bull,* (New York: Ballantine Books, 1993), 66. Hereafter cited as Utley-*The Lance.*

[243] Jerome A. Green, *American Carnage: Wounded Knee, 1890*, (Norman: University of Oklahoma Press, 2014), 13.

The brutality of the Indian–white confrontation is vividly illustrated by this photograph of a hunter, Ralph Morrison, who was killed and scalped by Cheyenne near Fort Dodge, Kansas, on 7 December, 1868. The two military men are Lieutenant Philip Reade, of the Third Infantry, and John O. Austin, Chief of Scouts. Incidents like these led to the establishment of Fort Sill and to the appointment of George A. Custer.

Chapter 5

The Fetterman Massacre of 1866

"offered with eighty men to ride through the whole Sioux Nation!" Capt.
William J. Fetterman.

"Great Father sends us presents and wants a new road. But White Chief goes with soldiers, to steal road before Indians say yes or not."
Red Cloud, Oglala Sioux Chief.

"They will not sell their hunting grounds to the white man for a road. They will not give you the road unless you whip them."
Standing Elk, Brule' Sioux Chief.

It was the unsuccessful Treaty of 1866 which was the direct cause of Red Cloud's War which lasted from 1866 to 1868. The failure of these negotia-tions had a devastating impact on Fort Phil Kearney, the Bozeman Trail, Colonel Carrington and Captain William J. Fetterman. Fetterman, who the massacre is named after, is cited for the supposed famous quote he made in reference to the lack of respect he had for the Indians' fighting ability. He stated that "with eighty men I could ride through the entire Sioux nation."[1] Later in the chapter, we will more closely examine the accuracy and validity of this quotation.

We are investigating the Fetterman battle because examples of Indian butchery were often found in the aftermath of battles between the Indians and the U.S. Army. One of the most brutal was the results of the battle of Fort Phil Kearney, also known as the "Fetterman Massacre," which took place on December 21st, 1866. Fort Kearney was built to protect the travel-ers, settlers, and gold seekers on the Bozeman Trail heading for Virginia City, Montana.

The paramount motivation for the founding of Fort Phil Kearney and the other forts on the Bozeman Trail, Fort Reno and Fort C. F. Smith, came about due to the gold discoveries in Montana and Idaho in 1863. It became necessary, in 1865-1866, to protect the newly established road that led from Fort Laramie to the gold fields of Montana, especially Virginia City. With the ending of the Civil War, the nation had accumulated an enormous amount of debt. These gold fields were seen as a primary way to reduce this debt; this new trail had to be protected. The Bozeman Trail was named after John Bozeman who was an unsuccessful miner from the gold fields of Colorado. Bozeman and his partner, John Jacobs, had discovered a trail that extended from Bannack, Montana, southeast along the eastern side of the Big Horn Mountains, through the Powder River country along the Oregon Trail to Fort Laramie in Wyoming.

The situation at Fort Phil Kearney, which is located in north-central Wyoming, was a classic confrontation between the U.S. Army and the Sioux Indians. The fort was built along with two other forts, Fort Reno and Fort C.F. Smith, to protect the Bozeman Trail. Fort Phil Kearney was situated right on the Bozeman Trail, approximately 200 miles northwest of Fort Laramie. It was located between the Big Horn Mountains and the Powder River in order to control the important valleys that were so necessary to traveling and transportation into and out of the Montana gold fields dis-covered in 1863. One must also remember the tremendous impact of the California gold rush of 1849 and the Colorado gold rush of 1859. All of these gold finds generated additional traffic of settlers and gold seekers on the Oregon, California and Bozeman Trails.

As stated earlier, government agents at Fort Laramie in the early part of 1866 had begun negotiating another treaty with the Sioux and Northern Cheyenne Indians. This treaty again raised the issue of safe travel and the building of forts along the Bozeman Trail. Two of the Sioux chiefs, members of the Brule' tribe, Spotted Tail and Standing Elk, agreed to the treaty and remained friendly. However, there were several Indian chiefs who vehe-mently opposed the treaty, especially Chief Red Cloud, an Oglala Sioux. At the very time the negotiations were going on, Colonel Carrington and his troops unfortunately arrived a few miles from Fort Laramie. Red Cloud resented the presence of these new troops. During the negotiations, he stood up and said, "Great Father sends us presents and wants new road. But White Chief goes with soldiers, to steal road before Indians says yes or no."[2] Red Cloud vigorously disagreed and bolted from the negotiations and immediately went on the warpath against the idea of building any forts on the Bozeman Trail.

In addition to the abrupt departure of Red Cloud, Colonel Carrington discovered a major problem with the supplies he was supposed to be issued at Fort Laramie. He had expected to get 100,000 rounds of ammunition but was begrudgingly issued only 1,000 rounds. He had also expected to obtain fresh horses, but he was told that none were available. When he had arrived at Fort Laramie, he had 700 soldiers of which 500 were raw recruits; they were untrained and infantry men, not cavalry, which would have better served his mission. "They were armed for the most part with old-fashioned muzzle-loading Springfield muskets, though the 35 members of the band had Spencer breech-loading carbines."[3] What an utterly bizarre idea; arm the band with the best rifles of the entire command. Carrington and his troops prepared to travel up the Bozeman Trail. He found himself very disil-lusioned with his circumstances.

> The only significant acquisition for his expedition were twenty-six wagons loaded with provisions. Mules were available, but the drivers would have to be furnished from his command, removing half a company of men from combat readiness in case of sudden attack enroute. A hasty inspection of the boxes and barrels also revealed that much of the food was inedible. The pilot bread, or hard tack, was so stale it had turned dark, and was so hard it could not be bitten, could scarcely be broken with a metal tool. 'The flour drawn at Laramie,' said Carrington, 'was musty, caked and very poor.' And nowhere on the post could be found utensils for baking it.[4]

Carrington could have only been apprehensive with the composition of his command. He was tasked to build a series of forts, three on the Bozeman Trail in hostile territory, and he was under-manned. His troops were primarily raw recruits. After staffing the other two forts, he was left with approximately 500 soldiers, 150 civilian contractors, and a number of women and children at the fort. He was equipped with outdated rifles, and his ammunition was dramatically inadequate. He had not acquired the number of fresh horses he had wanted, and his food supplies were stale. Obviously, he was not prepared to wage any kind of sustained conflict against the hostile Sioux tribes of Red Cloud. Departing from Fort Laramie, Carrington's command arrived at Fort Reno on the 28th of June. He departed Fort Reno on the 9th of July and arrived at the sight that was to become Fort Phil Kearney on July 13th, 1866. After hazardous construction, the fort was completed in early December.

During the building of the fort, it was necessary to use small detachments of wood cutters to provide the wood necessary and provide firewood. "The incessant labor of chopping, hauling, and hewing wood, with saw-mills full in operation, with ditching and such other varied duty that claimed attention day by day, was the execution of plans and drawings of Colonel Carrington, matured at old Fort Kearney in the early spring."[5]

These wood trains would venture several miles from the fort and were under constant threat of Indian attack. Fort Phil Kearney was constantly under Indian scrutiny with them directly demonstrating in front of the fort. They also attacked any military forces who strayed far from the fort. Based upon the advice of Jim Bridger, Carrington "located Fort Phil Kearney on a strategic plateau at the junction of the Big and Little Pineys. This soon became an impressive log-stockade post, 600 by 800 feet in size, which Inspector-General W. B. Hazen pronounced 'the best he had seen, except-ing one in British, built by the Hudson's Bay Company.'"[6] This statement acknowledged the fort building skills of Col. Carrington. It also reflected on the necessity of completing the fort before the brutal winter of the Rocky Mountains arrived.

Many of the junior officers were critical of Carrington spending so much effort in completing the fort rather than launching aggressive attacks against the Indians.They considered him an unskilled and ineffective officer because he had no combat experience. Having experienced the Rocky Mountains, myself during sub-zero winter weather, it was imperative for them to complete the fort before winter or many of the occupants of the fort would freeze to death. During the construction, there were two temperatures reported, 38 and 42 degrees below zero. The completion of the fort was a life or death situation; a factor that some of the junior officers dismissed.

In reference to the geography surrounding the fort, the area was dominated with prominent hills. The Montana Road, also known as the Boze-man Trail, came in from the southeast. The most important hill was Lodge Trail Ridge which was 2 miles from the fort and another adjacent hill which came to be known as Massacre Hill. This description is important because Lodge Trail Ridge became the nexus of the massacre. The funda-mental question became, why did Capt. Fetterman go beyond Lodge Trail Ridge on the 21st of December and disobey Col. Carrington's direct orders?

In reference to the officer corps, several of the junior officers disliked Colonel Carrington's leadership style and considered him a restrained, cautious leader with whom they disagreed. Some of these junior officers were angered that a desk-sitting officer, one without any fighting experience, had been promoted to fort commander. Three of these disgruntled officers were Lt. Grummond, Capt. Brown and Capt. Fetterman. Fetterman had very lit-tle respect for the Indians' fighting ability. Most of his fighting experience had been obtained in the Civil War, not fighting Indians with their exten-sive use of hit-and-run guerrilla tactics. As previously stated, he is supposed to have made the following two boastful comments:

...offered with eighty men to ride through the whole Sioux Nation.[7]
...a single company of Regulars could whip a thousand Indians, and that a full regiment, officially announced from headquarters to be on the way to reinforce the troops, could whip the entire array of hostile tribes.[8]

One must make note of the fact that there are several sources that attribute the famous quote, "...offered with eighty men to ride through the whole Sioux Nation," to Captain William Judd Fetterman. The only problem with assigning this direct quote to Fetterman is that it is totally false. The only statement that can be directly associated with Fetterman is the one above making reference to "...a single company of Regulars could whip a thousand Indians..." Both Margaret and Frances's books contain this quote, but make no reference to the eighty man quote. None, whatsoever.

The very first use of this direct quote was made in Cyrus Townsend Brady's book, *Indian Fights and Fighters*, published in 1904. Frances Grum-mond Carrington had been previously married to Lt. George W. Grum-mond; he was killed in the massacre. However, her 1910 book includes Col. Carrington's first recorded specific reference to the "eighty men" quote. It is only stated in Colonel Carrington's own personal memorial address, "Delivered at the Monument on Massacre Hill, Sheridan County, Wyo-ming, July 3, 1908." That quote states:

> Fetterman, gallant through the entire Civil War from the time he joined my regiment in 1861, was impatient, and wanted to fight. He said, "I can take eighty men and go to Tongue River." To this boast my Chief Guide, the veteran James Bridger, replied in my presence, "Your men who fought down South are crazy! They don't know anything about fighting Indians."[9]

In reference to the second quote, "a company of regulars could whip a thousand, and a regiment could whip the whole array of hostile tribes," it can be found in both of Carrington's wives' books with minor differences. In Margaret's book, *Absaraka: Home of the Crows*, (1868) it stated:

> Two days after Captain Fetterman arrived, impressed with the opinion, to which he had often given language, that, "a company of regulars could whip a thousand, and a regiment could whip the whole array of hostile tribes," he was permitted to make the experiment of lying in the cottonwood thickets of Big Piney from two o'clock until ten o'clock in the morning, using the hobbled mules for live bait to decoy the aborigines.[10]

In Frances' book, *My Army Life and the Fort Phil Kearney Massacre*, (1910) it stated:

> Brevet Lieutenant Colonel Fetterman, recently arrived from recruiting service, with no antecedent experience on the frontier, expressed the opinion that a "single company of Regulars could whip a thousand Indians, and that a full regiment, officially announced from headquarters to be on the way to reinforce the troops, could whip the entire array of hostile tribes. He was warmly seconded by Captain Brown and Lieutenant Grummond.[11]

Some have suggested that, since the number of soldiers killed was 81, it seems to fulfill Fetterman's supposed famous quote. The major problem with this train of thought is that the empirical evidence supports the quote originating with Cyrus Townsend Brady in 1904 and later with Col. Car-rington in 1908, some 42 years after the battle.

Dee Brown's study, *The Fetterman Massacre*, originally published in 1962 and then republished in 1971, references both quotes and uses the sources of Margaret Carrington's book, *Absaraka*, (1868) and Hebard and Brinin-stool's book, *The Bozeman Trail*, (1921).[12] The problem with Hebard and Brininstool's book is, although they reference the two famous quotes, they offer no footnote citations to substantiate the validity of their statements. There is no end to the academic speculation as to whether or not these two quotes can be utilized to condemn Fetterman for supposedly violating Car-rington's direct orders to not pursue the Indians beyond Lodge Trail Ridge.

The best explanation of the evolution of the importance of the quote "eighty men," is, in my opinion, presented by John H. Monnett in his book, *Where A Hundred Soldiers were Killed: The Struggle for the Powder River Coun-try in 1866 and the Making of the Fetterman Myth*, (2008). He also wrote an article published in Wild West Magazine, December 2010, *The Falsehoods of Fetterman's Fight*.[13] Monnett begins the evolutionary trail of the quote to Cyrus Townsend Brady's book, *Indian Fights and Fighters*, originally pub-lished in 1904. He stated that Brady conducted a thorough interview with Col. Carrington in 1903 before he published his book. Monnett offers the following explanation for the origination of the "eighty men" quote and says, "the statement is surely a literary contrivance of Brady's with Car-rington's approval...But it was Brady who penned the legacy, setting up a historical irony that has been profusely repeated since 1904."[14] The only problem with that statement is that Monnett seems to be guessing about Brady's "literary contrivance," and he offers no way to prove his statement other than his calculated conjecture.

The reality of the quote is that it can only be attributed to Brady or Carrington. It could have come out of the interview that Brady had with Carrington in 1903 and published in 1904, as Monnett states. Carrington's only mention of the quote is made by him in his memorial speech in 1908. Brady's book went on to become a classic work of the American West and has influenced decades of future writers and historians. The book has since been republished in paperback in 1971, and in it Brady leads into the quote by describing the lack of respect that most of the white soldiers had for the Indians. He said:

> They had the popular idea that one white man, especially if he were a soldier, was good for a dozen Indians; and although fifteen hundred lodges of Indians were known to be encamped on the Powder River, and there were probably between five and six thousand braves in the vicinity, they were constantly suggesting expeditions of all sorts with their scanty force. Some of them, including Fetterman and Brown, 'offered with eighty men to ride through the whole Sioux Nation!'" While the mettle of the Sioux Nation had not yet been fairly tried by these men, Carrington was wise enough to perceive that such folly meant inevitable destruction, and his consent was sternly refused.
>
> The total force available at the fort, including prisoners, teamsters, citizens and employees, was about three hundred and fifty—barely enough to hold the fort, should the Indians make an attack upon it.[15]

The following are background facts of the incident that involved the actions of Captain William J. Fetterman. He was a newly arrived officer serving at Fort Phil Kearney in December of 1866 under the command of Colonel Henry B. Carrington. The fort was under constant Indian observa-tion and attacks since its completion, especially the wood train expeditions that continually left the fort for lumber. To get some idea of the impact of the Indians' destructive attacks on the fort between the 26th of July and the 21st of December, Margaret Carrington, the Colonel's first wife, stated that the Indians during this time period, had:

> ...killed ninety-one enlisted men and five officers of our army, and killed fifty-eight citizens and wounded twenty more, and captured and drove away three hundred and six oxen and cows, three hundred and four mules, and one hundred and sixty-one horses. During this time, they appeared in front of Fort Phil Kearney, making hostile demonstrations and committing hostile acts, fifty-one different times, and attacked nearly every train and person that attempted to pass over the Montana Road.[16]

This level of hostile activity clearly shows that Fort Phil Kearney was in a very tenuous position and under constant harassment and attack. Consider-ing the hostile environment, one would have expected the officers to use caution when leaving the fort.

In addition to Col. Carrington's concerns for his officers and soldiers, he also had to worry about the safety and well-being of all the civilians including the wives and children who had accompanied their men to this outpost in the West. The following are the orders that Col. Carrington gave, as recalled by Sgt. Fessenden, a member of the band, if the fort was in danger of being overrun:

> The colonel gave orders that as soon as the Indians made the expected attack, the children and women should enter the magazine, and the men should hold the fort as long as possible. When they could hold it no longer, they were to get behind the wagons that surrounded the magazine, and when the colonel saw that all was lost, he would himself blow up the magazine and take the lives of all, rather than allow the Indians to capture any of the inmates alive. [17]

This clearly shows the ingrained horror that the frontier soldiers and their families had about having the fiendish rapists and butchers get their hands on white women and children. Better a merciful death at their own hands rather than the hideous experience of the butchering savages.

As a prelude to the massacre of the 21st, a major attack took place on the 6th of December between the garrison and Indians. In this incident, Colonel Carrington took part along with Capt. Fetterman, Capt. Brown and Lieutenants Wands, Grummond and Bingham. They were all involved in a disorganized attack against decoying Indians. This was Col. Carrington's first combat mission, and he seemed to be confused and disorganized. Lieu-tenants Bingham and Grummond had acted irresponsibly and abandoned their men during the heat of battle to pursue one Indian. Yes, that's right, one Indian. [18]

During this haphazard operation, one group of soldiers broke ranks and began a disorganized retreat, wherein Capt. Brown and Lt. Wands had to threaten these soldiers with their guns and said they would shoot them if they didn't halt. "Bingham had left his confused company of green recruits to ride to his death; Grummond had disobeyed Carrington and almost met the same fate as Bingham." [19] During the battle, Lt. Grummond had an angry confrontation with Colonel Carrington about not supporting a group of surrounded men. "Grummond was infuriated at Carrington for not coming to the rescue of the surrounded men and angrily asked whether the Colonel was a fool or a coward to allow his men to be cut to pieces without offering help."[20] It must be noted here that a Lieutenant angrily criticizing a full "Bird Colonel"(this term is derived from the silver eagles on a full colonel's epaulets) on the field of battle is unheard of in reference to military discipline and chain of command. It is of interest that Car-rington never made mention of the incident in any of his formal reports or testimony.

During the heat of the battle, Col. Carrington had sent a direct, specific written order for Capt. Powell to lead reinforcements to assist the troops in the field. Instead of obeying Carrington's direct order from the Post Commander, Powell sent a junior Lt. to go in his place and remained in his quarters; a highly unusual reaction to an ordered rescue mission. This is of interest because, during the testimony offered after the battle, Capt. Powell is Carrington's most vocal critic. Why didn't he respond to his Com-mander's direct written orders? There seems to be no evidence to explain it! In reference to the conclusion of the battle on the 6th, "not an officer or man in the field that day could take any pride in his accomplishments. Blunders, disobedience of orders, misunderstandings, recklessness, coward-ice, had almost brought disaster to the fort's defenders."[21] Clearly, the officer corps at Fort Phil Kearney lacked the necessary understanding of Indian fighting tactics and had simply relied upon their Civil War experience. A major drawback was also the total lack of fighting experience that Col. Carrington had as Post Commander. His junior officers were accustomed to the traditional, straight line fighting tactics of the Civil War and were absolutely of no use against the highly mobile, hit-andrun guerrilla tactics of the Plains Indians.

Two soldiers were killed in this fight, Lt. Bingham and Sgt. Bowers. As stated, Lt. Bingham's cavalry had run into some difficulties because of his reckless charge; and his men were retreating in a disastrous and unorganized manner. Rather than staying with his men and trying to organize them, Bingham, for some unknown reason, charged ahead leaving his men behind. One of Bingham's troopers suggested that the Lieutenant's horse "ran away with him and he could not restrain it."[22] Bingham's body was found with over fifty arrows shot into him. I will continue to ask the same question throughout this book. How many Indian arrows does it take to kill a single white man? Just another clear-cut example of Indian brutality! There is another sad example of a runaway horse that took place at the battle of the Little Big Horn. One soldier's horse panicked and took him down Medi-cine Trail Coulee, across the Little Big Horn River, right into the middle of the Sioux camp with the same mournful results.

The number of Indians referenced in this battle on December 6th were estimated to be between 200 and 300.[23] This number is important because it serves to prove that Carrington, Fetterman, Grummond and Brown all knew that there were large numbers of Indians in the immediate vicinity of the fort. There could be no excuse not to expect large numbers of Indians on the 19th and 21st of December. This decoy ambush plan was commonly used by the Indians to entice inexperienced soldiers into a dangerous situ-ation. It was very simple; send a few Indians on horseback to confront and bait the soldiers, lead them over a hill or piece of terrain where their line of sight was blocked, and then draw them into a trap with large numbers of Indians waiting on the other side of the hill.[24] Mrs. Frances Grummond Carrington described the Indian tactics as follows:

> At every recollection of the vast numbers that threatened us, it still remains a mystery why, with their superior numbers and better arms, they did not overwhelm and kill every one of us. I know that Indians generally fight under cover and by stealth, and rarely in the open field unless when in great numbers they have decoyed the whites into separate parties, to destroy them in detail. But that does not solve the mystery of their holding back until after the fort was completed, when the troops living in their tents might have been an easy prey.[25]

Frances' closing thought poses just one more problem about this com-plicated historical event. After the encounter on the 6th, Capt. Fetterman stated that he had "learned a lesson, and this Indian war has become a hand-to-hand fight, requiring the utmost caution, and he wants no more such risks."[26] It is quite interesting that he makes such a statement; and then, 15 days later, he is supposed to have recklessly led his men into the same kind of decoy trap. It certainly causes one to doubt that he would learn such a lesson and then so quickly forget it. The tactics used on the 6th set an example for the tactics that Fetterman used on the 21st. On the 6th, Fetterman took his command to relieve the wood train which was west of Sullivant Hills. Col. Carrington took his command almost due north, along the eastern edge of Lodge Trail Ridge to head off the hopefully retreating Indians. Fetterman and Carrington were to meet in a pincher movement and trap the withdrawing Indians between them. This tactic, of crossing Lodge Trail Ridge, seemed to have become the agreed upon strategy to cut off any Indian retreat. As we will see on the 21st, Fetterman does not go west to relieve the wood train, but goes directly north as if he were going to cut off a retreat of the attacking Indians. However, after the battle on

December 6th, Col. Carrington determined that any expedition that went beyond Lodge Trail Ridge would be put in a dangerous situation; he would not let it happen again.

On December 19th, the Indians had again attacked a wood train. Carrington sent Capt. Powell to go the aid of the attacked wood train, and they returned safely to the fort. The instructions that Col. Carrington gave to Capt. Powell were to relieve the train and, emphatically, not to pursue the Indians beyond Lodge Trail Ridge. He stated: "Heed the lessons of the 6th. Do not pursue Indians across Lodge Trail Ridge."[27] Capt. Powell fol-lowed Col. Carrington's orders to the letter and did not let his command pursue the Indians over Lodge Trail Ridge. Lt. Grummond, who was again in charge of the mounted infantry, obeyed orders; there was no ambush massacre on the 19th of December.

It has been suggested that Lt. Grummond had been a reckless officer based upon his past performance in the Civil War and on the 6th of December. During the attack on the 6th, Lt. Grummond had started out with Col. Carrington but foolishly broke away without permission and joined Lt. Bingham in their common pursuit of about thirty Indians off to the east. One source reported that, "...Lieutenants Bingham and Grummond disobeyed orders and pursued Indian decoy parties into an ambush that resulted in the death of Bingham and one non-commissioned officer. Only the stern discipline and timely action taken by Captain Fetterman, who advanced towards the sounds of the guns prevented a larger tragedy on that day."[28] Lt. Grummond ran out of ammunition for his pistol and had to fight his way out with just his saber, barely escaping death. He had also acquired a reputation for irresponsible action during his tour of duty in the Civil War.

> Indeed Grummond's irrational behavior on December 6 was in line with such bizarre actions as he had displayed in combat during the Civil War, especially his near lethal orders issued on the heights of Kennesawe Moun-tain two years previously. That behavior had been just one of the several rash exhibitions that prompted Grummond's court-martial in 1864 along with allegations by his own subordinates that he was unfit for command. The impulse to follow his own irresponsible course with almost suicidal consequences, in both the Civil War and on December 6, the ferocity of his saber combat that ultimately saved his life, and his uncontrolled and insubor-dinate public display of rage at his commander afterward are more suggestive of irrational behavior than anything exhibited that day by Capt. William J. Fetterman.[29]

The battle of Kennesawe Mountain, Georgia, took place on the 27th of July 1864 and was the strategic battle of a month-long bitter conflict that was part of the Atlanta Campaign. The opposing leaders were Confederate Joseph E. Johnson and Union General William Tecumseh Sherman. It involved over 200,000 Confederate and Union soldiers. It was a costly Union victory.[30]

Another important individual is Capt. Frederick H. Brown. Brown was involved in the December 6th battle along with Fetterman, Grummond, Bingham and Wands. He had to threaten to use force against some of the retreating troops of Lt. Bingham, who was killed in the battle. But it seems that Brown did not heed the lessons of that fateful day. After the unevent-ful attack of the 19th, on the evening of the 20th, Fetterman and Brown requested that they be allowed to take a combined force of 50 mounted soldiers and 50 civilians "in an expedition to Tongue River to clear out the Indians. Both men were convinced that if the hostile villages were destroyed, the fort could settle down to a peaceful winter."[31] Carrington sternly refused this request and stated that such a large command would severely weaken the fort's defensive posture and military readiness. Margaret Carrington recalled their request and specifically describes Capt. Brown's behavior towards Indians that night of the 20th, just before the eventful day of the 21st.

> Captain Brown's repeated dashes, especially on the 23rd of September, had inspired him with perfectly reckless daring in pursuit of Indians; and only the night before the massacre he had made a call, with spurs fastened in the button-holes of his coat, leggings wrapped, and two revolvers accessible, declaring by way of explanation, that he was ready by day and night, and must have one scalp before leaving for Laramie, to which he had been ordered. He had inspired Captain Fetterman, who had been but a short time in the country, and already had great contempt for our adversaries, with the same mad determination to chase whenever they could, regardless of numbers...[32]

Frances Carrington's recollections of Capt. Brown are similar to Margaret's, and she stated:

> Captain Frederick Brown, just promoted and about to leave for the East, had been the district and regimental quartermaster in charge of all stock and properties and was always foremost in their protection, so that he asked for "one more chance," as he called it, "to bring in the scalp of Red Cloud himself."[33]

The evidence clearly describes the past behavior of Lt. Grummond and Capt. Brown as irresponsible soldiers when it came to their estimation of the fighting abilities of the Plains Indians.

Cyrus T. Brady, in his famous book, *Indian Fights and Fighters,* (1904, 1971), also shows that Carrington's junior officers, Fetterman, Brown, and Grum-mond, had little regard for the Indians fighting prowess. It was reported that even with five to six thousand Indians in the area, "they were consistently suggesting expeditions of all sorts with their scanty force. Some of them, including Fetterman and Brown, 'offered with eighty men to ride through the whole Sioux Nation!'"[34] Obviously, this is the famous quote; but more importantly, it shows a close relationship between Fetterman and Brown. Brady further stated: "Some of the officers, therefore, covertly sneering at the caution of their commander, were burning for an opportunity to distin-guish themselves on this account, and had practically determined to make or take one at the first chance. Fetterman and Brown, unfortunately, were the chief malcontents."[35] Brown had volunteered to accompany his friends, Fetterman and Grummond, on that infamous day, the 21st of December. These agreeing and consistent descriptions of Capt. Brown and Lt. Grum-mond clearly suggest that they were prone to excitable and reckless behav-ior when in pursuit of Indians. These two inexperienced Indian fighters, although having confronted a large Indian attack on the 6th of December, seemed to have allowed themselves to forget those valuable lessons. The excitement of the chase seems to have over-powered their good judgment.

The following is an examination of the numerical superiority and weap-onry that the Indians had in reference to the Fetterman massacre of Decem-ber 21st, 1866. The term "massacre" is somewhat misleading in reference to this incident. It was really an ambush. Capt. Fetterman, Capt. Brown and Lt. Grummond went in hot pursuit of Indians right into a perfectly planned ambush. It can only be viewed as a massacre when one takes into account the number of Indians, between 1,500 and 2,000, that was estimated by Capt. Ten Eyck.[36] Some have even suggested as many as 3,000. This mas-sive number of Indians ambushed 81 U.S. soldiers under the command of Fetterman and Grummond. If we use the number of Indians as 2,000, the odds were twenty-five to one in favor of the Indians. Another example of the "brave" fighting tactics of the Plains Indians. Never fight unless you have overwhelming numerical superiority over your enemy, or otherwise hit-and-run away. The primary weapon of the Indians was the bow and arrow. They expertly used them to a very deadly affect. These were supplemented with war clubs, lances and a few revolvers.

One source, Dee Brown, states that the Indians used almost 40,000 arrows in the Fetterman ambush. "The last task of all was recovering arrows from the field of battle. Almost forty thousand had been fired, a thousand for each minute of the fighting, and those which had not found a human target or were not blunted or broken were quickly collected and replaced in quivers."[37] Now comes the common-sense question. How did Dee Brown come up with this fantastic number of arrows? But he offers no footnote or endnote to validate this excessive claim. It seems that we are again manufacturing absurd facts to embellish one's interpretation. Forty thousand arrows are alot of arrows. Let us not forget that Dee Brown also made the accusation that Col. Chivington's soldiers were poorly trained and drunk the night before the Sand Creek battle. He also made these statements without any empirical evidence to substantiate that charge. Dee Brown seems to have developed a reputation for historical fabrications!

Considering the number and weaponry of the Indians, we will now also investigate the number and weaponry of the soldiers. Fetterman was first to leave the fort with 50 infantry troops. They were armed with antiquated Springfield muzzle-loading muskets. The Springfield rifle was produced in two variant models; one, the 1861 model and the second, the 1863 model. Both variants used a .58 minnie ball with percussion lock action. By the end of the Civil War, muzzle-loaders were considered obsolete. After Fetterman left the fort, Lt. Grummond led the cavalry relief column which was composed of 27 mounted troops, plus 2 other civilians who also volunteered to go, Isaac Fischer and James Wheatley; that gives us the famous number of 81 men when we add in Fetterman and Grummond.

Grummond's cavalry had just recently been issued the Spencer repeating carbines that had initially been given to the Regimental Band. The Spencer carbine was a .52 caliber, manually operated lever-action repeating rifle. It was loaded through the butt of the rifle. It held a magazine that con-tained seven cartridges. In some cases, it would be issued with the Blakesless cartridge box that could hold between six to thirteen separate magazines. Thank God someone had the intelligence to issue these good weapons to the cavalry. The obvious question becomes, who thought the Regimen-tal Band should initially have the best military weapons? The bureaucratic military mind never ceases to amaze me! Never! The best overall weapons were held by the two civilian volunteers, Fischer and Wheatley, who had Henry Repeating rifles. The Henry was a .44 caliber, lever action, breech-loading rifle which held sixteen rounds in a tube magazine; sixteen rounds without having to reload. That is a substantial amount of firepower in one gun for the time. After the battle, a large number of empty cartridge shells were found around their bodies indicating they had made the Indians pay a steep price for their lives.

The actual historic incident took place beginning with another attack upon a wood train. The wood cutting pinery was about 5 miles from the fort. Carrington had ordered the wood train to leave the fort at about 10:00 a.m. on the 21st. In light of the attacks on the 6th and 19th Carrington sent out a larger escort for the wood train. It consisted of approximately 90 men, a combination of soldiers and civilian teamsters. At around 11:00 a.m., the lookouts on Picket Hill signaled that the wood train was under attack by a substantial number of Indians. This time Captain Fetterman, citing sen-iority over Capt. Powell, requested to lead the infantry to the rescue with Lieutenant Grummond in charge of the cavalry; and he was allowed to do so. [38] Colonel Carrington, based upon the experiences of the 6th and 19th of December, again made his orders very specific. Mrs. Grummond, later to become Col. Carrington's second wife, reported:

> The instructions of Colonel Carrington to Fetterman were distinctly and peremptorily given within my hearing and were repeated on the parade-ground when the line was formed, "Support the wood-train, relieve it and report to me." To my husband was given the order, "Report to Captain Fetterman, implicitly obey orders, and never leave him." Solicitude on my behalf prompted Lieutenant Wands to urge my husband "for his family's sake to be prudent and avoid rash movements, or any pursuit;" and with these orders ringing in their ears they left the gate. Before they were out of hearing Colonel Carrington sprang upon the "banquet" inside the stockade (the sen-try walk), halted the column, and in clear tones, heard by everybody, repeated his orders more minutely, "Under no circumstances must you cross Lodge Trail Ridge;" and the column moved quickly from sight.[39]

Another source that confirmed Fetterman's decision not to follow Car-rington's specific orders is the following. It came from one Alexander Brown, former Sergeant, troop D, 2nd U.S. Cavalry, who was stationed at Fort Kearney at the time of the massacre. Sgt. Brown stated:

> I was standing alongside of Colonel Carrington on that fatal day of Decem-ber 21, 1866, when he told Colonel Fetterman to take the men that were not on duty and go and relieve the wood train, but not to proceed or pursue the Indians over Lodge Trail Ridge. He disobeyed orders and consequently he and his command were wiped out. The following day we brought in the bodies and they were horribly mutilated.This is a true version of that terrible and tragic Fetterman disaster.[40]

241

So here we have another primary source who confirmed Colonel Carrington's direct orders, Sgt. Brown, an eye-witness. The same comments are reported in a respected secondary source, J. Cecil Alter's book, *Jim Bridger* (1925, 1950, 1962) It stated:

> Shortly after Captain Fetterman arrived at Fort Phil Kearny, impressed with his own opinion, to which he had often given language, that "a company of regulars could whip a thousand; and a regiment could whip the whole array of hostile tribes...
>
> In a speech made later, Colonel Carrington quoted Captains Fetterman and Brown: "I can take eighty men and go to the Tongue River through all the Sioux forces." To this boast, my Chief Guide, the veteran James Bridger, replied in my presence: "Your men who fought down South are crazy! They don't know anything about fighting Indians."[41]

An additional source stated that Colonel Carrington had just "issued the same instructions to Capt. Powell two days before and several others at the fort including Surgeon Hines, Lieutenant Wands and Sgt. Alexander Brown, and others at least inferred at a later date that Fetterman had disobeyed Car-rington's order."[42]

It is of interest to note that some sources seem to completely overlook the importance of Lieutenant A. H. Wands' role and testimony in the massa-cre. Wands was a 1st Lieutenant of the 18th U.S. Infantry and 28 years old on the day of the ambush. He was the Regimental Quarter Master and Acting Adjutant on the day of the ambush. He repeated Carrington's orders about not going beyond Lodge Trail Ridge to Lt. Grummond. Here is Lt. A. H. Wands' direct testimony provided in the "Records Relating to Investigations of the Ft. Philip Kearney (or Fetterman) Massacre:

> Colonel Carrington directed me to inform Lieutenant Grummond that his orders were to join Colonel Fetterman's (Capt. Fetterman was a Brevet Lt. Colonel) command, report to and receive all his orders from Colonel Fetterman, and also tell Colonel Fetterman, and to remember himself that this command was to go out and succor or relieve the wood train, bring it back if necessary, or if Colonel Fetterman thought best, take the train to the woods (it being then on its way out,) and bring it back, under no circumstances were they to cross the bluff in pursuit of Indians. I gave those instructions to Lieutenant Grummond, and while the Corporal of the guard was unlocking the gate, I returned to Lieutenant Grummond and repeated them, and asked him if he thoroughly understood them. He replied he did, and would obey them to the letter.

Lieutenant Grummond left the Post with his detachment of cavalry, and had proceeded about two hundred yards, when he was called back by Colo-nel Carrington, who was on the sentinel's platform at the time, and who called out in a loud voice, repeating the same instructions given Lieutenant Grummond by me, and asking him if he understood them. He replied, I do.

Lieutenant Grummond's command was seen to join Colonel Fetter-man, about a mile from the fort. Instead of proceeding to the wood train as ordered, the command crossed Piney Creek to its opposite bank, and proceeded up a long ridge on the opposite side of the creek from the wood train, and about three miles from the crossing, to a point about two miles from where the wood train was corralled. They were then seen to halt on the crest of the ridge, about four miles from the post. There were about forty or fifty Indians riding around the command, firing at them during the march from the crossing of the Creek up the ridges, and the command returning the fire.[43]

We also have a letter written by Dr. Hines to his brother, John, on the 1st of January, 1867, supporting the same issue that they both disobeyed orders. Dr. Hines, who was not a friend of Col. Carrington, wrote: "Instead of obeying orders, these officers (than whom were none better or braver in the service) allowed themselves to be decoyed from the position ordered to be taken and the whole command butchered, (eighty-one officers and men.)"[44] One may, therefore, conclude that there is substantial evidence to defend the argument that Captain Fetterman and Lt. Grummond had both disobeyed Col. Carrington's direct orders. We have the testimony of Francis Grummond (later to be Mrs. H. Carrington), Sgt. Brown, Lieutenant A.H. Wands, and Surgeon Dr. Hines. We have no proof of the famous "eighty men" quote; but we do have four primary sources that all agree that Fetterman, Brown and Grummond disobeyed Col. Carrington's orders about crossing Lodge Trail Ridge. One must keep in mind the fact that Capt. Brown joined Fetterman on his own volition without any permission from Col. Carrington. Clearly, Fetterman and Grummond violated Carrington's two direct orders and headed north around Lodge Trail Ridge.[45] Fetterman supposedly had been baited by the ambush plan and chased a band of Indi-ans, about 50, around the northern slope of Lodge Trail Ridge.

One can only guess as to why Grummond and Fetterman allowed them-selves to be drawn into this predictable trap; there were two previous exam-ples of it on the 6th and 19th of December. Why did they disregard the two previous lessons? We will never know! There are all kinds of speculation and guesswork as to why these men went after the Indians having supposedly learned their lesson. One can only consider the fact that this situation had three of the most disgruntled officers of Carrington's command together, and also Capt. Brown's statement about collecting the scalp of Red Cloud. Brown had just been given orders to rotate out of Fort Phil Kearney and to report to another post. He was supposed to leave Fort Kearney the very next day. Could this trio of officers have coalesced into an ambitious and daring group of soldiers determined to give one of them a last chance to get his desired trophy, an "Indian Scalp." Just another supposition to add to the already long list.

Fetterman and his command left the fort about 11:15 a.m. It took Grummond about fifteen minutes to get his cavalry organized and mounted. He left the fort at 11:30 a.m. Col. Carrington realized that he had not sent a surgeon with Fetterman and ordered Dr. Hines and two orderlies to ride to the wood train and, if they weren't needed there, to proceed to Capt. Fetterman. Dr. Hines had barely left the fort when the lookout on Picket Hill signaled that the wood train was no longer under attack. Now, another controversy develops in that Monnett states Fetterman also saw the lookout's signal and knew that the wood train was no longer in danger. Having seen this signal, Fetterman supposedly decided to go around Lodge Trail Ridge and attempt to cut off the retreating Indians. This reasoning provided Fetterman with a legitimate excuse to pursue the Indians around Lodge Trail Ridge. He was not disobeying orders but responding to the changing conditions of the battlefield. But no other source substantiates this fact; and it is, therefore, impossible to determine whether or not Fetterman saw the signal from Picket Hill. But what is more interesting is to read exactly what Col. Carrington had to say about Fetterman's decision to go around Lodge Trail Ridge. Carrington stated:

> Fetterman's command had been joined by Grummond's just west of the ordinary ferry crossing. It moved in good order. I remarked the fact that he, [Fetterman] had deployed his men as skirmishers, and was evidently moving wisely up the creek and along the southern slope of Lodge Trail Ridge, with good promise of cutting off the Indians as they should withdraw, repulsed at the train, and his position giving him perfect vantage ground to save the train if the Indians pressed the attack. It is true that the usual course was to follow the road directly to the train, but the course adopted was not an error, unless there was then a purpose to disobey orders.[46]

This is truly a startling statement by Carrington because he basically agrees with Fetterman's strategy and movements and offers no criticism of him at all. What is even more interesting is that the above statement was written on the 4th of January, 1867, after the battle had taken place. It was furnished by Carrington to the special Sanborn Commission which met at Fort McPherson, Nebraska, in the spring of 1867. Here is just another contradiction associated with the battle. If Fetterman had made a wise decision, on his own, under the premise of cutting off the retreating Indians and "the course adopted was not an error," then why charge him with disobeying orders? This might be the classic military contrivance; if you attack and win you're a hero; if you attack and lose then you are the scapegoat.

It could have also been an attempt to lessen the disgrace of such a horri-ble defeat; who knows! This document "supposedly" got lost in bureaucratic channels and was never used to support or defend Carrington until it was reported to the Acting Secretary of the Interior on the 5th of April, 1887. This document came to be known as Senate Executive Document No. 33, 50th Congress, 1st session, 1887. That is correct, it had been missing or "purposely" misplaced for about 20 years. On April 5, 1887, the U.S. Senate called the Secretary of the Interior for a copy of Carrington's report made in the spring of 1867; and Sec. Hoke produced the long-missing report. The report was 146 typewritten pages. Hoke explained the missing report, missing for 20 years, by stating: "These papers were found, after long search, among waste rubbish in the basement of the building."[47] We shall deal in depth with this missing report at the end of the chapter. As Shakespeare said in Hamlet, "There is something rotten in the state of Denmark."

At about 12:00 noon, Fetterman led his combined force to the crest of the hill and found himself confronted by decoys riding back and forth entic-ing his command. Lt. Grummond had joined Fetterman and had advanced ahead of the infantry with his cavalry out on the flanks of the command. Brown, on his own initiative, had joined Fetterman and Grummond in their pursuit of the Indians. Capt. Brown "asked for 'one more chance,' as he called it, 'to bring in the scalp of Red Cloud himself.'"[48] A few minutes after noon, Fetterman and his command crossed the ridge of Lodge Trail Ridge and followed the Bozeman Trail heading for the Peno Creek valley. Scattered gunfire could be heard coming from the area beyond the ridge by the personnel at the fort. As Fetterman and Grummond's troops proceeded on to Peno flats, the Indians sprung their trap. The harsh reality, however, was that "two thousand Sioux, Cheyenne and Arapaho, were waiting in concealment in the high grass of the flats and behind the rocky ridges on either side of the trail."[49] For approximately 20 minutes intense gunfire was heard by those at the fort and then the gunfire slowly tapered off. The entire battle taking about 40 minutes was over about 1:00 p.m.

The dead bodies of the two commands, infantry led by Fetterman and the cavalry led by Grummond, were located far beyond Lodge Trail Ridge on the flats of Peno Creek. They had become separated by several hun-dred yards; the cavalry was in front of the infantry. An interesting testimony made by Mitch Boyer, a renowned Indian scout and interpreter, described the location of the advance troops. He stated "… that some of the soldiers were a mile in advance of the others, …the advance soldiers were killed in retreating to the main body…"[50] This testimony, if accurate, places the cavalry quite a distance in front of the infantry. The empirical evidence clearly shows that both commands had gone around Lodge Trail Ridge with Grummond and the cavalry leading the way. Could the cavalry have gone ahead in hot pursuit, and Fetterman and Brown felt compelled by the dangerous military circumstances to provide support and aid to Grum-mond who had recklessly advanced on his own? Could Grummond's horse have nervously bolted and carried him away similar to the circumstances of Lt. Bingham on the 6th of December? We will never know! What can-not be challenged is the fact that Fetterman, Brown and Grummond had gone beyond Lodge Trail Ridge into a classic Indian decoy ambush. Sev-enty-nine soldiers and 2 civilians had been killed at the Fetterman battle; 81 men.

In reference to the number of Indians killed and wounded at the battle, no accurate numbers can be easily discerned. Fetterman's combined com-mand had been annihilated, "But the Indians paid dearly for this quick vic-tory, many more dying among the boulders on the ridge than had lost lives against the infantrymen on the road below."[51]

> Among the Indians were many wounded and dead, although exactly how many will never be known. Estimates of the participants varied from ten to a hundred dead, and from sixty to three hundred wounded. The more reli-able informants believed at least sixty were killed on the field, and of about three hundred wounded probably a hundred had died. Many years later, Red Cloud would recall the names of eleven Oglalas killed in the fighting and several others of the tribe who died later of wounds. White Elk, a Cheyenne, often said that more Indians were killed in the Fetterman fight than in the Custer fight ten years later.[52]

A very interesting comment; but, as you will see, the numbers vary con-siderably based upon the sources that are used. This kind of creative Indian math is used in reference to all the battles fought between the Indians and soldiers, whether it be the Sioux Uprising of 1862, Sand Creek, the Fet-terman battle, the Washita battle, the Little Big Horn or Wounded Knee. I will always present what I believe to be the most accurate figures that the evidence supports or seems most reasonable. In reference to the Fetterman fight, I believe that the number 60 killed and about three hundred wounded are the most reasonable presented. Of these three hundred wounded, prob-ably one hundred ended up dead. Let's do a little comparative analysis and see the differences that each author presents in reference to the number of dead Indians.

1. J. P. Dunn, *Massacre of the Mountains*, (1886). "They [the Indians] concede a loss of four Minneconjous, three Brules, three Ogallalles, one Cheyenne and one Arapaho, killed, and about sixty wounded, of whom several died and many were permanently maimed... This estimate is unquestionably below the reality. There is scarcely a doubt that each of the sixty-five blood spots on the field meant a dead Indian."[53] "But years later the Cheyennes said that the dead warriors, laid out side by side, made two long rows, perhaps fifty or sixty men." Dunn states possibly 65 dead, unknown wounded.

2. Cyrus Townsend Brady, *Indian Fights and Fighters,* (1904). 60 gouts of blood, probably dead, unknown wounded. "The Indian loss was very heavy, but could not exactly be determined."

3. Eli S. Ricker, *Interviews of Tablets 15 and 16.* (1906, 1907). Expanded and republished as *Voices of the American West, Volume 1: The Indian Interviews of Eli S. Ricker, 1903-1919,* (2005). Edited and with an introduction by Richard E. Jensen. American Horse Interview: "The Indians had only 7 killed and 8 wounded." American Horse also stated that he killed Capt. Fetterman with a club and his knife.

4. George B. Grinnell, *The Fighting Cheyennes,* (1915). White Elk inter-view, in reference to the number dead: "The number of Indians was very great. Arapahoes and Cheyennes there were a good many hun-dred, and there were three times as many Sioux."

5. Grace R. Hebard and E. A. Brininstool, *The BozemanTrail,* (1921). 14 dead, unknown wounded. Republished in 1960 as *BozemanTrail,Two Volumes in One*, with Introduction by General Charles King.Volume 1. "One Arapahoe, two Cheyennes and eleven Sioux were killed. 14 dead and unknown number of wounded."

6. James H. Cook, *Fifty Years on the Old Frontier,* (1923), republished in 1980. "Major Ten Eyck wanted me to learn, if possible, the number of Indians killed and wounded by Fetterman's command before they gave up their lives. When I asked Red Cloud for this information, his reply was that few Indians, eleven in all, he thought, were killed outright during the fight, but that a number were wounded, many of them so badly that they died later on in the camps which were

quickly scattered all over the country. Red Cloud also told me that in this fight, his sub-chief, American Horse, killed Colonel Fetterman. American Horse told me the same. 11 killed, many wounded."[54]

7. Paul I. Wellman, *Death on Horseback*, (1934). Cites the exact J. P. Dunn quotations presented above on pages 496 and 500 in which Indians initially admitted 12 killed and 60 wounded. Later Cheyennes admit to at least 50 or 60 dead.

8. Robert B. David, *Finn Burnett, Frontiersman,* (1937). "Red Cloud in later years admitted that the Sioux lost 180 warriors who were killed in that fateful day of the massacre…"[55]

9. Dee Brown, *Fetterman Massacre,* (1962). "Among the Indians were many wounded and dead, although exactly how many will never be known. Estimates of the participants varied from ten to a hun-dred dead, and from sixty to three hundred wounded. The more reli-able informants believed at least sixty were killed on the field, and of about three hundred wounded probably a hundred more died… White Elk, a Cheyenne, often said that more Indians were killed in the Fetterman fight than in the Custer fight ten years later. But whatever the casualties, the victory was not a cheap one for the com-bined tribes of Tongue River."[56] That makes for a possibility of 160 dead and 150 wounded.

10. Robert A. Murray, *Military Posts in the Powder River Country,* (1968). Indian interview between Half Yellow Face and James F. Bradley: "Some Crows who saw the fight and other Crows who later talked to some of the participants made estimates ranging from sixteen to one hundred Indians killed, and some summed it up as one hundred killed or dead of wounds."

11. Dee Brown, *Bury My Heart at Wounded Knee*, (1970). "Casualties were heavy among the Indians, almost 200 hundred dead and wounded. Because of the intense cold, they decided to take the wounded back to the temporary camp, where they could be kept from freezing."

12. Robert Utley, *Frontier Regulars,* (1973). "Estimates of Indian casual-ties range from a mere handful to a hundred killed and wounded."

13. Shannon D. Smith, *Give Me Eighty Men,* (2008). "Meanwhile, the Lakota and their allies celebrated their spectacular victory and also mourned the loss of a great number of their warriors.Years later, Red Cloud told James Cook eleven warriors died at that battle, but many more were wounded so badly that they died in their camps."[57]

14. Stanley Vestal, *Jim Bridger, Mountain Man: A Biography,* (1946, 1970). "Jim heard that Only fourteen or fifteen Sioux had been killed and

three or four Cheyennes." "Yet, of all the officers Bridger had worked with, Carrington had been the most willing to listen to men who knew the country and the cussed Injuns. Jim went around the rest of his days defending the Colonel when anyone blamed him---as many did."

15. John H. Monnett, *Where a Hundred Soldiers Were Killed*, (2008). "They ranged (for killed) anywhere from ten to three hundred. Most of the Indian accounts assert that many warriors died of wounds after they had been returned to their camps on Tongue River." Many of these deaths were attributed to the freezing weather at the time of the battle. In his first book, Monnett goes on to present a chart of "Estimated Claims of Indian Casualties at the Fetterman Fight and Sources." In this chart, he lists 21 Indians killed; and he provides vari-ous estimates given by seven Indians and one U.S. Army soldier, Sgt. Fessenden of the 18th Infantry. Fessenden suggests that 150 Indians were killed in the battle and 150 more died from mortal wounds, for a total killed of 300. Monnett considers this estimate to be hear-say evidence because it was provided by Indian squaws who lived around the fort. Of the seven Indians, White Elk, a Cheyenne, gives the highest estimate of between 52 and 62 killed. The others all gave, in my opinion, ridiculously low total numbers: 10 killed, 14 killed, 14 plus killed, 3 killed, 2 killed and lastly, many killed.[58]

16. John H. Monnett, *Eye Witness to the Fetterman Fight: Indian Views,* (2017). Monnett's latest book presents interviews with eleven dif-ferent Indians organized by tribal affiliation. One Miniconjou, eight Oglala, and four Northern Cheyenne. There is an inconsistency of the number of Indians killed by many of the interviewees.

   a. American Horse stated that "The Indians had 7 killed and 8 wounded."[59]

   b. Mitch Boyer cites, "there were eight Indians killed on the battle ground and fifty wounded and twenty-two of the wounded after-wards died."[60] Giving a total of thirty killed.

   c. George Bent said that fourteen Indians were killed.[61]

   d. Two Moons stated that, "The Cheyenne had two men killed in this fight, the Arapahos one and the Sioux eleven."[62] Giving a total of fourteen.

   e. White Elk reported: "Only two Cheyennes were killed. The Sioux were laid out side-by-side and made two long rows, perhaps fifty or sixty men. (Giving a total of 62). The numbers of Indians were very great. Of Arapahoes and Cheyennes there were a good many hundred, and there were three times as many Sioux. White Elk believes that in the Fetterman fight there were more men than in the Custer fight."63

f. Monnett presents an Appendix A which listed "Claimed Indian Warriors Killed or Mortally Wounded as twenty-three.

g. One U.S. Army dog killed by the Cheyenne. "After all were dead, a dog was seen running away, barking and someone called out: 'All are dead but the dog; let him carry the news to the fort,' but someone else cried out: 'No, do not let even a dog get away;' and a young man shot at it with his arrow and killed it."64 Earlier in the book Monnett offers a contradictory statement made by Fire Thunder which stated: "The only living thing was a dog. We didn't kill the dog because he looked too sweet."65

The evidence presented, in the sixteen books and Monnett's two charts, clearly show the Indian propensity to dramatically report low numbers for their killed in action immediately after the battle. This vast number of estimated killed clearly reinforces Col. W. A. Graham's statement: "Indian accounts contradicted each other to such an extent the I found them irrec-oncilable."66 Another problem with accurately counting Indian dead is that the Indians always attempted to remove all their dead from the battlefield; this further complicates an accurate body count. Determining the number of Indian casualties, especially after an Indian victory, will always remain a historical problem.

An interesting statistic and question comes to us out of the biography of *Finn Burnett, Frontiersman,* written by Robert B. David (1937). Burnett was a civilian contactor who worked at the fort during the massacre. David wrote: "Red Cloud in later years admitted that the Sioux lost 180 warriors who were killed in that fateful day of the massacre, as well as an almost unbe-lievable number of wounded, many of whom died later of their wounds. And, while this battle was terrible in its brutality and needlessness, yet the Sioux loss had been so great that plans for the total destruction of Forts Phil Kearny, Reno, and C.F. Smith were halted by Chief Red Cloud for the time being."67

This statement provides a reasonable explanation to the previously posed question by Margaret Carrington: "Why the Indians didn't attack the Fort after the massacre?" The fort's manpower had been dramatically reduced and the snow fall, which rose as high as the stockade walls, would have made an attack seem like the next logical thing to do. However, if the Indian casualties were as high as David suggests, then this factor would readily explain why there was no follow-up attack on any of the forts. That question is a fundamental one that many of the authors on this subject, including myself, seem to have forgotten to ask! It is amazing how one little piece of information can illuminate a previous problem about the topic.

Crazy Horse was believed to be the Indian chief who led the decoy Indians and had overall command of the Indians at the Fetterman battle. He also plays a major role in the battle of the Rosebud and, of course, the Little Big Horn in 1876. Red Cloud's involvement in this battle is controversial because there are sources that say he was there, including his own interview with famed western historian James A. Cook. In this interview, Red Cloud stated that, "his sub-chief, American Horse, killed Fetterman. American Horse has told me the same. These old Chiefs often talked with me about the details of this fight." [68] The following statement that Capt. Fetterman did not kill himself is that of the Sioux Indian Chief American Horse: "Controversy has arisen as to the exact conditions under which Fetterman and Brown died. Many years after the battle Chief American Horse (Sioux) positively asserted to a competent authority (Captain James H. Cook) that he, personally, killed Captain Fetterman by knocking him off his horse with a war club and stabbing him to death." [69]

However, another famed western historian, George B. Grinnell, reports that, "...it is stated that the Indians were led by Red Cloud, the Ogalala chief, who, however, according to all Indian testimony, was not present..." [70] Dee Brown states that, "Years later in his old age Red Cloud claimed to have directed the fighting, but the testimony of several Indian participants indicates that the Ogalala leader was not present." [71] If we cannot validate the presence of the famed Red Cloud, how can we accept the egotistical testimony of American Horse? As John Monnett reports," ...the reminis-cences of these warriors are filtered through the pens of white ethnolo-gists and chroniclers and latter day Indian descendants who interviewed them..." [72] One of the main factors that we must take into account about these interviews is that many of them were conducted in the 1890's and early 1900's.

Many of these old chiefs were in their late 70's and early 80's; their memories would obviously be questionable. These interviews were made some 25 to 45 years after the battle, and this time factor must be taken into consideration when ascertaining their accuracy. It must also be noted that many of the Indian interviews were notoriously unreliable. They would often tell their white interviewers what they thought they wanted to hear and, in many cases, decreased the number of Indians killed to embellish their own supposed fighting superiority to the white soldiers. In both the Fetterman battle and the Little Big Horn, some Indian participants accused the soldiers of panic and suicide, implying cowardice of the soldiers. Chief American Horse, several decades later in an interview with Eli S. Ricker, personally claimed to have killed Capt. Fetterman and stated that the Indi-ans had causalities of 7 killed and 8 wounded.[73]

The standard interpretation says that Captain Fetterman and Captain Fred Brown were supposedly found together with gunshot wounds to their heads. Bullet holes through the left temples of Captain Fetterman and Cap-tain Brown "from weapons held so close that the powder burned into their faces, showed that these officers had 'saved a shot for themselves,' as they had often said they would do, rather than fall into the hands of the Indians."[74] The double-suicide theory was supported as recorded in the writings of Margaret Carrington. She stated: "Captains Fetterman and Brown were at the point nearest the fort, each with a revolver shot in the left temple, and so scorched with powder as to leave no doubt that they shot each other when hope had fled."[75] Colonel Carrington's testimony stated that, "Fet-terman and Brown had each a revolver shot in the left temple. Brown had always declared he would reserve a shot for himself as a last resort, so I am convinced that these two brave men fell, each by the other's hand rather than undergo the slow torture inflicted upon others."[76] Therefore, based upon the consensus view and the sources cited above, one may conclude that there seems to be general agreement about the double-suicide theory.

There is, however, substantial contradictory evidence that challenges the double-suicide theory. The direct testimony of Dr. Samuel M. Horton, who had served as Chief Medical Officer of the Mountain District, and Post Surgeon of Fort Phil Kearney, did not support the double-suicide theory. In his testimony, he stated:

> Capt. Brown's body showed gashes inside of both thighs, to the bone, from his body to his knees, both ears had been cut off and his body otherwise horribly mutilated and a hole made in his left temple [caused?] by a small pistol ball; the latter most probably caused his death...Col. Fetterman's body showed his thorax to have been cut crosswise with a knife, deep into the viscera; his throat and entire neck were cut to the cervical spine all around. I believe that mutilation caused his death.[77]

If we are to believe Surgeon Dr. Samuel Horton, and there is no reason why we should not, considering his professional training as a physician, another myth of the Fetterman battle falls to more recent research. One may conclude that the pro double-suicide sources, primarily Col. Carrington and Margaret Carrington, made a simple and honest mistake based upon hearing of the temple bullet wound to Capt. Brown, or that they purposely lied. Then the question becomes, why would they lie? I see no advantage to them for conjuring up such a fabrication. It might be that they wanted to embellish Capt. Fetterman's reputation as a brave and heroic sol-dier, who having led his men into a disastrous ambush, died a gallant death with his comrade-in-arms, Capt. Brown. That would certainly make for a more acceptable end to a soldier's life than simply the result of Indian guile and deception.

Col. Carrington, after hearing the gunfire beyond Lodge Trail Ridge, sent an additional relief column led by Dr. Hines, between 12:15 and 12:30 p.m., to the wood train to provide additional support. He stated:

> I was ordered, perhaps an hour after they had left the Fort, by Colonel Car-rington, to go to the wood train. His orderly was to accompany me, and a Mr. Phillips, a citizen, was also to accompany me.
>
> I was afterwards joined by Lieutenant Matson, and a mounted infantry-man, we joining with some employees of the Quarter Master's Department in one or two wagons.
>
> We followed the road toward the wood train, and were satisfied the wood train was safe.
>
> My orders were after being satisfied of the safety of the wood train, to cross to the command of Brevet Lieutenant Col. Fetterman.
>
> Following this road for two miles or more, we then determined to join the command under Colonel Fetterman.
>
> Passing down the side of the defile between Big and Little Piney, we reached the Big Piney. We tried to find a crossing but could not, and were obliged to go lower down the stream to where the road crosses. The firing at this time was very rapid, and the Indians appearing on Lodge Trail, between us and the command, we came to the conclusion that the command was surrounded, and rode into the post for reinforcements. This was done as expeditiously as possible.
>
> Captain Ten Eyck was then sent out, with which command Lieut. Mat-son, myself, and the others who had been out, joined. We crossed the Big Piney, at the regular crossing, on the ice, marched up the road nearly oppo-site the Indian picket left on Lodge Trail ridge, and he descended, joining other Indians there. We then took a position on Lodge Trail ridge, where we received reinforcements and ammunition.
>
> We remained about one hour. The Indians were gradually moving off on horseback. A few remained near the bodies. Captain Ten Eyck, and some of the men fired at them to drive them off. They were from six to nine hundred

yards distant. The Indians were apparently waiting to gather some things. Captain Ten Eyck then advanced his line to those bodies, which were by the road side.[78]

When the relief column from the fort, led by Ten Eyck, finally got to what is now known as "Massacre Ridge," they found the grotesquely mutilated bodies of the 79 U. S. soldiers and two civilians, Isaac Fisher and James S. Wheatley. Carrington reported, on the first day after the battle, what he found on that wind-swept ridge was horrifying. "Naked, frozen hard as stone, all the bodies had been hacked to pieces."[79] Carrington's official report, which was kept from public knowledge by devious members of the War Department or the Interior Department bureaucrats claiming that it was lost, was not released until 20 years after the event in 1887. He described the horrible truth about the butchery and mutilation.

> Eyes torn out and laid on rocks; noses cut off; ears cut off; chins hewn off, teeth chopped out; joints of fingers; brains taken out and placed on rocks with other members of the body; entrails taken out and exposed; hands cut off; feet cut off. Arms taken out from sockets, private parts severed and inde-cently placed on the person. Eyes, ears, mouth, and arms penetrated with spearheads, sticks, and arrows; ribs slashed to separation with knives; skulls severed in every form, from chin to crown; muscles of calves, thighs, stomach, breast, back, arms and cheeks taken out. Punctures upon every sensitive part of the body, even to the soles of feet and palms of the hand.[80]

In addition to Col. Carrington's description, we also have the testimony of Capt. Ten Eyck before the Sanborn Commission taken on the 5th of July 1867. Capt. Ten Eyck was the first to arrive at the battle site and the very first to see the horribly mutilated bodies. He stated, "Some with their ears cut off, some with their bowels hanging out, from being cut through the abdomen, and a few with their bodies charred from burning, and some with their noses cut off."[81] Another eye-witness to the battlefield carnage was Finn Burnett, a civilian and sutler's assistant at Fort Phil Kearney on the date of the massacre. He described the process of loading the bodies for return to the fort as follows:

> Everyone worked in grim silence on that day. Scarcely a word was spo-ken, so tragic was the grief on every side. The women of the garrison were overcome with sorrow, and the men found themselves confronted with the extreme possibility of complete massacre for the entire crippled post.

It was terrible work to load the frozen corpses into the wagons. The ground was fairly sodden with blood, the smell of which frightened the mules until they were well-nigh unmanageable. A man was obliged to hold the head of every animal while the other teamsters loaded the naked, muti-lated remains like cordwood in the wagon-boxes. When the first wagon had been half loaded, the mules began to lurch and kick, until they succeeded in throwing the men aside. Turning the wagon around, they overturned it in their frenzy, and the bodies were dumped out before the animals could be recaptured and subdued. It was a terrible sight and a horrible job. Finally, all the dead were removed to the fort, and there they were dressed in new uniforms and placed in boxes for burial.[82]

In reference to the charred bodies, J. P. Dunn describes one of the methods that the Sioux used to burn captured prisoners: "they fasten a man, naked, to the ground, lying on his back, with arms and legs stretched out and fastened to pegs; then they build a fire on his stomach and keep it up until he dies, occasionally touching a burning brand to other portions of his body, gouging out an eye, or otherwise adding to the agony of the victim."[83]

These are classic examples of the horrendous, brutal mutilations that the American Indians inflicted upon army soldiers, white settlers, stage coach drivers, passengers, teamsters and any other unsuspecting victims that they came across. A really disgusting instance of their barbarism was that, "some of the dead at the Fetterman fight in December 1866 were found with their genitals cut off and placed in their mouths, apparently another mutilation perpetrated on the vanquished foe to make their life in the hereafter less fulfilling."[84]

To further substantiate this horrible culture of butchery, one source stated, in reference to the scalping and mutilation of Capt. Brown that, "How Brown was scalped is arguable as he was almost bald. He had some hair but it later was discovered that Brown had been mutilated, perhaps scalped, below the waist."[85] One of the men who helped prepare Capt. Brown's body for burial recalled that, "The privates of Capt. Brown were severed and placed in his mouth… and considering the extreme cold weather they could not be extricated."[86] My God, what unimaginable butchery and brutality!

As for Lt. Grummond, his head was "crushed with a war club and he had almost been decapitated; the Indians had cut off all of his fingers and filled his body with arrows."[87] One always hears about the wailings of the poor Indian women, but very little concern is spent upon the wives of the white soldiers and civilians who had to confront the butchered bodies of their beloved husbands. As a reflection on the character of Col. Carrrington, it was he who cut off a lock of Lt. Grummond's hair and gave it to the young pregnant wife of the Lt. when his body was brought in the evening after the battle. "Also, that evening Margaret Carrington, following the duty of the commandant's wife, consoled James Wheatley's nineteen-year-old widow, whom Finn Burnett described as a 'beautiful girl...and a splendid soldier.'"[88]

Very little concern is ever given to the sorrow and heartache that these white women had to endure. They had followed their men to the western frontier with hopes of making a new life together, raising their own families, and spending the rest of their lives with the men they loved. But then, in an instant, they had to identify the butchered bodies of their dismembered husbands and confront a sad and unknown future. All their hopes and dreams had been shattered by the Indian savages. I think Margaret Carrington said it best when she described the difficulties of living on the Plains. There seems to have been a well-known saying which came to be known as the triple. "The triplet of 'I never could, I never would, and I never will,' became almost obsolete; and in their place was these other impulses, 'I wouldn't, but I must and I will' or 'I could, I can, and I do!'[89] ...But any life on the plains is a good school, and its practical suggestions take all the starch and false pride as to work completely out of the unfortunate human creature who expects the spoon to be carried to the mouth by attendants, and a metropolitan table to be spread by the hands of a striker."[90]

I mention brave women and children here because far too often we forget about their courageous and significant contributions. "Always Remember the Ladies" is the famous quote that Abigail Adams made to her husband, John Adams, 2nd President of the United States. Specifically, in reference to the Fetterman massacre, the diaries of Margaret Irvin Carrington and Frances C. Carrington provide eye-witness accounts of the lives, experi-ences, and fears of officers' wives in the American West. In addition to the officers' wives, one must also not forget the difficult existence of the enlisted men's wives. Those who could accompany their husbands also shared the harsh experiences of the West. But rather than involve themselves in after-noon teas and poetry reading, they had to take in extra money by doing laborious tasks such as baking and soldiers' laundry. The existence of the wives, both officers and enlisted, were obviously not as hazardous as those of the soldiers; but there was always the horrible reality of kidnapping, captiv-ity, brutal rape, and murder.

A great primary source of women's contributions to the West is the multi-series volume of books titled, *Covered Wagon Women: Diaries & Letters from the Western Trails,* edited and compiled by Kenneth L. Holmes. Each volume covers a specific time period. The following volumes will be most useful for our investigation: Volume 8, 1862-1865, Volume 9, 1864-1868, and Volume 10, 1875-1883. I believe there are 11 volumes in the set. While we are discussing the women, we must also remember the children traveling across the West. The diaries of the Carrington women will be discussed further when we examine the actual day of the fight and the aftermath.

The strength and fortitude of these women and their families can readily be admired for their bravery and courage. Let us not forget their resilient children who followed their parents. Col. Carrington had two sons, Jimmy and Harry, who were brought with them to Fort Kearney. One source stated that, "Colonel Carrington's young son Jimmy also glimpsed the corpses and parts of corpses as they came into the fort in the wagons. Years later he would still have nightmares. 'How many times,' he wrote, 'I awoke in the dark in terror, to see again the tortured bodies and bloody arrows of that night.' "[91] What a horrible nightmare for any young child to have to bear for the rest of his life. These are the "real" memories that would haunt the human soul until death. Not a very flattering portrait of the so-called "Noble" Red man. But quite forgivable by the apologists for the Indians; after all it's just their culture! Dare I question the sincerity of the apologists? That would be like saying today, in reference to the Muslim Jihadists, forgive them for cutting off the heads of Westerners and Americans and hanging their burned bodies from a bridge; after all, it's just their culture.

When the recovery patrol returned to the fort, led by Captain Tenador (Ten) Eyck, the wagons contained the white, marble-like corpses of forty-nine of Fetterman's troops. The wagons which carried the dead soldiers "were slowly driven within, bearing their dead but precious harvest from the field of blood...with the heart-rending news, almost tenderly whispered by the soldiers themselves, that 'no more were to come in...'"[92] When Colonel Carrington returned the next day to gather the rest of the patrol, for his first sight of the massacred troops, he found, naked and frozen hard as stone, the remaining bodies of the ill-fated soldiers. Mrs. Carrington, the commander's wife, described the burial procedure as follows: "...the making of coffins and digging in the hard, frozen earth for a burial place, when the cold was so intense that the men worked in fifteen-minute reliefs..."[93]

Carrington had also found one man with 105 arrows in his naked body; he had also been scalped. The only man not mutilated was the company bugler, Adolph Metzler. It was believed that Metzler had killed several Indi-ans with his bugle in hand-to- hand combat beating them over the head with his battered copper instrument; he had fought very bravely. The Indi-ans did not mutilate enemies who they respected on the battlefield. Metzler was the only soldier found untouched and he was wrapped in a buffalo robe.[94]

The only living thing found on the battlefield was a gray mount horse named Dapple Dave which had belonged to the 2nd Cavalry. "The horse lay near the boulders, blood oozing from a dozen arrow wounds. Ten Eyck ordered a soldier to put the animal out of its misery…"[95] I mention this because the only living thing found on the battlefield at the Little Big Horn was a horse that belonged to Capt. Myles Keogh, named Comanche. It was more fortunate then Dapple Dave in that it was not as seriously wounded and was provided careful medical treatment that saved him. Comanche went on to become the 7th Cavalry's "venerated regimental mascot." He became one of the two horses to be given a military funeral with full military honors. After his death, his remains were sent to the Uni-versity of Kansas, where he is preserved and can still be viewed today on the second floor of Dyche's Hall. Just a little historical fact that makes "History" fascinating!

On the night of that sorrowful massacre, a kind gesture was made by a gallant man named "Portugee" Phillips. Phillips real name was John Phil-lips. He got the name "Portugee" because he was born in the Azore Islands off the coast of Portugal. He was originally a Portuguese citizen. He is another one of the extraordinary, but little known, famous personalities of the American West. There is a monument to "Portugee" Phillips that is a very short distance from the entrance to Fort Phil Kearney. There is a monument to celebrate the heroic bravery of his 236 mile, four day ride to Fort Laramie, in below zero blizzard conditions, to report the sad news of the Fetterman Massacre.

John "Portugee" Phillips was born in 1832 on one of the islands of the Azores, Pico. They are approximately 850 miles off the west coast of Por-tugal located in the North Atlantic Ocean. When he was 18 years old, he left the Azores on a whaling ship headed for the California gold fields. Between 1850 and 1865, he wandered the West following the gold boom-towns of California, Oregon, Idaho and Montana. While gold mining in the Big Horn Mountain area, he and some of his fellow gold miners came across Fort Phil Kearney; and in September of 1866, he signed on as a water carrier for a civilian contractor at the fort.[96]

There is nothing really to make him stand out in a crowd of gold miners and mountain men. However, on the night of the massacre, he supposedly offered his wolf robe to the recent widow, Mrs. Frances Grummond, who was pregnant at the time with her first child. Phillips went to Mrs. Grummond to "express his sympathy with her; that, overcome by his interest in her condition and the imminent danger of all concerned and weeping with sorrow over her loss, he said, 'I will go as the messenger if it costs me my life,' and then presented to her his own wolf robe to remember him by if he was never heard from again!"[97] That is a heart-warming gesture made by a simple gentleman to a young grieving widow carrying her first unborn child. This is the strength, perseverance, and unbelievable courage displayed by the men and women of the western frontier.

As Phillips made his kind gesture, Colonel Carrington overheard his statement about being a messenger and took him up on it. Carrington wrote two dispatches, one to General Cooke, and one to General Grant. He explained the sad plight of his forces and the loss of Capt. Fetterman's troops. He also requested additional troops, as he had done numerous times before, to defend his isolated fort with additional officers and men. He also again requested additional military supplies in the form of rifles and ammunition. He stated: "I hear nothing of my arms that left Leavenworth September 15th. Additional cavalry ordered to join have not reported their arrival...Give me at least two companies of cavalry forth with, well-armed, or four companies of infantry exclusive of what I need at Reno and C. F. Smith...Give me officers and men. Only the new Spencer arms should be sent..."[98] His requests illustrated the basic problem with the western military outposts, undermanned and ill-equipped; this was clearly the fault of higher headquarters in not providing the necessary soldiers and supplies needed to successfully accomplish their assigned mission.

Phillips left late on the night of the 21st of December heading for Fort Laramie. His journey took him first to the telegraph office at Horseshoe station, then to Fort Reno, and eventually to Fort Laramie. It was a grueling four-day journey that covered 236 miles. It has been suggested that Phil-lips did not make a part of this arduous trip alone. One source stated that Phillips had arrived at Horseshoe station with one other individual, William Bailey. Phillips then rode the last 40 miles to Fort Laramie alone.[99] Another source stated that Phillips arrived at Horseshoe station with two other men, Robert Bailey and a man named Dixon, at around 10:00 a.m. on Christmas day.[100] Whether or not Phillips made the ride accompanied or unaccompa-nied is "much ado about nothing."

He volunteered and completed the dangerous journey and for that he can be considered an unsung hero of the American est. Frances C. Car-rington best sums up his journey, "Whatever may be the reasons of any making the claim of sharing the trip with him, John Phillips was the mes-senger who singly braved the toils and dangers of the service rendered and no man can share the glory of his achievement. For daring heroism, neither the Ride of Paul Revere nor that of Sheridan can be compared with it, although not commemorated either by poetry or song, he deserves undying fame for his *midnight ride*."[101] For his remaining years, he worked as a cou-rier, contractor for the army, and a rancher. He remained in the Laramie-Cheyenne area and passed away in 1883.

Having completed the investigation of the Fetterman ambush and the historic ride of "Portugee" Phillips, we must now confront the aftermath of the battle. The usual political "witch-hunt" began for a victim to be sacrificed to the news media and Washington's political power elites. The aftermath of the battle led to the expected response from the military high command to any appalling incident that cast shadows on a governmental institution's reputation, in this case the army. Blame for the massacre was initially assigned to Colonel Carrington. Some members of the military brass decided Carrington was their man, at least at first, and the newspapers helped distort the truth.

> In newspapers and illustrated weekly he was in most cases the target of uniformed journalists who held him solely responsible for the "Fetterman Massacre."…The Department of Interior's Office of Indian Affairs issued statements absolving the "friendly Indians" and placing all the blame on Carrington. He was the victim of a public trial of which he was unaware for some weeks, and in which he was given no opportunity to present his side of the affair.[102]

The following newspaper reports clearly indicate that they were filled with fabrications and sensational distortions that had no basis in reality. The *New York Time*s reported on December 27, 1866, that an estimated 11,000 Indian warriors had attacked the fort. It also stated that, "'It is thought that the post was captured by treachery,' the reporter wrote, 'as the force there should have been able to stand a siege, and it seems hardly possible that it could have been captured by Indian assault.'"[103] One article in the *Chicago Republican* on the 3rd of January, 1867, stated that Col. Carrington "had not allowed pickets on the stockade to carry loaded weapons and to salute all Indians in the spirit of friendship and accused Carrington of 'cowardice and treachery.'"[104] On the 16th of January, the *Chicago Tribune* reported a most damaging and malicious lie describing Christmas day at the fort, "how all the officers and men were making merry as if nothing had happened: 'Never during our course of human events have we been blessed with the liberty of viewing so much obscenity, debauchery, and drunkenness. The whole garrison was on the 'bust.'"[105]

In stark contrast to the above reports, on that Christmas day, William R. Curtis, assisted in the preparation of Capt. Brown's frozen body. He "could not escape the memory of the awful sight. 'The privates of Capt. Brown were severed and placed in his mouth,' Curtis told Pvt. William Camp, 'and considering the extreme cold weather they could not be extricated.'"[106] This shows the incredulous viciousness of the loathsome press. The burial of the victims of the 21st could not take place until the 26th of December due to the intensely cold and frozen ground. The *Tribune* on the 2nd of February continued its malicious lies by stating that "Carrington [was] sit-ting beside a barracks stove 'gassing with some of the boys' at 2:30 in the morning following the battle."[107] The warped and unlimited distortions of the press in reference to the Fetterman battle are truly astonishing.

Margaret Carrington in her book, *Absaraka,* took on the challenge of defending her husband's reputation, as any loving wife would do, criticiz-ing some of the most outlandish newspaper reports. She stated: "It was, of course, to be expected that the Illustrated Papers should act promptly and perspicuously, with all the embellishment and accuracy which wood engraving affords...it was equally certain and necessary that a 'special artist,' some 'actual observer,' or a 'special correspondent,' should furnish the edi-tor's sanctum with the right material for his use in advance of the mails... but statesmen as well as editors, those who never saw a live Indian out of a city show, devised theory upon theory, to the great delight of their own complacent souls and with all the wonderful wisdom of absolute igno-rance."[108] Here are two more of her eloquent responses to the slanderous charges of the press:

> Not to name those papers and thus arouse invidious distinctions where so many showed brilliant powers of imagination, a few choice selections will do honor to them all and injustice to none.
>
> Albany, a city set on a hill, Argus-eyed and sagacious, had a corresponding preeminence in the way of invention and preciseness of detail. It portrayed, as "from reliable information," the fearful climax, "when the last band of survivors were driven to the gates of the fort, knocking and screaming in vain for admission; when the last cartridge from revolver, carbine, and rifle was expended; when the sabers and butts of muskets were broken; and when, leaning against the gates weary and bleeding and all resistance fruitless, all fell in one heap of mangled humanity, unsupported and uncared for. This sketch closed its recital with the startling announcement that the command-ing officer, whom it doomed to future obloquy, with two full companies, was looking on, afraid either to fire or open the gates lest the garrison within should be massacred by the infuriated savages and the post be sacked!...

One "Illustrated Paper" had a report "from the only eye-witness of the massacre." This person was said, "to have been cut off from his party by Indi-ans, and from a thicket only two hundred and fifty yards distant from the fight he saw the repeated charges of the cavalry, the dashing adventures of officers and men, and the last shot discharged by the last survivor through his own brain..."

To those who were present under the shadow of such a calamity, it seemed harsh and brutal that, more than two thousand miles away, there should be such a quick and morbid ambition to criticize and abuse...[109]

Quite an intelligent and literate lady, and a job very well done! You, the reader, know that the battle was fought some 4 to 5 miles from the fort, not at the fort's main gate. You also know that there were no surviving "eye-witnesses" to this battle other than the Indians. The newspapers at the time, especially those in the Midwest and back East, had their own agenda which was the protection of the "Noble" Red man from the brutal tactics of the U.S. Army.

It is now time to examine the historical background of the continuous animosity that existed between the Bureau of Indian Affairs and the Army throughout the Indian Wars.

This struggle had been raging off and on since 1849 when control of Indian affairs was transferred from the War Department to the Interior Department. It was the viewpoint of the military that the bureau had been corrupted by politicians who were dishonest, and working at cross purposes with national policy. It was the viewpoint of the Interior Department that Indian affairs could be better administered by civilians with humanitarian objectives. Each frequently accused the other of endangering lives, and neither overlooked an opportunity to make the other appear blameworthy.[110]

The Indians were always "friendly," "innocent" and free from blame. Accord-ing to the Bureau, they could do no wrong. Their constant request for guns and ammunition was an innocuous request so that they could do their seasonal hunting; they would never use these guns and ammunition to kill white people! Oh no, heaven forbid!! This so-called protective policy was in reality a delusional policy. It was fabricated to shield the Indians from the aggression and the brutality of the army and other evil white men. How-ever, its real primary motivation was to protect and further the monetary interests of the Indian agents, the Indian Bureau and their political backers in the Department of the Interior in Washington, D.C.

An excellent observation of the Indian Bureau's ridiculous policy towards the massacre is that given by Margaret I. Carrington when she stated:

A tenderhearted, sympathetic, but a temporary attache` of the Indian Bureau knew just how the massacre occurred---viz., that the poor, hungry, starving women of the Sioux had come to beg, and their husbands had come to ask a little powder for hunting and to have an order revoked as to gifts of arms to Indians, and being fired upon, they became desperate and took immediate vengeance.[111]

It was these kinds of completely erroneous and falsified statements that continuously aggravated the officers in the field and the army's leadership, especially Generals Sherman and Sheridan, that led to the constant hostili-ties between the Army and the Indian Bureau.

Another piece of evidence that criticizes the government, both the Indian Bureau and the Army, is the testimony presented by Mr. J.B. Weston. Weston was a civilian stock owner and Nebraska lawyer who was at the fort the day of the massacre. He stated that one of the fundamental causes of the Indian War that was being waged in the Powder River country was "Stupid and criminal management of our Indian Affairs by the U.S. Government. The Government, as represented by the Officials of the Indian Bureau, has never seemed to have any clear understanding of the Indian problem. Instead of preparing the way for the inevitable advance of civilization over this country, they have, as far as my observation has gone, been absorbed in some scheme of personal [s]peculation."[112] He further stated that when the Indian Bureau strategies have been ineffective and brought on a war, "the War Department has failed to appreciate its extent and magnitude; has sent a military force to this country so small, inadequate, and insufficient in num-bers, arms and supplies, that instead of conquering a peace, it has aggravated and augmented the troubles."[113]

It would hard to disagree with Mr. Weston's conclusions. Capt. Powell's testimony before the Sanborn Commission stated suggests stated that, "the paroled prisoners, being without guard, seemed to exercise their pleasure, if such it should be called, of breaking into the Commissary and stealing provisions, and also breaking into the Sutler's Store, which facts came under my official notice. The mounted detachment amused themselves principally with card playing, horse racing and getting drunk. The rest of the garrison performed their accustomed details in a very loose manner."[114]

Weston also identified one of the major treaty fallacies of the Indian Bureau, of providing guns and ammunition to the Indians, supposedly for the yearly hunting parties. One can recall that Col. Carrington was supposed to get 100,000 rounds of ammunition at Fort Laramie but was only pro-vided 1,000 rounds.[115] Weston stated that, "...Col. Carrington was unable to get his expected supplies of ammunition from Fort Laramie, but the same was furnished to the Indians, at the time of the Treaty, and employed by them afterwards against the Whites in this country, in perpetuating the most terrible butcheries and culminating in the Fort Phil Kearney massacre of Dec. 21st.,"[116] Clearly, the major faults of the Indian Bureau, which included the corruption of selling free annuities, falsifying claims against the govern-ment, and, most importantly, issuing guns and ammunition to the Indians under the treaty's conditions, would eventually be used against the army troops and frontier settlers.

There were two investigations launched to find out the "truth" of what caused the terrible massacre at Fort Phil Kearney. One must recall that the 79 troops and 2 civilians killed, 81 total, at the Fort Kearney massacre was the largest number of causalities in the Indian wars until the Little Big Horn battle of June 25th, 1876. The total killed at the battle of the Little Big Horn was approximately 268 men.

The first investigation was initiated by President Andrew Johnson and came to be known as the Sanborn Commission. The first meeting took place on the 2nd of March, 1867, in Omaha, Nebraska. The second investi-gation was a Military Court of Inquiry appointed by General Grant under the direction of the President. The first meeting of this Court of Inquiry was supposed to take place on the 1st of April but didn't have its first meet-ing until the 9th of May 1867; it also began its hearings in Omaha.

The Sanborn Commission had as its members, Generals John B. Sanborn (what a surprise), Alfred Sully, N.B. Buford, Colonel E.S. Parker, Indian trader G.P. Beauvais, and Fort Phil Kearney sutler Jefferson T. Kinney. It first took testimony between March 2nd and March 11th at Omaha and then moved to Fort McPherson, Nebraska. Testimony was taken here from March 20th to the 27th and included testimony by Col. Carrington, who was now post commander at McPherson. Carrington provided an extensive collection of letters, official messages, reports, documents and testimony pertaining to the incident.

Most of the Commission seemed satisfied with Carrington's presentation of his evidence and they did not call any other witnesses at Fort McPherson, which must have displeased Carrington for he complained that his orderly, Archibald Sample, three other enlisted men, and William Bailey, a civilian guide who had come with Carrington from Fort Phil Kearney, were not called. Carrington's testimony and supporting documents were hidden away in the files of the Department of the Interior for 20 years, while the Sen-ate Committee of Indian Affairs published derogatory statements by the commissioner of Indian affairs and letters from personal enemies of Carrington, including Dr. Hines and General Cooke. It was not until 1887, that Carrington persuaded the U.S. Senate to make public his official report and his testimony given before the Commission at Fort McPherson.[117]

In addition to the negative comments of General Cooke, there were other critical commentaries made by Commissioner Bogey, Lt. Bisbee and Capt. James Powell; Powell's being the most damaging.

General Cooke was the commander of the Mountain District/Department of the Platte and, therefore, Carrington's immediate superior officer. Cooke had given Carrington orders to not provide arms and ammunition to the Indians in July. That brought Carrington into disagreement with the Indian Commissioner Lewis V. Bogey. Bogey, as the head of the Indian Commission, argued that the Indians needed arms and ammunition to hunt and accused Carrington of provoking the Indians to attack. The following statements by Bogey clearly illustrate the asinine nature of the beliefs of the Indian Bureau. He stated that, "These Indians being in absolute want of guns and ammunition to make their winter hunt were on a friendly visit to the fort, desiring to communicate with the commanding officer…so that they might be enabled to procure their winter supply of buffalo."[118] Bogey further said:

> the whole affair seems incredible…and I find it difficult to account for the tragedy upon any other theory than that heretofore advanced by this office, to wit: that the Indians, almost in a state of starvation, having made repeated attempts at a conference, that they might make peace and obtain supplies for their families…were rendered desperate, and resorted to the stratagem which proved too successful. It seems as if the officer commanding could have avoided the catastrophe; and it seems also that men thus armed could have repelled an attack by all the Indians in Western Dakota.[119]

Obviously, Commissioner Bogey and the Indian Bureau were totally delu-sional about the real conditions that existed in the West.

In addition to the difficulties with the Indian Bureau, Gen. Cooke had ordered Carrington on September 27, 1866, to initiate offensive operations against the Indians as soon as possible and suggested he attack them in their winter camps. Carrington prepared to do this but continually requested additional arms, officers and troops to carry out this order. Cooke was not pleased with these continuous requests and considered Carrington to be incompetent and disobedient.

Also, Cooke had received letters of complaint from officers at Fort Phil Kearney that were critical of Carrington's ability as fort commander. As soon as Cooke heard of the massacre, without waiting for Carrington's full report, he moved to replace Carrington with Lt. Col. Wessells. The word-ing of the order made it sound like Carrington was being blamed for the massacre and was removed for his perceived incompetence. "Colonel H.B. Carrington, 18th United States Infantry, will be relieved from the command of Fort Phil Kearney by Brevet Brigadier General Wessells, and will proceed immediately to Fort Casper, to which post the headquarters of the new 18th Regiment have been heretofore ordered, and assume command of the post and that regiment."[120]

This really wasn't a demotion for Carrington. This move of commands had already been planned, but the quick timing of the order and the word-ing seems to have generated a major disagreement between Carrington and Cooke; a disagreement that would last 30 years. "Cooke meanwhile contin-ued to counter any possible criticism of his own responsibility in the Fetter-man affair by directing blame toward Carrington." Cooke stated: 'Colonel Carrington is very plausible,' he wrote General Grant on the 27th,'an ener-getic, industrious man in garrison; but it is too evident that he has not maintained discipline, and that his officers have no confidence in him.'"[121]

The following are excerpts from the testimony made by Lt. Bisbee before the Sanborn Commission. For the sake of clarity, I will use the Commis-sion's format of Question (Ques.) and Answer (Ans.).

Ques. What is your name and occupation?
Ans.   Wm. H. Bisbee, 1st Lieutenant and Brevet Captain in the 27th Infan-try, U.S.A., aidde-camp and Acting Assistant General on General Cooke's staff. (Please note that although Bisbee had been at Fort Phil Kearney, he had been transferred to Gen. Cooke's staff. Cooke was openly hostile to Col. Carrington as was Bisbee.)

Ques. How long a time have you known to elapse without any inspection of arms or ammunition?
Ans.   I can't recollect. One company might be inspected and another not. It was all done irregularly.

Ques. What was the feeling among the Officers, were they harmonious, or was there ill feeling existing towards each other, and towards the Commanding Officer?
Ans.   Almost without exception, it was harmonious, except a general feeling of disgust towards Colonel Carrington, in command of the troops.

Ques. What was the state of discipline in the garrison?

Ans. Very poor.
Ques. Were the orders issued by the Commanding Officer of the Post and district generally enforced?
Ans. They were not.
Ques. Were matters conducted there in an orderly manner, or in a disorderly and irregular manner?
Ans. Irregular and disorderly, generally.[122]

Obviously, Lt. Bisbee's testimony was critical and clearly suggested that the problems at Fort Phil Kearney were primarily the responsibility of Col. Carrington. The most derogatory testimony came from Capt. Powell before the Sanborn Commission on the 24th of July, 1867. I will use the same for-mat as above.

Ques. During the period last mentioned (5th of Nov. 1866 thru 21st of Dec. 1866), what was the discipline [sic] of the Post?
Ans. With the Company Officers it was good, with an effort on their part to discharge their duties to the best of their abilities. With the enlisted men it was chaotic.
Ques. In using the word chaotic, do you mean to understand that there was no discipline [sic] at the Post among the enlisted men?
Ans. I do.
Ques. What was the cause of the want of discipline [sic] at Fort Phil Kearney, during the time mentioned?
Ans. A want of proper support, Officially and personally, by the Company Commanders, from the Commanding Officer.
Ques. During that time, (between Nov. 5th and Dec. 21st) how did the enlisted men employ their time?
Ans. In answering the question, I shall have to answer it in various ways, as there were paroled prisoners from the Guard House in the garrison, and who had liberty of such, and there was a detachment of mounted men belonging to the Post from the different Companies, which had no direct or immediate Commander. The first party spoken of, the paroled prisoners, being without guard, seemed to exercise their pleasure, if such it should be called, of breaking into the Commissary and stealing provisions, and also breaking into the Sutler's Store, which facts came under my official notice. The mounted detachment amused themselves principally with card playing, horse racing and getting drunk. The rest of the garrison performed their accustomed details in a very loose manner.
Ques. You will please state all the facts, as far as you know, on that occasion. (the 19th of Dec. 1866)

Ans.   … Upon arriving at the Fort I reported to Col. Carrington and I think I stated to him at the same time, if he wished to haul timber from the Pinery he required a very large force, as I thought eighty or eighty-five men besides the teamsters was not too many.123

Ques.   Please state, as briefly as you can, such facts as have come to your knowledge connected with the death of Col. Fetterman and his party on the 21st of Dec. last.

Ans.   … Before moving his command from the Post, I saw Col. Carrington in conversation with Col. Fetterman, what orders or instructions Col. Carrington gave him I do not know but I observed that Col. Fetterman's command, in place of going to the relief of the wood train filed to the right and went on the Big Horn road. While they were moving along the Big Horn road, I endeavored to drive the Indians from their flanks and front by shelling them, which I succeeded in doing.

… After the elapse of this hour, about twelve o'clock, I requested Col. Carrington to arm all of the civilian employees at the Post, and at once send some person to the relief of Col. Fetterman with ammunition and wagons; Col. Carrington gave his consent to my request and asked my opinion upon the matter. I armed those men, had the wagons prepared, organized the detachment, consisting of employees and soldiers; Col. Carrington ordering Capt. Ten Eyck to take command.

After Capt. Eyck had left the garrison and reached the summit of some of the high hills where he could observe the battle field, he sent back a messenger, reporting to Col. Carrington that he could not find Col. Fetterman's party; the messenger also stated that he was of the opinion that the party was killed. Col. Carrington then asked my opinion again upon the subject, and I told him that I did not think they were dead, but had got to some place where they could protect themselves. He asked me what he should do, or words of like import. I told him to send word to Capt. Ten Eyck, that he was sent out there to fight, and he must get through to Fetterman's part; he did so.

Col. Carrington told me that he thought I had better take charge of the whole thing or something to that effect. I immediately assumed the duties of executive Officer of the Post, and had all the work stopped and prepared the men for action…

Ques.   …before Capt. Ten Eyck was started to the relief of Fetterman's party; please state the cause of the delay.

Ans.   I do not know the cause of the delay. Nearly all this time the Commander Officer was sitting on the top of his house, listening to the firing.

Ques.   …were there any fears expressed by the Officers of the garrison, as
to the safety of Col. Fetterman and party.

Ans.   When Col. Fetterman first went out there were fears expressed for
the safety of Col. Fetterman and party.[124]

The statements of Gen. Philip St. George Cooke and of Lt. Bisbee, who
was then serving as the aid-de-camp and member on General Cooke's staff,
were very critical of Col. Carrington. The comments of Commissioner of
Indian Affairs Lewis Bogey, and the damning testimony of Capt. Powell, the
first use of the number of 80 men, painted a very dire picture for Car-rington
in reference to the circumstances surrounding the attack. Powell and Bisbee
were clearly defending Fetterman and criticizing Carrington.

Powell's testimony has been used to suggest that Carrington had given
Fetterman specific orders not to relieve the wood train, but to take the Big
Horn Road and try an offensive maneuver to cut off the retreating Indians
attacking the wood train. The main problem with this statement is that four
other eye-witnesses clearly heard Carrington's orders not to go beyond
Lodge Trail Ridge. So there had to be another reason why Fetterman disobeyed orders, as mentioned previously, possibly to support an unwise impulsive cavalry attack led by Lt. Grummond. Powell's testimony also suggests
that Col. Carrington lost control of the situation and basically surrendered
command of the Post to him. Carrington continually asked for Powell's
opinions as the relief column of Capt. Ten Eyck was being organized. Powell stated: "Col. Carrington told me he thought I had better take charge of the
whole thing or something to that effect. I immediately assumed the duties of
Executive Officer of the Post, and I had all work stopped and pre-pared the
men for action."[125] J. W.Vaugnh offers the following assessment of Capt.
Powell's testimony:

> It is impossible to give full credence to Major Powell's statements
> because his claim that he drove the Indians from the flanks of Fetterman's
> command by shelling them is not substantiated by any other source. The
> shelling seems unlikely since it would have been as dangerous to the
> soldiers as to the Indi-ans. His statements that Colonel Carrington turned
> the command of the post over to him and that he assumed command are
> not confirmed by any other accounts.[126]

And adding insult to injury, as reported above, Powell stated in refer-ence
to the delay of sending out the relief column of Capt. Ten Eyck: "I do not
know the cause of the delay. Nearly all this time the Commanding Officer
was sitting on the top of his house, listening to the firing."[127] Col.

Carrington's response challenges Powell's observation by stating: "I went to the top of the house, on which was a lookout, and heard a few shots, apparently in the direction of Peno Creek. With my glass I could see neither Indian nor soldier." Carrington has himself using a spy-glass or individual telescope to search for the ongoing battle, not just sitting on the roof listening to gunfire as Powell alleges. You decide which one is more honest. In my opinion, knowing Powell's animosity towards Carrington, I stand by Carrington.

In defense of Col. Carrington, we have his own extensive testimony, filling 120 pages, and his specific Rebuttal to Capt. Powell's testimony, filling 15 pages. We also have the testimony of Mr. J. B. Weston, Lt. A.H. Wands, soldier George B. Mackey, and a supportive letter written by Jim Bridger. In addition, we have a statement made by Assistant Surgeon C.M. Hines in a letter to his brother, John, stating that, "No men were better armed. Instead of obeying orders, these officers (than whom there was none better or braver in the service) allowed themselves to be decoyed from the position ordered to be taken, and the whole command were butchered, (eighty-one officers and men.)"[128] Hines' letter is important because many sources cite him as being hostile towards Carrington; but in this letter, he clearly agrees with Carrington about the disobedience of orders. The disobedience of orders is the fundamental charge that Carrington makes against Fetterman and Grummond. In the following, I will deal with certain excerpts from Col. Carrington's extensive Rebuttal to Capt. Powell's testimony:

1st. Bvt. Major Powell states, "That the discipline of the enlisted men to be "chaotic", owing to want of proper support, officially and personally, by company commanders from the Commanding officer", meaning Col. Car-rington, successor to Capt. Ten Eyck as Post Commander.

Remarks. Col. Carrington personally superintended all important garrison details, nightly visited the sentries no matter who was the officer of the day, and invariably supported his officers, each and all, who conformed to Order No. 38, before given in evidence, the regulations of the Army and the Rules and Articles of War. Order No. 38, was enforced, although not according to the acceptance of Brevet Maj. Powell and Capt. W. H. Bisbee and said order illustrated Col. Carrington's system in the government of men.

Officers were <u>always</u> [supported?], when they were humane and just, as well as exact, and conformed to the orders of the Commanding officer…Strik-ing, cursing and other modes of brutal departure from Order No. 38, were not supported but reprehended, and Bvt. Major Powell's theory was most obnoxious to the spirit of the order…

2nd. Bvt. Major Powell, <u>states</u>, that, "Mounted Infantry formed a detachment from the different Companies, which detachment had not direct or immediate commander."

Remarks. …The Mounted Infantry were organized and officered according to General Pope's orders, and as appears from Colonel Carrington's evi-dence, were mounted, at a time, when they composed (within twenty) all the men of the Battalion. They were separately quartered, near their horses, and <u>never were without a direct and immediate commander</u>. The desire of Bvt. Maj. Powell to have a full company, with a Lieutenant, above all others, was natural but does not explain a statement which he knew to be without foundation.

3rd. Bvt. Maj. Powell, <u>states</u>, that, "The paroled prisoners being without guard, seemed to exercise their pleasure, if such it could be called, of break-ing into the Commissary and ste aling provisions and also breaking into the sutler's store, which facts came under his official notice."

Remarks. Bvt. Maj. Powell, <u>omits the fact</u>, that the prisoners were not paroled [sic], until the day of the massacre to make all men available for some duty;…

<u>Also; omits the fact</u>, that neither of the paroled prisoners was ever charged with, or suspected of the theft referred to:

<u>Also; omits the fact</u>, that there was but one robbery at the sutler's, when the east storeroom door was left open by the Carpenter, close by where the prisoners were under a tarpaulin, where they had to remain during the erection of the guard house, and that then, there was no sign of "breaking in."

<u>Also; omits the fact</u>, that a special sentinel was always at the Commissary building, day and night, even in the severest weather; that, an extra sentinel was posted in cases of reported theft, that the Quarter Master Sergeant and clerk were sometimes required to sleep inside, with arms, ordered, "to shoot whoever attempted to enter", and that with the exception of a few cans of blackberries and some syrup, the thefts at the Commissary were small and rare.

<u>Also; omits the fact</u>, that Bvt. Maj. Powell, did not disclose the names of those trespassers, or afford the Commanding officer the opportunity to punish.

4th. Bvt. Maj. Powell, states, that, "The mounted detachment amused themselves principally with card playing, horse racing and getting drunk." and "the rest of the garrison performed their accustomed duties in a very loose manner, viz, guard duties, fatigue duties in the Qr. M. and Com. Depts., and guard to wood trains."

Remarks. Bvt. Maj. Powell, omits the fact, that when two officers playfully tested their horses on the plain before the fort, and the Colonel found that high betting took place, even among the enlisted men, an order was promptly issued forbidding all racing and betting; notwithstanding such action was deemed by some officers as an unwarranted interference and affecting moral questions beyond the Colonel's control.

Also; omits the fact, that, it was the only show of a horse race; that, mounted Infantry never used their horses, except to go a few rods, to water, unless in pursuit of Indians, or on duty, as mail carriers or otherwise [sic].

Also; omits the fact, that card playing was never allowed men, on duty; and that probably alone, of all officers, except the Chaplin, the Colonel never played, under any circumstances, even socially.

Also; omits the fact, all half hours were called at night; that, often guards were changed half-hourly; that men could not, all, have two consecutive nights in bed; that all posts were carefully maintained and visited in all weather by the Colonel…

5th. Bvt. Maj. Powell, states, that, "There seemed to be a system of volunteer-ing; Officers going out in charge of men, from the number of about forty to about sixty, which custom seemed to have been tolerated by the Post Commander."

Remarks. Bvt. Maj. Powell, omits the fact, that there was a standing order, dated as early as September 13th issued by Col. Carrington, then District Commander, and sometimes enforced by guards at the gates, forbidding officers, soldiers, or citizens to go out without orders from the Command-ing officer.

Also; omits the fact, that a mounted detail was kept subject to the order of the Quarter Master, who often had to go out to see about his herds; and also, the fact, that the Officer of the day was expected, at once, to act, upon a sud-den alarm, so, that no time should be lost.

Also; omits the fact, that when, on the 6th of December, in the field, I sent Captain Powell to bring out reinforcements and an ambulance, Lieut. Arnold came, in his place.[129]

Col. Carrington's rebuttal of Capt. Powell's testimony is very comprehensive and specific. Carrington's rebuttal continues after the 5th one above, and includes 16 additional rebuttals in the same format, for a total of 21 rebuttals. In reference to the final rebuttal above, about the 6th of December, this incident was a very serious matter between Carrington and Powell. On the 6th, another attack had been launched by the Indians on a wood train; and Col. Carrington, with the support of Lt. Bingham, Lt. Grummond and Lt. Wands, left the fort to provide relief. The reference above to being "in the field" means that they were involved in combat operations. "When Carrington dispatched a written order to Fort Phil Kearney for reinforcements and an ambulance, he specifically asked for Capt. Powell to head the relief. But Powell remained in his quarters, ordering Lieutenant Wilbur Arnold to go in his place."[130] To refuse or ignore a written order from your Post Commander during an actual battle is the height of stupidity and insubordination, but there is no record of any punishment given out by Carrington.

Considering all of the voluminous quantities of testimony by individuals who had an axe to grind in reference to the Fetterman massacre, it is refreshing to get an opinion from "Old Gabe," Jim Bridger. Bridger's under-standing of the American West and its native inhabitants was unsurpassed as to the scope and comprehensive knowledge that he acquired over some 40-odd years.

Bridger wrote a supportive letter of Carrington for the *Army and Navy Journal* dated May 4, 1867. One must not forget that Bridger served as a scout and was at the fort on the day of the battle. He stated in this letter:

> Now as to the Philip Kearny massacre, it has been said that the Indians did not approach with hostile intent, but that the commanding officer, mistak-ing their intentions, fired on them, and thus brought on the fight. This is preposterous. Up to that time the Indians had been hanging around the fort every day, stealing stock on every opportunity, attacking the trains going to the woods, and even stealing up at night and shooting men connected with passing trains, while they were sitting around their campfires, within one hundred yards of the fort...Every person that knows anything of affairs in this country knows very well that the massacre at Fort Philip Kearny was planned weeks before, and that the Sioux, Cheyennes and Arapahos had been collecting together, in preparation for it, on the Tongue River, until they numbered 2,200 lodges. The intention was to attack Fort Philip Kearny first, and if they were successful to then attack Fort C. F. Smith... their vowed intention is to make a vigorous and determined attack on each of these three posts, and on all trains that may come along the road. Friendly Indians report that they are being supplied with ammunition by half-breed

traders connected with the Hudson's Bay Company. There is no use sending out commissioners to treat with them, as it will be only acting over again last Summer's scenes. They would be willing to enter into any temporary treaty to enable themselves to get fully supplied with powder with which to carry on the war. The only way to settle the question is to send out a suf-ficient number of troops to completely whip the hostile Sioux, Cheyennes and Arapahos and make them sue for peace. Unless this is done the road had better be abandoned and the country given up to the Indians.

I have been in this country among these Indians nearly forty-four years, and I am familiar with their past history, and my experience and knowledge of them is greater than can be gained by commissioners during the sittings of any council that may be held. I know that these Indians will not respect any treaty until they have been whipped into it.

May 4, 1867   James Bridger [131]

The Sanborn Commission had an unusual evolution in that it divided itself into 3 sub-commissions that further complicated the fact-gathering process. The entire group held its first meeting at Omaha, Nebraska on March 2nd, 1867. They then moved on to Fort McPherson and Fort Sedge-wick, where they divided up into three separate groups. One group was led by General Sully and Col. Parker; its responsibility was to interview the Missouri Sioux. The second group was led by Generals Sanborn and Buford, and Mr. Beauvais at Fort Laramie. They were to interview the Indi-ans around the fort and attempt to persuade them to come in for negotia-tions. The third group was a group of one, Mr. Jefferson T. Kinney. Kinney was in charge of the sutler's store at Fort Phil Kearney and had requested that testimony had to be taken at Fort Kearney for the investigation to be complete. Kinney was no friend of Col. Carrington and had a suit against the government for goods supposedly stolen by soldiers at the fort.

The Commission group led by General Buford made their report on the 6th of June. The group led by General Sanborn made their report on the 8th of July. Both of their reports acquitted Col. Carrington "of all blame for the Fetterman disaster because of his shortage of troops and supplies."[132]

> Sanborn reported the facts as he saw them, and instead of censuring Car-rington, gently absolved him from blame. "The difficulty 'in a nutshell,' " said Sanborn, "was that the commanding officer of the district was furnished no more troops or supplies for this state of war than he had been provided and furnished him in a profound state of peace. In regions where all was peace, as at Laramie in November, twelve companies were stationed, while in the regions where all was war, as at Phil Kearny, there were only five companies allowed.

Unfortunately for Carrington, Sanborn's favorable report was buried among derogatory statements from the Commissioner of Indian Affairs, comments of biased Indian agents, letters from personal enemies such as Surgeon C. M. Hines and an unidentified sergeant, excerpts from unfriendly newspapers, and the damning comments of General Cooke. All of these were published a few months later by the Senate's Commission on Indian Affairs.

As for Carrington's own testimony with its supporting documents, these papers were conveniently stored away by someone in authority in the Department of the Interior. For twenty-years they would remain hidden in the files, and for twenty years, Henry B. Carrington would fight a continuing battle to clear his tarnished reputation as a soldier.[133]

The Sanborn Commission, rather they condemn Carrington or Fetterman, concluded that Gen. Cooke was the main cause for all the problems that took place at Fort Phil Kearney. His issuance of the order of July 31st prevented the trading of guns and ammunition to the Indians. This conclusion was backed up by a scathing letter written by Lewis V. Bogey, the Commissioner of Indian Affairs on the 4th of February, 1867. It continued the ongoing argument between the Indian Bureau and the Army and also stated that, "An order issued by General Cooke, at Omaha, on the 31st day of July last…in relations to arms and ammunition, has had a very bad effect. I am satisfied that such orders are not only unwise, but really cruel, and therefore calculated to produce the very worst effect. Indians are men, and when hungry will, like us, resort to any means to obtain food, and as the chase is the only means of subsistence, if you deprive them of the power of procuring it, you certainly produce great dissatisfaction."[134] Again, ad nauseam, the Office of Indian Affairs promoted and defended its basic policy of giving the Indians guns and ammunition for their winter hunt. Continuing his criticism of the army, Bogey directly blamed Col. Carrington for the disaster and stated, "…although I regret the unfortunate death of so many brave soldiers, yet there can be no doubt that it was owing to the foolish and rash management of the officer in command at that post."[135]

As for the Commission of one, J. T. Kinney, meeting at Fort Phil Kearney, was tasked with gathering further evidence and to meet with the friendly "Mountain Crows." He started collecting evidence on the 5th of July and remained at the fort for a two-month period. He interviewed five important witnesses about the battle. They were Capt. Ten Eyck, Capt. Powell, Major Horton, Mr. J.B. Weston, and the famous scout, "Mitch" Boyer. Mitch Boyer made the famous statement to General Custer on the eve of the Lit-tle Big Horn, "General, I have been with these Indians for thirty years, and this is the largest village I have ever heard of."[136] To read Boyer's testimony before the Sanborn Commission see Appendix A in John S. Gray's book, Custer's Last Campaign (1991).

We will now briefly summarize Boyer's testimony gathered from Commissioner John F. Kinney's Report. This testimony took place at Fort Phil Kearney on the July 27, 1867. In reference to the number of Indians involved in the fight and the number of Indian casualties: "He said that there were 1800 Indians engaged in it and the great majority were Sioux, that there were some Arapahoes and Cheyennes engaged in it."[137] He gave unusually low numbers as to the number of Indians killed, wounded, and those who died from their wounds. He first reported "that there were eight Indians killed on the battle ground and about fifty wounded, twenty-two of whom died of their wounds..."[138] But he later goes on to state: "There were about 150 warriors of the Cheyennes under "Bull Head," who was killed. There were about sixty Arapahoes without any chief of their nation, but who were fighting under the Sioux."[139] Many sources have concluded that the freezing cold weather killed many of the wounded. Again, we have the contradictory testimony of an Indian.

In reference to the fighting ability of the soldiers, he said that, "the soldiers fought bravely, but by huddling together, gave the Indians a better opportunity to kill them than if they had scattered about. He said that the soldiers' ammunition did not give out, but they fired to the last. He said the Indians took all the ammunition the soldiers left, but some soldiers had none left."[140] This statement contradicts the statement made by some of the Indians that the soldiers committed suicide. The Indians who were attacked by Custer at the Little Big Horn made the same claims. It seems whenever the Indians win and they answer white men's questions about the battles, many claim the white suicide response. It seems they fear admitting that they killed the soldiers because the white men might become angry with them. The Indians at the Little Big Horn claimed exactly the same thing.

In reference to the fundamental question as to why the Indians fought the soldiers, he answered that, "the principle reason was that the whites were building forts in this country and traveling this road, driving off their game, and if they allowed it to go on, in two years they would not have anything for their children to eat." When Boyer was asked as to what the Indians intended to do the coming season, "He said that they were going to fight as long as they could, and if they did not stop traveling this road, they would keep on fighting..." In reference to the question if there could be peace with the Indians, Boyer responded, "No sir, not while the coun-try is occupied by soldiers and the whites travel the road..."[141] It seems rather obvious that if the U.S. Army and Federal Government had followed the recommendations of experienced mountain men and scouts, such as Jim Bridger and Mitch Boyer, there would not have been such bloodshed. Boyer's scouting expertise is considered by many to be second only to that of "Old Gabe;" that is quite a compliment! Sutler Kinney sent a copy of his findings to Mr. O.H. Browning, the Secretary of the Interior, on the 7th of October, 1867. Although Kinney's investigative report included the damning comments of Capt. Powell, his final report surprisingly does not criticize Carrington. Kinney's report said:

> ...under the Treaty of 1851 all of this territory had been awarded to the Crows but that the Sioux and Cheyenne now occupied it. He recommended that the territory be restored to the Crows and that the hostile Indians be driven onto reservations by the War Department. In a strongly worded docu-ment he contended that the Indians should not be allowed to stand in the way of progress and the building of settlements that were springing up in Montana. No further action or reports were made by the Sanborn Commis-sion, although the government followed the advice of the Commissioners Sanborn, Buford, and Beauvais and abandoned the Bozeman Trail and its forts in accordance with their suggestions.[142]

That is an unusual report considering the "hard feelings" that Kinney sup-posedly had against Carrington, in addition to the claim he had against the government for stolen goods at the fort.

Having finished with the reports and charges of the Sanborn Commis-sioners, one must now take a brief look at the Military Court of Inquiry; brief because it didn't last long nor did it accomplish anything. That court had been organized by a directive from President Andrew Johnson to Gen-eral Grant to investigate and report if any blame or wrongdoing had been done or any punitive action had to be taken against any of the military per-sonnel involved. Based upon the fact that the Sanborn Commission placed the blame, not on Carrington or Fetterman, but on General Cooke and the inept management of higher headquarters, the inquiry was quietly ter-minated. The "court of Inquiry was inexplicably suspended in June, 1867, probably to deflect criticism of the high command's possible negligence in the Fetterman Affair. Thus, the Sanborn report constitutes the significant historical document."[143] Carrington was cleared of all charges by both the Sanborn Commission and the Military Court of Inquiry but had to fight for 20 years to fully clear his name. It should be noted here that Monnett stated that the War Department suppressed Carrington's testimony and supporting documents for the next twenty years. Most other sources state that it was the Interior Department that purposely hid this document in the basement of its Washington building for twenty years.Vaughn stated in his book *Indian Fights,* that "Carrington then went to see Generals Sherman and Grant to secure the publication of his report, but the report remained buried in the dusty files of the Interior Department for twenty years. Carrington, after writing his friends to obtain evidence to offset Powell's testimony, received a letter from Wands dated November 27, 1867, which refuted most of Pow-ell's charges."[144]

The interesting thing about Carrington's charges in the Sanborn testimony against Fetterman and Grummond was that the only direct charge he stated was that of disobeying orders. There was no mention of the "give me eighty men" quote or the quote about "a single company of Regulars could whip a thousand Indians."[145] In his testimony to the Commission, on the 27th of December, 1866, he described the impulsive behavior of his young officers. He testified that, "...because most of the officers had not been with me in reconnaissance's [sic], and had recently arrived at Post, entirely unused to Indian warfare; because I knew the Indians to be in large numbers, I would not authorize them to make hazardous adventures. When Fetter-man and Brown asked for fifty mounted men to go with fifty citizens, on a trip to Tongue River, to destroy Indian villages [sic]."[146] This request might have served as a premonition for the "give me eighty men" quote that is so famously attributed to Fetterman. Carrington did not allow them to go because it would have dramatically reduced the fort's supply of horses and personnel. In reference to the problem of discipline brought up by Capt. Powell and Lt. Bisbee, Carrington stated that, "The want of discipline was not in the soldiers nor their commander. It was in Officers coming fresh to the command, who were unequal to the wiles of the Indians and despised my caution..."[147] In reference to the actual hostile conditions surrounding the settlement of the fort and the disobedience of orders, Carrington testi-fied that:

> Fort Phil Kearney was established amid hostilities. Fifty-one skirmishes have occurred. No disaster other than the usual incidents to border warfare occurred, until gross disobedience of orders sacrificed nearly eighty of the choice men of my command. I now know, that dissatisfied with my unwill-ingness to hazard the post, its stores, and the whole line for an uncertain attempt to strike Indians in their villages, (many times my numbers,) at least one of the Officers sacrificed deliberately determined, whenever obtaining a separate command, to pursue Indians after independent honor.
>
> Life was the forfeit--In the grave I bury disobedience. But I will vindicate the living and stand by my acts and record. It will stand as a simple fact that in

the face of constant night and day attacks; and in the heart of Indian country, the posts ordered to be established, were established during 1866...[148]

Carrington had presented quite a cogent defense of his reputation and the scurrilous charges that had been made against him. The only problem was that the Sanborn Report, as stated previously, was buried in the base-ment of the Department of the Interior until 1887. Secretary of the Inte-rior, Hoke Smith, said that, "These papers were found, after long search, among waste rubbish in the basement of the building."[149] The pernicious reports of the Indian Bureau, General Cooke, Capt. Powell, Lt. Bisbee and inaccurate "yellow journalistic" newspaper reports continued to haunt Col. Carrington. But he was cleared by both the Sanborn Commission and the Military Court of Inquiry. "By this late date many of the actors in the trag-edy were dead or forgotten. Old military feuds, however, die hard. William Bisbee, for one, never forgave Carrington. Bisbee and Fetterman had been close friends during the Civil War, and Bisbee preferred to believe that Fet-terman was blameless, and that Carrington had tried to shift the blame on Fetterman who was dead and could not reply."[150]

In addition to the charges against Fetterman and Grummond, Carrington left a living victim of the battle, one Capt. Ten Eyck, to confront an indirect charge of cowardice. Capt. Ten Eyck led the relief column sent by Car-rington to support the Fetterman command. Carrington's order to Ten Eyck was as follows: "You must unite with Fetterman, fire slowly and keep the men in hand.You could have saved two miles towards the scene of the battle, if you had taken Lodge Trail Ridge."[151] Ten Eyck's response to this allegation was: "My reason for taking the road was that I could accomplish the distance sooner, and with less fatigue to my men, there not being as much snow on the road, the ascent being more gradual, and the ridge being intersected by several deep ravines, that were partially filled with snow."[152] It wasn't until 1908 that Carrington set right the misconceptions of Captain Ten Eyck's behavior on the day of the battle. In a speech titled, *Equal Justice to Both Living and Dead*, presented on the dedication of the monument on Massacre Hill, Sheridan County, Wyoming, July 3, 1908, Carrington stated the following:

> I did not come here after a journey of twenty-five hundred miles, and at my advanced age, (84 at that time), entirely for my own gratification...I came deliberately, and under the spur of a most solemn and sacred duty, and your generosity and welcome show that duty conscientiously done never fails to find friends. It was not simply because so many years passed before Congress recognized the service rendered in 1866, but pitiful appeals from the family

of the brave Captain Ten Eyck were irresistible in their claim that I vindicate his good name at whatever risk of travel...

On the 21st of December the wood-train, as usual, took the trail just south of Sullivant Hill, as late as ten o'clock. The signal was soon given from Pilot Hill that the party was threatened by Indians. I started Capt. Brevet Lieutenant Colonel Fetterman with a strong detachment of troops to the relief of the train with positive orders, twice repeated, to "relieve the wood-train, escort it back in safety, but not to pursue Indians, under any conditions, and especially, not to cross Lodge Trail Ridge, north of the Fort..."

Fetterman, gallant through the entire Civil War from the time he joined my regiment in 1861, was impatient, and wanted to fight. He said, "I can take eighty men and go to Tongue River." To this boast my Chief Guide, the veteran James Bridger, replied in my presence, "Your men who fought down South are crazy! They don't know anything about fighting Indians..."

At the first shot I went to the balcony lookout, on my building...and had the "assembly" sounded...the Infantry and a few mounted men to guard their wagons were out of the Fort (Ten Eyck's command) and moving at a double-quick pace for the crossing, toward the scene of the conflict...

Ten Eyck, after crossing the creek, had gone to the nearest high hill, and in sight from the Fort, to get the bearing of the Fetterman party, and sent back my Orderly, Sample, who went with him, to tell me that "the Valley was full of Indians, challenging him to come down, but he could see nothing of Fetterman. I sent the Orderly back, followed by reinforcements, with this written order, "I send you forty men and ten thousand rounds of ammuni-tion. Join Fetterman at all hazards! Keep cool! You would have saved two miles to-day if you had gone as I directed over Lodge Trail Ridge." This was not a reprimand at all, but suggestive as to location of the enemy, as he could not otherwise know after the firing had ceased, and he could not judge as I could, on my lookout, of the locality in peril.

As a fact, Ten Eyck obeyed my order. He pressed on, kept his men in hand, rescued forty-nine dead bodies, and brought them home in safety without the loss of a man...

"Two Moons" (a Sioux Chief who participated in the battle) also described the Fetterman fight and stated that "when they saw more soldiers coming out (meaning Ten Eyck's party) they made a rush and killed them all before any fresh soldiers could get there." And yet for years the name of Ten Eyck was counted as a reproach, and the gallant service done was tortured into fear of the Indians, whereas he risked all the fight possible to save his fallen comrades, and it was the highest military art to have done just what he did do.[153]

Carrington reinforced his defense of Ten Eyck's conduct in a reprinted version of his brief pamphlet, *The Indian Question*, (1909). He clearly stated:

"The foregoing message to Captain Ten Eyck, was in no sense a rebuke, as it has been interpreted in many quarters: but a guiding suggestion… The chief incentives to my recent trip to Wyoming were to do justice to Captain Ten Eyck…by giving the exact facts on which was based the delayed publication of my own official report."[154] The only problem with Carrington's statements were that they were far too long from the incident, some 42 years, to really do Ten Eyck any good. The close-knit social system of the military is not at all forgiving when it comes to charges of cowardice, even if it is only hinted at. "The damage was done, however, and the ordinary prudence resulted in Ten Eyck's disgrace and in his being the victim of rumors and whispers behind his back that he detoured because of cowardice. Ten Eyck began drinking heavily and was permitted to retire from the army with the rank of Captain, another unfortunate casualty of the Fetterman massacre."[155]

Having dealt with the "blame game," first Col. Carrington, then Fetterman and Grummond, many have seemed to overlook the important role that might have been played by Captain Frederick H. Brown. Brown had been close friends with Fetterman and Grummond and was with Fetterman when they both died on Massacre Hill. When Fetterman initially joined the command, he had "…recently arrived from recruiting service, with no antecedent experience on the frontier, expressed the opinion that "a single company of Regulars could whip a thousand Indians…" "He was warmly seconded by Captain Brown and Lieutenant Grummond."[156] It seems that Brown had made a number of successful patrols against the Indians attacking around the fort. On the 23rd of September, there was an Indian attack on the picket on Pilot Hill and the Pinery train. Captain Brown was sent with a relief troop and quickly drove off the Indians. Margaret Carrington describes Capt. Brown's bravado in the following manner:

> Captain Brown's repeated dashes, and especially his success on the 23rd of September, had inspired him with perfectly reckless daring in pursuit of Indians; and only the night before the massacre he made a call, with spurs fastened in the button-holes of his coat, leggings wrapped, and two revolvers accessible, declaring, by the way of explanation, that he was ready by day and night, and must have *one scalp* before leaving for Laramie, to which place he had been ordered. He had inspired Captain Fetterman, who had been but a short time in the country, and already had great contempt for our adversaries, with the same mad determination to chase whenever they could, regardless of numbers; and together they planned an expedition of a week's travel trip to Tongue River valley, with a mixed party of ninety citizens and soldiers, to destroy the Indian villages and clear out all enemies. Disapproval of the plan did not change their belief in its feasibility and wisdom…[157]

As stated previously, Col. Carrington disapproved of their plan because of the detrimental impact it would have on the number of personnel and horses it would leave for defending the fort. Brown's past behavior stresses his predilection for reckless behavior.

Having examined the unpredictable behavior of Capt. Brown, one must now investigate the destiny of the main character of this historical drama, Col. Carrington. Fate, again, showed its total indifference to the human condition. After the battle on the 21st, the army ordered Carrington to transfer his command from Fort Kearney to Fort Casper during one of the coldest winters in Wyoming's past. The journey with his command left Fort Kearney on the 23rd of January, 1867. Carrington described this ordeal as follows: "Upon being relieved I moved to Fort Casper with regimental headquarters, staff and officers' families, with mercury at 38 degrees below zero (the second day), and having more than half my escort of sixty men frosted the first sixty-five miles, requiring two amputations at Reno."[158]

Colonel Carrington had the unfortunate luck of mistakenly shooting himself in the thigh during the trip from Fort Casper to Fort Laramie. This serious wound made it necessary to take a two-week convalescence before he continued to Fort McPherson where he then had to confront a com-mission investigating the battle. In 1870, four years after the battle, having survived the investigation process of two inquiries, Carrington retired from the army to become a professor of military science at Wabash College in Indiana. But fate would not leave him alone. In 1870, his first wife, Marga-ret, suddenly died of tuberculosis and left him a widower. He began a cor-respondence with Frances Grummond, and the two were wed in 1871. He remained at his teaching post in Indiana until 1878 when he and Frances moved back to Boston, Massachusetts. Frances published her famous book in 1910 and died a year later in October of 1911. Colonel Carrington died the year after in October of 1912; both husband and wife are buried in Hyde Park, Massachusetts.[159]

The circumstances involving Col. Carrington's two wives help explain the writing of the two early, important primary source books on the battle. Margaret's book was, as stated previously, published in 1868 under the title, *Absaraka: Home of the Crows.* Frances' book, *My Army Life and the Fort Phil Kearney Massacre*, was published in 1910. It must be noted again that neither of these books made any reference to the famous quote, "with eighty men, I could ride through the entire Sioux nation." One cannot help but ponder the possibility that the famous quote may have been a mistakenly distorted remembrance of the request by Brown and Fetterman to take ninety men and travel to Tongue River and "destroy the Indian villages and clear out all enemies." Ah, but just another intriguing supposition.

Both books did, however, include the famous quote, "a company of regulars could whip a thousand, and a regiment could whip the whole array of hostile tribes." In many cases, Frances' book is almost a word-for-word replication of Margaret's book. Carrington had Margaret's book reprinted, as previously reported, at least 5 times. He came out with his own edition, titled *Ab Sa Ra Ka: Land of the Massacre,* in 1879. This book included 6 additional chapters titled *Indian Affairs on the Plains.* These chapters discussed the Army-Indian conflicts between 1867 and 1877, to include the Battle of the Rosebud and the Little Big Horn. Many considered these reprints as part of his ongoing attempts to clear his own name.

Henry Carrington was definitely a member of the political and military elite class of his period. He was born in 1824 and grew up in Connecti-cut. He was highly educated and graduated from Yale in 1845. He became friends with the famous Washington Irving and taught natural science and Greek at Irving's college. He studied law at Yale and formed a law partnership with one William Dennison who later became Governor of Ohio in 1860. He was actively involved in Whig and Republican Party poli-tics and was also a fervent anti-slavery supporter. After the Civil War freed the slaves, many of the anti-slavery supporters became staunch supporters and protectors of the American Indian, including Henry Carrington. He became friends with a political power broker named Samuel P. Chase. Chase was a very famous lawyer who later became a U.S. Senator and Governor of Ohio. He served as the Secretary of the Treasury for Lincoln and also became the 6th Chief Justice of the U.S. Supreme Court. It was these elitist connections that got Carrington appointed as a full Colonel of the 18th U.S. Infantry in 1861, the unit he commanded at Fort Phil Kearney. In 1863, he was promoted to Brigadier General. His sole military experience, for which he was highly praised, involved the administrative duties dealing with the reorganization of the state militias in Ohio and Indiana.[160] Even with his limited battlefield experience, Carrington was quite an accomplished man. He received his LL.D. in 1873. In addition to his extensive law background, he was also a very prolific author and produced 10 books, primarily on the American Revolution. Of these, he wrote two books and a pamphlet on the American Indians, *Ab-Sa-Ra-Ka: Land of Massacre,* 1879, which was a copy of Margaret's first book with his additions, a small pamphlet titled, *The Indian Question,* 1884, and another book, *The Exodus of the Flat Head Indians,* 1902.

Having examined the evidence gathered in reference to the Fetterman Massacre, what can we now conclude? The most important conclusion is that the famous quotation, "give me eighty men…," lacks any evidence to prove its being said by Capt. Fetterman. There is absolutely no primary source document that supports that conclusion. The evidence indicates that the quote was first used by Brady in his book, *Indian Fights and Fighters* (1904), and then again by Carrington in his dedication speech before the Fetterman Massacre monument in 1908. After that the quote seems to have taken on a life of its own.

Another important fact that the evidence supports is that of the orders given to Fetterman and Grummond as they left to support the wood train. There are three eye-witnesses who distinctly heard Col. Carrington order these two officers not to go beyond Lodge Trail Ridge and only support and relieve the wood train. The first one is Francis Grummond Carrington, the Colonel's second wife. She stated: "The instructions of Colonel Carrington to Fetterman were distinctly and peremptorily given within my hearing and were repeated on the parade-ground when the line was formed, 'Support the wood train, relieve it and report to me.'"[161] She went on to say: "Before they were out of hearing Colonel Carrington sprang upon the banquet inside the stockade (the sentry walk), halted the column, and in clear tones, heard by everybody, repeated his orders more minutely 'Under no circum-stances must you cross Lodge Trail Ridge;' and the column moved quickly from sight."[162]

The second eye-witness is that of Sgt. Alexander Brown, who stated: "I was standing alongside of Colonel Carrington on that fatal day of Decem-ber 21,1866, when he told Colonel Fetterman to take the men that were not on duty and go to the relieve the wood train, but not to proceed or pursue the Indians over Lodge Trail Ridge. He disobeyed orders and conse-quently he and his command were wiped out."[163]

The third eye-witness was 1st Lt.Wands who stated: "Colonel Carrington directed me to inform Lt. Grummond that his orders were to join Col. Fet-terman's command, report to and receive all his orders from Colonel Fet-terman…under no circumstances were they to cross the bluff in pursuit of the Indians…Colonel Carrington, who was on the sentinels platform at the time, and who called out in a loud voice, repeating the same instructions given Lieutenant Grummond by me, asking him if he understood them. He replied, I do."[164]

One can obviously challenge Frances Carrington's statement as being sympathetic to Carrington because she was his wife; heaven forbid that she was just telling the truth. The simplicity of the statement, however, does not fit the analytical framework constructed by the conspiracy theorists. For them, both of the Carrington women must be purposely lying to protect their husband's reputation. But both Sgt. Alexander Brown and Lt. Wands' statements clearly support the order not to go beyond Lodge Trail Ridge. As also mentioned previously, there was a letter written by Dr. Hines, Asst. Surgeon, supposedly an enemy of Carrington, to his brother, John, on the 1st of January, 1867. He stated: "Instead of obeying orders, these officers (than whom there were none better or braver in the service) allowed themselves to be decoyed from the position ordered to take, and the whole command were butchered, (eighty-one officers and men.)"[165] The evidence provided by Frances Carrington, Sgt. Brown, Lt. Wands and Dr. Hines clearly sup-ports the statement that the orders to not go beyond Lodge Trail Ridge were given directly to Fetterman and Grummond.

Another important piece of evidence that clearly shows that Fetterman, Brown and Grummond went beyond Lodge Trail Ridge is the actual loca-tion of the bodies after the battle. The location of the bodies as reported by scout Mitch Boyer stated that, "…some of the soldiers were a mile in advance of the others…the advanced soldiers were killed in retreating to the main body…"[166] This assessment, made by one of the best scouts in the West, clearly indicates that Grummond had gone on ahead with his cavalry and had placed his command in a very dangerous position.

Common sense could suggest that Fetterman and Brown, seeing their friend in danger, rode to his defense and completed the trap. If this were the case, then the impulsive Grummond would bear a major responsibility for the disaster for leading his cavalry so far in front of the infantry. This is what Shannon D. Smith argues in her well written book, *Give Me Eighty Men: Women and the Myth of the Fetterman Fight* (2008).[167] She exonerates Fetter-man and blames Grummond by comparing their past military records and concludes that Grummond is the most likely to be reckless and impulsive.

Now we will discuss Doctor Horton's testimony regarding the horrible mutilated conditions of the soldiers of Fetterman's command:

From the appearance of all the persons in Col. Fettermans party I believe the majority of them were killed by clubs with which the Indians crushed their skulls and brains, after having falling wounded. A few were disembow-eled with knives which I believe was done after they were wounded. The brains of some of them were found lying beside their bodies, some of them were killed by arrows after they had fallen and were stripped, as their bod-ies contained a great number of arrows. One body had as high as sixty five arrows in it…

Capt. Browns body showed gashes inside of both thighs, to the bone, from his body to his knees, both ears had been cut off and his body otherwise mutilated and a hole made in his left temple [caused?] by a small pistol ball; the latter most probably caused his death. Lieut. Grummonds body showed his head to have been crushed by a club; and his legs were slightly scorched by fire.

One body was found with a large stake driven into it, as high as the chest. One body was found with one arm cut off at the shoulder joint. One body with both hands and both feet cut off, one with the entire head crushed away, except the lower jaw. All the bodies were more or less mutilated, and presented in nearly every instance a horrible sight, never to be forgotten by those who saw them.[168]

This butchering of U.S. Army soldiers clearly supports my initial proposi-tion that the most heinous mutilations were carried out by the Indians after their successful battle.

Another myth that has been incorrectly repeated for many years was the double-suicide theory. This theory stated that both Fetterman and Brown had committed suicide by shooting each other in the head to avoid Indian torture. Both wounds were supposed to be in the left temple of each man. However, if two men are standing side-by-side it would be extremely dif-ficult to accomplish. It would be more likely that one wound would be in the left temple and the other wound would be in the right temple. The only way two wounds could be in each left temple is if they were both directly facing each other; very unlikely, but possible. However, it really doesn't make any difference because the direct testimony of Dr. Horton clearly stated that Capt. (Brevet Lt. Colonel) Fetterman had died, not from a gunshot wound to the head, but by a slash across the throat. "Col. Fetterman's body showed his thorax to have been cut crosswise with a knife, deep into the viscera; his throat and entire neck were cut to the cervical spine all around. I believe that mutilation caused his death."[169] The direct testimony of Dr. Horton disproves the statement that both men had committed suicide by shoot-ing each other in the left temples. His testimony indicates that only Capt. Brown's body had showed gashes inside of both thighs, to the bone, from his body to his knees, both ears had been cut off and body otherwise horribly mutilated and a hole made in has left temple [caused?] by a small pistol ball; the latter most probably caused his death.[170]

The foundation of the initial charges against Fetterman all stem from the literary works of Margaret and Frances Carrington. The first com-ment that Margaret made was, "Two days after Captain Fetterman arrived, impressed with the opinion, to which he had often given language, that "a company of regulars could whip a thousand, and a regiment could whip the whole array of hostile tribes…'"[171] Her next reference to Fetterman is the attack on the 6th of December, when she references Fetterman's participa-tion in the fight, she said: "Captain Fetterman has been in, and says 'he has learned a lesson, and that this Indian war has become a hand-to-hand fight, requiring the utmost caution,' and he wants no more such risks."[172] What could possibly have caused him to forget such a dangerous lesson in less than 15 days?

After the battle on the 6th, Margaret Carrington said: "He (Capt. Brown) had inspired Captain Fetterman, who had been but a short time in the country, and already had great contempt for our adversaries…"[173] Obvi-ously, these contradictory statements about Fetterman's attitudes toward the Indians complicate the problem. Could it be that Capt. Brown had again inspired Capt. Fetterman on the 21st of December and, since Brown had stated a desire for scalps, threw caution to the wind, and proceeded reck-lessly in pursuit of the Indians. Captain Brown had stated that he, "must have one scalp before leaving for Laramie." He also said that he wanted to "have Red Cloud's scalp before he left."[174] What this does suggest is that Brown was probably more recklessly motivated to chase the Indians in "hot pursuit" than Fetterman. When you combine the young, ambitious, reck-lessness of the three officers involved, Brown, Grummond and Fetterman, one might have had an egotistical formula for disaster.

Let us now propose some possibilities as to why Fetterman, Brown and Grummond went beyond Lodge Trail Ridge.

One: Fetterman, having been confronted with new or different tactical conditions, he possibly saw the signal from Pilot Hill that the wood train was safe and he decided to utilize the strategy previously used successfully to cut-off the retreating Indians.

Two: Lt. Grummond recklessly led the Cavalry far ahead of the Infantry, at least a mile; and Fetterman and Brown felt an obligation to res-cue Grummond who had ridden into the ambush and then needed saving.

Three: That Fetterman and Carrington had both agreed on the "cut-off" tactic and Fetterman was just following Carrington's shared plan.

Four: Fetterman, under the influence of Grummond and especially Brown, who wanted "Red Cloud's scalp" before he left Fort Phil Kearney, allowed himself to by decoyed into the classic Indian ambush.

What conclusions can one make about the hypotheses generated by this examination of the evidence so far available?

One: the quote about, "Give me eighty Indians…" was not made by Capt. Fetterman.

Two: the theory regarding the double-suicide about Fetterman and Brown shooting each other in the left temples has been challenged by the testimony of Dr. Horton.

Three: that the orders to "not go beyond Lodge Trail Ridge," given to Fetterman and Grummond, have been substantiated by fiver sources: Margaret and Frances Carrington, 1st Lt. Wands, Sgt. Alexander Brown and Dr. Hines.

Four: that the location of the bodies of the Infantry and Cavalry clearly indicate that the two commands of men had gone around Lodge Trail Ridge and disobeyed Col. Carrington's direct orders.

Five: that the Cavalry was quite some distance in front of the Infantry, possibly a full mile, when the bodies were discovered, substantiated by Dr. Hines and the famous scout, Mitch Boyer.

Six: As to the overall blame for the massacre, Vaughn stated: "If anyone should be blamed for the disaster, it is the high command which allowed twelve companies of well-equipped soldiers to remain back in Fort Laramie while five companies of poorly armed infantrymen and one company of newly recruited cavalrymen were trying to fight off the Indians while building a new army post in the heart of their territory."[175]

The first to challenge the standard interpretation is the author, J.W. Vaughn in his book, *Indian Fights: New Facts on Seven Encounters,* (1966). He defends Capt. Fetterman and blames Colonel Carrington for not sending reinforcements to assist Fetterman. He suggests that Lt. Grummond might have played a bigger role in the massacre than previously reported. The second revisionist book is by Shannon D. (Calitri) Smith, *Give Me Eighty Men: Women and the Myth of the Fetterman Fight.* (2008). She suggests that Carrington and Fetterman agreed upon an offensive plan to go around Lodge Trail Ridge and that Carrington "never" gave the order about not going past Lodge Trail Ridge. Rather than disobeying the specific orders, Carrington and Fetterman decided together that a better military tactic was to go around the north rim of Lodge Trail Ridge and attempt to cut off the Indians attacking the wood train before they could retreat. Capt. Fetterman is not to blame based upon his past military service record; Lt. Grummond is the new culprit. There is also a third interpretation, *Where a Hundred Sol-diers Were Killed: The Struggle for the Powder River Country and the Making of the Fetterman Myth* (2008), written by John H. Monnett. It also agrees with Vaughn's interpretation.

Interpretation is the essence of historical research. Which sources can you muster and which make for the best and most reasonable analysis based upon the evidence that one has found. It always comes down to one's per-sonal interpretation of the sources gathered and how the evidence is pre-sented. In most cases, we have each of the authors defending their own analysis as the most accurate and correct. However, many historical authors are biased in their research; and they become enamored with their subject or are driven by a politically correct agenda. However, every once in a while, you come across a unique and common sense interpretation that hits like a bolt from the blue. In my opinion, this unique analysis is that of J.W. Vaughn in his book, *Indian Fights: New Facts on Seven Encounters,* (1966). He summarizes the Fetterman massacre as a disaster which was "one of the mis-fortunes of war, and none of the officers involved was to blame. In such an event, Fetterman, Brown, Grummond, and all their men were heroes who fell fighting overwhelming numbers of the enemy."[176] Rather than blaming Fetterman for a foolish decision, one might possibly blame von Clausewitz's "Fog of War," the ambiguity of the battlefield. Maybe they were all ill-fated victims of fate and the unknown misfortunes of war.

End Notes for Chapter 5.

[1] Grace Raymond Hebard, E.A. Brininstool, *The Bozeman Trail* (Charleston: Bib-lioBazaar, LLC, 1921, 2013), Vol. I, 305. Hereafter cited as Hebard/Brininstool Also Paul I. Wellman, *Death on the Prairie: The Thirty Struggle for the Western Plains* (Lincoln: The University of Nebraska Press, 1934), 38. Hereafter cited as Wellman.

[2] Ibid, 43.

[3] George Bird Grinnell, *The Fighting Cheyennes,* (Norman: University of Oklahoma Press, 1955),198. Hereafter cited as Grinnell-*Fighting.* Dee Brown, *Bury My Heart at Wounded Knee,* (New York: Holt, Rhinehart & Winston, 1970), 130. Hereafter cited as Brown-Wounded Knee. Brown, *Fetterman*, 41.

[4] Brown, *Fetterman*, 41.

[5] Francis C. Carrington, *My Army Life and the Fort Kearney Massacre.* (Lincoln: Uni-versity of Nebraska Press, 2004), 87. Hereafter cited as F. Carrington.

[6] Merrill J. Mattes, *Indians, Infants and Infantry: Andrew and Elizabeth Burt on the Frontier,* (Lincoln: University of Nebraska Press, 1988), 110. Hereafter cited as Mattes. Cyrus Townsend Brady, *Indian Fights and Fighters,* (Lincoln, University of Nebraska Press, 1971), 13. Hereafter cited as Brady, *Indian Fights.*

[7] Brady-*Indian Fights,* 23. Cyrus Townsend Brady, *The Sioux Indian Wars: From the Powder River to the Little Big Horn,* (New York: Barnes & Noble, 1992), 23. This

book was originally printed as *Indian Fights and Fighters* and is a word-for-word duplication of that book. I will only use the citation Brady-*Indian Fights*. John H. Monnett, *Where A Hundred Soldiers Were Killed,* (Albuquerque: University of New Mexico Press, 2008), 233. Hereafter cited as Monnett.

[8] F. Carrington, 261.Margaret Irvin Carrington, *Absaraka: Home of the Crows,* (Lincoln: University of Nebraska Press, 1983), 171. Hereafter cited as M. Carrington. Monnett, 98. F-Carrington, 119.

[9] F. Carrington, 253.

[10] M. Carrington, 170-171.

[11] F. Carrington, 119.

[12] Brown, *Fetterman,* 150. M. Carrington, 171. Hebard, 305.

[13] Monnett, 232-233. Also cited in John Monnett, *The Falsehoods of Fetterman's Fight, Wild West Magazine,* December, 2010,Vol. 23, No. 4, 40-41. Hereafter cited as Monnett, Wild West. The same article can be found online at: http://www. historynet.com/the-falsehoods-of-fettermans-fight.htm. 1-12. (accessed March 1, 2014).

[14] Ibid.

[15] Brady, 23.

[16] M. Carrington, 261

[17] Monnett, 147.

[18] J. W. *Vaughn, Indian Fights: New Facts on Seven Encounters,* (Norman: University of Oklahoma Press, 1966), 40. Hereafter cited as Vaughn. Brown, *Fetterman,* 162-63. Dunn, 491. F. Carrington, 131. Lt. William H. Bisbee, Testimony in Records Relating to Investigations of the Ft. Phillip Kearney Massacre, M740 roll 1 of 1, National Archives & Records Administration. page 3 of 6. Also known as the Sanborn Commission, March 11, 1867, at Omaha Nebraska. http://freepages. history.rootsweb.ancestry.com/~familyinformatio... Hereafter cited as cited as Testimony, M740. (accessed March 1, 2014).

[19] Vaughn, 40. Brown, *Fetterman,* 164.

[20] Vaughn. 40. Brown, *Fetterman,* 162. Monnett, 116.

[21] Brown, *Fetterman,* 164.

[22] Ibid, 165. F. Carrington, 133.Vaughn, 41. Monnett, 114. Shannon D. Smith, *Give Me Eighty Men:Women and the Myth of the Fetterman Fight,* (Lincoln: University of Nebraska Press, 2008), 93. Hereafter cited as Smith.

[23] M. Harrington, 195. Brady, 20.

[24] Grinnell, 200.

[25] F. Carrington, 127.

[26] M. Carrington, 195. Brown, *Fetterman,* 166. Monnett, 114.

[27] Brown, *Fetterman,* 169. Vaughn, 43.

[28] Monnett, 116.

[29] Ibid, 117.

[30] Russell W. Blount, Jr. *Clash at Kennesaw: June & July 1864.* (Gretna, Pelican Publishing Company, 2012). Also see Earl J. Hess, *Kennesaw Mountain: Sherman,*

Johnston, and the Atlanta Campaign. (Chapel Hill: University of North Carolina Press, 2013).

[31] Brown, *Fetterman*, 170.

[32] M. Carrington, 208-9. Monnett, 118. Vaughn, 43.

[33] F. Carrington, 143.

[34] Brady, 23.

[35] Ibid, 24.

[36] Vaughn, 62.

[37] Brown, *Fetterman*, 183.

[38] Brady, 28.

[39] F. Carrington, 144. M. Carrington, 202.

[40] Greene, *Indian War Veterans*, 89.

[41] J. Cecil Alter, *Jim Bridger*, (Norman, University of Oklahoma Press, 1962), 330. Hereafter cited as Alter. It must be noted that this quote in Alter's book refers back to Frances C. Carrington's book, *My Army Life*, 253; this is what makes the research process so much fun!

[42] Monnett, 132.

[43] A. H. Wands's testimony, M740. 9-10.

[44] Dr. Hine's letter found in U.S. Congress. 39th. 2nd sess. House executive docu-ment, No. 71, 14.

[45] Dunn, 499.

[46] Brown, *Fetterman,* 176. U.S. Congress. 50th. 1st sess. Senate executive document 33. 44. Found on line at Hathi Trust. sent by digref@loc.gov. http://hdl.han-dle.net/2027/uc1.b3986360?urlappend=%3Bseq=355.(accessed February 28, 2014).

[47] Vaughn, 197.

[48] F. Carrington, 132 and 143. Brown, *Fetterman*, 150.

[49] Brown, *Fetterman*, 173 and 178.

[50] John S. Gray, *Custer's Last Campaign: Mitch Boyer and the Littler Big Horn Recon-structed*, (Lincoln: University of Nebraska Press, 1991), Appendix A, Michael Boyer on the Fetterman Massacre to Commissioner J.K. Kinney of the Sanborn Commission, 403. Hereafter cited as Gray/Boyer's testimony.

[51] Brown, *Fetterman*, 182.

[52] Ibid, 183.

[53] Dunn, 500.

[54] Cook, 198.

[55] Robert B. David, *Finn Burnett, Frontiersman,* (Glendale: Arthur Clark Publishing, 1937), 130. Hereafter cited as David.

[56] Brown-*Fetterman,* 183.

[57] Smith, 120. Might I dare be so bold to identify Smith as an Indian sympa-thizer due to her identification of the "spectacular victory" of the Indians. Is this really a "spectacular" victory considering the odds were 2,000 Indians against 81 Americans. 81 Americans who were mutilated and horribly butchered beyond

recognition. Especially in light of the fact that White Elk, a Cheyenne, stated that, "more Indians were killed in the Fetterman fight than in the Custer fight ten years later." I believe so! She also teaches history at the Oglala Lakota College on the Pine Ridge Indian Reservation. Can one wonder where her sympathies lie! There is also a mistake in her book in reference to the endnote 23 in Chapter 6, 121. She cites Cook's book, *Fifty Years on the Old Frontie*r, endnote 23 211 in her Endnotes in the back of the book and she cites Cook, page 229. When one goes to page 229 in Cook's book, new edition paperback, copyright 1980, there is no reference to Fetterman, there is only references to, *Troubles in New Mexico*. Cook's references to the Fetterman battle are on pages 197–198.

[58] Monnett, 152.

[59] John H. Monnett, ed., *Eyewitness to the Fetterman Fight: Indian Views*, (Norman: University of Oklahoma Press, 2017) 57. Hereafter cited as Monnett-*Eyewitness*.

[60] Ibid., 89.

[61] Ibid., 104.

[62] Ibid., 105.

[63] Ibid., 116.

[64] Ibid.

[65] Ibid., 52.

[66] W. A. Graham, *The Custer Myth: A Source Book of Custeriana*, (New York: Bonanza Books, 1953), 3. Hereafter cited as W.A. Graham.

[67] Robert B. David, *Finn Burnett, Frontiersman*, originally published in 1937 by Arthur H. Clark Co. Newly republished (Mechanicsburg: Stackpole Books, 2003), 130. Hereafter cited as David, *Finn Burnett*.

[68] Cooke, 198.

[69] Hebard, Vol. I, 312, fn. 86. Cook, 198.

[70] Grinnell, 200.

[71] Brown-*Fetterman*, 178.

[72] Monnett, 130.

[73] Hebard, Vol. I, 312. Richard E. Jensen, ed., *Voices of the American West: The Indian Interviews of Eli. S. Ricker,1903-1919.* (Lincoln: University of Nebraska Press, 2005), 280-81. Hereafter known as Jensen.

[74] M. Carrington, 268. Brown, *Fetterman*, 189. Dunn, 495-496.

[75] M. Carrington, 208. Dunn, 495. Hebard and Brininstool, Vol. I, 312-13.

[76] Col. H.B. Carrington's testimony, M740, 12 Hereafter cited as Carrington's testimony.

[77] Dr. Samuel Horton's testimony, M740, 3. Hereafter cited as Horton's testimony. Monnett, 147.

[78] Dr. C. M. Hines's testimony, M740, 3-4. Hereafter cites as Hines's testimony. Brown-*Fetterman*, 48-49.

[79] Thomas Goodrich, *Scalp Dance: Indian Warfare on the High Plains, 1865-1879,* (Mechanicsburg: Stack pole Books, 1997) p. 29. Hereafter cited as Goodrich. Brown-*Fetterman*, 188.

[80] Monnett, 150-51. Goodrich, 29-30. Brown-*Fetterman*, 188. Horton's testimony, M740, Page 3 of 5. U.S. Congress. 50th. 1st sess. Senate executive document 33, 41.

[81] Capt. Ten Eyck's testimony, M740, 12. Hereafter cited as Ten Eyck's testimony.

[82] David, *Finn Burnett*, 129. Brown, *Fetterman*, 197.

[83] Dunn, 489-90.

[84] Douglas D. Scott, P. Willey and Melissa A. Connor, *They Died with Custer: Soldiers' Bones from the Battle of the Little Big Horn*, (Norman: University of Oklahoma Press, 1998), 314 Hereafter cited as Scott, Willey, and Connor.

[85] Monnett, 271, fn. 93.

[86] Ibid, 187.

[87] Ibid, 149.

[88] Ibid, 150. David, *Finn Burnett*, 130.

[89] Monnett, 39. M. Carrington, 174-175

[90] M. Carrington, 174-75.

[91] Monnett, 148.

[92] F. Carrington, 148.

[93] Ibid, 155. Dunn, 499.

[94] Vestal, 292. Monnett, 149. Vaughn, 70. Goodrich, 30.

[95] Brown, *Fetterman*, 189.

[96] John D. McDermott, *'Portraits of Fort Phil Kearny.' The Famous Ride of John "Portu-guese" Phillips.* 2. http://www.philkearny.vcn.com/phillips.htm. Hereafter cited as McDermott. (accessed September 15, 2015).

[97] F. Carrington, 149, 169. Brown-*Fetterman*, 192.

[98] F. Carrington, 167. Brown-*Fetterman*, 193.

[99] Brown-*Fetterman*, 193-195.

[100] McDermott, page 3 of 6.

[101] F. Carrington, 166-167.

[102] Brown-*Fetterman,* p. 213.

[103] Monnett, 187.

[104] Ibid, 188.

[105] Ibid.

[106] Ibid., 187.

[107] Ibid.

[108] M. Carrington, 218-19.

[109] Ibid, 221-22. Monnett, 188.

[110] Brown-*Fetterman*, 215.

[111] M. Carrington, 223. Henry B. Carrington, *Ab Sa Ra Ka: Land of Massacre,* (London: J.B. Lippincott & Co, 1879), 223. Henry Carrington basically reprinted his 1st wife's book, Margaret Carrington, *Absaraka: Home of the Crows*, word for word from pages 13 to 258. In his book on page 259 he begins 6 new chapters and titles them *Indian Affairs on the Plains*, it runs from 259 to 354. On page 355 he has another new chapter titled, Honor to Whom Honor, and ends at page

360 and then he has an Appendix that runs from 361 to 378. The volume cited is the 5th Edition of Mrs. Carrington's Narrative.

[112] Mr. J.P. Weston's, testimony, M740, 5. http://freepages.history.rootsweb.ances-try.com/~familyinformatio… Hereafter cited as Weston's testimony. (accessed September 15, 2015).

[113] Ibid.

[114] Vaughn, 183. Capt. Powell's testimony, M740, page 3 of 14. Accessed on 3/1/2014. http://freepages.history.rootsweb.ancestry.com/~familyinformatio… Hereafter cited as Capt. Powell's testimony, M740. (accessed September 16, 2014).

[115] Brown-*Fetterman*, 41.

[116] Weston's, testimony, M740, page 3 of 8.

[117] Vaughn, 20.

[118] Brown-*Fetterman*, 214.

[119] Ibid. U.S. Congress. 39th. 2nd sess. House executive document No. 71, 15

[120] Brown-*Fetterman*, 207. U. S. Congress. 39th. 2nd sess. Senate executive document 15, 3.

[121] Brown-*Fetterman*, 208.

[122] Lt. Bisbee's testimony, M740, 5 Hereafter cited as Bisbee's testimony.

[123] Capt. Powell's testimony, M740, 6

[124] Ibid, pages 2–12 of 14. Vaughn, 55-56.

[125] Capt. Powell's testimony, M740, 9.

[126] Vaughn, 56.

[127] Capt. Powell's testimony, M740, 12.

[128] C.M. Hines letter January 1, 1867. *Letter from the Secretary of the Interior*. U. S. Congress, 39th. 2nd sess. House executive document, No.71, 25. http://freepages. history.ancestry.com/~familyinformatio… (accessed September 17,2014.)

[129] H. Carrington's Rebuttal Testimony, to Capt. Powell's Testimony, 2-6. http:// freepages.history.rootsweb.ancestry.com/~familyinformatio… (accessed Sep-tember 17, 2014). Vaughn, Appendix B, 206-211.

[130] Brown-*Fetterman*, 165.

[131] Ibid, 216-17. Monnett, 222.

[132] Vaughn, 19-21, and fn. 6, 21.

[133] Brown-*Fetterman*, 218. Monnett, 223.

[134] Lewis V. Bogey, *Letter from the Secretary of the Interior*, U.S. Congress. 39th. 2nd sess. House Exec. Doc., No. 71, 3. http://freepages.history.rootsweb.ancestry. com/~familyinformation… (accessed September 17,2014).

[135] Ibid, page 4 of 26.

[136] Gray/Boyer, 243.

[137] Ibid., 402.

[138] Ibid.

[139] Ibid.

[140] Ibid.

[141] Ibid., 403.

[142] Vaughn, fn. 6, 21-22.

[143] Monnett, 220.

[144] Vaughn, 86-87.

[145] M. Carrington, 171. F. Carrington, 119. Monnett, 227.

[146] H. Carrington testimony, 5, December 27, 1866, 30. Hereafter cited as H. Carrington's testimony, 5.

[147] Ibid, 32.

[148] Ibid, 34. Monnett, 221.

[149] Vaughn, Appendix A, 197.

[150] Brown-Fetterman, 226.

[151] H. Carrington's testimony, 5, 27. H. Carrington, *Ab Sa Ra Ka: Land of Massacre*, 369.

[152] Capt. Ten Eyck's testimony before the Sanborn Commission, July 5th, 1867. 10. (accessed 1 March, 2014). http://freepages.history.rootsweb.ancestry.com/~familyinformatio... Hereafter cited as Ten Eyck's testimony. Vaughn, 61. (accessed March 1, 2014).

[153] F. Carrington, 251-255.

[154] Henry Carrington, *The Indian Question*, (Boston: n.p., 1884), fn. p. 26. Reprinted 1973 New York: Sol Lewis.

[155] Vaughn, 64.

[156] F. Carrington, 119.

[157] M. Carrington, 208-209. Monnett, 104. Vaughn, 42-43. In reference to the quote in bold print, it comes directly from M. Carington, but Monnett iden-tifies a letter written by George Webber and gives him credit, as the source; Monnett, page 105.

[158] Dee Brown, *Fetterman*, 209. H. Carrington's testimony, 5th Page, page 34 of 49.

[159] Shannon S. Calitri, in the Introduction to F. Carrington's book, *My Army Life*, xix. Hereafter cited as Calitri-*F. Carrington.*

[160] Calitri- *F. Carrington*, vii.

[161] F. *Carring*ton, 144. M. Carrington, 201-202.

[162] F. Carrington. Ibid.

[163] Greene, *Indian War Veterans*, 89.

[164] Wands' testimony, M740, pages 9 and 10 of 12.

[165] Dr. Hine's letter found in U.S. Congress. 39th. 2nd sess. House executive docu-ment, no 71, 14

[166] Gray/*Boyer*, 403. Monnett, 137.

[167] The main criticism that I have with Smith's book is the incestuous intellectual agenda she promotes in reference to the politically correct Feminist Gender Studies programs so politically correct in today's universities. There is no free-dom of speech in the academic universities they only allow speakers that blindly parrot their own ideas and intellectually fabricated agendas.

[168] Dr. Horton's testimony, M740, 3-4

[169] Ibid.

[170] Ibid., 3.

[171] M. Carrington, 171.

[172] Ibid, 195. Monnett, 115.

[173] M. Carrington, 208-209.

[174] F. Carrington, 132. Stanley Vestal, *Warpath:The True Story of the Fighting Sioux Told in a Biography of Chief White Bull,* (Lincoln: University of Nebraska Press, 1984), 59. Hereafter known as Vestal, *Warpath.*

[175] Vaughn. 90.

[176] Ibid.

This picture above is of Robert McGee who was unfortunate to have been scalped while he was still alive. But he did obviously survive. The incident of his scalping took place when he was just 13 years old. He and his family were travelling on the Santa Fe Trail in Kansas on their way to New Mexico. They were attacked by a band of marauding Sioux Indians.

Bibliography

[i] *The American Heritage College Dictionary,* 4th ed., s. v. "polemic." Hereafter cited as *AHCD.*

[ii] J. P. Dunn, Jr., *Massacres of the Mountains: A History of the Indian Wars of the Far West,*

(Mechanicsburg: Stackpole Books, 2002), 489-490. Originally published in 1886. Hereafter

cited as J. P. Dunn.

[iii] Revisionist History, https//en.wikipedia.org/wiki/Revisionist history, pg. 1

[iv] James McPherson, "From the President: Revisionist Historians," *Perspectives on History,*

American Historical Association, (September 2003) pg. 1 of 5.

[v] E.H. Carr, *What is History?* (London: Cox and Wyman Ltd, 1961), 30. Hereafter cited as Carr-

History.

[vi] Ibid., 28.

[7] Utley, *Indian Wars,* vi-vii.

[8] http://en.wikipedia.org. wiki/Revisionist_history_1 Hereafter cited as Wikipedia Revisionist.

[9.] James M. McPherson, "Revisionist Historians," *Perspectives on History,* September, (2003):

Pg. 1 of 5. http://www.historians.org/publications-and-directories/perspective-on-history/

september-2003/revisionist-historians. Retrieved 2 August 2016.

[x] Charles A. Beard, *An Economic Interpretation of the Constitution of the United States,*

(New York: The Free Press, 1913) 17. Hereafter cited Beard.

[xi] Brinkley, Appendix, A-12.

[xii] Ibid. William A. McClenaghan, *Magruder's American Government,*

(Newton: Allyn and Bacon, Inc. 1987), 729. Hereafter cited as *Magruder's.*

[xiii] Julius W. Pratt, *Back Doors to War: The Roosevelt Foreign Policy, 1933-1941, The*

American Historical Review Vol. 58 No. 1 (Oct., 1952) 150-152. Hereafter cited as Pratt.

[xiv] Robert Dallek, *Franklin D. Roosevelt and* American Foreign Policy, 1932-1945, (Oxford:

Oxford University Press, 1979), 307. Hereafter cited as Dallek.

R.J.C. Butow, *How*

Roosevelt Attacked Japan at Pearl Harbor: *Myth Masquerading as History, Prologue: The*

U.S. National Archives and Records Administratioon. Fall 1996, Vol.

28, No. 3, pg. 3 of 19. Hereafter cited as Butow. https://www. archives.gov/publications/prologue/1996/fall/butow.html

xv David Bergamini, *Japan's Imperial Conspiracy: How Emperor Hirohito led Japan into War*

against the West, (New York: William Morrow and Company, 1971), 1079-1081. Hereafter

cited as Bergimini.

xvi Utley, *Indian Wars*, v-vi.

xvii Cyrus T. Brady. *Indian Fights and Fighters,* (Lincoln: University of Nebraska Press, 1971),

193. Hereafter cited as Brady-*Indian Fights*.

xviii Utley, *Indian Wars*, 246.

xix Foley-*Missionary*, 17

xx Mark Twain, "The Noble Red Man", *The Galaxy*, Vol. 10, Issue 3, Sept. 1870, 426-429.

http://www.jrbooksonline.com/comparison_burton_twain. htm. http://nationalvanguard.org/2015/02//the-noble-red-man/ Hereafter cited as *Twain.*

xxi Morse H. Coffin, *The Battle of Sand Creek,* ed. Alan W. Farley, (Waco: W.M. Morrison-

Publisher, 1965, originally published in 1878), 4. Hereafter cited as Coffin.

xxii Richard G. Hardorff, *Hokahey! A Good Day to Die: The Indian Casualties of the Custer Fight,*

(Lincoln: University of Nebraska Press, 1993), 12. Hereafter cited as Hardorff-*Hokahey.*

xxiii Stacey Makes Good, "Sioux is Not Even a Word," *Lakota Country Times,* Pine Ridge Indian

Reservation, no dated provided. Hereafter cited as Stacey Makes Good. Hardorff-*Hokahey,*

14.

xxiv John G. Neihardt, *Black Elk Speaks,* (New York: MJF BOOKS, 1932), 56. Hereafter cited as

Neihardt, Black Elk. *Setting the Record Straight About Native Languages: A Good Day To*

Die, Hokahey.

http://www.answers.com/Q/How_do_you_say_today_is_a_good_day_to_

die_in_the_Indian language. Hereafter cited as www.answers. http://www.native-languages.org/iaq20.htm.

[xxv] http://dickshovel.com/wasichu.html, pg. 1.

[xxvi] Aaron Huey, "The Black Hills Are Not for Sale," *Harpers*, 26 November 2011, http://nativeamericannetroots.net/diary/tag/He%20Sapa, pg. 4 of 35.

[xxvii] www.native-languages, pg. 1.

[xxviii] *AHCD., s. v. "native."*

[xxix] *AHCD., s. v. "battle."*

[xxx] Ibid., s. v. "massacre."

Index

Made in the USA
Columbia, SC
08 February 2019